MW00560267

Extrasensory perception (ES[] observed since antiquity. Re[] given to the methodological appr[] twenty year (1974–1995) $20M pru_giaiil, popularly known by its last codename Star Gate, various US Government agencies, such as the Army, Navy, CIA, and DIA (Defense Intelligence Agency), have utilized RV for operational intelligence purposes. In a declassified memo, the US Army Intelligence and Security Command (INSCOM) briefed Senator Samuel A. Nunn Jr. (D), (then) Chairman of the Senate Arms Committee, stating: "...Center Lane [codename of the RV intelligence collection program at the time] has demonstrated that important foreign intelligence and counterintelligence may be obtained through the use of Remote Viewing...."

While the US was using ESP to spy on the Soviets, they too, were using ESP to spy upon the US. *ESP Wars: East & West* tells the complete inside story from both points of view using the significant firsthand experience of two of the authors (May & McMoneagle) and extensive interviews with their counterparts in the former KGB and Soviet Military.

ESP Wars is the only account written by people with firsthand memory of the US side from 1975-1995 and to have access to the Russian counterpart to Star Gate. The story has humor, intrigue, details of both programs, and the history of ESP for military purposes. Additionally, the Appendix has selected US government documents and a transcript of a successful operational remote viewing.

Panta Rei is an imprint of Crossroad Press.

First Crossroad Press edition

ESP WARS
EAST & WEST

AN ACCOUNT OF THE MILITARY USE OF PSYCHIC ESPIONAGE AS NARRATED BY THE KEY RUSSIAN AND AMERICAN PLAYERS

BY

EDWIN C. MAY, PH.D.
VICTOR RUBEL, PH.D.
JOSEPH W. McMONEAGLE
LOYD AUERBACH, M.S.

DEDICATION

The following individuals contributed greatly to the material in *ESP Wars,* through interviews and contributed writings. We include their biographies to show the high level of our source material.

Lieutenant General, Alexei Yuryevich Savin, Ph.D.

Alexei Savin was born in 1946 in Moscow. His father was an aviation officer (later he became Major General of the Air Forces); his mother was a dramatic actor and singer. He graduated from the Sebastopol Naval School in 1969 as a "naval aircraft radio operator" with the rank of lieutenant engineer. After graduating, he started working at the Institute of Theoretical Cybernetics (today the Scientific Research Institute of Aviation Systems) in a military reception office. While working there for the next 16 years, he wrote a number of scientific papers about the development of combat aviation. In 1986, he was offered the post of senior officer in the Armaments Directorate of the Defense Ministry of the USSR.

In 1989, the Chief of the Armaments Directorate ordered him to assemble a commission of medical doctors, physicists, and military and civilian scientists to examine psychics. As a result of Savin's report to the Ministry of Defense, he was sent to the General Staff. The Chief of that organization, Army General Mikhail Moiseyev, appointed him to be a head of the special top-secret department of the General Staff called Military Unit 10003, reporting directly to Moiseyev.

The focus of Savin's work was the "Hidden Human Potentialities and Super-Capabilities Development Program," which included developing extraordinary mental capabilities, and manifesting exceptional creative potential and extrasensory capabilities. At the same time, Savin's department searched for breakthrough trends in the creation of new types of weapons.

For about 15 years, Alexei Savin worked at the General Staff, conducting R&D on ESP and the other areas. He and his staff created the largest ever military program on ESP and Human Potential research (in the world), and collaborated with the Russian Academy of Science. They trained groups of psychics-operatives for Marine, Air Forces and other Army branches, and actively tested psychics' work in real combat operations in Chechnya (which he personally supervised, and where he was also wounded and was decorated with a medal).

Under Alexei Savin's command, his department became a full Directorate of the General Staff with 50 employees (both, military and civilian) and many subcontractors (organizations and individuals) with an average financing of about $4,000,000 a year. Savin was personal adviser to the Prime Minister of the USSR Valentin Pavlov, several Secretaries of the Security Counsel of Russia, and Heads of the General Staff. Russian President Dmitry Medvedev also was in contact with him, seeking advice.

Alexei Savin has achieved a rank of Lieutenant General and holds Ph.D. degrees in Technical and Philosophical sciences. He is an Academician of the Russian Academy of Natural Sciences and honorary member of many scientific and professional societies. He wrote many scientific and professional (military) papers and four books, including the most recent *A.Yu. Savin, D.N. Fonarev. A Guide for Eternity* (Moscow, Vega, 2009, in Russian).

Major General Boris Konstantinovich Ratnikov

Boris Ratnikov was born in 1944 in the village of Kurovo, not far from Moscow. He graduated from the Aviation Institute in 1969 and went to work in the design office of the Scientific Research Institute of Aviation in the town of Zhukovsky. While working there for three years, he applied to work for the KGB. After finishing the KGB Officers School in Minsk, he worked for several years as a regional operative in the Municipal Department of the KGB in Ramenskoye (a town near Moscow), at various classified aviation enterprises, supervising their operations.

In 1981, he was sent to Afghanistan where he took part in numerous intelligence and combat operations. On his return, he worked in aircraft security at the Moscow department of the KGB for nearly three years. Subsequently, he left the KGB and accepted an invitation from Alexander Korzhakov to serve as his assistant in the Security Department for the Supreme Soviet of the Russian Republic, of which Boris Yeltsin had recently become chairman.

Serving in the Security Department, he became a direct participant of the coup in August 1991, which ended in the collapse of the USSR and the fall of communism. Soon after, he became the Deputy Head of the Federal Security Service, supervising analysis, operations, staff, technical and other services. There, he established a special parapsychological department and used many ESP techniques for security and intelligence. This service applied psychic techniques to international politics and to defending key Russian political figures against enemy psychic scanning and potential psychic attacks.

He appointed Major General Georgii Rogozin for this work. Rogozin later became the Deputy Head of the Yeltsin's Presidential Security Service and widely known in Russia as "the astrologer and the psychic No.1" of the Russian Secret and Security Services. Together with Rogozin, Boris Ratnikov conducted many ESP experiments and intelligence operations, and developed a number of special ESP techniques for security services. Ratnikov personally supervised many security operations, defending the Russian President Boris Yeltsyn and other top Russian political figures.

Boris Ratnikov achieved a rank of Major General. He wrote many professional (military) papers and public articles published in the Russian press and has given a number of interviews for major Russian TV channels. Together with General Rogozin, he wrote the book *Beyond the Known* (Moscow, Vega, 2009, in Russian) about some results of their work with ESP.

We dedicate this book to those heroes both in the US and in Russia who, at times, put their careers at risk in defending the value of ESP not only for spying but also because of its vast implications across the totality of human experience. We still have a long way to go before the unfettered acceptance of ESP as a normal human experience.

We are deeply grateful to a handful of dedicated US members of Congress, Agency Directors, and Intelligence officers without whose commitment the US program may not have survived for over 20 years let alone being started; yet, because of a fear of public ridicule, they have asked us to keep their names confidential. They know who they are and we hope that, not long from now, you all may know their names.

ACKNOWLEDGMENTS

We would like to thank Kristine Lewis for her editing time and expertise, and Sonali Marwaha for her final edits, formatting work. On a personal note, the authors and editors are especially appreciative of our families who have remained out steadfast supporters through the good times and bad sometimes for decades. Without their support the book would not have been possible.

Very special thanks go to Ms. Sally Rhine Feather for allowing us to publish a rare photograph of her parents (page 51).

CONTENTS

FOREWORD

"ESP Wars" sounds like something from a science fiction novel. Yet what you have before you is a book written with contributions by military men and scientists, generals and Ph.Ds., some of whom directed the largest military ESP programs in the US and Russia. Psychic espionage, telepathy, psychotronic generators, and the psychic work that military intelligence, the CIA, and the KGB engaged in are among the many topics covered in this book.

It has repeatedly been said that intelligence services and military personnel around the world exhibit a special interest in parapsychology, the field of science that studies psychic phenomena and abilities. In the absence of authentic information from the agencies involved, there has been much misunderstanding and many unsubstantiated claims made about these programs. In reality, some military and intelligence agencies do view psychic means of gathering data and influencing people as a means of waging a new type of war—ESP Wars. This particular interest in parapsychology has allowed the opportunity to create new and unique types of espionage and weapons. This is why work in these areas has been, and continues to be, conducted in recent decades in many countries, above all in the USSR/Russia and the US, which were until relatively recently major geopolitical adversaries.

The most extensive work in the field of military ESP and parapsychology was conducted in Russia by a special Directorate of the General Staff known as secret Military Unit 10003 under the leadership of Lieutenant General Alexei Savin, Ph.D. Much work was done in the Federal Security Service and the Presidential Security/Secret Service—special services, which emerged from the 9th Directorate of the KGB—under the direction of Major

Generals Boris Ratnikov and Georgii Rogozin, who served as Vice Directors of these services. Parapsychological research and ESP operations in the Ministry of Internal Affairs were directed by the Colonel of Internal Services, Colonel (and Professor) Vyacheslav Zvonikov, M.D.

The Star Gate program, the most extensive military ESP program in the US, was conducted by military intelligence and CIA from 1972 until 1995. Its main goal was the application of extrasensory perception for military purposes, primarily the use of remote viewing to gather information about military installations in the USSR. Dr. Edwin May was the director of this program during the last decade of its operation. Joe McMoneagle, a professional intelligence agent of the highest caliber, was officially registered as Agent 001, and became the project's most successful psychic.

Naturally, all these programs were classified as top-secret. But, times have changed. The history of the Communist Bloc has come to an end, the strategic parity of forces has changed, and many military secrets are no longer secret. Former opponents have become friends, have had the opportunity to share their experiences, achievements and plans for the future and have started to work together. One result is the book you are holding in your hands. I know that other books have been planned, and more than one television production company has expressed interest in becoming involved, so it is entirely possible that there will be a series of documentary films based on this and subsequent books. You have before you the first book, which I recommend to your attention in every possible way.

I'd like to make some general remarks concerning the material presented.

Non-military research in parapsychology in both the Soviet Union and the United States did not fundamentally differ either in its focus or level. Scientists set the same goals, based their work on the same principles, used similar techniques and equipment, and their results were also similar. With respect to the military research, there were some differences. In the US, a major emphasis was placed on working with operative psychics and remote viewing. In other words, the focus was, on the extrasensory retrieval of information about the potential enemy's important installations, as was distinctly defined in the Star Gate program. Although similar work was done in the Soviet Union and Russia, there were two features that fundamentally distinguished it.

First, psychics were physically on site during combat operations, such as in Chechnya. This surprised Americans, because in fact, their presence wasn't necessary in working with ESP. But there were substantial reasons for this, and General Savin will discuss them.

Second, more attention was placed on developing hardware in working with the psyche and on developing unusual methods to influence material objects, what later became fashionably known as "psychotronic generators" or "psychotronic weapons." The constraint of Marxist-Leninist ideology contributed in part to this approach because from its point of view, hardware was more "material" than the "mystical fluids" of psychics. Hardware research was conducted in many classified scientific research institutes, and civilian scientists also submitted design proposals for hardware. In all honesty, it should be pointed out that 90% of these proposals, designs and research projects were unsuccessful, and mostly the result of errors, scientific incompetence or simply deceit. As for the remaining 10%, they were, and still remain, utterly unique designs that were frequently ahead of their time and which created the foundation for future technologies. We will begin talking about them in this book.

Because of perestroika beginning in the early 1990s, and with it the change of ideology and the political system in the USSR, then in Russia, a massive military program of research into, and the development of, extraordinary human capacities was initiated. It was conducted by a special Directorate of the General Staff of the Armed Forces in Russia. Under the direction of Lieutenant General Alexei Savin, a large body of research was conducted into various aspects of the effects of energy and information, traditionally identified with parapsychology and ESP. Groups of military-psychics were trained for operations in different branches of the Armed Forces, primarily the Navy and Air Force, and psychics were trained and used in operations during military conflicts in Chechnya. But most importantly, unique techniques of developing extraordinary human abilities and qualitatively increasing intellectual and spiritual levels were developed and carefully tested in practice.

The Federal Security Service and President's Security Service of Russia tackled the challenges of protecting high-level government officials, as well as the collection and analysis of politically significant information. Major Generals Boris Ratnikov and Georgii Rogozin used many parapsychological techniques in these special security services. Other defense and law enforcement agencies began systematically using psychics in their work in the 1990s. The Ministry of Internal Affairs under Colonel Vyacheslav Zvonikov did their own parapsychological research, training of psychics and operative work. All these efforts needed to be systematized and as Deputy Director of the KGB in the early 1990s, I devoted much energy to coordinating the parapsychological research done by various security departments.

Employing psychics in operations is far from the most important consideration here—parapsychology and ESP are much broader than this. This work began from trivial motives in both the USSR and the US: to overtake the enemy, not to allow the enemy to retrieve data from our facilities or to affect them. During that time, it was to obtain information about the enemy and, whenever possible, to influence him by parapsychological means. But the range of phenomenal human abilities is extraordinarily broad: it includes clairvoyance and telepathy, mentally moving objects, diagnosing and treating illness, and using energy and information to exert influence on various environments. This range goes beyond any confines that utilitarian military goals can impose, which points to the altogether different significance of extrasensory phenomena within the network of complex evolutionary processes. Moreover, in the process of seeking the mechanisms of how extraordinary capacities arise, and in the course of their development and operative use, we saw that the individuals who engaged in this research were transformed, their values were changed, and their cultural and intellectual levels improved.

From my point of view, this constitutes the most important result of our work in the field of parapsychology and ESP, although it lies outside the scope of the initial challenges set by the security services and military departments. I am convinced that it is precisely these results of our work that will most significantly contribute to strengthening the mutual understanding between people and will, in some way, help solve the difficult problems facing the human community as a whole today.

—Nikolai Sham
Major General
Deputy Director of KGB (Ret.)

INTRODUCTION

ESP WARS: REALITY OR IMAGINATION?

War has been an integral part of human history from the very beginning and has become ever more sophisticated. While one can definitely argue that advancement in weaponry from stone knives and spears to nuclear, laser, radiological, and biological weapons may not make one feel any safer, warfare has evolved as our science and technology has evolved—and often our science and technology has evolved—because of war. Intelligence gathering, like the use of weaponry, has been an integral part of the history of warfare from the very beginning, and has taken some new forms with technology-based spying. However, the use of human assets in gathering information on one's enemies continues as it has from the start of human history.

If someone from an ancient culture had been bold and creative enough to hint at the possibility of the technological weapons of today, it would have seemed pure fantasy, though they would not have scoffed at the idea of magical or psychic weapons or spying. In many conflicts in the past, and for many rulers at the head of the different sides of those conflicts, utilizing prophets, seers, psychics, mediums, and self-professed magic-wielders has been part of their status quo; one more intelligence asset to use.

Today, technology being what it is, speculations can run wild on tech-based weaponry with only the reaction being "maybe someday" or even "we already have those secret weapons." On the other hand, the immediate reaction of many to any suggestion that someday we might use ESP phenomena—precognition, remote viewing, and psychokinesis—in warfare and espionage is of downright disbelief. After all, many people, especially scientists, seem to seriously doubt or outright deny the existence of such things.

Would it surprise you to learn we're not talking about some distant future? That we're actually talking about the recent past and present? That ESP has already been added to the arsenal of modern warfare both in the former Soviet Union—now in Russia—and the United States, as well as other countries around the world? Maybe it's a surprise to you, or maybe it isn't.

For decades, people all over the world have heard or seen snippets of news about psychics being used to spy and even to attempt mind control, and have gobbled up these reports with great interest—whether the reports had any truth to them or not. Revelations and speculations about psychic research in the Soviet Union caused much discussion on this side of the Iron Curtain. Confirmation that the American Military was conducting its own form of psychic espionage came in the mid-1990s—though some of the work was declassified earlier—only fueled a fire of interest in this area that had only slightly diminished since the fall of the USSR.

Before the fall of the Iron Curtain, some information had come out about the USSR's research on psychic applications for warfare—especially in the popular press and media—but very little about what might or might not have continued since the fall of communism in Russia. In the US, it wasn't until 1995 that the full declassification of the military intelligence psychic spying program last known by the code name STAR GATE happened with its closure, that the public found out for sure that there was any sort of American psychic espionage program. Even researchers conducting more public scientific research on ESP in general and Remote Viewing in particular had no real knowledge of such a military application or the STAR GATE program.

Even well before the declassification of STAR GATE and the declassification of similar programs in Russia, there had been considerable public interest in whether ESP was being used by the military and intelligence communities, and if so, how. This interest has already spawned a number of books on the topic published in the US. If you've read any of them, our book will stand out as somewhat different, as those books fall short in two important respects.

First and foremost, they failed to discuss, or in most cases even mention, the activity in the former Soviet Union and later, in Russia. Additionally, they entirely missed the greater perspective of what went on with those programs. They were written by retired military or civilian personnel who held non-management positions and were in the operational side of STAR GATE—that is, the psychic spying part—and/or were involved for only a fraction of the 20 year span of the total effort.[1]

So, besides being focused only on one side of the ESP Wars (the US), they were presenting only a part of the whole, missing the behind the scenes story of how and why these programs even began, how they garnered and continued support in the halls of government and with the military, and why they ceased.

Even the Russian books on this subject have never described the major Russian military ESP program at the General Staff level and have not told the story about its home—Military Unit 10003— due to its top secret status. As with the American books focusing on only one side of the ESP Wars, the Russian books skipped their "enemy's" side of the story, the STAR GATE program. In Russia, there have been a number of TV programs and publications in press about parapsychological work in the Presidential Security Service, but they were unable to tell this story consistently for the limited information they had.

This book brings together the real stories of the American and Soviet/Russian ESP programs, what actually went on in those programs, and how ESP was used in intelligence gathering and other applications. The book also covers the greater story of why these major powers saw fit to put stock in something so many academics dismiss out of turn, how they found practical value for Military and Intelligence operations, and the competition in this series of ESP Wars.

Perhaps most important to this two-level story are the sources of information in the book.

First author Edwin C. May, Ph.D. was in the middle of it all from 1975-1995, and served as the Director of the contracting side of STAR GATE for the last 10 years of its life. A well-respected researcher in his own right, Dr. May dealt with all sides of the program—from the individual viewers to the military and government personnel watching over and funding STAR GATE. One of the project's best (and best known) remote viewers, Joseph McMoneagle, provided source material and perspective of one of the psychic "spies."

Second author Dr. Victor Rubel, Ph.D., coordinated the development of this international project from the beginning. His work as a manager, a historian and a scholar-writer was invaluable in putting this book together.

Drs. May and Rubel have made certain that the Russian story is well told by interviewing and garnering other information from Russian military sources. One source is Lt. General Alexei Yu. Savin, Ph.D., who was the head of the special ESP Division (Military Unit 10003) of the General Staff, which is the Russian equivalent of the Joint Chiefs of Staff. Another Russian source is KGB Major General Boris Ratnikov. His duties, in part, included being the Deputy Head of the Federal Service of Security and Head of its special parapsychological department. That service applied psychic techniques to international politics and to defending key Russian political figures against enemy psychic scanning and potential psychic attacks.

This book provides a tapestry of personal stories of the major players from the American and Russian sides. We have joined forces with our former adversaries to document ESP Wars from both sides of the Iron Curtain during the cold war and after. We also wanted to describe some of the differences in the approach from both camps, and especially from the Russian side, and reveal some of the strongly felt ideologies that had been suppressed during the Soviet era.

We were determined to keep our story non-technical yet give insight into what went on behind the scenes and to personalize the individual players. Third author Loyd Auerbach, who's written several more popular books and articles about parapsychology and psychic experiences for the general public, is here to make sure we keep the story flowing and interesting—sort of as the readers' representative.

So, what are ESP Wars?

ESP Wars are wars fought using extrasensory means instead of bombs and bullets. They probably cannot be separated from other kinds of warfare, at least conceptually, as perhaps, the only difference is the method and means of the "fighting"—just as one can't much separate wars of today with those of a thousand years ago other than by the weapons and tactics.

ESP, or extrasensory perception, is a term coined by Dr. J. B. Rhine in the 1930's. It covers information gathering by the mind without the use of the normal senses, logical inference or intuition. In other words, ESP is the acquisition of information by mental means alone.

ESP traditionally covers three areas or subcategories of abilities or experiences: telepathy (mind-to-mind information exchange), clairvoyance (real time information perception) and precognition (awareness of information from the future). In modern laboratory experiments, it is possible to ensure that there is not, nor even could be, any sensory leakage of information whatsoever. According to May, precognition may be the only form of ESP as it can account for what appears to be telepathy or clairvoyance.

In historical anecdotes and in the "field" (in real life), where it is difficult to know or control the circumstances, claims of ESP abound. These kinds of mostly first-hand personal experiences are difficult to consider as evidential of ESP from the scientific perspective. At best, they serve a valuable function, challenging modern researchers to see what aspects of these claims can be teased into the laboratory, studied under the best possible scientific methodology and eventually understood well enough to use psychic abilities in practical applications. Thus, although we will describe historical accounts of the use of ESP in warfare, keep in mind that these are personal accounts and must be properly considered only as anecdotal reports and not blindly accepted as having happened as remembered or reported. Even so, these stories are important, since they form a foundation for the use of ESP, show us patterns in the experiences that we can bring into the laboratory, indicate potential real-world applications, and show that the experiences are actually quite common around the world—even though what's behind them is not yet understood.

The general field of study of ESP is called by a number of different names, but the most common is parapsychology. Within the US Government's STAR GATE program, the researchers defined a new term, anomalous cognition (AC). Cognition as in becoming aware of information, knowing something, and anomalous as in ways we currently do not understand. In other words, it is awareness or knowing or gaining information about something using a process we are still trying to figure out. The term "remote viewing" refers mainly to anomalous cognition—typically an extrasensory perception of a location or other target hidden from the senses by distance, and is primarily associated with a methodological approach in laboratory studies.

In this book, we will use various terms interchangeably—psychic functioning, ESP, AC and the Greek letter psi—but they all basically mean the same thing. The broader concept of psi also includes the possibility to influence the physical world by mental means alone— that is, not using the known sensory or motor actions of the brain and body.[2] Most people know it as telekinesis or simply "mind over matter," while parapsychologists use the term psychokinesis (PK).

We know that the study of ESP remains controversial, and even dismissed by a large number of academics, even though the experiences continue to be reported and with some rare exceptions, only parapsychologists seem interested in fully exploring what's behind the experiences. At first sight, many of the claims of psychic functioning seem to lie outside of what we currently understand in physics, psychology and physiology. Therefore, for many people, the immediate and quite proper response to psychic claims is huge and even amused—or belligerent—skepticism or disbelief. Think of how entertaining but ridiculous the stories are that one finds easily in the world's tabloid newspapers.

On the other hand, substantial peer-reviewed scientific literature that meets all the requirements of modern science strongly supports the existence of ESP. These reports can be found in small circulation (as with so many scientific publications), peer-reviewed scientific/ technical journals, and residing on the back shelves of some public and university libraries.

While parapsychologists apply the term ESP to cover informational abilities and experiences vs. the physical-affect ones (PK), we use the term ESP here in a broader way. Certainly part of warfare is gathering intelligence—just trying to figure out what your enemy is up to. Most of this book is about that particular use. However, our expanded concept of ESP includes physical interactions at a distance, that is, to cause your adversaries physical distress, make them ill or, perhaps even kill them. This might be done directly by a shaman/psychic or by using some device, often referred to as a psychotronic weapon that had been activated by that individual to cause the damage to the enemy.

It's not our primary purpose to convince you that psychic functioning is real—though that conclusion will be hard for most readers to avoid. We're not going to dump studies and evidence on you. Throughout the book, we'll offer some implications and evidence for its validity, especially in the context of the US and Russian remote viewing programs.

For example, were you aware that Jessica Utts, a professor of statistics at the University of California at Irvine (formerly at UC Davis), was hired with other experts indirectly by the CIA through the American Institutes for Research to provide a statistical critical review of the evidence for psychic functioning or ESP? As part of her analysis, she stated:

"Using the standards applied to any other area of science, it is concluded that psychic functioning has been well established. The results of the studies examined are far beyond what is expected by chance. Arguments that these results could be due to methodological flaws in the experiments are soundly refuted. Effects of similar magnitude to those found in government sponsored research at SRI and SAIC have been replicated at a number of laboratories across the world. Such consistency cannot be readily explained by claims of flaws or fraud."[3]

Apparently unbeknownst to many academics and scientists— mainly because they either haven't looked or because their beliefs about ESP turn them away from such considerations—there is a host of technical reviews of the experimental literature of parapsychology, known as meta-analyses, which clump together most of the available published research directed toward a particular topic. Professor Utts published one such review paper in the prestigious statistical journal Statistical Sciences, and Cornell University psychology professor Daryl Bem, along with the late Charles Honorton, published a notable review in Psychological Bulletin of the literature investigating a type of ESP known as the ganzfeld—a procedure where psi is observed when the participant is in a mildly altered state of consciousness.[4]

In other words, contrary to what so many academics and professional debunkers state, there is scientific evidence for the existence of ESP, based on well-controlled laboratory research, and some of it is indeed repeatable.

There is a second form of evidence that one might consider more circumstantial. It arises from the simple fact of the long-term existence and successful functioning of the military ESP programs in the United States and Russia, from the stature of the scientists involved in them, and from their extensive high-level, and enduring support they received from within their respective governments and academic worlds. If these programs were ineffective, they would have shut down at the very beginning.

The last Prime Minister of the USSR, Valentin Pavlov, was a great supporter of the Russian ESP program and was fascinated by the results. In both countries, many eminent scientists, including academicians and Nobel laureates, supported these programs. On the American side, remote viewer Joe McMoneagle was given the most prestigious award possible in peacetime for his excellence in providing psychic intelligence. His Legion of Merit award citation reads in part:

"...[McMoneagle] used his talents and expertise in the execution of more than 200 missions, addressing over 150 essential elements of information. These EEI [essential elements of information] contained critical intelligence reported at the highest echelons of our military and government, including such national level agencies as the Joint Chiefs of Staff, DIA, NSA, CIA, DEA, and the Secret Service, producing crucial and vital intelligence unavailable from any other source..."

You may be wondering how it happened that the Russian side of the story herein has as its sources the very high-level military/intelligence personnel so directly involved in their psychic spying/warfare programs.

In 1992, Ed May and his late colleague, Ms. Larissa Vilenskaya, traveled to Moscow in what would turn out to be the first of many visits. Although most of that trip was devoted to exploring the world of non-government sponsored ESP activity, they did begin to see hints of a much larger, government-condoned, military program.

During their second visit, they hit pay dirt. They met General

Savin and some of his colleagues who could not have been more cordial—perhaps surprisingly since the fall of the Soviet Union was still so recent. After a number of formal meetings, it became clear to both May and Savin that Russia and the US could benefit substantially if they joined forces to address problems of common interest, such as counter-terrorism. Over the next many, nearly annual visits, May and Savin became friends.

Finally, in the year 2000, May, Vilenskaya and McMoneagle visited Savin and quite a number of the members of the Russian ESP group at the Military Unit 10003. At that time, General Savin allowed them to take a number of photographs and said he would officially cooperate with the US side, as they wrote up a report for US Intelligence Community about our extensive contacts. As we will see, nothing came of that; the full cooperation between the two sides, as imagined by May and Savin never occurred.

After May learned that Savin had retired, he wrote a personal letter to the General, suggesting that they join together to document what had happened with the use of psychics on both sides during and after the Cold War. May suggested that both the former Soviets and the Americans would be able to tell stories, reveal names, and document examples that had never been seen in public before. The first result is this book.

The book is divided into four parts, as we do want to talk about the past and future, but mainly to underscore the differences and value of approaches from the West and the East. The first part gives a sketch of the roots of ESP Wars from ancient to modern times and discusses some of the military and political ESP activity during World War II and the Cold War.

The next two sections describe the personal journeys and first-hand material of the leading participants, from the US and Soviet/Russian perspectives, respectively. In both, you'll get an idea of what prompted the development of the programs, the politics within the governments and respective military and intelligence communities, and why the programs came to an end—of what they evolved into. Naturally, we'll also look at the psychic tasks and missions of both sides in the ESP Wars.

Part four brings the two sides together by first discussing the closure of the programs and the opening of discussions between the two sides of the ESP Wars. Following that is the last chapter in which we attempt to draw some conclusions and make predictions for the future of ESP and how it can serve humanity in ways better than the applications in the ESP Wars. We'll discuss why ESP can and should eventually become one of the turning points for modern science's understanding of what we are as human beings, and our potential.

For your information, we've included a selection of recently declassified documents from the US program as Appendix A.

In future books, we hope to delve more deeply in this story, give material not known to the general public, and provide peer-reviewed scientific results and analyses. Perhaps by that time we will be able to facilitate for declassification of even more remarkable material that we collected during our work. In any case, we hope that this material will bring some new significant perspectives to ESP and its role in our lives.

ESP WARS: East and West provides the previously untold bigger story of what the US was doing in the psychic spying business, what the Russians—as successors to the Soviets—were doing on their side, and what both East and West found in actually doing ESP on a practical level that supports the existence of this ability that humans possess, which is so often dismissed without consideration by mainstream science, yet remains clearly and perpetually in the public consciousness and beliefs.

It's a story that encompasses government and military involvement in and management of an intelligence-gathering program using extrasensory perception that had its roots in the Cold War with the Soviet Union and continued well after the dissolution of that nation.

It's also a story of the "missions" the remote viewers were tasked with, of the applications of ESP in the context of spying, and of the people in the program themselves.

And it's a story of the official Russian work in psychic intelligence that was a legacy of the USSR—a story never told in the West until this time by sources within their program.

Not only does the material in this book lend credence to the growing body of knowledge that supports the existence and effective applications of psychic functioning, it discusses the high-level involvement of both the US and Russian governments that reached all the way to the West Wing of the Whitehouse and to the Kremlin.

ESP WARS: East and West places you with the people inside the psychic arms race the US and USSR/Russia found themselves in from the perspectives of both the "weapons" (ESP and the remote viewers) and those military and government personnel on both sides effectively pulling the "triggers."

One final note: several of the people involved in the history of the STAR GATE program did not want their real names used in this book, for whatever reason. In such cases, we will put quotes around the name and italicize it, if for no other reason than your own information.

NOTES

1) There is, however, a partial exception to this general rule. Mr. Dale E. Graff, has written two authoritative books about STAR GATE first from his perspective as a civilian working for the US Air Force in the Foreign Technology Division at Wright-Patterson Air Force base in Ohio, and later working for the Defense Intelligence Agency. As a contracting officer's technical representative, he monitored the ESP government contracts and later became the director for the Ft. Meade psychic spying unit. Dale had direct involvement from 1976 to 1993. Yet, Tracks in the Psychic Wilderness, which was published in 1998 and his second book, River Dreams, which was published in 2000, could not have told the story from neither the complete point of view or from the Russian perspective.

2) Generally, we can extend the meaning of ESP from Extra Sensory Perception to Extra Sensory Performance, which includes psychic influence.

3) The full American Institutes for Research Report can be found on line at www.lfr.org/LFR/csl/library/AirReport.pdf.

4) It is interesting to note, that both these reviews, along with much of the published literature, led Utts to her conclusion cited above

for the CIA. It inspired one of parapsychology's most informed critics, psychology professor Ray Hyman of the University of Oregon, to remark from the stage of the 20th anniversary of the Committee to Scientifically Investigate the Claims of the Paranormal (CSICOP) that there is no longer any doubt that some kind of information transfer anomaly exists, and we must now invest resources to explore and understand that anomaly.

THE ROOTS
OF MODERN ESP WARS

CHAPTER 1

ANCIENT TRADITIONS, HISTORY AND ESP: SETTING THE STAGE FOR ESP WARS

People all over the world have been having psychic experiences— especially ESP experiences—since the very start of any sort of written historical record, and according to archeological evidence they've been attempting contact with spirits, divine and extraordinary sources of information since our beginnings. It was those and other experiences that made a number of scientists in the 19th century curious about applying the scientific method to understand just what was going on (detailed in the next chapter).

Over 130 years of research under laboratory conditions, field investigation, surveys, interviews, and even real-world attempts to apply ESP and PK by a relatively small group of scientists and others have provided a large body of data that ranges from strictly statistical experimental results to clear examples of application of psi under controlled conditions to purely anecdotal evidence. Over the past 50 years, the improvement in laboratory techniques and sophistication in research designs and the numerous meta-analyses of the scientific data has further established the robustness of the phenomenon. While some put forth a theory of "quantum consciousness" and spirituality as an explanation for psi phenomena, others seek the answer for its occurrence in some of the systems of the brain based on principles of classical physics.

Studying ESP, which comes primarily from people's perceptions, requires understanding the range of the experiences and abilities reported. Applying ESP requires some understanding of how people have seemingly used ESP in the past, and the circumstances under which they seem to have the most success. If people have been experiencing and applying ESP throughout our existence, then studying accounts from ancient through more recent times to find patterns in the experiences and applications of ESP and support for their existence makes quite a bit of sense.

ESP itself is considered to be perception above or beyond normal sensory perception as currently defined. One of the issues in parapsychological work is that research on ESP may find that there is something very sensory about the flow of information, but not sensory as we understand the senses and perception today. More mainstream research on perception and information processing in the brain may also uncover such "new" senses, but also may not connect such new understanding to what people have called ESP abilities until that point in time.

ESP has been most often called the "sixth sense," in reference to our "normal" five senses as most people understand them: sight, hearing, smell, touch, and taste. However, mainstream science has redefined and expanded the concept of the senses to include behavioral abilities of balance and acceleration, temperature sensing, and kinesthetic sense. Senses of time and even rhythm have been identified. There is clear evidence that some birds, animals, and fish have a magnetic sense, and humans may as well. In other words, as we expand our understanding of how our bodies sense the environment, we may find that there's nothing extrasensory about ESP at all. Or we may find that there is a different process than the senses that accounts for ESP.

In this chapter and the next, we're going to do a little time-traveling to see how our modern ideas of ESP—and the research and applications—have evolved. More than that, these chapters give the foundation of the ESP Wars of the 20th and 21st centuries, foundations that were first built by ancient peoples and their shamanic and magical traditions. Given the nations involved in the ESP Wars we're discussing, we'll focus particularly on ideas and experiences in recorded history from the central Asian regions, the European perspectives of the Middle Ages and Renaissance Period, and the formation of the Theosophical Society and Spiritualism and their influence on the development of the Societies for Psychical Research in Europe, culminating in the contemporary scientific laboratory investigations into psi and the failed and successful attempts to apply ESP in espionage and warfare.

Both the descriptions of psychic experiences, as well as specific applications of ESP and PK can be found in historical records and literature going back thousands of years. Beliefs in magic and extraordinary powers go back even further than the written word, something we're well aware of thanks to oral traditions, arts and artifacts. One of the terms most often associated with magic-users, practitioners of healing arts, or seers that are not in more mainstream religions is "Shaman"—a term taken from the Tungusic languages of eastern Siberia, specifically the Yakut—an especially appropriate origin given the Soviet/Russian side of the ESP Wars we'll be discussing in this book.

Shamanism—or forms of it—is considered to be humanity's most ancient and most universal religion and, at the same time, a healing system and a way to solve various life problems. The most fundamental elements of shamanic practice are altered states of consciousness and engaging in practices involving mythological archetypes. The history of various cultures—and specifically shamanic practices—suggests that there exists a deep internal connection between human spirituality and the manifestation of psychic abilities, which is consistent with similar statements by various religious and spiritual traditions. This link has remained strong over the centuries. Its existence across cultures is a pointer towards the universality of the concept of psychic abilities.

In altered states of consciousness, the shaman is said to acquire new powers and capacities such as clairvoyance and telepathy in order to address the problems confronting him. With his ability to see the "invisible," the shaman becomes an intermediary between two worlds—the physical world of people and the world of spirits. More than that, the shaman is a warrior in battles with the unseen, a protector and healer, a spy master (with the spies being "spirits"), and more. In a world of scarce resources, ancient societies had to use any and all resources in their arsenal in order to survive, including otherworldly ones. Shamans and other seers and magic users would often use their abilities to determine where hunters might find the best game, where they might gather naturally-growing vegetation, and where and when to plant crops. Such practices continue to this day amongst indigenous peoples around the world and have their analogue in psychics who offer advice on investments, business, and agriculture.

One of the shaman's primary missions was to fight in the "underworld" for the interests of his fellow tribesmen. Thus, one of his main challenges was to do battle with the invisible (an early ESP war). The Russian anthropologist S. I. Weinstein describes the battle of a very old and physically ailing Tuvan shaman with an evil spirit:[1]

One could feel that his suit and tambourine were too heavy for the old man, and the doubt whether Shonchur would be able to move around in this attire arose in my mind involuntarily... Suddenly the shaman... jumped up abruptly. He made several movements, which surprised me with their ease and freedom... he was nearly dancing... He covered himself with the tambourine as if it were a shield, and ran and jumped around the yurt with ease, chasing the evil spirit without opening his eyes, and, strangely enough, without brushing up against anyone present... He continued to jump, and finally overtook the enemy. The battle began. The enemies fell down and rolled around on the yurt floor. The shaman pressed his tambourine firmly down on the evil spirit.

1.   The tambourine served not only as a musical instrument, but also as a weapon, and it was frequently the repository of the shaman's vital power. There was a widespread belief among some native peoples in the East, such as a few Altai tribes of Central Asia, that if you destroy a tambourine, its shaman owner would also die.

Shamans have most often used their powers to help rather than harm people, and they did so while in altered states of consciousness. However, when conflicts arose between tribes, shamans were expected to ensure victory for their tribe by summoning the spirits for help for finding out what the enemy's intentions were and/or and putting the hex on the enemy. I. M. Suslov, a Russian anthropologist, describes such an extrasensory shamanic battle during a traditional shamanic ritual called a kamlaniye, which he witnessed in Siberia in 1927. His account is based on the song that the shaman sang:

The shaman jumped to his feet. Then he summoned his best assistant spirits with a disturbing song. The bumumuki spirits controlled by the shaman turned into cows, horses, and reindeer and, somewhere in the darkness under the protection of the assistant spirits, they formed into a detachment. The detachment of avengers rushed toward the enemies. Leading the spirits was the soul of the shaman in the shape of a wolf, astride the rootstock of a young a larch....[2]

Being human themselves, shamans would sometimes succumb to ordinary human passions and leave their higher aspirations behind in favor of more mercenary aims. They'd endeavor to use their extrasensory abilities for acquiring power, riches, or revenge. In the modern anthropological literature, there are some descriptions of the personal battles between shamans, where the shamans who were battling for dominance faced one another in their full ritual garb, festooned with protective amulets. Looking each other straight in the eye they would begin their shamanic dancing and singing as they accompanied themselves on their tambourines. When they finished singing, they would lie down on the earth head by head, close their eyes, and plunge spiritually into other worlds or dimensions. From time to time their bodies would shudder, and rattles and groans would emanate from them, showing observers that a battle was being waged somewhere in far off space. The apparent battle could go on for many hours. The result reportedly was sometimes the death of one of the combatants.

Anthropologists researching Siberian shamanism have reported that when a shaman died during one of these battles, his disciples and children who were considered an integral part of him, often died as well—especially those under the age of three. Moreover, the disciples and children could die even before the shaman did; they were unable to survive the battle internally because their primary source of life force was destroyed in the spirit world. In some reported cases, the shaman would sacrifice his dependents in exchange for his own life. Examples of this occurrence have been found among the Nanai and Iglich peoples in the Amur River region of Central Asia even in the 20th century.

There are legends among the Yakuts and other Siberian peoples which describe numerous psychic battles between shamans. Similar accounts can be found in shamanic and other magical traditions all over the world, suggesting that the battles, the ESP Wars, in which shamans and similar individuals took part, were even more frequent than battles fought on a more physical basis. In modern times, we see examples of psychic battles on this scale in movies, TV, comic books and science fiction, fantasy and horror literature.

Siberian shamanism has one other curious connection to ESP not very widely known: the mysterious illness known as meryacheniye, which afflicted large groups of the populations of Siberia and the Far North until the 20th century. Sometimes this affliction erupted entirely spontaneously, but more often, it arose during shamanic rituals. In an altered state of consciousness, participants in shamanic rituals would imitate one another's movements and unconditionally execute whatever commands they were given. Some physicians regard meryacheniye as an induced mass hysteria and have even used the term "mental plague" to describe it.

Similar psychological states have been observed in Western Europe and Asia during periods of outbreaks of religious fanaticism, but there are ways in which meryacheniye differs from them. Several authors have observed that people occasionally imitated one another's movements without even seeing one another, evidence that some form of ESP might have been involved.

While meryacheniye was not well studied, based on accounts there is little doubt shamans and tribal leaders have at times tried to use meryacheniye for their own aims, including military ones. With total mind control, a shaman could easily turn his followers into an army. This may sound like something from a fantasy or horror novel, but we are talking about actual beliefs and local history of the region. Stories abound that such things actually happened.

Tales such as these reveal a certain universal pattern—in Jungian terms, the archetype of the "Warring Magicians."

In many cultures and societies, the role of the shaman gradually changed or was taken over by all sorts of magicians, sorcerers, priests, oracles, prophets, and healers. Rulers, military leaders, and many others sought out these magicians and prophets, trying to secure their support whether to help or harm their own people or those they would conquer or defend against. It's unlikely all—or perhaps even any majority—of these magicians' possessed genuine psychic powers, but nearly all tried to exaggerate the glory of their "otherworldly" powers and their victories in extrasensory battles.

Sorcery, prophecy, and divination have been the constant

companions of people throughout the ages. Written accounts of the use of magic and prophecy can be found in records of early cultures in Mesopotamia, India, Egypt, and China. Among those ancient peoples, the priests of the Sumerians, Akkadians, Babylonians, Assyrians, ancient Aryans, Chinese, and Egyptians in particular sought secret knowledge. The modern word 'magician' derives from the ancient Persian word magush which represents "priest" in the Zoroastrian religion.

An account from the year 522 BCE narrates the rise in power of a magician who became the king of the vast Persian Empire, which stretched across a large part of the civilized world at that time. The inscription carved into the Behistun cliff near the city of Kermanshah, reads, "And the magician Gaumata took both Persia and other countries from Cambyses, invaded them, appropriated them, and became king. Not a single man—neither Persian nor Mede nor anyone from our clan—could take the kingdom away from the magician Gaumata." However, his apparent extrasensory powers failed him in the fierce struggle for power, and the magician Gaumata was killed just half a year after he ascended to the throne.

The Warring Magicians archetype has been manifested in mythmaking, legends, and fairy tales that are so widely a part of folk culture, and can also be found in the texts of numerous religions. The following Biblical text is an example of the broad folk popularity of the Warring Magicians archetype in Ancient Egypt and Central Asia:

And Moses and Aaron went in unto Pharaoh, and they did so as the Lord had commanded: and Aaron cast down his rod before Pharaoh, and before his servants, and it became a serpent. Then Pharaoh also called the wise men and the sorcerers: now the magicians of Egypt, they also did in like manner with their enchantments. For they cast down every man his rod, and they became serpents: but Aaron's rod swallowed up their rods (Exodus 7:10-12).

Since ancient times, there have been psychological techniques that appear to allow an individual to "turn on" ESP. Such techniques typically do put the individual in some altered state of consciousness, or occur in naturally occurring altered states such as sleep and dreaming.

Dreams are one area where the shaman or the individuals taking on that role would intervene, generally providing interpretation for guidance—though sometimes themselves being the dreamers with precognitive advice for those consulting them. As far back as the time of the ancient Mesopotamian and Egyptian civilizations, we can find records of people working with dreams, interpreting them, and applying the interpretations or predictions to the workings of the society. Historical accounts from around the world provide us with examples of precognition in the form of dreams being used by those in power or wanting to grab power, whether the rulers or their advisors had the dreams themselves.

Other magicians spoke of communing with the spirits or the gods to gain insight into what the enemy might be doing, or what their own rulers ought to do next to ensure safety for their people or victory in a battle, war, or conquest. Some allowed the gods or spirits to speak directly through them, which we call "channeling." In parts of the ancient world, temple oracles were often the means by which answers from the "gods" were delivered in response to the peoples questions. Priests were said to have obtained these answers through divination practices or human mediums, who may have acquired information via extrasensory channels. It is quite likely that the mediums were naturally psychically gifted, although some method of inducing altered states of consciousness was more often used.

One of the more famous "channelers" of divine sources in ancient times was the Oracle at the temple of the god Apollo at Delphi in Greece. From the 8th Century BCE and for the next 1200 years, citizens and rulers alike sought advice in Delphi. The Delphic Oracle spoke with the words of Apollo. The priestess, the Pythia, reportedly entered an altered state of consciousness with some sort of incense or smoke and would become the medium or channel through which divine wisdom would pass. According to some sources, young and easily hypnotized girls were chosen to serve as the Pythia to deliver oracles while in trance. Other sources claim that the smoke, which could have had psychoactive properties, put the Pythia into a clairvoyant or precognitive state. Although the spoken words were generally then interpreted by other priests and applied to the "client" or problem at hand, there are direct reports of the "psychicness" of the Pythia.

Probably the first clear remote viewing experiment in recorded history—and one of the most widely known military predictions of the past—occurred when King Croesus of the wealthy state of Lydia decided to test the Oracle's powers before actually asking for the Pythia's advice. The Pythia was to focus on an unknown target involving the king of Lydia and describe it. In trance, the Oracle described what she perceived—which apparently related to the ruler having some turtle soup—and surprised the king with her accuracy. That led him to ask the more essential military question.

The father of the aforementioned Cambyses, King Cyrus the Great, had founded the Persian Empire. King Croesus wanted to stop the growth of Persian power and began to prepare a military campaign against Cyrus. So, he asked the Oracle the traditional question of whether to wage war. The Oracle's process left him with a statement: if Croesus attacked Persia, he would destroy a great kingdom. It also advised him to unite with the most powerful of the Greek states.

Although Croesus was already allied with the Egyptian Pharaoh and the King of Babylon, he followed the Oracle's recommendation and made an alliance with Sparta. Now that he was confident of blessings from the gods, Croesus began the Persian campaign in 547 BCE. At first, he experienced success, which convinced him that the prophecy was correct. But his advance was hampered in central Anatolia. In the meantime, winter had come, and at that time, it was customary to disband armies for the winter. Reassured by the prophecy and his successes, Croesus followed the custom. However, Cyrus took advantage of Croesus, attacked him, and took him prisoner.

As it turned out, the great kingdom that Croesus would destroy would be his own.

An important lesson here is that if you are going to ask an oracle a question—especially an oracle presenting information that is subject to some degree of interpretation—you'd better be certain of the exact meaning of the question, and be as specific as possible. He was told about the defeat of a great army if he attacked the Persians, and assumed the enemy would lose. But the army that was defeated was his own.

Misinterpretation—or "reading into"—the advice given by a psychic advisor or channeler or diviner is a fundamental problem of the process. One might simply argue that for the Pythia to have predicted a great army would be defeated when asked about a military campaign was both easy and obvious since when two armies clash, usually one side will be defeated. But King Croesus, looking for confirmation that he would prove victorious, blinded himself to the nuances of her prediction. Like many people who visit psychics, he heard only what he wanted to hear.

While arguably the most famous of the Delphic prophecies, an even more striking example from history illustrates the issue of interpretation and misinterpretation.

The Roman Emperor Nero became aware of the warning given by the Pythia, "Beware of the 73rd year." Nero decided that this prediction referred to his age, and because he was only a bit older than 30 at the time, it did not disturb him very much. However, within a year Nero lost his power as a result of a coup in which he was abandoned even by his own bodyguards. The loss of power lead to his suicide.

The misinterpretation? It turned out that the prediction referred to Galba, the ruler of Spain, who dethroned Nero and became emperor at the age of 73.

Throughout history, the question of interpreting the data obtained through extrasensory means has been one of the enigmas of parapsychology. There is no simple and unambiguous answer.

Aside from such prophecies, the ancient Greeks provided us with accounts of their philosophers who had other ESP abilities. The well-known philosopher and mystic Pythagoras (6th century BCE) was believed to be able to read the thoughts of those he conversed and debated with, and to see their past and future as well. According to one legend, Pythagoras received his training in these skills from Egyptian priests.

The secret Pythagorean doctrine of the magic of numbers was one of the most interesting attempts of the Greeks to connect rational thinking and logic with the mysterious irrational world of prophecies, magic rituals, and supernatural forces. The Eleusinian mysteries played a considerable role in this. The mysteries were actually highly revered ceremonies and rituals held in honor of the Greek Gods Demeter and Persephone, which almost all of the outstanding Greek philosophers took part in. It was believed that these mysteries opened up the world of spirituality and ESP to participants through altered states of consciousness. Thus, the Greeks can be considered a major connecting link between the magical world of the East and modern western culture, given the philosophical legacy that is at the heart of much of western culture and reasoning.

A well-known adage traditionally attributed to the ancient Greeks, but expressed on a grander scale in the spiritual traditions of India is, "Know yourself and you will know the world." One of its meanings is to discover extrasensory abilities through which we can gain information about the universe.

These traditions developed long ago in the practice of yoga in India, and we can find detailed accounts in the ancient Indian epics the Mahabharata and the Ramayana, which date back three to five thousand years. Patañjali presented the practices of the yogis in a systematic form in the Yoga-Sutras which are dated at about the 2nd century BCE.

In the Yoga Sutras, it's noted that various ESP abilities or special powers called siddhis appear as a natural outcome of achieving a certain degree of psychophysical development. They develop after the practitioner reaches the stage of meditation, which is the sixth stage of the eight stages of Raja Yoga. This Indian tradition emphasizes the ethical aspects of psi abilities and cautions against the use of it for personal gain, as it recognizes the adverse consequences that may occur because of such abilities. Both the Mahabharata and Ramayana are full of descriptions of yogis who engage in practices of great austerity and mortification in order to acquire extrasensory powers.

We still don't have reliable modern scientific research which can confirm the efficacy of yoga for the development of psychic abilities. However, there is some evidence to show that yoga enhances extra-sensory powers, and the authors of this book have met people who have stated this based on their personal experience.

Part of the framework of such abilities in India involved concepts of vital energy; similar concepts were developed in ancient China, where it's called Qi, sometimes written as Chi (both pronounced "chee"). Work with Qi currents that run through the body's energy meridians (pathways for the energy) often led Chinese doctors and Taoist masters to manifest ESP and PK-related phenomena. There are many cases described in Chinese manuscripts, and of course, martial artists have made such claims for quite some time.

According to legend and traditional beliefs, Buddhist masters possessed psychic powers. Legend has it that when Tibetan king Trisong-Detsen invited the guru Padmasambhava to establish Buddhism in Tibet in the 8th century, he had to endure a multitude of psychic and spiritual battles with the deities of the local Bon religion.

The Tibetan yogi Milarepa Jetsun (1052-1135 CE) narrates his own interesting experience of ESP used for ulterior motives. Considering this story only as a myth, it is a representation of the function of the Jungian Warring Magicians archetype.

When Milarepa's father died, his uncle and aunt seized all his property, including his house and land. They humiliated Milarepa, his mother and his sister, starved them, and forced them to do the hardest manual labor. His mother wanted Milarepa to study black magic in order to take revenge on his relatives. He found a lama with magic powers who trained Milarepa in the practice of destructive rituals. Milarepa recounts[3]:

I struck a blow at my enemies on the wedding day of my uncle's eldest son. All my uncle's supporters were invited to the wedding feast. His sons and his bride and also the people who were hostile towards us had gathered. There were thirty-five people in all... I followed the instructions for seven days... And that very night the patron deities actually appeared with the bleeding heads and hearts of thirty-five people. They piled them in a heap and said, 'Is this what you wanted as you continuously appealed to us these past days?'... [On the wedding day]... the stallions and mares tied below the house went berserk and began to thrash around and jostle one other. Several stallions broke loose... and eventually one of them hit the supporting column with such force that it broke, and the entire house came crashing down. Thirty-five people perished, including the bride and all of her uncle's sons. The sky was filled with smoke and clouds of dust. The corpses of the men, women, children and animals who perished were intermingled with the house debris.

Milarepa's mother publicly announced that this was her son's magical revenge. Some of the villagers were horrified by what had been done and turned against her. And then at his mother's request, Milarepa sent a hailstorm to their fields and destroyed their crops:

In the meantime, I placed the ritual device for unleashing my magical powers on a hillside facing the valley, and began casting spells, but not a single cloud appeared, not even one the size of a sparrow. I began invoking the names of the gods and retold the history of our misfortunes and described the cruelty of the neighbors and beat the earth with my garments and began to weep from despair. A dark, huge and heavy cloud suddenly appeared out of nowhere, and when it descended over the valley, the most powerful hailstorm began, leaving not a single sheaf in the fields. The hail fell three times and dug deep ravines in the hillsides. The loud wailing of hopeless and grief issued from the mouths of the villagers.

Afterwards, Milarepa bitterly regretted his deeds and soon became one of the renowned Buddhist devotees:

I felt deep remorse that I had done so much harm through black magic... I so longed to live the religious life that I even forgot to eat. I couldn't find rest day or night, and was not even able to sleep.

With regard to testimonials on the use of magic and ESP, it's important to keep in mind both the tendency to mythologize or make folklore that which people witness and may not completely understand—past and present—and the Jungian concept of synchronicity, or giving meaning and even cause and effect relationships to two purely coincidental events.

The traditions of the martial arts of Kung Fu and Tai-Chi are associated with the name of another Buddhist master, Bodhidharma (440-528 CE), who brought sacred Buddhist teachings to China from India. These teachings and traditions were further developed in places like the Shaolin monastery and led to a more meditative form of Buddhism that required some physical exercise that could keep balance in the body. In addition, the monks needed ways to defend themselves against attackers in the mountainous areas such as that around the monastery. Legend has it that the meditation, breathing, and energy exercises of the Shaolin evolved into Kung Fu.

The Shaolin monks and other Eastern martial arts schools

developed and preserved the traditions over the course of 1500 years, and presuppose systematic work with energy (Qi) in the body (and outside) and with extrasensory abilities. They even include concepts and practices of energetic "non-contact" combat and self-defense, which modern secret services and military special forces have tried to add to their arsenals.

In medieval Japan, exercises that led to the development of extrasensory—or at least enhanced sensory—capacities were typical in training saboteur spies and scouts called ninjas ("nin"-secret, "ja" - a person). For instance, in order to develop night vision, children were reportedly placed for several days or even weeks in a cave into which daylight could barely penetrate, and the children would be forced to move deeper and deeper in darkness. When light was reduced to a minimum, they would acquire the ability to see in total darkness. This was partly related to training the sensitivity of the retina. However, we cannot rule out its use to develop the extrasensory power of clairvoyance or some form of "eye-less sight." These abilities were reinforced through the systematic repetition of such trainings. The possession of these abilities very often (but not always) assisted in the individual's inner development.

Back in the West in the first millennium CE and beyond, magic users and the extrasensory gifted were held in varying degrees of respect or contempt or even fear depending on the local cultural background and folklore, and how the Church had (or had not) taken hold. Still, rulers or other powerful men might sidestep any misgivings that resulted from their embracing of the Christian faith to gain insight into their enemies and their futures. ESP Wars and battles were still in the arsenal of the rich and powerful and the military, even if they had to hide their use of such weapons and spyware.

The Middle Ages brought a new attitude towards psychic abilities and experiences, and created a different kind of application of ESP in warfare. While previously, it was apparently gifted individuals involved in both sides of psychic conflicts, in the 16th century the Catholic Church and other denominations of Christianity declared effective war against people with ESP and/or PK on a mass scale, condemning innocents by the tens of thousands in the process: the witch-hunts were on!

The Church found itself in a very ambiguous position. On the one hand, both Jesus and many saints performed miracles that were, if true, extrasensory in nature. On the other hand, the Church tried in every possible way to deny that ordinary people possessed these abilities. Since it was impossible to deny the obvious, people with ESP were declared "Satan's messengers" who operated "with all power and signs and lying wonders." (2 Thessalonians 2:9)

The number of executions for sorcery and witchcraft before the 13th century was rather insignificant. It was only after Pope Innocent VIII's "Sorcerer's bill", "Summis desiderantes" in 1484 that real witch-hunts became widespread, with a peak during the 16th and 17th centuries, and hundreds of thousands burned at the stake, hanged, or otherwise executed or imprisoned. It's possible this began because of an exercise of political power (as with the Inquisition in Spain) or perhaps members of the Church actually feared individuals who possessed psychic abilities could see other dimensions of the universe and divinity and/or could see through the politics of the religion. Or perhaps they were jealous (or afraid) that such people might have had a real connection with the Divine.

During this period having psychic powers and being caught trying to demonstrate it virtually assured death. Perhaps after several generations, this might have altered the gene pool, though one cannot calculate the number of those executed who might have had more than the normal smattering of psychic experiences or abilities.

In fact, there were numerous reasons seemingly behind why people were accused. Actually demonstrating something psychic or practicing an occult or magical or folk healing art were reasons that undoubtedly accounted for only a small number of victims of the witch-hunts. Disbelieving in Church doctrine, or practicing a non-Christian religion at the very least often resulted in expulsion from a locale and at the worst led to being accused of witchcraft. Being old, infirm, maimed, orphaned, or ill put many in the "witch" category. Unmarried or widowed women who owned property coveted by others were accused in order to take that property, and in many cases, the accusation was used to remove political or even business rivals.

As it happens, the witch-hunts during the 16th and 17th centuries (perhaps ironically) coincided with the time of the Enlightenment, and a considerable number of the active "witch hunters" were actually "humanists"—educated philosophers, writers, lawyers and doctors. It seems to us that different factors are combined here, just as in any difficult social phenomenon. By the time, the witch-hunts petered out, the Catholic Church and some of the other denominations had already passed the peak of their political power.

One exercise of the power of the Church did indeed have to do with apparent psychic abilities, though this is not limited to only Christianity. There are numerous accounts in the Old Testament and the history of Judaism of the powers of prophets to provide the words of God to humanity, as shamans and other magic workers had done for thousands of years in communication with their gods or spirits. Some of the miracles of the Old Testament might be interpreted as the use of psychokinesis.

The history of early Christianity and the Catholic Church portrays miracles on the part of Jesus and many saints coming after him. Saints such as Gerald of Aurillac, Catherine of Siena, Nicholas of Torentino, Melangell of Wales, and Paola Frassinetti were all healers with apparently extraordinary powers. This tradition of canonizing healers has continued through until today.

Another sign or power that indicated the presence of the divine in a pious individual was (self) levitation. St. Teresa of Avila was one who reportedly levitated on occasion, including an incident where it occurred without her thought or desire.

The 17th century saint, Joseph of Cupertino, known today as the patron saint of pilots and astronauts, is the one saint in history who probably flew more often than Sally Field in the TV show The Flying Nun. His levitations reportedly began shortly after he became a priest. Not merely content to float above the ground, he was apparently able to fly even with others on his back. Sources vary as to how often he "flew" for witnesses, with some saying as many as over 100 times. It should also be noted that St. Joseph did much in the way of healing. That he was a priest was possibly why he was not accused of witchcraft; however, he did get in some trouble with the Inquisitors in Naples, who ended up sending him to a monastery.

The powers of the saints were not used, as far as we know, for warfare. However, on occasion war was at the heart of the situation in which the miracles seemed to happen. One such case is that of Saint Joan of Arc, and her story is a great one for analyzing the use of ESP in war.

Born in 1412, Joan had heard voices since childhood. These disembodied voices told her that her mission in life was to save her homeland. When she announced this mission, Joan was sent to the court of the French Dauphin (the heir apparent to the throne of France). After many interrogations, he informed those present that Joan shared a certain secret with him, that no one except God knew or could know, and that this was why he trusted her completely. It is assumed that Joan found out the Dauphin's personal prayer telepathically and repeated it to him out loud word for word.

As a result, Joan was given an army and she went on to lead the French in several important victories during the Hundred Years War. One important victory was to break the siege of Orleans, the last barrier that kept the English from capturing all of France. The battle was reportedly won in a most incredible way. As some historians point out, the English made inexplicable mistakes and simply threw down their arms. Their course of action was so strange that it is easy to try to explain it with supernatural reasons, and these have been attributed to Joan of Arc.

Many people witnessed Joan's gift of prophecy. She would casually say, "Wait, in three days we will take the city," or "Be patient, in an hour you will win," and what she said would come true. Ultimately, France retained its sovereignty. Still, apparently, the Church or simply politics got the best of her situation, and she was burnt at the stake as a witch in 1431 at the age of 19. The Catholic Church beatified her in 1902 and she was later canonized as a saint in 1920.

It is interesting to note that real precognition does not always result in real-world success. As a counterpoint to Joan of Arc's case, we can look at an example from Russian medieval history.

Russian chronicles of the 17th century preserved a story of the scholarly monk Sylvester Medvedev, who hid the volkhv (clairvoyant sorcerer) Dmitrii Silin in his cell for three years. Volkhvs in ancient Russia were the successors of the pre-Christian, virtually shamanic traditions, and the Orthodox Church strongly opposed them. But the Orthodox monk Sylvester wanted to use Silin's ESP powers to become Russia's patriarch, and to also help his patron prince Vasilii Golitsyn become Tsar of Muscovy.

At the time, Golitsyn was the de facto head of the government while Tsarevna Sofia Alekseyevna acted as regent for her young brothers Ivan V and Peter I (later Peter the Great). Golitsyn's attempt at a governmental coup and Medvedev's dream of becoming patriarch ended in their executions. The volkhv Silin already knew this and told the conspirators about it, but it did not stop them.

Their legal case investigation[4] stated:

And Sylvester Medvedev told him to look into the sun: how will Prince Golitsyn fare and will he be Tsar of Muscovy?... and would he, Sylvester become patriarch? And he, Silin, taking heed of Sylvester's words, went to the Bell Tower of Ivan the Great and looked into the sun twice. And in the sun he saw that all the great princes wore their crowns on their heads as usual, but that prince Vasilii Golitsyn's crown was dangling around his chest and all sides of him, and that he, the prince, stood there somberly and then walked around in circles; and that Tsarevna Sofya Alekseevna was sad and troubled, and that Silvester was gloomy... And it seemed that he, Sylvester Medvedev, told Silin to go to prince Golitsyn. And the prince asked: would he be a great man in Muscovy? And Silin told him that he would not undertake it, and that it would not come to pass, that nothing would happen.

The age of Enlightenment, with its emphasis on science and reason, set ESP into the background for a time, while interest in magic and the supernatural remained. The focus was now on a rational understanding of psychic phenomena and what was called "supernatural" and developing theories to account for them.

The famous German doctor Franz Anton Mesmer (1734-1815), who had a medical practice in Vienna, became one of the foremost proponents of this time. Mesmer is, of course, whom "mesmerism"— which evolved into hypnosis—is named after.

Confronted with several difficult cases, Mesmer tried using strong magnets to treat his patients. He based this on Paracelsus's ideas about influence of magnetic "fluids" on the body. Many of his patients recovered, which convinced Mesmer of the existence of "animal magnetism" by which a person can "be recharged" by the planets and can, in turn, charge other objects. Mesmer proclaimed his discovery and became very popular. However, conflicts with the other doctors and the academic world dogged him to the end of his life.

A host of later research in the ESP field arose from Mesmer's work, particularly attempts to create accumulators of biological energy. Hypnosis was the active power of his healing process, even though it took a very long time for any official recognition of this method by members of the scientific and medical communities. Hypnosis was also one of the topics for study mentioned in the charter of the Society for Psychical Research when it formed in 1882.

Mesmer's ideas were echoed in the works of the well-known German scientist and chemist Baron Karl von Reichenbach, the inventor of kerosene and paraffin. He speculated on the existence of certain "vital energy" which he named Odkraft that emanates from organic and inorganic bodies and can be perceived by very sensitive people. Reichenbach began to experiment with "odic energy" and published the results in highly reputable journals such as The Annals of Physics and Chemistry. His results were confirmed in independent experiments. Today we know this phenomenon by the term "biofield."

On the psychic side of things, the 18th century Swedish scholar Emanuel Swedenborg experienced a spiritual renaissance late in life. Convinced he was receiving divine information, Swedenborg purportedly channeled information from angels (who may have been human souls in life) and God for a number of years. In addition, he evidenced remote viewing and telepathic abilities. His teachings had some effect on the development of spiritualism in the next century, which we discuss in the following chapter.

During this time period, there were psychically focused individuals in Russia as well. Eighteenth century Circassian monk Login Kochkaryov made predictions of Napoleon's war with Russia and the First World War to General-Governor Pyotr Dmitrievich Yeropkin and to the Empress Catherine II in Moscow.

As the story goes, this strange wandering monk came to Moscow in January, 1789. As he was walking past the merchant Akhlopkov's house, he suddenly ran up to it and began throwing handfuls of snow into the windows. The police arrived, and the man told them his name was Login Kochkaryov. He further told them he saw the house on fire and hurried to put out the fire. Kochkaryov was detained for disturbing the peace. The following day, however, the merchant's house did catch fire.

The Moscow Governor-General Pyotr Dmitrievich Eropkin was then informed of the incident, and when Eropkin personally interrogated him, Kochkaryov predicted that Russia would be at war with Napoleon in 1812. The governor snidely expressed a desire to find out something about the near future. The monk immediately replied, "No later than tomorrow you can look forward to great unexpected joy." The next day, to Eropkin's considerable amazement, the Empress sent him the gift of a gold snuff box, encrusted with precious stones, with her portrait. This reward for devoted service was nearly the equivalent of a medal!

Then the governor sent Login Kochkaryov off to the Empress with this letter[5]:

This man, despite his insight and wondrous gift of prophesying the future, can call into being disastrous consequences, for he has predicted that overwhelming hostile forces will invade Russia and capture Moscow, of which not a single stone will remain standing. This prediction can cause great mental agitation.

In St. Petersburg, Kochkaryov was subjected to "special" observation by local medics and other learned men. He had an audience with Empress Catherine II, after which she wrote to Eropkin:

Pyotr Dmitrievich, the man whom you sent, Kochkaryov, is very unusual. He also predicted to us that there would be a war in 1812 that would destroy Moscow, and that this war would end in our victory. He also predicted a war at the beginning of the 20th century involving many peoples.

Kochkaryov made further predictions to Catherine that there would be a long war in the Caucasus and that many Asian lands would be unified under the Russian Empire. The rest of what the seer told the Empress has remained a mystery because all other traces of the soothsayer have been lost. But it can be suggested that Russia's calm reaction to the news of Napoleon's invasion and the strategy to withdraw from active military operations could probably have been the result of the Russian imperial house knowing about the onset and the outcome of the war.

It's important to note that alongside what we believe was real ESP phenomena have been cases of cheating, deception, and fraud. It's sometimes difficult to say which label—real or fraud—to apply to every instance in records throughout recorded history. One such case, which occurred after the rise of Spiritualism in the West, is something that happened to Friedrich Wilhelm II, King of Prussia.

Fraud, yes—but certainly a somewhat comic example of the application of psychic advice to military decisions. Or so it was believed by the King.

In 1871, the King of Prussia was persuaded to join the Order of Gold Rosicrucians, secretly directed by his French "big brothers." Later, when Prussia was at war with France, Friedrich Wilhelm was called away from a ball by a Rosicrucian password, and the ghost of his grandfather Friedrich II appeared in a dark hall before the king. "The grandfather's ghost" advised Friedrich Wilhelm not to interfere in France's affairs.

Impressed by this séance, the King never gave the order to attack Paris and stopped the Prussian army near Verdun. Due to the inexplicable indecision of the Prussian command, the badly organized and poorly trained French armies unexpectedly gained victory in the battle at Valmy.

That ghost was actually the French actor Fleury.

There was a quite a focus on messages and advice from spirits that came out of the influence of Spiritualism in the mid-1800s. Spiritualism was also key in the beginnings of the field of psychical research, and its successor parapsychology, and the popularization of psychic and spiritual powers in the West—leading to new attempts to bend ESP to war, and leading into our next chapter.

NOTES:

1) Quoted from Basilov V.N. The Elects by Spirits, M. Politizdat., 1984 (in Russian)

2) Also quoted from Basilov V.N. The Elects by Spirits, M. Politizdat., 1984 (in Russian)

3) Milarepa: The Great Yogi of Tibet." Translated into Russian by O. Tumanova.

4) I. Kozlovsky. Sylvester Medvedev, Kiev, 1895 (in Russian)

5) Alexander Gorbovsky

CHAPTER 2

MORE MODERN INTEREST IN ESP FOR SPYING AND WARFARE: FROM SPIRITUALISM TO NAZI OCCULTISM—EAST, WEST & IN-BETWEEN

An unprecedented explosion of mass interest in psychic and spiritual phenomena characterized the second half of the 19th century that affected countries in the East and the West, and included the more or less official beginnings of parapsychology with the founding of the Society for Psychical Research (SPR) in Great Britain in 1882. There were several major and minor influences operating in the early days of psychical research: the popularity of mesmerism, von Reichenbach's writings, theosophy, and the burgeoning spiritualist movement and the rise of rational empiricism in science, both of the latter which were occurring around the mid-1800s.

Rational and empirical thought in science at the time shaped how early researchers looked at the experiences and phenomena. From the start their aim was to collect empirical data about the psychic and spiritual events in the world so that they could truly explain just one more part of the vast range of human experience.

On the other hand, healing by means of the laying-on of hands, conversations about telepathy and eyeless vision, and especially conjuring spirits and conversing with the dead became popular with all the social classes. However, it was the spiritualist movement that really set the stage for just what would be studied, though it was not the whole of the stage's psychic scenery—and setting the stage specifically for the ESP Wars of the 20th century.

EAST AND WEST

Spiritualism had a very humble beginning. While the various phenomena under the "spiritual" umbrella had been happening for thousands of years, and in the early 1840s the works of Emanuel Swedenborg were influencing many in that direction, it was the experiences of two sisters living near Rochester, New York that in 1848 crystallized (and popularized) interest in psychic occurrences. Margaretta and Katherine Fox demonstrated some kind of contact with spirits that resulted in rapping noises produced to answer questions.

The wave of interest and spiritual contact spread a bit in the United States, but for some reason—possibly due to a lack of an overall, organized movement—it more or less subsided until about the time of the Civil War. However, the "movement" had begun to spread to Great Britain, also with interest in the popular Fox sisters, beginning in the 1850s.

Here in the States, while the movement was less organized, there were waves of interest in spirit contact during and after the War Between the States and the First World War with so many lives lost during warfare, there was a natural urge for people who had lost loved ones to want to try to contact them. In addition, due to the death of their child, Mary Todd Lincoln and Abraham Lincoln (especially the former) took part in various spiritualistic activities.

People of every economic stratum were equally seized by an enthusiasm for meetings with mediums, conjuring spirits, spinning saucers, and turning tables. Families held séances in their parlors, day and night, and psychic games were quite popular play for adults and children alike. The popular (and controversial) Ouija Board came out of these home-based activities.

But it wasn't just the United Kingdom and North America. Before World War I, there were over 2000 spiritualist circles in Germany, 3000 in France, 3500 in Russia—with 1000 in St. Petersburg alone. In response to this craze, the Physical Society of St. Petersburg University even organized a commission on mediums in 1875. The commission, headed by the world-renowned scientist Dmitri Mendeleyev, who devised the Periodic Table of the Elements, built a special instrument: a table with a pressure gauge that recorded the pressure exerted by participants' hands during séances. After completing its research, the commission concluded that, "Spiritualist phenomena arise either from unconscious movements or from conscious deceit, and that spiritualist teaching (the belief in spirits) is superstition." However, this statement made no impression on the public at large—mediums continued to "conquer" the world with their popularity.

At the same time, Western European civilization began to discover Eastern philosophy along with the practices of Hindu and Buddhist yoga. Societies that studied and practiced occultism and Eastern doctrines began appearing everywhere. Elena Blavatskaya, better known as Madame Blavatsky, and Colonel Henry Olcott founded the Theosophical Society, arguably the most famous of these societies, on November 17, 1875 in New York. The Society had the declared purpose of researching previously unstudied laws of nature and human capabilities on the basis of a synthesis of Eastern and Western spiritual achievements. But there is no doubt that Madame Blavatsky's hidden agenda was the creation of a new world religion, as this can be seen even in her choice of the term theosophy, which means "divine wisdom" in Greek. Despite claims that it was intended to be a religion, theosophy alongside mediumship, became a real influence on modern parapsychology especially in the East, and Madame Blavatsky became a name that is well-known even today.

Elena Petrovna Blavatskaya was born in 1831 in Russia into a wealthy and distinguished aristocratic family from one of the dynastic lines of the Dolgoruky princes who founded Moscow. According to her aunt, Elena demonstrated special mental powers as well as a lively and penetrating mind from early childhood. Her grandfather was the governor of Astrakhan, a region where many Kalmyk Buddhists lived. This gave Elena the opportunity to become acquainted with Eastern teachings at an early age. She married at seventeen, but soon left her husband and set off to travel around the world. She visited many countries during the next quarter century, and claimed that after repeated attempts to get into Tibet, she eventually succeeded in making two trips there. In 1873 she went to America, where she met Colonel Henry Olcott, who aided her in founding the Theosophical movement in 1875.

Although the foundation of Theosophy, Blavatskaya's main works, The Secret Doctrine and Isis Unveiled, are essentially an improbable mix of eastern legends, scraps of philosophy, attacks on science, travel notes, mediumistic revelations and simple fairy tales, they made a huge impression on an American and European reading public that was captivated by the East, and served as the underpinning of the Theosophical movement. American inventor Thomas Edison, French astronomer Camille Flammarion, and the eminent English psychologist William James were among the many celebrities of the day who belonged to the Theosophical Society.

It is difficult to exaggerate the enormous influence that the Theosophical society had on esoteric thought around the world. Theosophical societies sprang up in Germany in 1884, in France in 1893, in Russia in 1908 and in many other countries. The Theosophical Society was first based in the US, but its founders then moved its headquarters to India in 1879. Several years later, Blavatskaya—Madame Blavatsky— moved to Europe.

THE WEST

In general, the developing scientific world regarded Theosophy and Spiritualism as dubious. However, with a spiritualist movement focusing so much public attention on psychic phenomena in England, the interest of several scholars was piqued. This led to the foundation of the Society for Psychical Research (SPR) in 1882. Among the founders were intellectual spiritualists, theosophists, and scientists associated with Cambridge University, including Henry Sidgwick and Frederick W. H. Myers, with Sidgwick assuming the role of the SPR's first president.

In 1885, following a visit by Sir William Barrett to the United States, the American Society for Psychical Research was founded in Boston. Famed psychologist William James and astronomer-mathematician Simon Newcomb inspired the formation of the ASPR, with Newcomb as its first president. Richard Hodgson came from Britain to the United States in 1887 to take over as executive secretary of the ASPR, which became an official branch of the British SPR, remaining as such until Hodgson's death in 1905. Professor James H. Hyslop, a former professor of logic at Columbia University, became the newly re-organized ASPR's secretary and director, making it independent of the SPR and bringing the technical methods of the scientist to psychical research in the United States.

The French Society for Psychical Research was also founded in 1885, and the Russian Society of Experimental Psychology formed a commission to study the phenomenon of "mind reading" in 1890.

During the years between the founding of the SPR and ASPR and Hyslop's death in 1920, the major thrust of both organizations was an interest in the phenomena brought to light by spiritualist mediums. Many of these early investigators were quite stubborn and often skeptical, and brought up the important question when dealing with apparent communication with spirits: further information received by a medium is passed by an actual spirit entity, or through the medium's own clairvoyant or telepathic reception of the same information from "records" or from living sources.

In general, all of the organizations sought to distinguish real paranormal phenomena from charlatanism and to investigate them as a branch of science. Besides the work with mediums, they did surveys of the public's psychic experiences, investigated reported cases of apparitions, hauntings and poltergeists, and studied cases of spontaneous telepathy and precognition that had been confirmed by witnesses. One of the most extensive surveys was conducted by the SPR. The "Census of Hallucinations" was conducted in 1889-90, studying over 17,000 replies from the British public and asking questions about apparitional and other psychic experiences. Much was accomplished in research, even though the researchers themselves were sometimes greatly disappointed by the results— especially when investigating or studying spirit mediums.

The tests that the SPR conducted, contrary to the intentions of their members to find actual phenomena, helped to expose deception more often than confirming any reality of mediumistic phenomena. Some positive results with spirit mediums were often overshadowed by fraud and even scandal.

With the Theosophical Society, a scandal broke out that would be the first in a long series that exposed cases of fraud by theosophists. Emma Coulomb, who worked in the Society's headquarters, exposed a number of the tricks that the theosophists were using to fool the public after apparently failing to convince Blavatsky to pay her for silence on the matter. Her story immediately appeared in the newspapers. As a result of this and other scandals, several theosophical societies, including the German one, were disbanded. Madame Blavatsky died in 1891.

There were other issues of opposition with spiritualist mediums both within and without the scientific community that affected the SPR somewhat, and the ASPR more directly. Between 1923 and 1941, the American SPR tried various means to popularize psychical research, which led to some loss of prestige. A splinter group was formed in Boston in 1925 as the Boston Society for Psychical Research. The fascination of some of its more prominent members with the antics of medium Mina Crandon of Boston (known as "Margery") caused a wide split in the attitudes of members and outside observers alike when a great controversy over her legitimacy arose out of work carried on by a number of investigators, most notably Harry Houdini, who complained that she was a complete fraud who had even offered sexual favors to investigators in return for an endorsement as a genuine medium. Other colorful personalities also used accusations of fraud against Margery as publicity for themselves, and in fact, the controversy over Margery's legitimacy as a medium/psychic continues to this day, with some histories of the period suggesting that Houdini planted evidence to frame Mrs. Crandon.

The Margery mediumship brought to a head the controversy over fraudulent mediums that still goes on (with accusations of fraud tossed at any supposedly gifted psychic). In some respects, it pushed researchers in a direction that firmly established the field of parapsychology as an experimental science.

When ASPR President Hyslop died, William McDougall succeeded to the presidency of the ASPR, and became one of the two people really responsible for the rise of what we call parapsychology. McDougall, a psychologist from Oxford, came over to teach at Harvard while also serving as ASPR president. His influence on the other important figure, a young biologist by the name of Joseph Banks Rhine, led Rhine to follow McDougall to Duke University in 1927.

Luckily for McDougall and Rhine, they were able to avoid

becoming embroiled in the scandalous situation of the Margery mediumship, keeping a skeptical, noncommittal attitude about her genuineness as a medium. Rhine and his wife Louisa followed McDougall to Duke in 1927 for postdoctoral studies, and along with McDougall were really interested in making studies of psychic phenomena acceptable to the academic world, and to research scientists, in the controlled experimental situation of the laboratory. They wished to do more than merely see psi at work: they sought patterns and explanations for the displays that the investigators witnessed. They wished to gather data that would lead to some kind of answers to prove the existence of this newly investigated phenomena. They also wished to show the universal nature of psychic abilities, that all people shared the talents seemingly evidenced by so called psychics and mediums. In addition, bringing psychical research into the laboratory with "normal" subjects and controlled conditions could reduce the chance of dealing with fraudulent subjects out for publicity

As it happens, they were not the first researchers to give psychic phenomena the laboratory treatment. Over in France, in the early 20th century, Rene Warcollier conducted what might be considered the first remote viewing experiments, though often these were telepathy experiments with senders focusing on drawings, rather than location descriptions. Warcollier, in collaboration with Gardner Murphy, also conducted transatlantic telepathy experiments in the early 1920s.

In the United States, psychologist John Coover conducted various ESP experiments in a laboratory at Stanford University, under funding by Thomas Stanford. Coover's results were generally negative (no better than chance) according to his report published in 1917, though later reassessment of the data presented showed there was actually statistical significance displayed. One of the more interesting studies he performed had to do with a person knowing when they were being stared at, a commonly reported experience, and one that is the subject of much current parapsychological research.

Even with these earlier researchers making their mark, it was McDougall and then the Rhines who really kick-started the field of parapsychology under that name. Coined by Max Dessoir of Germany several years before, J. B. Rhine, with McDougall's approval, adopted the term "parapsychology" to somewhat distance his laboratory/academic studies of psychic phenomena from the work of the psychical researchers. The original sense of his use of the word parapsychology related to experimental and quantitative studies of psi, more or less as a subset of the broad category of psychical research, although today we use the terms interchangeably, along with the term "psi research."

During the early work by McDougall and the Rhines, the terms "extrasensory perception" and "psychokinesis" were introduced with ESP covering the informational psychic abilities, and PK relating to the interactional ones. ESP is probably a poor term, since there may not be anything extra about this information channel, or even anything sensory. Yet it does seem to mimic the way we normally perceive things ("seeing" a vision that may be precognitive in nature). Psi, the 23rd letter of the Greek alphabet, was finally introduced as a more or less generic heading covering both ESP and PK.

After one year at Duke, Rhine joined the staff of the Department of Psychology. His area of specialization began with experiments on telepathy and clairvoyance, and later with psychokinesis and precognition. During his first few years there, psychologist Karl Zener, a colleague of Rhine's, developed the ESP cards so familiar to all, in order to simplify the statistics involved in collecting the data. The initial results of those early tests were less than inspiring, until some long distance telepathy tests were conducted in 1933, later written up by Rhine in his book Extra Sensory Perception. These experiments, with participants J. G. Pratt (who later worked with Rhine as a parapsychologist) and Herbert Pearce achieved significant scores and stirred controversy around those scores that continues to this day.

The Parapsychology Laboratory was started on its own in 1935, with the Journal of Parapsychology beginning publication in 1937. Initial emphasis of the Laboratory was on strict, experimentally controlled investigations, and this was stated in the Journal's first issue as the way of psi research for the future (by McDougall). While this was not the first time controlled laboratory experiments had been conducted, it was the first time an organization/laboratory had been set up for continued statistical analysis of psi effects. Rhine's research also deals with subsequent periods of the history of parapsychology, which we will discuss later in this book.

In the US and the UK, there were numerous stellar performers in the ranks of mediums from the late 19th to early 20th centuries, some working as mental mediums (messages from the deceased), some as physical mediums (those dim or dark room séance folks who had things moving around and ectoplasm appearing) or both. Fraud was rampant, unfortunately, though there were mediums who seemed genuine to the researchers who investigated them, and some who were a bit "mixed."

Most of the physical mediums would conduct their séances in near or total darkness, quite possibly because the phonies and stage performers created an expectation in lay audiences that this was the only way for the spirits to come forth. However, such conditions left lots of room for fraudulently produced effects.

A rare photo of J. B. Rhine and his wife, Louisa

One of the most famous and controversial physical mediums of the nineteenth century, Daniel Dunglas Home, stayed away from total darkness in his séances. Of course, it might be argued that he never did a séance, as no spirits were contacted. Among the effects reportedly produced by Home were raps on tables and walls, levitation of articles on a table or of the table itself, self-levitation (including one reported incident where he levitated horizontally out of one window and returned through another in a different part of the room), temporary immunity to fire with the apparent ability to transfer the ability, though in a limited way, to others, and continued physical events occurring until well after the formal séance.

Spirits? From the descriptions of Home and other similar physical mediums, it would appear they were more gifted with psychokinesis than with any sort of spirit contact abilities. However, his reported feats fit in with reports of shamans and other mystics around the world who were either channeling or were given such powers by divine or spiritual entities.

Another physical medium who claimed to be getting her powers from the spirit world was Eusapia Palladino. A stout, Italian woman of the late 19th and early 20th centuries, Palladino was known to produce a wide range of physical events in her séances, including raps, levitations, curtain movements, breezes, partial materializations of some wispy forms, "cold" fire and fights, and more, some of it in full light. Palladino was also known for faking effects for the clients and researchers. Apparently, she admitted doing this because it was easier on her to fake the effects than to "really" produce them. Even given this proclivity to take the easy way out, the researchers and magicians who studied her still found much that was inexplicable, including the bizarre loss of weight during séances (those where they could detect no fraud). In fact, the weight loss was common for her, with the average being only a few pounds.

Researchers from all over studied Palladino—but not without problems. An 1895 study by the British SPR yielded what has been called the "Cambridge Fiasco." The researchers of the SPR were apparently unprepared to study Palladino under appropriate controlled conditions. According to the late parapsychologist D. Scott Rogo, because the SPR had not kept up on the European literature about her, they were unaware of her ability to fake things. Of course, Palladino, not hit with many controls, took the easy way out and apparently faked it.

The SPR was embarrassed about the situation, though three more SPR investigators, Everard Fielding, W. W. Baggally, and Hereward Carrington, did give Palladino another go. This time, after careful controls, they reported that Palladino was genuine. The account of the investigation, known as the "Fielding Report,"[1] described hundreds of separate phenomena reportedly manifested under stringent conditions.

While there were probably hundreds (if not thousands) of mental mediums operating in the late 1800s and early 1900s, probably two of the more famous of the period were Lenore Piper and Gladys Osborne Leonard.

Mrs. Piper came under scrutiny of the psychical researchers in the US in the 1890s, primarily Richard Hodgson. Mrs. Piper had a number of spirit "controls" who either spoke through her or came through in automatic writing, including fictional controls (in other words, the person the "spirit" claimed to be never really lived). In addition, Mrs. Piper apparently could gain information from both the dead and the living. While telepathy of living sources was often the preferred explanation for how some of the information received by mediums like Mrs. Piper could be true, Hodgson became convinced that her sources were often the deceased.

Gladys Leonard, a medium from Great Britain, began channeling early in the twentieth century. Feda, her control, was apparently the Hindu wife of one of Leonard's ancestors. Feda gave no direct evidence that could be used to verify her existence, though as with a number of the reincarnation cases, sufficiently detailed records that could sort out any verifiable information from what Mrs. Leonard already knew about her ancestor probably didn't exist. Leonard was thoroughly investigated for fraud by researchers, and was extremely successful with a number of complex tasks that appeared to limit the possibility of her telepathically picking up information from the minds of those sitting in the séance.

Better-known, though not nearly as well investigated, was the medium/channeler Edgar Cayce. Born in Kentucky, in 1877, the man known as "the sleeping prophet" was apparently capable of all sorts of readings for people with no more information than a name and address, indicating he was likely a bit of a remote viewer. His readings were typically directed at the health of the individual, and were reportedly more than a bit accurate. Prescribing treatments that are rooted less in medicine than in folk medicine—much like shamanic practitioners—many people reported being helped by

Cayce's advice. Cayce had no working knowledge of medicine (which showed, according to some critics, in the inaccuracies of many readings). Readings also included those concerning past lives, and Cayce often spoke while in trance of the ancient civilization of Atlantis.

Cayce first worked as a salesman, though he did report having psychic experiences even as a child. It was not until after he sought out a hypnotist to help him with an apparently incurable throat ailment that his true "calling" became evident. In "trance," Cayce was apparently able to both diagnose and offer a cure for his own ailment. It was suggested he try this same technique with others, and subsequently he began diagnosing and suggesting treatment through a self-induced trance state.

During his lifetime, Cayce conducted approximately thirty thousand health readings. In 1931, Cayce founded the Association for Research and Enlightenment (ARE) in Virginia Beach, Virginia. The ARE supports some research and education and has thousands of members and local groups around the world, though primarily in the United States. Cayce died in 1945, having left his personal mark on the lives of tens of thousands of people through his readings, and millions more through his writings. His books are still in print and easily obtained, and his readings are available online.

After the West's initial enthusiasm towards psi phenomena in the early part of the 20th century, the 1930s saw a rise in criticism of extrasensory perception and mysticism with members of the scientific community reacting negatively to the activities of the psi community. Even Rhine's serious research and several scientific papers on ESP during this time could not sway popular scientific opinion. The first few years of the Rhine work produced little in the way of knowledge of how psi functions, although there did pop up clusters of well-scoring subjects in the early days, and a few effects led to looking at attitude and personality influences on the occurrence of psi. In 1940, in a volume by Rhine, J. G. Pratt, and a few others entitled Extra Sensory Perception after Sixty Years, the Rhine work was summarized. The volume describes 145 ESP experiments in which more than 75,000 people participated. In 106 of them, the results surpassed the number predicted by probability theory. Rhine summarized various approaches to the study of paranormal phenomena and invited his scientific colleagues and critics to write independent chapters; however, the negative attitude prevailed and only three of them responded due to continuing severe pressure from the academic world. Nevertheless, Rhine's book still played an historical role. He never gave up, and continually refined his laboratory methodology in the fight to gain acceptance for parapsychology among the wider scientific community.

Around that same time (1941), the ASPR was reorganized and reconstructed under the guidance of Dr. George H. Hyslop (Professor Hyslop's son), bringing together under one roof the old ASPR and the Boston SPR. At the initial meeting, Dr. Gardner Murphy, a prominent psychologist, was elected to the Board of Trustees and named Chairman of the ASPR Research Committee. This became a commitment to doing some laboratory research, and an element of continuity and relationship to the work done at the Duke Parapsychology Laboratory.

Scandal, fraud, and an emphasis on direction towards laboratory interest in psi and away from investigations of mediumship, as well as technological development in the world in general, pushed the mystique of the medium into the background of psychical research. Parapsychologists, as they were now more frequently called, were more interested in proving to the world the existence of psi phenomena and learning how it works through controlled situations with average people than they were in watching tables tilt and ectoplasm form, at least in the US and UK. Even the attitudes of the public began to shift. While people still went to see mediums, psychics, and fortunetellers, they did so in a more private manner, as technology seemed to ridicule those practices, especially in light of the fraud controversies surrounding so many mediums.

THE EAST

In some parts of the world, Eastern mysticism was often mixed up with ideas of the "occult" and "black magic," and some seemingly psychic figures often added to those connections, whether deserved or not. Take for example the case of one of history's darker-seeming characters, Grigory Rasputin (1869-1916)—thought by some to be a practitioner of the "black arts."

The "sacred elder" was a peasant by birth who gained a reputation as a mystic with healing powers and second sight. Sometimes called the "Mad Monk" due to his religious practices, a mythology has sprung up around him and his role in the court of the Romanovs and their fall from power. In 1905, the healer was sent for to help Alexis, the son of Tsar Nicholas II and Tsarina Alexandra. The boy suffered from hemophilia and somehow Rasputin was able to provide some relief or healing—or so it seemed.

From then on, he became a favorite of the Russian imperial couple during that period, having promoted the reshuffling of ministers and the destruction of the government's apparatus through his hypnotic influence, extrasensory abilities, and intrigues. Stories of his influence over the court, his sexual antics, drinking, taking bribes, and sometimes bizarre behavior affected his reputation and that of the court. One could definitely say his presence exerted influence over many political decisions made, whether it was his own charismatic advice or simply the way others approached the Tsar and Tsarina while he was present. Some historians "credit" him with the weakening of power of the imperial family, making it easier for their ouster.

Besides tales of his ESP and what some called his unnatural ability to influence those around him, including predictions of a coming war before the start (or even the inkling of the start) of WWI, there is much mythology built up around his assassination and specifically how he died. After no effect from eating poisoned cakes, according to accounts Rasputin was apparently shot, stabbed, beaten, and drowned before death claimed him.

Early 20th century scientific investigation of ESP was, of course, not limited to the US and UK, or even France and Germany, as research in Russia had also begun in earnest. The Russian scientists Vladimir Bekhterev, Vladimir Durov, Bernard Kazhinsky and Leonid Vasiliev are among the pioneers who began serious scientific research into the phenomena of telepathy and mental suggestion. The prominent Russian neurophysiologist and psychiatrist Vladimir Bekhterev, who had a longtime scientific interest in psychic phenomena, was the founder of the Psychoneurological Institute in 1907, and the Institute of the Study of the Brain and Mental Activity in 1918 in St. Petersburg (Leningrad). At the suggestion of the celebrated animal trainer Vladimir Durov, he conducted a series of joint experiments using mental suggestion with animals as subjects. Bekhterev describes how they began their teamwork[2]:

A number of experiments of this type were conducted in my apartment with a small male dog named Pikki, by nature a very lively and smart fox terrier... The experiments were conducted after the dinner hour with several members of my family, including two doctors, O. Bekhtereva-Nikonova and E. Vorobyova present...

Pikki easily carried out all mental tasks [of those present]... In order to be fully confident...I decided to conduct a similar experiment myself, without telling anyone what it would be. My task was to have the dog jump up on a round chair located about two sazhens [sazhen is an old Russian measure of length, equivalent to 2.13 meters] from the grand piano and to sit there. As in our previous experiments, the dog was invited to jump up on the chair; while I was concentrating on the shape of the round chair, I looked into the dog's eyes, and Pikki bolted from me at a breakneck speed and ran around the dining table many times. I considered the experiment a failure, but I recalled that I had concentrated exclusively on the shape of the round chair, forgetting that I should have begun concentrating on having the dog move toward the round chair and jump on it. So I decided to repeat the experiment, without telling anyone about the error, and corrected myself as I just described.

I invited the dog to jump up on the chair again and took its muzzle between my palms. I began thinking that the dog should run to the round chair located about one sazhen behind me, jump on it and remain there. After concentrating for about half to three quarters of a minute, I released the dog, and within an instant the dog was already sitting on the round chair. As I mentioned earlier, no one except me knew about the task that Pikki had executed in this case, because I did not consult with any one about it and, nevertheless, Pikki guessed my secret without the slightest difficulty.

Bekhterev and Durov subsequently conducted several thousand experiments in their study of human and animal telepathy. Some of the experiments were conducted at the Bekhterev Brain Institute in Leningrad, while others were done in Moscow, mainly at the Laboratory of Practical Zoo-psychology, which Durov founded. In a single year (1921), 1278 experiments of mental suggestion to animals were conducted there: 696 of them were successful, and 582 were unsuccessful. Scientists at Moscow University also took part in conducting experiments and processing their results.

In 1919, Bernard Kazhinsky, an electrical engineer who worked in Durov's laboratory, began investigating the electromagnetic nature of telepathy or "brain radio" as it was then called. These experiments were conducted in chambers shielded by metal and other materials. In 1923, Kazhinsky published his results in the book The Transfer of Thoughts. Two years later Kazhinsky met Bekhterev, who invited him to work on a device for the electromagnetic enhancement of mental suggestion at his Brain Institute. Kazhinsky created a device in early 1927 but it proved unable to exert the desired effect on the telepathy process. The work was soon brought to an abrupt standstill in December 1927, due to the sudden death of Bekhterev by poisoning. Many authors suspect the state police—the OGPU—had a hand in this, as there were rumors that Bekhterev had diagnosed Stalin with paranoia.

Bekhterev's pupil and collaborator, the physiologist Professor Leonid Vasiliev succeeded him as head of research in telepathy at the Brain Institute. At this time, the Narkomat (Ministry) of Defense began to show interest in this research, assigning Vasiliev with testing the hypothesis of the electromagnetic nature of telepathy. Vasiliev's method was to first place the subject in a metal chamber, then repeat the experiment outside the chambers. The manifestation of telepathy did not disappear when metal screens that block electromagnetic waves were used to shield individuals, prompting Vasiliev to conclude that electromagnetic waves were not the carriers of mental signals. However, the opposite results were received at the recently established Institute of Biophysics by academician Peter Lazarev and Professor Sergei Turlygin, who even determined that the length of a wave of brain radiation was 1.8-2.1 mm. Pavlov's Institute of Physiology also took part in this research.

Biologist Alexander Gurvich made an interesting contribution to the understanding of the nature of psi phenomena. In his attempt to understand the process of plant morphogenesis, he came to believe in the existence of specific biological fields that shape live objects as they grow and that ensure their development, and he was the first scientist to introduce the concept of a morphogenetic field in his

1922 paper On Embryonic Fields. Gurvich worked on developing the concept of a biofield, and introduced this term into scientific jargon. A classical academic scientist, Professor Gurvich always had a lively interest in the work of the Brain Institute, and sought to explain the phenomenon of telepathy from the point of view of biological fields. His works were widely published in the West in the 1920s and 1930s, and have found further elaboration in Rupert Sheldrake's ideas about morphic fields and morphic resonance, which became very popular towards end of 20th century.

V. K. Chekhovsky, an engineer who had conducted experiments in telepathy independently in the past, arrived at the Brain Institute in the mid-1920s. He worked with a group of people to try to simultaneously transfer the same thought to a recipient, called "collective inductor." The Institute's academic council and Bekhterev became personally interested in Chekhovksy's research and responded to it positively. With this support, Chekhovsky launched efforts to open a branch of the Brain Institute in Moscow.

During this period of scientific research in Russia, there is a strange account of an attempt to use the ancient magic of involtatsiya[3] to overthrow the ruling regime. This is how the well-known biophysicist Alexander Chizhevsky (1897-1964), who also studied telepathy and was well acquainted with the participants in this process, describes it[4]:

This work made it possible to hide another more dangerous activity. A baker's dozen of like-minded men, including Chekhovksy, gathered weekly on Thursday evenings to commune together at his apartment [opposite the building of OGPU] on Lubyanka Street, observing the strictest rules of conspiracy. Silently draping certain cloaks over their shoulders and donning strange headdresses, they took their places around an extended table with rounded-off edges. In front of each member lay a book inscribed with mysterious letters. In the center of the table stood a skillfully sculpted wax bust of... Stalin himself! The wax head was covered with Stalin's own hair that had been bought for an outrageous sum of money from Stalin's hairdresser. Sometimes in the center of the table, instead of the bust there would be a photo of Stalin's head, shot from behind. The photograph was as difficult to obtain as his hair, but the people who gathered there needed an exact image of the nape of the leader's neck.

Then the action would begin: special verbal formulaic incantations were pronounced as the nape of the leader's neck in the photo or the nape of his wax bust was pierced with a steel needle. This area is known as the occipital area: the centers that govern breathing and heartbeat, and the medulla oblongata are located there. The people gathered there passionately wished to destroy these vitally important parts of the leader.

Eventually the appropriate security services found out about this criminal intention. On one of those Thursdays, the criminal community was neutralized. Representatives of these same security services suddenly appeared and arrested all the participants, or so they thought. They laid an ambush in the apartment. But when an unusually dressed person appeared in that empty apartment the next day, the guards, who had been waiting in, bolted from the strange apartment in a panic. It turned out that one of the participants managed to conceal himself in some nook, and hid there, without anyone noticing him. When he couldn't bear hiding out any longer, he decided to leave the secret shelter "come what may," and as he was leaving, he frightened the ambush party to death, and they ran away. This was how he gained his freedom, and this is how this case became known to the public.

Chekhovsky and Teger, the group's two leaders, were arrested by the OGPU along with two dozen participants. In 1928, both leaders were exiled to Solovki; Teger was then moved to Central Asia due to illness, and Chekhovsky was shot in October 1929 after leading an attempted prison break.

GERMANY AND SHAMBHALA

In Germany, the Thule Society, which was destined to play an exceptional role in the fate of Europe, was founded on August 17, 1918. It was a Masonic organization, the Munich branch of the German Order (established in 1912) that incorporated the mystical pan-Germanism of Guido von List, theosophy, and other fashionable occult currents of the time. As a political act, members of the Society organized the German Workers' Party in 1918 (later the National Socialist German Workers' Party or NSGWP), which Adolf

Hitler joined the following year.

The young Führer quickly found spiritual teachers and friends there, including Dietrich Eckart, Alfred Rosenberg, and Rudolf Hess, who became one of his closest associates. The young Hess was passionately interested in mysticism and astrology, and was a student of Professor Karl Haushofer at Munich University, whose geopolitical theories impressed Hess deeply. Hess introduced his friend Adolf to Haushofer, and from that point on the Professor became one of the Führer's main spiritual instructors—a reputation later as Hitler's spiritual director. Haushofer's ideas quickly found their way into Hitler's Mein Kampf, and after Hitler came to power, Haushofer's geopolitical and mystical theories became extraordinarily popular in Germany. One of them was an idea that the supermen who would rule the world would come from the mythical hidden city of Shambhala in Tibet.

Karl Haushofer served in the diplomatic service in Asia from 1887, and then as a brigade general during WWI. It was rumored that he possessed powerful extrasensory powers, that he could predict the movement of enemy troops, and even show exactly where and when shells and bombs would hit. In other words, a participant in ESP warfare.

After the war, in 1921, he became a professor at Munich University. This was his public face, but there was another side to him about which Haushofer usually kept silent. He was in touch with Blavatskaya, and, possibly, with George Gurdjieff, one of the most prominent mystical and spiritual teachers of the 20th century whose teachings also related to Shambhala.

Legends about Gurdjieff abound. Born in the city of Aleksandropol in the Caucasus to a Greek father and an Armenian mother, as a child he was tremendously attracted to esoteric and spiritual knowledge, which his father and the Father Superior of a local orthodox cathedral cultivated in him. From the mid-1890s, he spent approximately 15 years traveling in the East, including studies with the Sufis and living in Tibet for some time. Gurdjieff claimed that he "had the possibility to get into the holy of holies of almost all the secret organizations, such as, the occult, religious, philosophical, political, and mystical societies inaccessible to the ordinary person..."

Gurdjieff, Haushofer, Hitler, Blavatskaya, and artist Nikolai Roerich all tried to find Shambhala—the mythical land of spiritual teachers. They organized a number of expeditions to search for it, and their objectives ranged from seeking higher knowledge to seeking higher powers. The esoteric western public trembled at the sound of expressions like the "warriors of Shambhala" and at the mythological descriptions of the battles of the armies of Good and Evil and the use of higher forces and fantastic types of weapons. Both the Nazis and the communists were looking for Shambhala. As a result, for many people at that time, Shambhala became a symbol of ESP Wars rather than a symbol of spirituality.

THE EAST

One of these expeditions to find Shambhala was led by Professor Alexander Barchenko and planned by a special department of the OGPU. Barchenko had long been deeply interested in parapsychology, and had conducted experiments in telepathy while studying at the Department of Medicine at Yurievsky University from 1905-1911. In 1920, he met academician Bekhterev, and was sent by the Brain Institute to the Kola Peninsula to study the mysterious disease of meryacheniye, described in the previous chapter.

After spending time in the north, Barchenko came to the conclusion that the northern peoples descended from the ancient Arctic civilization of Hyperborea, and in 1922, he set off on a new expedition to investigate this idea. Barchenko's reports about the remnants of the Hyperborean civilization created a sensation, but Barchenko still needed financing. Consequently, he sent a letter to Felix Dzerzhinsky, the head of OGPU, in which he described his research and requested support. This information aroused the interest of the special services. In December of 1924, Barchenko was summoned to Moscow to report to the board of the OGPU. There he met Gleb Bokii, the head of the Special Department of OGPU.

On Lenin's instructions, Bokii's Special Department engaged in cryptography, breaking codes and gathering compromising material to discredit Bolshevik leaders. Bokii had money and the latest equipment. He organized the Laboratory of Neuro-Energy at the Special Department to study parapsychological phenomena and appointed Barchenko as its head.

Barchenko also convinced Bokii to organize an expedition to Shambhala. The main objective of this undertaking was to seek higher knowledge and higher powers. Bokii allocated a huge sum for the expedition—100,000 rubles (the equivalent of more than $500,000 at the time). The expedition was planned for the summer of 1925, but it fell through due to opposition from Trilisser, the head of espionage, and Chicherin, the Minister of Foreign Affairs. Bokii's Special Department functioned for an additional twelve years, but Bokii and Barchenko were arrested during the wave of purges in 1937. They were later shot on charges of organizing an attempt to assassinate Stalin. All the parapsychological research was terminated, and the research materials disappeared without a trace into the archives of the NKVD.

In the Soviet Union, Stalin was now "clearing the space" of potential extrasensory threats, the reality of which he had no doubt. Magic had to be on his side and no one else's—though perhaps Stalin believed he already had enough power, so it was better still to do without it altogether. Books on occultism were removed from shelves all across the country, members of esoteric groups were sent to camps and shot. Within a few years, occultism in Russia virtually ceased to exist and the only parapsychological research conducted at the time—Professor Vasiliev's work at the Brain Institute—was completely shut down.

How was this different from a witch-hunt or the next round of an ESP war?

GERMANY AND THE NAZIS

Spiritualism and theosophy did have its influence in Germany, but Rudolf Steiner, the former head of the German Theosophical Society, resigned from it as a sign of dissent in 1913. That same year he established the new Anthroposophical Society, based on the belief in the existence of an intellectually understandable spiritual world. His lectures attracted huge audiences, and he was especially popular with students and society women. He even attracted important followers such as General Helmut Johan Ludwig von Moltke, Jr., chief of the General Staff of the German Army during World War I. This relationship ended badly, probably because Steiner was not held in high esteem by some at the time, including a new name on the German scene, Adolph Hitler.

As historian Anton Pervushin writes, "Even back in the days of the Weimar republic, when Nazis had no real power in Germany, Hitler gave orders to eliminate Steiner. He accused the founder of anthroposophy of using 'black magic' to subjugate von Moltke, thereby causing Germany's defeat in the First World War. Plans were made to assassinate Steiner, but he secretly left Germany in the summer of 1922, never to return."

Also involved with the Nazis was Erik Jan Hanussen, the so-called "Prophet of the Third Reich." Born Jewish, as Hermann Steinschneider in Vienna, he took up stage mentalism (mind reading) and magic in his teens, and joined the army at the end of WWI. He adopted the stage name and persona of a self-proclaimed Danish count, as well as claims of incredible psychic and hypnotic powers. His fame grew in the 1920s, when he moved to Berlin and created a "Palace of the Occult." He invested money in a number of high-ranking Nazis, and was introduced to Hitler in 1932. He publicly supported Hitler and the Nazi regime, especially in his published writings in his own astrological publication and in columns for several Berlin journals. He prophesized that Hitler would lead the Reich into a new age for Germany. It is believed he had some influence with Hitler, especially the dictator's interests in the occult and magic, and arguably helped Hitler's rise to power as Chancellor of Germany.

There are assumptions that he believed that hitching himself to the Nazis would protect him from any reprisals even in light of his Jewish background. He was quite wealthy, had achieved fame and secured favors for friends. However, in 1932 attempts to expose him as a charlatan led to revelations of his real name and heritage. Hanussen responded by refuting the claims, presenting papers showing he was the son of Danish nobility, raised by a Jewish couple after his parents died in an accident.

Apparently, the self-proclaimed psychic did not foresee his own fate, as in early 1933 he was arrested by the Nazis for using forged papers and shot. It is likely that no matter how much influence he might have had with Hitler and others of the rising Third

Reich, his background and perpetrated fraud was too much of an embarrassment for the Nazis.

Was he genuinely clairvoyant or simply a psychic fraud? This is hard to say; however, some of his published predictions did come true, and others did not—par for the course for any psychic making predictions of an uncertain future. But Hanussen's influence or, at the very least, participation can be seen when looking at the Nazis' fascination and eventual obsession with the occult, definitely securing Erik Jan Hanussen's place in the history of ESP Wars.

All totalitarian regimes seem to operate in the same way. When Hitler came to power in Germany, he, too, began to persecute those involved in the occult. But given his regime's connections with the Thule mystical society, the reason why Hitler engaged in this persecution, even more than Stalin, seemed to be his desire to eliminate any potential competition. Nazi doctrine clearly had roots in mysticism, and numerous books, films and television shows have documented the Nazi obsession with the occult, and the influence of the occult on Nazi actions and beliefs.

Heinrich Himmler, another fan of mysticism, assisted Hitler in every possible way in the difficult business of Nazi spirituality. As head of the SS, the Nazi party's elite military, Himmler transformed it into an organization with mystical rituals and symbolism with one of the goals of using ESP for military purposes.

In 1937, a new division was formed within the structure of the SS: "Ahnenerbe" (Ancestral Heritage). Its initial task was to study Germany's historical and cultural heritage; however, the SS turned it into an organization that oversaw the development of secret weapons and information of parapsychological, mystical, and occult nature. From 1938-1939 the SS and the Ahnenerbe took an active part in preparing an expedition to Tibet that was headed by Ernst Schafer. The expedition's goals were the establishment of political contacts, the classification of the races in Tibet, the discernment of the residual signs of physical Nordic traits, the search for Shambhala, the study of the Bon religion's magic practices, and research into ESP techniques that could potentially be used by the Nazi regime. The expedition was received in Lhasa with respect, and the Tibetan authorities gave Schafer their general support. In spite of its success, the expedition soon had to curtail its activities on orders from

Himmler due to the approach of World War II.

In spite of his passion for Tibet, Hitler had an even greater obsession with magical and religious artifacts. He was especially obsessed with the Holy Lance, also called the Spear of Destiny, which ostensibly would have granted power over the entire world. According to legend, the centurion Gaius Cassius had used this spear to "mercifully pierce" the side of Jesus Christ to end his torment. Young Adolf had seen this relic—or at least something purported to be the relic—in a museum at the Hofburg palace in Vienna, and it had made quite an impression on him. Hitler's goal was to acquire this spear, which he did after the Anschluss with Austria. Thus, the major battle of the magic war had already been won in 1938. All that remained was a mere trifle: the conquest of the entire world.

This obsession with the mystical also led to rumored attempts to find other magical, occult, and religious artifacts—where the idea of the Nazi search for the lost Ark of the Covenant in the film Raiders of the Lost Ark comes from. According to some accounts from WWII, groups of Nazis canvassed parts of the world to uncover items of power or look for lost or hidden lands to raid for weapons and technology to help Hitler's goals.

Others in Nazi Germany aided in furthering their ESP war. In 1942, Navy Captain Hans Roider advanced the theory that the English would use a pendulum to locate German submarines. Working with a pendulum (or resonator) is a standard ESP or dowsing procedure, and is used to answer a question from the response of the pendulum. The pendulum, which is hard to hold still, changes the direction or frequency of its oscillations when it is placed over an assigned point on a map when an operator makes a correct guess. The movement is caused by unconsciously controlled minor muscle movements called the Ideomotor Response, acting ostensibly in such cases on information received via ESP in the unconscious. The idea was understood and welcomed, and the Ahnenerbe organized the Pendulum Institute in order to locate sites for military purposes.

The Institute's best-known operation was the search for Mussolini. When Benito Mussolini was arrested in Italy in September 1943, Hitler ordered "il Duche" found and rescued. But the intelligence services could not find him, and ESP was brought into the operation.

The Pendulum Institute recruited a group of psychics, who spent all day without taking work breaks, holding plum-bobs suspended over maps. These psychics had no success with indicating Mussolini's location, and the search was transferred back to the Intelligence Services. Covert operations expert, Otto Scorseni, eventually liberated the Italian dictator, and Hitler bestowed much kindness on Scorseni, whereas the psychics were severely reprimanded.

THE EAST

East of Germany, Stalin, despite trying to wipe out occultism and its practitioners in the Soviet Union, was also trying to get help from the mystical and parapsychological sources. An interesting case of Stalin's participation in ESP-based warfare is the story of the curse on opening Tamerlane's tomb, and its history can serve as an example of the types of synchronicity that Carl Jung described. It also illustrates Stalin's attitude to other-worldly matters and his obvious unwillingness to confront magic forces.

Nicknamed the Iron Lame Man because of an injury, Tamerlane (Timur, 1336-1405), a descendant of one of Genghis Khan's commanders, conquered huge territories stretching from India to the Mediterranean Sea in the 14th century. His incredible cruelty was legendary: he built walls from the bodies of living people, covered them with lime, and erected towers made of tens of thousands of severed heads. Tamerlane made Samarkand the capital of his empire and when he died, he was buried there in the magnificent mausoleum of Gur-e Amir. On the tomb, in addition to a multitude of Tamerlane's names, there was a warning to all who wished to unseal the tomb: "Those who disturb Timur's rest will bring disasters upon themselves, and brutal wars will break out around the world." And this is indeed what came to pass.

For about five centuries nobody dared to disturb Timur's remains, not even the Bolsheviks—neither during the revolution, nor the civil war, nor afterwards. But Stalin was irresistibly drawn to everything that was connected with the great conquerors and rulers of the past. He hinted in every way possible at how similar he was to Peter I and naturally found it impossible to ignore a relic such as Tamerlane's tomb on Soviet land.

In June 1941, a scientific expedition went to Samarkand with the purpose of opening the tomb, and studying the extant remains, and creating a portrait of the conqueror based on those remains, and then exhibit them. Unexpected obstacles and equipment breakdowns delayed the expedition's work. When he learned about the expedition's purpose, eighty-year-old Maksud Alayev, the custodian of the monument, was horrified and pointed out the warning inscription to the visitors. The expedition participants were overly cautious and wanted to play it safe, so they sent a report [about the curse] to Moscow. Orders came back to arrest Alayev for spreading rumors and panic and to open the tomb immediately.

Witnesses relate that right before the tomb was opened, several elderly clan leaders came to see the expedition participants to repeat their warning that war would break out if they opened Timur's tomb. At the exact moment the tomb was opened, the lights in the mausoleum went out. But nobody dared to disobey the orders from Moscow, and on June 19, 1941, Tamerlane's sarcophagus was opened.

War began 48 hours later—early in the morning on June 21, Germany attacked the Soviet Union. This war truly did turn out to be one of the most brutal wars in the history of mankind.

Later, expedition operative Malik Kayumov related this story to Marshal Zhukov, who took it seriously and conveyed it to Stalin. On December 20, 1942, Timur's remains were re-interred with full burial rites, and the mausoleum of Gur-e Amir was restored during the height of the war. Remarkably, this date coincided with the Soviet victory at Stalingrad, one of the most crucial battles of World War II.

THE WEST AND WWII

There are accounts of the British utilizing psychic resources to fight their own ESP Wars against the Nazis. One such account has groups of practitioners of what became known as Wicca erecting a "cone of power" to stave off a possible German invasion of England, another puts the onus on psychic Dion Fortune's ceremonial magic group.

There are rumors that during WWII, Winston Churchill

consulted medium Helen Duncan for advice, though there are also interpretations of historical accounts and records that Churchill himself was a believer in spiritualism and a psychic who used his powers to defend England.

There are many other episodes in the history up to and including World War II with psychic associations, enough to produce an entire volume. We just wanted to show that there was some historical background for the ESP Wars which came later on, and truly whet your appetite for the better documented use of psychic abilities you'll be reading about.

NOTES

1) Fielding, Everard, W. W. Baggally, and Hereward Carrington. "Report on a Series of Sittings with Eusapia Palladino." Proceedings of the Society for Psychical Research, vol. 23, 1909, pp. 309-569.

2) A report presented by V. M. Bekhterev at a conference held at the Institute of the Brain and Mental Activity in November 1919.

3) Occult term, meaning influence on people by means of paranormal energy

4) From an article by I. V. Mirzalis. "A. L. Chizhevsky's Unsolved Secret."

CHAPTER 3

THE ESP COLD WAR

The Cold War between the US and the USSR began almost immediately after the end of WWII. The legacy of the Nazi occult/psychic programs had not extended past the collapse of the Reich, and attempts at military use of ESP rested primarily with the two superpowers. However, the two sides had very different approaches to using ESP for military purposes. Much of what was conceived of, pursued, and achieved was seemingly stoked as much by a lack of information coupled with misinformation as a lack of understanding of the potential extent of ESP as a tool for espionage.

THE WEST

By the end of the 1940s, the US was the leader in ESP research, especially due to the dedicated work of J. B. Rhine and his colleagues. Rhine's experiments at Duke University were controversial, though the statistics were impressive to many mathematicians. The apparent successful findings caused serious criticism, perhaps more because of the supporting evidence that ESP actually existed—an idea to this day still hard for many in the sciences to even consider possible. His research was reviewed in the prestigious journal Science by George R. Price, a well-known chemist and geneticist. Price acknowledged that if Rhine's results were true, they were revolutionary. But since he could not identify any technical or procedural flaws in the work or think of any other viable explanation for the results, he concluded that the results must be fraudulent. His assertion sparked a lively debate in Science in 1956, though two decades later, Price apologized in the same journal for his original assertion.[1]

Rhine was instrumental in promoting parapsychological research and professionalizing it, as well as creating popular interest in the subject. In fact, one of the things Duke University was most known for in the public eye was Rhine's research on ESP and PK and the parapsychology lab there. This fact was so well known that until relatively recently, people continued to associate Duke and psi research and believed there was still a parapsychology lab there, even though the lab moved off campus in 1965 with Rhine's retirement from the university and leaving no formal with Duke. Not finished with his research in parapsychology, Rhine founded the Foundation for Research on the Nature of Man (FRNM), also in Duke's home town of Durham, North Carolina. The Foundation, a non-profit corporation, was seen as the umbrella organization under which other programs could function, one of those being the Institute for Parapsychology. J. B. and researcher-wife Louisa Rhine oversaw much in the way of research as well as the training and development of a number of parapsychologists until their deaths in the 1980s. Besides the research at the Institute, educational and publishing activities have also been a focus since the 1960s. It may be that the public's association between a parapsychology research center and Duke University was furthered by both existing in Durham.

In 1995, in honor of its founders J. B. and Louisa Rhine, the Foundation was re-christened as the Rhine Research Center and continues its programs of research, education, and publication of The Journal of Parapsychology. 1995, by the way, marked the centenary of the birth of J. B. Rhine.

In 1957, the Parapsychological Association was founded. Still, the world's only organization looking at scientific research of psi phenomena, abilities and experiences, it's composed of professional parapsychologists and people with a professional interest specifically in the subject. In 1969, after an impassioned plea by anthropologist Margaret Mead, the organization was admitted as an affiliate of the American Association for the Advancement of Science, the most prestigious science organization in the US. Attempts by some members of the scientific community to oppose its membership were unsuccessful. Although this was seen by some as evidence that parapsychology was becoming a legitimate science, the sad fact is that this struggle continues even today.

Since Rhine's day, parapsychology research blossomed as best it could in the United States even with funding on the low end for such scientific endeavors. A number of universities including Princeton, University of California at Davis and Santa Barbara, and Syracuse University embarked on small programs. Of these, the Princeton Engineering Anomalous Research (PEAR) laboratory was the longest lived of these, having shut down relatively recently with the retirement of Dr. Robert Jahn. Today, the state of publicly funded ESP research is not good at all, due to dwindling funding sources over the last 30 years.

In the UK, the University of Edinburgh began education and research in parapsychology thanks to a bequest from the late writer and philosopher Arthur Koestler. The University established the Koestler Chair of Parapsychology in the Psychology Department, held for a majority of time by the late Dr. Robert Morris. Many of today's psi researchers have studied under Dr. Morris in Edinburgh, and the UK has over 20 universities with graduates of the Koestler Unit teaching and researching.

In the US, perhaps the best funded research was under US government sponsorship first at SRI International and later Science Applications International Corporation (SAIC), where psi research and applications thrived for over 20 years, as you'll see shortly.

As you saw in the last chapter, the history of ESP Wars has some ties to many a controversial figure of the first half of the 20th century connected to Europe, the USSR, and the US.

Another leading figure investigating paranormal phenomena during the early 20th century whose reach extended past WWII into the Cold War era was Wilhelm Reich, a psychiatrist and student of Sigmund Freud. Reich fled Europe in 1939 and settled in the US where he maintained a thriving psychoanalytic practice, conducted research on what he called "orgone energy," and designed "orgone energy accumulators" that he claimed improved people's health. In 1954, the US Food and Drug Administration brought legal action against his use of an unverified medical device. Reich refused to appear in court and defiantly declared that the court did not possess the competence to pass judgments concerning scientific discoveries. He was found in contempt of court and sentenced to two years in prison for violating an interstate injunction against shipping orgone equipment and literature. All of Reich's equipment was destroyed at his estate in Maine, and over six tons of his books and publications, many of which were unrelated to the subject of orgone, were burned in a public incinerator in New York City.

Reich died of a heart attack on November 3, 1957 during his eighth month of imprisonment in a federal prison. However, his ideas about accumulating biological and mental energy did not die with him. Instead, they soon resurfaced in attempts to create psychotronic generators in Europe and the USSR.[2]

As all conspiracy junkies will tell you, military and intelligence organizations in the US had an interest in and attempted to develop methods of mind control, and as a natural next step, became increasingly interested in parapsychology and ESP. Beginning in 1945 with "Operation Paperclip," which imported and employed Nazi experts in brainwashing and torture, operations with names like "Chatter" (1947), "Bluebird" (1950), and "Artichoke" (1951) soon followed and served as bases for the new large-scale MK-ULTRA Project. MK-ULTRA was launched by CIA Director Allen Dulles on April 13, 1953, and directed by Sydney Gottlieb.

In this covert program, the CIA pursued a variety of goals: acquiring the ability to manipulate foreign leaders, finding new methods to obtain and send information without a subject's knowledge, enhancing or diluting the effect of alcohol and other drugs, causing panic and disorientation, strengthening mental abilities and perceptual acuity, and a range of other objectives. Their research techniques included experiments using hypnosis and psychotropic substances, noise loops, drugs to induce coma, and many other harsh methods. Many experiments were conducted without the knowledge of the patients involved—drugs were simply mixed into their food, or some other substance or influence that wasn't immediately perceptible was used.

In 1964, MK-ULTRA was renamed MK-SEARCH. The Cold War was on, and the program allocated many resources in the search for a perfect "truth drug" for use in interrogating suspected Soviet spies. Any and all sorts of other possible methods of mind control were investigated—a huge number of experiments with LSD and other psychedelics and drugs were conducted.

In the mid-1970s, it was disclosed that the CIA had conducted illegal experiments on American citizens in the 1950s and 1960s. Numerous references can be found in the press of the time, especially in the New York Times. The disclosure led to a Congressional investigation headed by the Church Committee and the Rockefeller Commission. President Gerald Ford followed their recommendations and issued the First Executive Order on Intelligence Service Activities in 1976 that prohibited, among other things, using drugs on human subjects without their consent. Presidents Carter and Reagan subsequently expanded this directive to apply to any type of experimentation on human subjects.[3]

Many MK-ULTRA Project experiments involved various aspects of parapsychology. The major reason for the CIA's great interest in researching ESP was its potential both as a means of mental manipulation and as a method of covertly sending and receiving information. During experiments in which subjects were under the influence of LSD or hypnosis, some people entered altered states of consciousness in which they manifested ESP phenomena. Project MK-ULTRA was right in the middle of the ESP Cold War.

Unfortunately, we may never learn about the details of the project experiments as a Congressional investigation in 1975 revealed that Richard Helms, then director of the CIA, ordered all the MK-ULTRA files destroyed in 1973 to cover up the real nature and magnitude of the project's research work. Nevertheless, some of the research was revealed through the testimony of project participants and eyewitnesses. While not all of this testimony may have been true, one case deserves special attention in view of its enormous role in the escalation of the use of ESP in the cold war between the USA and the USSR, as well as in the development of parapsychology in both countries: telepathic experiments aboard a nuclear sub.

This particular story began in 1957 when the Rand Corporation think tank, which was engaged in secret research for the government, sent a report to President Eisenhower in which it recommended conducting telepathic experiments involving a submarine under the ice in the Arctic. Direct radio communication with a submerged submarine is not possible because radio waves do not travel through water. As this was before submarines had retractable antennae, a sub had to surface to receive or send radio messages, making their location discoverable. However, they still could not penetrate the polar ice, leaving no means of communication while in that area. The Rand Corporation concluded that it was logical to try telepathic communication.

Experiments were conducted on July 25, 1958, while the USS Nautilus—our first nuclear submarine—was under the Arctic ice for the better part of 16 days. Colonel William Bauers headed the project. The "psychic transmitter" was a student from Duke University named "Smith," located at the Westinghouse Laboratory in Friendship, Maryland. Meanwhile, the "psychic receiver", a lieutenant in the US Navy named "Jones," was on the submarine. Twice a day, an automatic machine shuffled 1,000 Zener cards at an appointed time and dispensed five cards per minute to Smith. He concentrated on each symbol, tried to send it mentally, and then sketched it on a sheet of paper. Each sheet with the five drawn symbols was placed in a sealed envelope. Colonel Bauers recorded the time of the experiment and locked each envelope in a safe.

On the submarine, Jones simultaneously drew the card symbols, which he received telepathically, and then he sealed his drawings in an envelope that he gave to the captain of the Nautilus. The submarine returned to port, the envelopes were opened and the results were compared: they showed a remarkable level of correspondence—70% (112 out of 160), instead of the 20% expected by chance guessing. The odds of this occurring by chance are less than 1 in 8,000,000,000!

A remarkable statistic like this, leads detractors and proponents of parapsychology alike to be skeptical about the Nautilus reports, if only because results like this simply are not seen under controlled laboratory conditions.

Dr. Richard S. Broughton, the former director of the Rhine Research Center, and someone quite familiar with the Rhine legacy thought that there was some grain of truth to the card-guessing experiment on the Nautilus. But in general, he was unable to confirm that notorious experiment. In an e-mail dated 2 June 2008 from Broughton to Ed May, and used with permission, Dr. Broughton recalled:

Well, on the basis of what I can remember from the odd document or two that I encountered in Rhine's safe (as distinct from the documents that he transferred to Duke), parts of that account are true. But, as you yourself have encountered, the little grains of truth do not amount to a conspiracy or any widespread use of psi by the CIA or other government bodies.

I do recall seeing copies, stamped secret (or some such thing) relating to at least one funding agreement dated in the early 1950s with the Navy. My recollection was that it didn't specify what research was involved, as if that was in other documents, but I believe I was told by people who would have known (Dorothy Pope or Fay David) that it was funding for Pratt's experiments with homing pigeons (which always were a bit of an anomaly in the Duke program).

I also think there is some grain of truth to the card-guessing experiment on the Nautilus, but it was more of one of those one-shot demonstrations rather than any substantial program [editor's emphasis]. I never ran across any documents that would have suggested any systematic work. The fact that it may have used the Duke card shuffler is one of those details that story tellers add to increase apparent veracity, but that would simply have been one of the routine procedures in place at the lab in those days. They are widely pictured in all Rhine's books.

Certainly, Rhine had his own share of contacts in the military and he had applied for funding on at least a few occasions, and sometimes got it. Also, in the 50s and perhaps later he was strongly anti-communist (as evidenced in some of his unpublished talks), seeing parapsychology as scientific evidence to counter Soviet Materialism. It would not be surprising that any applications for funding might use that perspective to help sell.

It's worth adding that it is rumored that Rhine himself did not believe a word of the Nautilus experiment. True or not, the story has implications for later Soviet involvement in the ESP Wars.

The US Navy denied that it was involved in these experiments, but many details of this case point to the fact that US intelligence services deliberately used disinformation against the Soviets: the information first appeared in the foreign press, the French magazine Constellation, and the source of the information was never disclosed. Regardless of the Navy denial, indirect data suggest that the US was installing new sound detectors in the oceans to detect Soviet submarines at this time, and so they needed to distract attention away from this project.

The telepathic experiments on the Nautilus did not come up with anything new as many similar experiments had been conducted in the 1920s and 1930s in both the US and in Soviet Union. All that was new was that, if true, the Navy tested the practical use of telepathy.

THE EAST

Regardless of its veracity, the information about the Nautilus experiments was taken rather seriously in the Soviet Union, although with an understanding of the possibility it was disinformation.

The USSR had been in the deepest "ESP depression" from the post-war period onward from Stalin's final years through Khrushchev's early years as leader. During this time, the discipline of psychology was not even considered a legitimate science, much less parapsychology. There were no scholarly degrees granted in psychology; they were replaced by degrees in pedagogy. It wasn't until 1956 that the first specialized journal Questions of Psychology started as a publication. This was all due to ideology: psychology and parapsychology were considered too "idealistic," and their development was in constant conflict with Marxist-Leninist doctrine.

There were other disciplines that shared the fate of being disregarded; the champions of the purity of communist views also regarded cybernetics and genetics as pseudo-sciences. This perception, as it turns out, was quite misleading. As our former adversaries have revealed in this book, the Soviet era was far from entirely embracing the doctrine of unadulterated materialism given their continued belief in spiritualism and shamanistic beliefs.

From the late 1930s to the late 1950s there was no research conducted on telepathy in the USSR, except for a small series of research work done in 1952 by Professor S. Turlygin and physician-psychotherapist Dmitry Mirza at the Institute of Biophysics of the USSR Academy of Sciences. When Khrushchev came to power, the situation began to improve. In March, 1958, a discussion about renewing research into telepathy began at the Biophysics Institute but no decision was made. However, at the end of 1958 a small telepathy research laboratory headed by Dmitry Mirza was opened at the scientific research institute Electrom of the USSR Academy of Sciences.

Lt. Colonel Igor Poletaev, a cadre officer and expert in cybernetics, who had been involved in research there, tried to acquire financing for telepathy research from the Ministry of Defense. He submitted an official report to military organizations, but got a lukewarm response. Things changed after information about the experiments on the Nautilus was disclosed.

On March 26, 1960, Poletaev submitted the following official report again, but this time directly to Marshal Rodion Malinovsky, the Minister of Defense of the USSR[4]:

In March 1960 Professor Leonid Vasiliev (the head of the Physiology Department of Leningrad State University) reported that the American Armed Forces have adopted telepathy (the transfer of thoughts at a distance without the use of technical means) as a means of communicating with submarines at sea. Professor Vasiliev received this information from one of his colleagues in Paris. Articles with a brief mention of this fact appeared in two French magazines (I am attaching the translations of these articles). Scientific research into telepathy has been conducted for a long time, but major US research organizations—RAND Corporation, Westinghouse, Bell Telephone Company and others—joined in this work in late 1957. Research has been conducted intensively and successfully. On the basis of this research, an experiment was undertaken involving information transfer by means of telepathic communication from a naval base to the submarine Nautilus which was submerged under Arctic ice at a distance of 2000 km from the base. The experiment was successful.

The transfer was conducted in the five-symbol alphabet of Zener cards, and it resulted in a score of 70% correct symbols. Considering that self-corrective codes could be designed today based on information theory which would allow for error correction in a communication channel, (if this information is reliable) these results make us confident that telepathy could be used to establish effective communication, especially military communication.

It should also be noted that no other means of communication could have been used during the Nautilus experiment: specifically, radio communication was impossible because the boat was submerged. Without getting into a discussion about the reliability of the aforementioned information, we must acknowledge that the danger of disregarding these reports is too great in the event that a new psychological weapon with which we are unfamiliar is used against the USSR. I consider it my duty to report the above mentioned facts directly to you with urgency.

As far as I know, successful research into telepathy was conducted in the Soviet Union on behalf of the People's Commissariat of Defense in the 1930s at the I. P. Pavlov Institute of Physiology (Leningrad) under the direction of Professor Leonid Vasiliev. Although the results were positive, further research was stopped. Reports about the findings of this research are still stored in the archives of the Pavlov Institute.

In September 1958, at your orders, the Director of the Main Military Medical Administration had several meetings with Professors Vasiliev and Gulyaev about the possibility of renewing research into telepathy for military and military-medical applications. However, for some reason, the research work was postponed, and it has not yet resumed.

At present Gulyaev and Vasiliev, the main Soviet experts in telepathy (who demonstrated the possibility of telepathic communication with shielded radio-waves 25 years ago) have stated that they are ready and able to continue research into telepathy.

As is evident from the official report, the possibility of disinformation or simply a false report in the media was considered from the very beginning, but that wasn't the essential point. Most likely, the well-known Soviet scientists Vasiliev and Poletaev simply decided to take advantage of a favorable situation to break through the ideological barrier and obtain military funding for research that they considered promising. As for the Soviet military command, when it came to any new potential weapon, they always felt it was important not to lag behind America. The fact that parapsychological research in America was being expanded was known in the Soviet Union and, even if there had been no specific report about the Nautilus, some other information would have resulted in a similar outcome.

In any case, Marshal Malinovsky's response was not long in

coming. Later in 1960, a special laboratory for the study of telepathic phenomena was established under Professor Vasiliev's direction at Leningrad University's Institute of Physiology of Biology with powerful assistance and financing from the Ministry of Defense. Some of Vasiliev's books, including Mysterious Phenomena of the Human Psyche, Experimental Research into Mental Suggestion, and others were published at this time. These books were extremely popular with students and young scientists, as were discussions about telepathy during those years. The laboratory engaged in academic research as well as fulfilling orders for the Ministry of Defense, under Vasiliev's direction until his death in February, 1966.

At the time, and even extending to today, the question of how ESP works remains one of parapsychology's main scientific challenges. However, the use of ESP in warfare does not require an explanation as to "how" it works. That it works, that there were successful applications was sufficient for both the US and Russian military to justify continuing in this area.

In 1961, the Institute of Information Transfer (IPPI) was created within the system of the USSR Academy of Sciences. Located in Moscow, it was a semi-secret scientific institution where the overwhelming majority of subjects studied were classified. Almost from the IPPI's inception, the study of information processes in living systems and bio-information was established in addition to the study of cybernetics, computer science and the design of electronic communication technology. This was where ESP research flourished, and did so because research there was conducted in the most rigorous scientific way and incorporated the newest state of the art equipment. One specific example as to how ESP fit in here was IPPI's research attempts to design equipment to record telepathic signals.

In March 1962, the Academy of Sciences made the decision to transfer Dmitry Mirza's telepathy laboratory from there to the IPPI. The Institute's initial budget, estimated at the huge sum of 10 million rubles (over $15 million at the exchange rate of that time), was increased annually—more than any research money put into parapsychology in the west.

Vasiliev's laboratory and the IPPI were only the harbingers of what was to come. From the mid-1960s, the number of scientific institutions in the USSR involved in some way with parapsychological research increased rapidly. In addition to secret research establishments, the major universities in the USSR— Moscow, Leningrad, Novosibirsk, and others—were also engaged in ESP research. Most of the secret scientific institutes touched upon parapsychological subjects to some degree, but the stigma of "idealistic materialism" remained. Researchers tried to circumvent the intrigue and separate what they were doing from the baggage of psychic terminology by giving parapsychological research projects entirely respectable scientific names. They tried to reproduce ESP phenomena in every possible way with "material" devices, much as one sees amateur ghost hunters on TV trying to detect the "paranormal" with electronic devices today. To many people, ESP is connected to the spiritual and the possibility of survival after death. Thus, there was substantial effort to make ESP fall exclusively into the domain of the "material"—physics and physiology. The USSR was not alone for inventing euphemisms to obscure the interest in parapsychology. Under Star Gate, the Americans used them as well—Enhanced Human Performance, Novel Information Transfer, and Psychoenergetics to name but a few.

The Soviet work resulted in the creation of a large variety of psychotronic generators—"psychically charged" hardware devices that ostensibly could store and later direct the psychic energy for whatever purpose—and accumulators of every kind imaginable. The overwhelming majority of them did not work, but a few did, and we will talk about those in another chapter. Later, it became fashionable to call all these devices "psychotronic weapons."

Another example of secret Soviet research was the extensive program of telepathic research on humans and animals conducted from 1965 to 1968. This was conducted at the semi-secret Novosibirsk Institute of Automation and Electrometry of the Siberian branch of the USSR Academy of Sciences, under the direction of Captain First Class (Colonel) V. P. Perov, who held a Ph.D. in Technical Sciences. The results of the research were not declassified and published until 10 years later, in the mid-1970s.

A possible breakthrough in understanding the nature of ESP phenomena was made in Czechoslovakia in the 1960s, which was a part of the Communist Block at that time. It grew out of the clinical research done at the Prague Psychiatric Center by Stanislav Grof, who resided in the US for quite some time, into non-ordinary states of consciousness. By its very nature, this research dealt with many types of paranormal phenomena. Grof's work showed that[5]:

...from a broader perspective, there is no reason to separate so-called paranormal phenomena into a special category. Since many types of transpersonal experiences rather typically involve access to new information about the universe through extrasensory channels, the clear boundary between psychology and parapsychology disappears....

Pressure to conform to the communist ideology was weaker in Czechoslovakia than in the USSR. This led to the situation where a large association of parapsychologists were working in Prague. There was probably more parapsychological research in the small nation of Czechoslovakia in the 1960s and 1970s than in the whole of the vast Soviet Union. Czechoslovak parapsychologists were also engaged in the creation of psychotronic generators. Unfortunately, these breakthroughs were largely stymied by the invasion of Soviet troops and violent change of the Czechoslovak government during events of the Prague Spring of 1967. The political regime had become tougher, and many interesting research efforts were curtailed or stopped.

By no means did all ESP researchers in the USSR want to work for the state, nor could they. Some of them chose not to collaborate for moral reasons: it was a matter of critical importance to them that the KGB and the Ministry of Defense were trying to use the experimental findings of parapsychological research for political and military purposes. Others simply would not be accepted by secret research establishments because of their biographies or due to a lack of formal education, but they remained very interested in parapsychology and wanted to be involved with it. The number of these enthusiasts grew steadily, and in 1965 they succeeded in convincing the A. S. Popov Scientific and Technical Society of Radio Engineering, Electronics and Communication (NTORES) to establish a new section specifically committed to research into extrasensory phenomena (NTORES is analogous to the American IEEE).

Professor Ippolit M. Kogan, who held a Ph.D. in Physical and

Mathematical Sciences, was the head of the new section which was primarily devoted to studying telepathy though avoided using this term in favor of the official sounding "biological communication." The group had many other interests, including research on psychokinesis, clairvoyance, psychic diagnostics, and psychic healings.

Three years later, the group succeeded in setting up equipment in their Bio-Information Laboratory in a basement on Maly Vuzovsky Lane in Moscow. The members who worked there in the evenings conducted very serious research work without any expensive or ultra-precise equipment at their disposal. Most of the work was done by these psi enthusiasts on a volunteer basis, and they received no compensation for their work. The experiments they conducted in long-distance telepathic communication—sessions with Yuri Kamensky and Karl Nikolaiev from Moscow to Leningrad and back—are widely known today.

Less well known are the experiments on clairvoyant recognition of hidden images done by Yuri Korabelnikov and Ludmila Tishchenko. Moscow University Professor Vladimir Raikov, a well-known physician and hypnotist, also worked with the laboratory and conducted ESP experiments during hypnosis sessions. Barbara Ivanova ran a successful group of healers at the laboratory, Karl Nikolaev's group trained in telepathic abilities, and Larissa Vilenskaya's group did research on "skin vision" there. Vilenskaya came to the US in 1975 and later joined the Star Gate program when it was at Science Applications International Corporation.

Interestingly enough, the level of the Bio-Information group's research was so serious that reports that reached the West were perceived as information leaks about supposed secret research. To this day, it is still possible to find descriptions in the Western press of experiments, such as those done by Nikolaiev, as examples of "KGB experiments." This is a bitter irony given that the majority of researchers engaged in the work at the Bio-Information Laboratory regarded the KGB extremely negatively, and often had to overcome opposition from the authorities.

The Western press wrote a great deal about the persecution of amateur parapsychologists in the USSR. Most of what they wrote was true, but statements made by some western authors about the full support of parapsychology in the USSR by the state were pure promotion. In general, the state suppressed parapsychology on purely ideological grounds rather than encouraging it. The study of paranormal phenomena advanced primarily due to the enthusiasm of these amateur researchers and the work that they did.

One Russian psychic from this time period, Sergey Vronsky, deserves our special attention. Vronsky lived in Yurmala, Latvia, where he earned money on the side using his ESP abilities to help a former schoolmate who was an investigator. As with psychic detectives in the West, he psychically searched for missing people and objects. From time to time, he traveled to Moscow and gave underground lectures on astrology and ESP. Many psychics who later became well-known in Russia studied with him, such as the remarkable psychic Vladimir Safonov, who is a player in later aspects of the Soviet ESP Wars.

Shortly thereafter, the KGB also began working with Vronsky's psychic abilities in their operations in similar fashion: he solved crimes and prevented accidents with the help of ESP. Some KGB officers who we'll "meet" later in this book also studied ESP with Vronsky.

From 1968 on, Sergei Vronsky gave lectures and conducted practical training at the aforementioned Bio-Information Laboratory. Vronsky even received official permission to engage in astrology, but only under the name of cosmos-biology. At that time, he cast horoscopes for a number of top officials and leaders of the USSR. Through it all, he remained above popular ideology: he accepted very small fees or none at all, and always refused "dirty" money.

Jumping a little ahead to after the end of the cold war, Vronsky enjoyed a revival in popularity. The press and TV began featuring pieces about him. He wrote several bestsellers, including the twelve-volume series Classical Astrology that became his magnum opus. He taught astrology in a number of educational institutions and gave many public lectures. A generation of astrologers and psychics of the 1990s developed under his tutelage.

Sergei Vronsky played an enormous role in the revival of astrology and parapsychology in Russia during the post-war period. The entire constellation of well-known psychics and astrologers is obliged to him for their knowledge and abilities; among them we can mention Intelligence Services Major General George Rogozin, Vladimir Safonov, Larissa Vilenskaya, and others. Sergei Vronsky was a man not only of profound knowledge and extraordinary abilities, but also a man with a great soul. In spite of a difficult, occasionally brutal life, he always maintained his love for people. Vronsky died on January 10, 1998. In one of his last conversations with journalists Vronsky said, "I am not at liberty to tell the whole truth… There is a principle that an individual initiated into a great secret must carry it away with him."

Vronsky's biography contains many contradictory elements and pieces of information which are hard to believe. Nonetheless, we can say without doubt that Vronsky made a substantial and singular contribution to parapsychology and to the history of the ESP Wars. Indeed, his life provides the perfect bridge for our story as we move forward to explore the use of ESP on both sides of the Cold War.

At about the time of Vronsky's Cold War activities, the luminescence of objects displayed with high-frequency photography was re-discovered for the second time in the USSR. This phenomenon, called electrography, was originally discovered in 1895 by Yakov Narkevich-Yodko of Belarus. It was subsequently forgotten and newly discovered in the 1940s by Simeon and Valentina Kirlian, who named it the "Kirlian Effect" and obtained a patent on the method in 1949. It was revealed that any living object placed in a high frequency field when photographed appears to emanate luminescence—to glow with an aura of sorts—and whose nature depends on the object's state. This was of immediate interest to parapsychologists, and in due course "Kirlianography," or Kirlian photography as we came to know it in the West became a standard method used in both civilian and military parapsychological research.

Many researchers are still convinced that what we see in Kirlian photographs are biological fields and the mysterious aura. However, carefully controlled experiments in the West have demonstrated that the effects are due to the more mundane corona discharges common in strong electric fields. The Soviet scientists V. I. Inyushin and V. G. Adamenko discovered "phantom effects" in the damaged leaves of plants that they had photographed using the Kirlian method, the effect made popular by American researchers such as Thelma Moss of UCLA. The effect was called "phantom" as the "aura" in the photographs of severed leaves of plants still looked whole, as if the entire leaf was still present. According to Inyushin and Adamenko, this research suggested the existence of an underlying energetic structure upon which biological objects build their physical form, a phenomenon that Alexander Gurvich had theoretically predicted and named morphogenetic fields back in the 1920s.

The publication of the booklet In the World of Wonderful Categories by the Kirlians in 1957 caused a real sensation in the scientific world. It appeared that the Kirlian effect could be applied in diagnosing illness, determining the activity of drugs, testing psychological states, discovering defects in materials and in dozens of other areas, including potential applications for the military, intelligence services and for crime detection.

For example, Konstantin Korotkov, a scientist at the Leningrad Polytechnic Institute, used the Kirlian methodology to study the changes in the luminosity of the finger pads of the deceased. He concluded that this method could be used to quite accurately determine the nature of a person's death: whether the cause of death was natural or violent, whether it was a suicide or due to a wrongly prescribed drug. Professor Korotkov continued studying the energetic activity of human organs several days after death, and concluded that individuals go through several stages after death, a process which he described in the book Light after the Life: A Scientific Journey into the Spiritual World.

The Kirlian method gained wide recognition in the West. Several international conferences on the Kirlian effect were held in New York in the 1960s and 1970s, and an institute was founded to research the phenomenon in the US. Eventually, a special international association was established. At that point, the Academy of Sciences in the USSR suddenly began to recommend its use. By the early 1990s about 50 copyrights and patents for various inventions based on the Kirlian effect were granted in the USSR, an appreciable number of them involved ESP aspects, while others involved use by the military.

Here the West and East differ again. Many scientists in the West were skeptical of Kirlian photography and many of the stated conclusions and applications. Research was conducted that demonstrates a different—a Western scientific—perspective: controlling for environmental variables, such as humidity, finger pressure, and other factors, the "aura" around the fingertip is a well-understood corona discharge, which may be modulated by the emotional state of the participant.

All of this interest in psi in the USSR spawned a number of legends among Soviet parapsychologists. One such legend claims that Nikita Khrushchev gave permission for ESP research in the USSR after his trip to India. While there, he had seen yogis who appeared able to stop the activity of their hearts at any time and some who did not seem to experience bodily pain while lying on nail-studded boards. Khrushchev decided that the KGB and the Soviet army would become even more efficient and invulnerable if they mastered the "miracles" that these yogis performed. Of course, it may be difficult to believe Khrushchev believed such activities simply based on the claims, given that methods of the fakirs to do those things had been known by magicians and many others for quite some time.

As appealing as these legends might be, we must nevertheless acknowledge that the main stimulus to the renewal of ESP research in the USSR in the early 1960s was information that similar research was being conducted for military use by the MK-ULTRA Project and the US Navy, at Professor Rhine's laboratory and at a number of firms, institutes and universities in the US and Western Europe.

As it turns out, the Soviets were justifying their ESP programs by saying the West was doing it also. Ironically, government and military programs in the West were doing the exact same thing, justifying their programs on the basis that the Soviets were doing it!

The Soviet Union responded to the reports from the US with a steadily increasing amount of parapsychological research and with efforts to develop a psychotronic weapon. Although the KGB did not operate an integrated program of parapsychological research, the magnitude of this research in the USSR during 60s and early 70s compelled the US to begin the research, which evolved into the Star Gate program—the next round of the ESP Wars.

NOTES

1) Charles Honorton and Diane C. Ferrari conducted a modern analysis of over 50 years of Zener card experiments involving over 2,000,000 individual card guesses. They addressed all kinds of possible problems such as only publishing the experiments that "worked," or those that contained sloppy protocols or analyses accounted for the results. The bottom line is that there is a small, but statistically robust, definitive effect. The reference, Honorton & Ferrari (1989). "Future Telling:" A Meta-Analysis of Forced-Choice Precognition Experiments, 1935-1987, Journal of Parapsychology, 53, 281-308, can be found on the web at www.lfr.org/LFR/csl/library/HonortonFerrari.pdf

2) In addition to the alarm, Reich caused in psychoanalytic circles with his overt emphasis on the body and his claims to cure cancer, Reich was also investigated by Federal authorities because of his past membership in the Austrian and German Communist parties.

3) These rulings had long-term implications for the US Star Gate Program. The rules governing the use of humans in experiments that were funded by the Department of Defense, were more stringent in protecting the rights of individuals than were similar rules in the private sector under the Health and Human Services Agency.

4) A copy of the official report was declassified and sent for publication by I. A. Poletaev in 1968.

5) Stanislav Grof, M.D. The Adventure of Self Discovery, State University of New York Press, 1988, N.Y., p.162.

ESP IN THE MILITARY

THE WEST

CHAPTER 4

BEHIND THE SCENES OF THE STAR GATE PROGRAM: VIEW FROM THE DIRECTOR

Authors' Note: With three authors and content in a book that could easily be a first person narrative at times, it's always difficult to decide whether to jump from a personal narration to more of a third person reporting. To make it easier on our readers, we opted for the third—but we do underscore that this story is Ed May's experience.

In late 1975, Edwin C. May joined an on-going, highly classified program at what was then Stanford Research Institute (now SRI International) as a consultant. The program and its personnel were to study extrasensory perception under the label "remote viewing" and its application for gathering information for the US military and intelligence communities. Up until that point, by academic training, degree and for a career, May was a nuclear physicist. The program director, Dr. Harold (Hal) Puthoff, called May into his office, pulled material out of an imposing safe, and showed it to May. He received his SECRET government clearance and his career took a major turn.

"What he showed me blew my mind," said May. "Even to this day, thirty six years later, I still get goose bumps thinking about the then classified examples he showed me." From that point forward, May has made ESP research his profession, applying it to problems involving the US national interest. Most of his friends to this day remain dumbfounded that he managed to make this seemingly illogical transition. In this chapter, we learn the story of Ed May's life-changing career shift from academic physics research to directing the US Government's secret ESP spying program, now known as Star Gate, and his part in both the operations (the remote viewing "missions") and the military/government bureaucratic process to keep it going.

What Puthoff showed him has been declassified, but at the time, this required government clearances to view. To give some idea of what was in the material, the following is a report of a remote viewing session from Puthoff and Russell Targ's final report to the CIA, dated December 1, 1975. Note that the viewer, S1, was later identified as retired police commissioner Pat Price.

Date: 1 June 1973, 1700 hours, Menlo Park, California.

Protocol: Coordinates 38°23'45"to 48"N, 79°25'00"W were given (with no further description) by experimenter Dr. H.E. Puthoff to subject Sl by telephone to initiate experiment.

On the morning of 4 June 1973, Sl's written response (dated 2 June 1973, 1250 to 1350 hours, Lake Tahoe, California) was received in the mail:

Looked at general area from altitude of about 1500 ft. above highest terrain. On my left forward quadrant is a peak in a chain of mountains, elevation approximately 4996 ft. above sea level. Slopes are grayish slate covered with variety of broadleaf trees, vines, shrubbery, and undergrowth. I am facing about 3° to 5° west of north. Looking down the mountain to the right (east) side is a roadway—freeway, country style—curves then heads ENE to a fairly large city about 30 to 40 miles distant. This area was a battleground in the Civil War—low rolling hills, creeks, few lakes or reservoirs. There is a smaller town a little SE about 15 to 20 miles distant with small settlements, village type, very rural, scattered around. Looking across the peak, 2500 to 3000 ft. mountains stretch out for a hundred or so miles. Area is essentially wooded. Some of the westerly slopes are eroded and gully washed—looks like strip-mining, coal mainly.

Weather at this time is cloudy, rainy. Temperature at my altitude about 54°F—high cumulo nimbus clouds to about 25,000 to 30,000 ft. Clear area, but turbulent, between that level and some cirro stratus at 46,000 ft. Air mass in that strip moving WNW to SE.

1318 hours—Perceived that peak area has large underground storage areas. Road comes up back side of mountains (west slopes), fairly well concealed, looks deliberately so. It's cut under trees where possible—would be very hard to detect flying over area. Looks like former missile site—bases for launchers still there, but area now houses record storage area, microfilm, file cabinets; as you go into underground area through aluminum rolled up doors, first areas filled with records, etc. Rooms about 100-ft long, 40-ft wide, 20-ft ceilings, with concrete supporting pilasters, flare-shaped. Temperature cool—fluorescent lighted. Personnel, Army 5th Corps Engineers. M/Sgt. Long on desk placard on grey steel desk—file cabinets security locked—combination locks, steel rods through eyebolts. Beyond these rooms, heading east, are several bays with computers, communication equipment, large maps, display type, overlays. Personnel, Army Signal Corps. Elevators.

1330 hours—Looked over general area from original location again—valleys quite hazy, lightning about 30 miles north along mountain ridge. Temperature drop about 6°F, it's about 48°F. Looking for other significances: see warm air mass moving in from SW colliding with cool air mass about 100 miles ESE from my viewpoint. Air is very turbulent—tornado type; birds in my area seeking heavy cover. There is a fairly large river that I can see about 15 to 20 miles north and slightly west; runs NE then curves in wide valley running SW to NE; river then runs SE. Area to east: low rolling hills. Quite a few Civil War monuments. A marble colonnade type: 'In this area was fought the battle of Lynchburg where many brave men of the Union and Confederate Army's (sic) fell. We dedicate this area to all peace loving people of the future—Daughters G.A.R.'

On a later date Sl was asked to return to the West Virginia site with the goal of obtaining information on code words, if possible. In response, Sl supplied the following information:

Top of desk had papers labeled "Flytrap" and "Minerva". File cabinet on north wall labeled "Operation Pool" … (third word unreadable).

Folders inside cabinet labeled "Cueball", "14 Ball", "Ball", "8 Ball", and "Rackup". Name of site vaguely seems like Hayfork or Haystack. Personnel: Col. R.J. Hamilton, Maj. Gen. George R. Nash, Major John C. Calhoun (??).

Urals Site (S1)

After obtaining a reading on the West Virginia site, Sl volunteered that he had scanned the other side of the globe for a Communist Bloc equivalent and found one located in the Urals at 65°00′57″N, 59°59′59″E, described as follows:

Elevation, 6200 ft. Scrubby brush, tundra-type ground hummocks, rocky outcroppings, mountains with fairly steep slopes. Facing north, about 60 miles ground slopes to marshland. Mountain chain runs off to right about 35° east of north. Facing south, mountains run fairly north and south. Facing west, mountains drop down to foothills for 60 miles or so; some rivers running roughly north. Facing east, mountains are rather abrupt, dropping to rolling hills and to flat land. Area site underground, reinforced concrete, doorways of steel of the roll-up type. Unusually high ratio of women to men, at least at night. I see some helipads, concrete. Light rail tracks run from pads to another set of rails that parallel the doors into the mountain.

Thirty miles north (5° west of north) of the site is a radar installation with one large (165 ft.) dish and two small fast-track dishes.

The two reports for the West Virginia Site, and the report for the Urals Site were verified by personnel in the sponsor organization as being substantially correct. The results of the evaluation are contained in a separate report filed with the COTR [Contracting Office Technical Representative].

As it turns out, the West Virginia site was a very secret National Security Agency (NSA) listening post, and Pat's data spawned a substantial internal security investigation that showed no wrongdoing on the part of the SRI team or Pat. All this happened before the internet and tools like Google Earth. In essence, it was data like this from Pat and others during those early days of the project that cemented the US Government's commitment to the remote viewing programs for the next twenty years.

While the above engendered much curiosity on the part of Ed May, others would (and do) look at such reports with great skepticism and even downright disbelief. How did May even get to that point, and why did that push him in the new and different life direction? "Unlike many of my colleagues, I never had any experience with matters psychic," said May. "I did not awake one night to find my deceased grandmother at the foot of my bed, nor had I experienced or even heard of an out-of-body experience." So what happened to bring a nuclear physicist so far into the ESP Wars? To get to the answer to that question, first a bit of background on Dr. Edwin C. May.

Born in Boston just before the US entered World War II, his father was a Navy man, and as with many military families, he moved to various posts in the US until his father finally saw action in the Pacific theater. After the war, the family settled on a ranch near Tucson, Arizona. Even in his early years, he was fascinated with all things Russian, arguably setting some of his future path. Studying the World Book Encyclopedia, he taught himself the Cyrillic alphabet and learned some of the geography of Russia. "When Sputnik began orbiting the Earth, I could not wait to run outside to watch this 'star' glide silently overhead—for me, this was quite a thrill."

His high school education at a boarding school in Tucson was instrumental in shaping his career. In his senior year (1958), he took physics from a teacher who added beginning calculus as part of the course, which for the time was most unusual. This stimulated his interest in the subject, and he did quite well at it.

His mother, who had spent much of her life before he was born in Boston, wanted him to apply to Massachusetts Institute of Technology (MIT) in Cambridge. "I told her it was merely an engineering school; that I had a higher calling, being destined for physics." Ultimately, he ended up at the University of Rochester, NY, anxious to start his new life as a physics major. He applied for the advanced physics course and was accepted.

While he did not do well in most of his other subjects in college, physics was his one real success. He excelled in the physics laboratory, especially in nuclear instrumentation, high-speed electronics, and gamma ray angular correlation measurements—advanced fields for a college senior at that time. "Fortunately, my physics professors wrote glowing graduate school recommendations that offset my otherwise mediocre grades."

As with so many other American college students, he spent his summers working. Beginning in 1960 and continuing for the next five summers, he worked at the Rand Corporation, located right on the beach in Santa Monica, CA. Rand, while a private company, was mostly a "think tank" for the US Air Force. "As a child I had learned basic piloting skills as a member of the Civil Air Patrol cadet program, so working for the Air Force, even indirectly, was a particular thrill. This was also my introduction to the world of state secrets in that security clearances were required even for summer employees." While his work was mostly in atmospheric physics, he did analyze some intelligence, mostly in the nuclear domain. Thus began a lifelong career on the edges of the intelligence community as a contributing analyst.

In 1962, after graduating from the University of Rochester, he began his doctoral studies at the Carnegie Institute of Technology in Pittsburgh (now known as Carnegie-Mellon University). His first day there set another precedent for his life, as May describes:

"While wandering lost through one of the faculty buildings, I saw an Asian Indian hunched over an apparatus that I immediately recognized from my work at Rochester.

Curious, I went in and asked, 'Isn't that a gamma-gamma angular correlation setup?'

"The Indian said, 'Yes, and who are you?'

"We struck up a conversation, and it turned out he was Professor S. Jha, one of the best-known and respected researchers in nuclear structure and Mösbauer studies. Within weeks I began working for Jha in his laboratory."

Unfortunately, Professor Jha and his laboratory were May's only real contact with academia. Still young (22), he spent most of his time outside the lab in non-academic pursuits like so many other college and graduate students time enjoying extended lunches, learning to play a bagpipe (perhaps not so common!), and partying in general. Physics as an academic pursuit had not yet become his main agenda.

May's lifestyle choices caught up with him in early 1964 when the physics department asked him to leave. The timing was bad, as this revelation was followed immediately by a "friendly" request by the US Army to appear for a draft induction physical exam. US involvement in the Vietnam War had just begun.

"Believe me, there is no more effective wake-up call for a young man than the threat of being drafted. I told Professor Jha my tale of woe and fortunately, he responded with a wonderful solution. One of his research contracts was with the US Navy and he was able to hire me as a laboratory technician under that project. By a stroke of luck, as an employee in the defense industry, I could avoid going to war in Vietnam."

May worked for Jha until late in 1964. Then one day, he was led down the street to the University of Pittsburgh, into the office of Professor Bernard L. Cohen, one of the top experimentalists in nuclear structure and reaction mechanisms.

As May recalls, Jha said, "Bernie, this fellow has had some academic difficulty in my department, but he is simply one of the best experimentalists I have ever watched at work in a lab. You should have him in your department and he should work for you."

The recommendation took, and Edwin May began his second graduate school career. "With fire in my belly, I was able to work with a mature and focused intensity."

He joined the University of Pittsburgh as a Ph.D. candidate and began working in the accelerator laboratory under Professor Cohen. Jha's faith in him proved to be well-founded, as he did well in academics, learned a great deal about experimental methodologies and hardware, and wrote a Ph.D. dissertation entitled, "Nuclear Reaction Studies via the (p,pn) Reaction on Light Nuclei and the (d,pn) Reaction on Medium to Heavy Nuclei."

During his studies at the University of Pittsburgh, May met another Indian who would become a trusted friend and indirectly provide another career influence: S. Gangadharan, or "Gangs" for short. Although he was getting his Ph.D. in nuclear chemistry, their experimental work was quite similar, so they helped each other. That was the beginning of a 40-year friendship that ended suddenly in 2000 with the unexpected passing of Gangs. In the interim, he introduced May to his family, and Gangs became the main link to the large network of close friends and associates in India that he retains to this day.

*The late Dr. S. Gangadharan (Gangs)—Director, Board of Radiation and
Isotope Technology, Bhabha Atomic Research Center, India*

May received his Ph.D. in 1968 and headed for his first post-doctoral assignment in the physics department and cyclotron laboratory at the University of California at Davis.

During his post-doctoral appointment at UC Davis, May had his first real exposure to the world of psi. He attended a conference that was organized by Professor Charles Tart, a well-known and respected psychologist who at that time was mostly interested in altered states of consciousness. One of the speakers was a very businesslike person named Robert Monroe who talked about something he had never heard of before: out-of-body experiences. These were new and fascinating ideas to May, and he wasted no time in buying Monroe's book, Journeys Out of the Body.

"If this down-to-earth fellow could get out of his body, surely I could do it more easily, being an inquiring scientist and all," said May. "That arrogance turned out to be totally unjustified. I tried for many months to get out of my body with no luck at all, and set the whole thing aside as foolishness."

At the end of his post-doctoral appointment, he moved to San Francisco to explore his newfound freedom. During part of the year, he taught physics in the so-called Free University of San Francisco and immersed himself in activities typical of California in the 1970s. These included attending a lecture on serious parapsychology research by Charles Honorton, who became a leader in parapsychological research. "The way he explained the subject piqued my interest as it sounded to me like 'real' science, with testable hypotheses and solid statistical analyses." May had dinner with Honorton, and was offered sound answers to all his questions. "But I remained unconvinced that any of these interesting ideas were true."

After a bit of library research, he discovered that, in India, many of the concepts he had been learning about were generally accepted as fact. He was drawn to India, where he had visited his old friend Gangadharan (Gangs) in 1970 (and fell in love with the country). By then, Gangs was actively pursuing his career at the Bhabha Atomic Research Center in Mumbai. He wrote to his friend and described his newfound interest in psychic phenomena. "I explained that if even a small fraction of what I heard about parapsychology were true, then the implications for physics were boundless. So I proposed that I come to India and focus our effort on psychic phenomena for a year of collaborative research."

In order to get there, in 1973, May and Gangadharan shared a scheme. At that time, the US Congress had passed Public Law 480, which allowed India to pay its financial debt to the US in its national, soft currency, the Rupee. As a result, the US had approximately one billion US dollars' worth of Indian Rupees that, by law, could not be exchanged anywhere into international hard currency. Thus, academics could benefit by submitting research proposals on any topic whatsoever, and if the cover page indicated that the funds for the research were to come from Public Law 480, the proposals often were not even sent out for peer review! The US was anxious to use these Indian Rupees. While researchers could spend nearly unlimited amounts of money in India, they could not, for example, purchase an international flight, because that had to be done in hard currency. They had to come up with their own funds for that.

Their scheme involved a neutron-activation device developed at the University of California at Berkeley that allowed archaeologists to determine if some ancient clay pottery shard was made from local clay—that is, from the soil near where the shard was found—or if it came from some other, perhaps distant place. In this way, archaeologists could map the trading routes of peoples of the ancient world.

They wanted to use Public Law 480 funds to do just that with the substantial number of clay pots lying in museums all over India. "If truth be told, it was an excuse to use government funds to pay for travel all over India—and also to explore some important science."

May had decided to look into the yogis in India rather than the clay pots, and thought that could be a hard sell. However, much to his surprise he received an enthusiastic response from Gangs explaining that he had always been interested in the paranormal. May began doing his homework for the trip by reading much of the English-language literature of those who had gone before in parapsychology. As part of his preparations, he built an elaborate random number generator device (long before personal computers) and gathered other gear to measure psychokinesis, the purported capacity of mind over matter.

"As an arrogant young scientist, I of course assumed that I could easily surpass the work of my predecessors, armed with my extensive Indian connections." Thus, off he went in August 1974 to live with Gangs, his wife Mahalakshmi, and their new son Ramprasad at Anushakti Nagar ("atomic energy city"), expecting to make Nobel Prize-winning discoveries of mind over matter.

However, after nearly a year of fascinating experiences in South India, May had to admit that he had not in fact witnessed any truly paranormal phenomena. "Looking back on that year, I feel ashamed of my own arrogance, cultural ignorance, and general naiveté. I now know that what I had undertaken should not be the job of Westerners, no matter how kindly they regard the culture. The challenge is to examine critically a culturally embedded concept such as 'psi' phenomena. Being outsiders, we cannot comprehend the faith and emotional structures that support the beliefs. Objectivity is impossible, since we risk being overly critical one moment and emotionally captivated the next, either of these consequences being detrimental to a scientific inquiry. Additionally, my outsider status profoundly affected the way people interacted with me, distorting my impressions further."

While scientific research on siddhis—the Sanskrit term for psi abilities—is a possibility, it is difficult to separate superstition, magic tricks and outright fraud in the search for true psi experiences. Fighting to eradicate superstition is a task that the rationalists in Indian society, as in any other culture, are faced with. Some of May's experiences during this time can be found in an article he wrote on the topic for Psychic magazine.[1]

As his stay in India was approaching its end, he wrote a ten-page letter to Charles Honorton suggesting a number of ways in which they could collaborate at the laboratory at Maimonides Medical Center in Brooklyn, NY, where Honorton was working. In response to May's request, he received a one-word answer: "Yes!"

AN INTRODUCTION TO SERIOUS ESP RESEARCH

Maimonides had been the site of extensive parapsychological research with dream telepathy by Drs. Montague Ullman and Stanley Krippner, and had expanded their parapsychological research to include a number of other areas and researchers. "From the spring of 1975 to the following winter, my ESP research went into high gear," said May, "as I studied serious parapsychology research with a master [Honorton] and saw substantial evidence for the existence of ESP. I was hooked."

During his time working with Honorton, he met an artist and psychic, Ingo Swann, who was involved in psychokinesis experiments at the Stanford Research Institute (SRI) near San Francisco. Swann was curious about May's technical and experimental background, and they became friends. Over several months, they conducted a few pilot studies together, with Swann as a psychic participant at Maimonides.

Charles Honorton: Maimonides (1975)

In the end, Ingo encouraged Dr. Harold Puthoff, the SRI program's director, to hire Ed to help with the on-going psychokinesis experiments. Thus, it was Ingo Swan who really got May started on his twenty-year career investigating and utilizing psychic phenomena, something for which he said he "will be eternally grateful."

However, unknown to May at the time, some elements of the research program at SRI were classified as Top Secret, and were being funded by the CIA.

Except for rare earlier instances, the US government became seriously interested in using ESP for military and intelligence applications only after 1972. Since then, a number of authors, including remote viewer Joseph McMoneagle, have written about the participation of the government in its 20-year, 20-million-dollar program that came to be known as Star Gate. The early history of this program has been described by Puthoff and Targ in their 1976 book, Mind Reach. However, many aspects of the project were under strict secrecy guidelines or considered classified information, and thus were not mentioned at all in that book. As of this writing, however, most of the project data and methods are either in the public domain or have been otherwise declassified, which is why we can tell the true story of what happened there.

May joined the SRI team first in 1975 as a consultant and became a full-time employee as a senior research physicist the following year. Once his "Secret" clearance was in effect, he learned what was really going on inside the walls of the Star Gate program. The quality of the data astounded May, and it frustrated him how few people on the outside understood the truth about extrasensory perception.

In 1982, Russell Targ left the program and in 1985, Harold Puthoff stepped out of the program as well. Thus, the directorship of the Star Gate program was passed to Edwin C. May.

THE ESP PROGRAM ON MAY'S WATCH

From the inception of the project under the CIA's auspices in 1972 through 1979, the SRI program had three primary responsibilities.

First, to use ESP to obtain information about potential threats from the Soviet Union, other Eastern Bloc countries, and the People's Republic of China. Second, to assess the credibility and accuracy of intelligence regarding ESP research that was slowly filtering out from the Soviet Union. Finally, though with minimal support, to conduct basic and applied research. Basic research concerned the fundamental physics, physiology, and psychology of ESP, whereas applied research sought ways to make the end-product information more accurate and reliable.

It is a sad fact that modern military decision makers are extremely hesitant to finance programs based on a putative extrasensory capability. During the Cold War, Senator William Proxmire invented a prize—the Golden Fleece Award—as a way of embarrassing government officials who routinely funded all sorts of silly projects. Thanks to academic prejudice and often ridiculous portrayals of psychic phenomena in the media, the study of ESP possessed a high "giggle" factor, regardless of the quality of the work. Both this giggle factor and the Fleece Award had a chilling effect in the funding community for ESP research. As a result, when May became the project director at SRI, more than forty percent of his time was spent attempting to raise funds so that the program could continue.

There were many successful applications of ESP within the project at SRI, and later at Science Applications International Corporation (SAIC). We'll address some of those successes in a later chapter, but one example is an intelligence-like success that was never formally part of the Star Gate program, having occurred later. It resulted from a desperate call from one of May's friends. While a leap ahead in time for Ed May's story, it demonstrates how useful the process of remote viewing can be, and how the process works for certain tasks.

On one of his many visits to Washington and the Defense Intelligence Agency (DIA)—the agency that gave SAIC a contract for research into ESP and its application—he met with Angela Ford. Angela was one of the DIA's most skillful remote viewers, and she introduced May to "Esther," who had been one of the managers of Bill Clinton's first-term primary campaign in 1993. Once elected, Clinton appointed Esther to a high position in one of the departments in the Executive Branch of the government. Here is Angela's photo.

Accomplished remote viewer: Angela D. Ford

May and Angela met "Esther" in her office, and he was impressed with her obvious and extensive connections to the Clinton family. On the wall or mounted elsewhere were a large number of photos, some of them signed, of Bill and "Esther" in various situations. There she was jogging with the President, playing with Socks, the family cat, chatting with Hillary, engaging in formal meetings, and so on—quite impressive, indeed.

"'Esther' and I went for dinner and enjoyed many in-depth discussions about the nature of reality, parapsychological phenomena of all kinds, and the politics of the day. Many meetings and dinners followed, and 'Esther' and I still maintain our friendship."

Sometime during Clinton's second term, May received a panicked telephone call from "Esther." It seems that her 20-something daughter had failed to show up at work and was missing.

"'Esther,' why the hell are you calling me?" May asked. "Given your position in the West Wing, you can have direct access to the FBI, the Secret Service, and local law enforcement. Why me?"

Understandably, she was in a bit of a panic, but she told him that the best efforts from government officials had been of no help. She urged him to ask some of the remote viewers to see whether they could help somehow. In the laboratory, this is called a "search task." Although searching for lost things, such as people, aircraft, weapons, or drugs seems an obvious thing to do with psychics, this generally turns out to be a very challenging task.

THE SEARCH TASK

Three basic approaches have worked for a search task in the field and in the laboratory. The first is to ask psychics to "stick a pin in a map" corresponding to the lost person. In May's experience, this approach usually doesn't work. When it does work, people often give this positive result undeserved attention.

A more effective technique is the standard remote viewing of a target such as the whereabouts of a missing person, in this case "Esther's" daughter. However, even this approach has its problems and an excellent remote viewing might not contribute much to actually finding the lost person.

Imagine the following scenario: We wish to find a Soviet submarine that is lurking underwater somewhere off the California coast. Fortunately, we have at our disposal a psychic viewer who is nearly perfect with her impressions. The viewer describes the interior of the sub exactly, describes the crewmembers in detail, provides the name of the Captain and his children, and tells what the crew ate for dinner that evening. We now have top-of-the-line accurate psychic data, but it in no way helps us to find the sub.

The viewer then takes a psychic "look outside" of the sub, which yields an amazingly accurate description of—you guessed it—water!

This is one example of how the intelligence value, in this case what is needed to find Esther's daughter, is often unrelated to the quality of the remote viewing. The quality of remote viewing can be excellent, but the value of the information worthless.

Fortunately, the real-world research provides a compromise. In the standard out-bound remote viewing protocol developed by Targ and Puthoff, an "agent" travels to some randomly chosen location and the viewer simply describes the surroundings where that person is currently located. This is the bread-and-butter laboratory remote viewing experiment.

How could this approach be used to locate a person?

That depends upon the accuracy and detail of the psychic response. In the ultimate case, suppose the viewer gives the street name and address of the hiding or lost person, then finding them is simply a job of going there and knocking at the appropriate door– assuming the person has not been moved, or assuming the task is to view where the person will be at a given point in the near future.

Dr. Nevin Lantz at SRI 1982

Back to "Esther's" story and her missing daughter. May hesitantly agreed to ask three of the best viewers to try to describe the physical surroundings and emotional circumstances where she was currently located.

One of these was Nevin D. Lantz, Ph.D. who holds a degree in clinical psychology. Nevin had been formally associated with the project at SRI since the 1980s and was in charge of identifying personality factors that predict psychic ability by working with various consultants and conducting specific experiments. Additionally, he tasked Joe McMoneagle and Angela D. Ford—then still an excellent government remote viewer—with attempting to locate the missing young woman.

Nevin responded with a detailed psychological profile of the missing woman and with the good news that she was not in physical harm's way, but had suffered a substantial psychological episode. Later they learned that this remote psychological assessment was accurate. A combination of the responses from Joe and Angela aided the FBI in recovering the missing woman. All's well that ends well.

Another success with the search task happened earlier. Though it may sound impossible to some, this approach or something conceptually similar, has worked spectacularly well in the past. Consider the case of trying to find US Army Brigadier General Dozier who was kidnapped from his home in Verona, Italy on the evening of December 17, 1981.Joe McMoneagle was asked to locate the General by using remote viewing to accurately draw Dozier's current location. Among the response data was a drawing of a unique circular park with a cathedral. As it turns out, by scouring maps and photographs for such a combination of structures, the searchers found one in the city of Padua, the place where General Dozier was rescued.

Dozier was briefed the following February at the Command's Special Compartmented Information Facility (SCIF—Bldg 4554) on the Grill Flame[2] psychic program–this was the unclassified name for the then-classified SRI program. Dozier was then asked to review sketches and narratives generated during the Grill Flame sessions for any correlation to places or events surrounding his kidnapping. Dozier was so impressed with the data that he suggested that senior government officials, military officers, and leading business and political personalities be instructed in what to "think" if they were kidnapped so that psychic searchers could more easily locate them.

As a postscript to "Esther's" story, since she was both relieved and especially happy at the outcome, May was convinced that the Star Gate project now enjoyed the attention of the West Wing of the White House and perhaps of the President, himself.

"So I sat back waiting for the flood of contract funds to appear in order to continue the research. Apparently, the only thing that happened was that a few of Joe's books on the topic were handed to the President. No contract funds were forthcoming, and I take responsibility for that. It is simply not a good fundraising technique to do something noteworthy, and then wait for money to be thrown in one's direction. Clearly one has to be much more proactive than that, whether in fundraising for a school project or for research at the cutting edge of science."

THE MID 1980'S

In 1986, the program had a rather substantial 5-year Army contract of $10 million. As a result of these resources, significant progress was made in all of our primary tasks. For the first time, May and his colleagues actually had a charter to conduct basic research to attempt to understand the underlying mechanisms of parapsychological phenomena as part of their role as scientific support of the Army/ DIA's in-house remote viewing group. Until this contract, they were required mostly to conduct operations-oriented research–in other words, investigations designed to improve the quality of the results and not expected to understand the mechanisms. Additionally, they continued to conduct foreign assessments—analysis of potential parapsychological threats from other countries, and to a limited degree, remote viewing on foreign sites.

The funding was never fully realized, as it happens. In the third year, it was cut in two, and after the fourth year, all the money vanished. So of the total $10M, only half of it actually came through.

One aspect of the large Army contract was that they were required to conform to the wishes of three separate Army-constituted panels, unlike any previous review panels (of which there were many): a Scientific Oversight Committee, an Institutional Review Board (a.k.a. Human Use Review Committee), and a Pentagon Policy Review Committee. All committee members were required to hold active security clearances. Let us emphasize that these committees were not "rubber-stamp" bodies. Rather, their members agreed to long-term commitments, and they all took their responsibilities very seriously. May commented, "As the recipient of their reviews, I can attest that the quality of our output improved substantially."

Perhaps the least active but arguably the most important group was the Pentagon Policy Oversight Committee. It consisted of three members of note, some drawn from the Defense Policy Board, whose sole responsibility was to determine whether or not their activity met the goals and objectives of the Department of Defense. Over the course of four years, May was asked to meet with this group in the Pentagon perhaps three times. Their reports were supportive of the activities, and the program and personnel passed muster with regard to the overall mission.

The second oversight committee may surprise many. The US Department of Defense is actually very concerned about the ethical treatment of humans who participate in DOD-directed experiments. While the folks at SRI might easily have asked the in-place Institutional Review Board (IRB) at Stanford University, which is also known by other names such as Human Use Review Committee or Ethics Committee to review their work, they did not. Rather, they built their own IRB from scratch, because the DOD requirements are actually stricter than for IRBs governed by the Department of Health and Human Services. The mix of professions for such an IRB, which are prescribed by law, included a member of the clergy, a layperson, a lawyer, and physicians of various types. Believe it or not, their clergy-person was a Buddhist priest who held a Secret security clearance. Within their IRB was who's who of the medical world, including one Nobel Laureate.

As with other IRBs, they were required to write up a detailed human-use protocol for each individual experiment in their contractual statement of work. This write-up had to explain why the experiment was being conducted. It had to cover the nature of its physical, financial, emotional, and health risks. It included the possible outcomes that were anticipated and what would be concluded accordingly. Finally, it had to cover the likelihood that each of these potential outcomes would meet the primary objective of the experiment. In other words, would all possible outcomes justify the use of human subjects?

All of the experimental participants were additionally required to undergo complete physical, psychological, and neuropsychological exams. If these revealed abnormalities of any kind, and May and his colleagues still wished that person to participate, they had to obtain a waiver from the person and his or her physician. This was a very time-consuming, but critically important task.

The final, and probably the most active panel was the Scientific Oversight Committee (SOC). For the first two years, there were twelve members that were drawn from lists of people supplied by the project personnel, and ones provided by the Army. The Army had the final decision regarding who would serve on the committee. They all were paid under the contract for their time and travel. A threshold requirement for serving on the SOC was that the member be skeptical of the putative parapsychological phenomena, but at the same time, open-minded enough to want to take the job seriously. Furthermore, their time commitment was substantial— the job was to last for the five-year duration of the contract. However, because in the third year of the contract the $2M budget was cut in half, May reluctantly had to reduce the SOC membership down to only five.

The SOC had three primary tasks: to review and approve the detailed experimental protocol for every experiment to be conducted under the Army contract; to exercise unannounced drop-in privileges in order to see firsthand what was happening; and to review critically, in writing, the final reports for each of the tasks in the contractual statement of work. There were 38 reports in the first year alone.

Because the group was highly professional, the first of the SOC's three tasks was rather straightforward. From time to time they did some protocol "tweaking," but for the most part, the protocols they submitted were approved directly, with little or no substantive change.

The SOC's second task—unannounced drop-in privileges— looked good on paper, but was hardly ever exercised. "I suppose this was to be expected, given that the Committee members were senior professionals with active individual careers," said May.

The main SOC action came with their third responsibility— critical review of the program's final reports. Once the reports were completed and had been copy-edited by SRI International (the new official name for Stanford Research Institute) professional editors, they were copied and sent to all the SOC members. The committee members were to review them as if they had been submitted to a scientific journal of which the member was editor-in-chief. They took notes and eventually provided their comments in writing directly to the Army's Contract Offices' Technical Representative (COTR). In this case, the representative was an Army officer with the rank of full Colonel who had been transferred to the Army Presidio in San Francisco, but whose full-time responsibility was to be in his office in our group at SRI. Their opinions were added to the final reports as an appendix.

In addition to their written opinions, the SRI program personnel hosted a two-day meeting each year during which they presented their results and discussed the outcomes with the SOC group in person. There was good news and bad— although the bad news should be construed as good. Because they were successful, they won 85% of the vigorous and sometimes loud arguments, but the better news was the 15% they lost. The program's scientific "product" so to speak, sharply improved, and that improvement manifested in two ways.

According to May, "First, we learned to approach all positive results from our experiments in a skeptical way: assume what we just saw was a mistake and set about finding it. If we failed to find an error, we could assume something interesting was happening. Secondly, because of the interdisciplinary nature of the SOC, our group was exposed to experimental and theoretical techniques that were outside of the training of our own researchers but could be incorporated with the SOC's assistance. My interaction with the SOC is among the highlights of my professional, academic research career."

However, there were frustrations. As an example to illustrate, one year they invited Professor Jessica Utts, a statistician, to work with them as a visiting scientist. During that year, with her assistance, the program improved upon the more traditional method of analyzing the results of remote viewing experiments by using more sophisticated statistical and mathematical approaches. One of the SOC members chaired the statistics department of one of the University of California's major campuses. This individual rejected the new approach without offering any scientific argument, saying that it was too complex and that there was too much room for subtle, unknown errors. "We all have heard the expression that ESP stands for 'Error Some Place,' which was his assumption, but even so, that statistician's response was quite unexpected."

As it turned out, May had the opportunity to show a single example (then highly classified) of a simulated operational remote viewing conducted as a test by an Air Force client, the full details of which will be found in Chapter 6. The target was the special high-energy electron accelerator located at Lawrence Livermore

Laboratory, nearly 50 miles east of San Francisco. Naturally, the experiment team had no information with regard to the target or its location—called "double-blind" in the parlance of laboratory experiments, since both the subjects and the experimenters were "blind" to the target. The Air Force provided 100 percent "ground truth" —absolute confirmation of what the actual target looked like—so that they could conduct the analysis using the statistical methods that had been developed, though those methods had been so easily rejected by this one SOC member just mentioned. "The visual correspondences were stunning!" according to May.

After the presentation, the same SOC member came up to May and excitedly proclaimed that he "got it!" Of course, May thought he meant the statistical approach, but this was a wrong assumption. This single, visually stunning example convinced him that remote viewing was real. Later, May took him aside in the parking lot and read him the riot act! "How dare you! Jessica and our team have worked a year dotting our I's and crossing our T's to assure the best possible statistical analysis, yet you summarily rejected that approach as being evidential! On the other hand you become convinced about remote viewing from a single example that I cannot defend statistically or scientifically." He was speechless.

It seems that May, and for that matter most of us, assume that science progresses on the basis of good scientific arguments and evidence, but we tend to leave out the emotional component. Robert Burton in a recent book, On Being Certain (St. Martin's Griffin, 2009) points out that modern neuroscience suggests that it is the emotional centers of the brain that become active as we become certain of our opinions and just about anything.

This is surprising to May, as "I had thought that scientists prefer to think that it is the logic and analysis portion of the brain that makes us certain. Maybe I experienced this with our statistician SOC member."

HOW WELL DID ESP INTELLIGENCE COLLECTION WORK AT SRI?

There was another approach to gathering intelligence besides direct ESP in which the US Government took an interest. Normally, when a new military policy, weapons system, or battle order is being considered, the proposed new system is evaluated critically. Often two teams of evaluators, designated as Red and Blue, are assembled to criticize or support the plan, respectively. The SRI group was awarded a contract to participate in a Red team to evaluate a proposal by the Carter Administration, and later by the Reagan Administration, to deploy the new MX missile system.

The proposals were variations on the theme of building many more missile launching facilities than there are missiles, then continually moving the missiles covertly among the various launching facilities—let's call it a nuclear shell game. The Congressional Budget Office originally estimated that procuring 200 MX missiles, building 5,800 shelters for them, and operating such a system would cost $28.3 billion dollars all the way through to the fiscal year 2000, while 300 MX missiles scattered about among 8,500 shelters would cost $37.6 billion dollars. The first option provided for one MX missile for every 29 shelters, while the second planned one missile for every 28 shelters. These were somewhat lower ratios than the one proposed by the Department of Defense, which suggested that there should be one missile for every 20 to 25 shelters.

Eventually, a "racetrack" idea gained favor. Each missile would be moved among the shelters located on spur roads radiating from a central, circular track. There would be about five such patterns, or clusters, in each of about 40 valleys in the deserts of Nevada and Utah. This racetrack system would allow transporters to shift missiles between shelters within 30 minutes, in time to escape incoming Soviet missiles after they have been launched. The racetracks would be about 56 kilometers in diameter.

The complexity and financial support that would have been required for this proposed system demonstrates how seriously the Carter Administration considered the concept. In fact, they were planning to move ahead as soon as possible. The US Air Force expected to begin site selection for the MX operation base test and training facility by 1980. Work on the first racetrack and shelters would begin by 1983, and the first ten MX missiles and 230 shelters were scheduled to be operational by 1986. The Soviets would not know where to aim their missiles in order to cause the most damage to the US's ability to retaliate, since our missiles would be moved continuously among the various shelters.

The question was whether or not this concept could be compromised using ESP. If so, we (the US) would have to assume that the Soviets could also accomplish this. Meaning, it would make no sense to build this vast system of racetracks and shelters in the first place.

The group's proposal, which was eventually approved, included the following elements in the statement of work. The following is what they were going to do with the money if the contract was awarded to SRI:

Assuming a 1-in-20 ratio of missiles-to-shelter mix, determine the statistics of MX system compromise as a function of beyond chance hitting by ESP practitioners. [In other words, what were the results necessary to statistically show "hits" by the viewers were better than chance.]

Conduct a screening program involving about 100 SRI employees and other experienced ESP practitioners, utilizing a 1-in-20 screening device with 100 trials for each participant.

Take the five best people from the screening and have each of them contribute 200 more trials.

From these data, estimate the potential vulnerability of the racetrack, or shell game concept.

In addition, they used a sophisticated statistical technique coupled with a form of ESP called "dowsing" to see if they could compromise the system.

In their final report to the Government, they showed that ESP practitioners were able to locate the hypothetical missile in twelve out of twelve trials, with a total of 452 circle selections. The correct hit rate was over two-and-one-half times what was expected in a one-in-ten game. The figure below shows a letter on US Senate stationery from Senator John W. Warner (R-Virginia) to the Secretary of Defense at the time, the Honorable Caspar W. Weinberger, describing the contribution to the MX missile program.

May doubts that the data they gathered as the sole reason that kept the system from being built, but on the other hand, the ESP research reports surely contributed in an important way toward that end.

Beginning in 1986, the Air Force became exceptionally interested in learning the degree to which remote viewing could provide useful information on directed-energy weapon systems. To test this idea, they awarded a contract to examine this question in three trials: one per year, for three years. As always, they used a double-blind protocol, meaning that no one who interacted with the remote viewers knew anything about the potential target or even, in this case, the identity of the client. A session would play out as follows: "We were usually given the Social Security number of an individual none of us had met. In addition, we were told that on a specific date this person would be somewhere in continental United States." The individual would be on-site with the actual targets, making the individual a beacon for the remote viewing. "As project director, I knew that the targets would be directed-energy systems of some kind, but beyond that I too did not know any specifics." In essence, the Social Security number was all the viewer would have as the targeting mechanism.

United States Senate
WASHINGTON, D.C. 20510

March 4, 1981

80 MAR 10 AM 9 07

OFFICE OF
THE SECRETARY OF DEFENSE

Honorable Caspar W. Weinberger
Secretary
Department of Defense
Washington, D. C. 20301

Dear Mr. Secretary:

Attached you will find a copy of a letter I recently received concerning an intelligence collecting technique known as "remote viewing" which, if feasible, could compromise the location – uncertainty aspect of the MX missile system, thus making the system vulnerable and obsolete.

I would like to request that the Department of Defense review this matter carefully and respond in writing to me regarding the concerns raised in the attached letter.

With best wishes, I am,

Sincerely,

John W. Warner

John W. Warner

JWW/jum

Enclosure

30350

Senator Warner's letter to the Secretary of Defense

Beginning at a specified time, Dr. Nevin Lantz, the project's psychologist and active researcher, would assign a task to the viewer at midnight and again once every eight hours, including the next day's midnight. That task was simple: describe the surroundings where the person to whom the Social Security number belonged was standing. So far, nothing particularly new or inventive was involved. The analysis of the result was a breakthrough not only for laboratory studies. If used properly, it could easily have been adapted to the real world of psychic spying.

Before any of the sessions with a client began, May worked with the sponsor to define three categories of things they wanted to know about the target. First and foremost was the target's function: why it was being developed. The Air Force had five or six different aspects in this category alone in which they were interested. The second category was physical relationships: an instrument, for example, might be under the building that was next to a truck. There were around ten such aspects. Lastly, they specified a rather long list of objects, similar to those one would expect from a traditional remote viewing.

For each of the targets, the Air Force filled out a table for each element in all three categories that was specific to each target to be used later and rated each to the degree to which each element was germane to that target and its location. After the psychic session, an analyst, who was blind to the target and its list of items, filled out the same table, but with regard to the degree to which each item was present in the psychic's response.

Armed with both tables, one for the intended target and one for the response, the computer could take over. Although mathematically complex—the process is known as "fuzzy set analysis"—three simple ideas emerged from the computation. The accuracy was defined as the percentage of the Air Force predefined target that was obtained by the psychic. The reliability was defined as the percentage of the psychic's response that was correct. And finally, the figure of merit was defined as the product of accuracy and reliability.

The way to obtain a high figure of merit was for the psychic to describe as much of the intended target as possible, but in as simple and minimal way as possible so as not to include many incorrect aspects. To get a hint of what a random response could be like in the absence of any psychic ability, they had determined in the laboratory that using a rough rule of thumb about a third of any site can be described by about a third of any response. Perhaps this may seem high, but this rule of thumb arose from considerable analyses of data collected in the laboratory.

How did this work out? Here's just one of three successful examples: Project Rose, a high frequency, high-power, microwave device in the New Mexico desert at Sandia National Laboratory.

Joe McMoneagle was the psychic on this trial. By the Air Force's own assessment, the accuracy, reliability, and figure of merit for this case were 80 percent, 69 percent, and 55 percent, respectively. Keep in mind that chance or just Joe being lucky would predict these numbers to be 33 percent, 33 percent, and 11 percent, respectively. The figure on the following page shows that the drawing and pictures were more impressive.

"In my thirty years of experience in ESP research, I consider this case to be among the very best," said May. "If this example had been an intelligence operation instead of a proof-of-principle session, an independent analyst would have no trouble whatsoever in identifying the target as a microwave device of some sort." The drawings on the right in Figure 2 clearly show easily identifiable elements, such as a waveguide and microwave horn. Joe went on to say that, this device was in a wrapped environment and was being used as some kind of test evaluator.

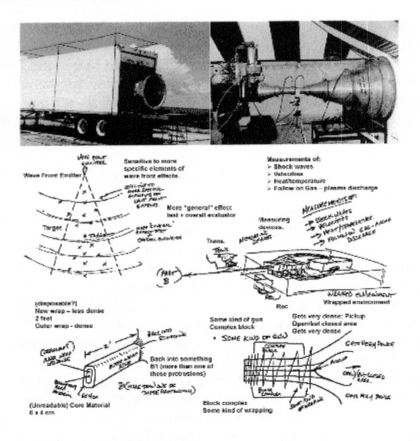

Microwave target test bed for directed energy weapons systems. Ed May has added typed versions of some of the written words for clarity. These appear in small boxes.

In fact, they were shining the microwaves on electronic instruments to test their sensitivity to high-energy microwave radiation. For May, the pièce de résistance is the drawing in the upper left side of Figure 2. "Perhaps it is not as visually compelling as other examples, but for me, at least, 'He nailed it!' Not only did Joe accurately describe exactly what was going on, but also by his drawing indicated the spread of the electromagnetic radiation, which matched the known beam angle of the device." The actual device is shown on the top of this figure.

The point in all this detail is important. They had developed a system of analysis with the potential of allowing an operations analyst looking at real psychic spying data to evaluate the results quantitatively. When combined with more traditional methods of intelligence collection, the military could assess more accurately whether or not to invest resources in solving the problem.

In short, did the psychic spying program work? "Yes," said May. "I realize, of course, that the 'official' US Government's response was 'No.' However, as I hope I have demonstrated here, the real answer is more complex." We'll see just how that complexity played out in the 1995 assessment of Star Gate and the closure of the project in Part 4.

NOT ALL HARD WORK

To be healthy individually and keep the group's morale high, the folks in the program played as hard as they worked. During the first year of the multi-million dollar contract, the budget was $1.875 million, spread across 38 separate tasks in the statement of work. Like military contractors everywhere, they had to endure substantial bureaucracy, and their struggles with typical silly corporate rules helped keep the serious work in perspective.

"For each of these 38 different tasks, I was required to provide quarterly reports and independent financial accounting," said May. "By the end of the first year, I was $500 overspent. I considered this an accounting miracle. It was less than a 0.03 percent error, and almost anyone would have thought that should have been good enough even for government work. But no! Our resident US Army colonel demanded that SRI find the error, and all my pleading about how wasteful that was in time and money fell on deaf colonel ears. I even offered to pay the difference out of my own bank account, but was told that the US Army had no known mechanism of accepting money from an individual. After a few weeks and many more complaints, the SRI accounting office found the discrepancy. I feel sure that SRI had to spend in overhead costs many times the $500 to satisfy the desires of this Army bean-counter."

As anyone in the corporate world can tell you, such mobilizations of resources to uncover errors or issues that cost far less than what the resources to uncover it had to spend is pretty common. It certainly should be no surprise that the military works the same way. However, such events always put undue stress on people, especially if they're already working hard on their own assigned projects. The need to blow off steam with a little harmless fun can lead to silliness, even in top-secret programs.

Because the project was highly classified at SRI International, it existed behind a set of cipher-locked doors, the offices lining one external wall of the geophysics building. Since only a few people had security access to the project, they could get away with things behind the locked doors that others in the building could not. One of these was to celebrate the birthdays of project people in fine style. Normally, this involved a bottle of champagne, a beautifully decorated cake from a local bakery, a signed card, and usually a number of small funny gifts, and, perhaps best of all, the rest of the afternoon to play.

So on the occasion of the aforementioned Army bean-counters birthday, they had some fun at his expense. Jim Salyer from the DIA, who had for a long time been resident with May and company, had a wickedly delightful sense of humor. Jim called the colonel out of his office and informed him of the group's usual birthday custom. Jim said, "To kick off the occasion, I put $5 into a hat and passed it around for contributions by the group. When the hat came back, it had $3.14 in it."

May continues: "What Jim had done was to replace our usual pretty tablecloth with old newspapers duct-taped together. The birthday cake was replaced with a cupcake with a bite taken out of it. The champagne replaced with a small and very cheap wine cooler. Jim had taken a Christmas card that an aunt had sent him and crossed out 'Merry Christmas' with a crayon and wrote in 'Happy Birthday.' This card had all of our signatures. As my gag gift, I brought a large jar of jellybeans, so that after the 'cake,' we could run a bean-counting contest.

"It was apparent that the irony of all this was lost on our colonel. He was clearly trying his best to be a good sport, but his shoulders were starting to droop. A little later, we brought out the real cake and champagne, and a good time was had by all."

Apparently, May was able to turn the tables on Jim Salyer, with a turnabout based on May's life outside of SRI. "When my sister turned 50, I was responsible for getting the cake for the party. I pulled a practical joke on her by getting a piece of foam rubber and paying a professional bakery to frost it with an appropriate Happy Birthday greeting. You can guess what happened when it was time for her to cut the cake.

"I had told Jim Salyer this story, and knew that when it came for Jim's 50th birthday, he would be on full alert. However, I got smart. I cut a corner out of the piece of foam rubber, asked the bakery to put a real piece of cake into the cutout corner, and frost the whole thing as above. The party behind closed doors went forward according to our custom.

May asked Jim to cut the cake and he balked.

"Are you kidding, May?" he said. "No way!"

May accused Salyer of being a "dumb-ass skeptical government worker." May proceeded to cut the real corner out for himself and began eating it. "I handed the knife to Jim to finish the job . . . GOT HIM!"

Regular social gatherings also helped with dealing with the stress of bureaucracy. Nearly every Friday afternoon, the group gathered in one of the laboratories that was a floor above their offices for something they called their psi video emporium. They brought in beer (violating SRI regulations) and popcorn, and rented a movie for the afternoon. On one such occasion, the group also included the aforementioned Army colonel, who believed he was "under cover," since no one was supposed to know he was an Army officer.

One of our staff was fishing through her popcorn and innocently, but loudly, proclaimed, "Hey! Look at this shrunken little kernel!"

Some of the attendees did know all about the Army officer for technical and administrative reasons and according to May, they "were all on the floor laughing!"

ON THE JOB TRAINING AS A PROJECT DIRECTOR

The military folks were not the only ones who presented the group with issues, as May points out with some of the foibles of SRI management itself. The following are examples of this. The first example is trivial, but revealing.

As mentioned, the program's suite of offices lay along one outer wall of the building. By definition, all of the offices had outside windows that offered thrilling views of other World War II-era drab office buildings and a freshly paved parking lot. In the group of twelve people, one was an administrative assistant—a formal SRI title for someone far more skilled than, say, a receptionist or secretary. A huge problem erupted with the management, as they were concerned that if the other administrative assistants in the building found out that the project's assistant had a window, all hell would break loose! Apparently, none of the other admins was allowed such a luxury. In typical managerial style, May had been presented with a problem with no obvious solution.

"Experimental physicists generally believe we can make stuff up as we go along, so I came up with a solution that I knew was so silly that even our witless managers could see it. I suggested that we board up one of the windows! That did it. I won, and there were no more complaints. But I had to promise not to discuss the fact that our administrative assistant was so very special that she could actually have a window."

May's second example is a bit more chilling.

Near the end of the final year for the Army contract, May received a call from a staffer for the Senate Select Committee for Intelligence, telling him that the senior member of that committee wanted to visit the project and specifically May himself. "Who was I to say no to such an important visitor?"

May continues, "As a loyal employee, I raced to my boss' office to inform him of our good fortune. He was star-struck, and started planning an elaborate welcome ceremony and lengthy marketing briefings to convince this senator to throw piles of dollars toward SRI programs having nothing to do with ESP," not exactly the reaction May had expected. May told him that this visit was unofficial, and that the senator merely wanted to review the ESP program. His boss then proceeded to lecture him about how the program was "small potatoes" compared to others at SRI, and that he fully intended to move forward as planned.

It is interesting to note that over the 17-year run of the psychic program at SRI International, the average amount of funding per year was a bit more than $750,000 USD. That this was "small potatoes" to other projects certainly puts the funding for ESP research in perspective, given that the amount was itself huge in comparison to publicly funded psi research.

Upon returning to his office, May called the Senate staffer. "As it turns out, I was the only person at SRI who was 'read-in' to a still highly classified aspect of our program, so I informed that staffer that the briefing would be classified at that particular level. And would he mind excusing any SRI personnel who might be in the room after the pleasantries were exchanged?" This was a very common practice in intelligence briefings.

During the visit, it all came to pass. Pleasantries were exchanged, welcoming speeches made, and then, like a punch to the gut of the management, they were all excused from the room given their lack of appropriate clearances. In other words, they were unable to do their marketing for other SRI projects/programs.

May found this was a bit of a shallow victory. His management was enraged at his actions, "But I could play innocent with some justification, in that I was not the person who made up our so-called 'bigot list' for our Special Access Program. But there was a bit of fallout."

The briefing to this special senator went exceptionally well, and laid the foundation for a good working relationship and later a friendship. The senator said he would put six million into the supplemental authorization markup earmarked for the program. But if appropriated, the money would not be available for about nine months, long after the current contract funds would have expired.

Back he went to the management, asking that they support the project's personnel for that period of time on overhead money, with the promise of six million at the end of nine months. The way both SRI and SAIC work financially is this: they are contract research organizations, so if the project director (May) was to land a big contract, his salary is paid via that contract even though his paycheck is issued by SRI/SAIC. They get the money from the contract. If he did not have a contract, he would still get paid for a while on what is called overhead funds that the corporations have accumulated over time as part of their fee structure. Usually they are not willing to support research staff for long from these accounts, but certainly for some time.

However, the circumstances of the senator's visit provided an important lesson: "One should never provoke one's bosses as I did by having them expelled from an important briefing." Even though this prospect of six million made great business sense, they denied his request, so that the ESP research program at SRI International was forced to close in September 1989 for lack of funds.

However, after a nine-month period, the program rose again from the ashes, May was able to find another home for Star Gate, which prospered at Science Applications International Corporation for another four years. In other words, SRI management lost out on the next contract because they were mad at May for sabotaging their efforts to co-opt the senator's visit–a visit specifically set up to spend time with May and his people.

For Ed May, dealing with the bureaucracy, the funding issues, and personnel–those involved directly in the program and those in management and other programs at SRI–many lessons were learned from his experience. "One is obvious: I learned to be a program manager with a substantial budget and a group of very bright people who often held firm and diverse opinions on nearly everything." But something more important may have happened to him and his worldview.

SHIFTING PERSPECTIVES

In modern consciousness studies, there is a spread of ideas about the nature of consciousness, ranging from the dualist's perspective— that some part of us, for example our soul or consciousness or some other non-material aspect, survives the death of our bodies —-to the materialist's point of view that mind and brain are the same with death the end of an individual's consciousness.

According to the latter view, our rich internal and subjective experience, the Mind, is an outgrowth (a.k.a. an emergent property) of the vast number of neurons in our brain and the even larger number of interconnections among them. "This is the view that I have arrived at based on the data, my experiences, and a growing accumulation of supportive research data," would be a good summation of a proponent's position. Currently this reductionist/materialist view is held by a very small minority of researchers currently active in trying to understand ESP, although it is easily the consensus within the neurosciences and research psychology communities.

During all this, the world itself was changing. The Soviet Union fell apart, and the Cold War was over. May's experiences with Star Gate, combined with this fact, led to something new: a sharing of knowledge with the Russians involved in their side of the ESP Wars and a clear understanding of how the Russians view ESP differently than we in America do.

Said May, "I have had the pleasure of visiting Moscow maybe a dozen times by now, and these former 'enemies' have become good friends. During one of my many visits to Moscow, I was meeting with three of my Russian colleagues and our host in his office. Major General Nikolai Sham, Deputy Director of the KGB (Ret.) who kindly wrote the foreword to this book, had also joined us. All those present, other than myself, had been members of the Communist Party, which officially implied they were firmly atheists and materialists. From our discussion of the nature of consciousness, we realized that there was one, and only one, materialist-atheist in the room... me! The rest were hardline idealists and theists. We had a great laugh over the obvious irony."

While atheism was part of the official Soviet dogma, on a working level it was simply ignored by many. Even the Russian Orthodox Church has its unofficial roots in Russian shamanism, and the good news is that in shamanistic traditions ESP is considered a good thing. Thus, May had no difficulty at all in getting the support of former very senior officials of the Soviet system, who were quite happy to come forward and admit their interest in ESP, which led to this book.

On the American side of things, however, we are generally a Protestant-influenced nation. In that tradition, ESP is too often considered the work of the Devil.

May and his folks have also enjoyed top level government supporters, which have include a Secretary of Defense and other agency directors, most all of whom have retired by now. None of them, however, are willing, as the spy stories say, to come in from the cold. According to May, "They will not allow me to mention their names, even though the evidence of their involvement in the programs is now part of public record."

Psychic phenomena have been part of the human experience ever since we, as a species, could communicate, or possibly even before the evolution of language in other species. With some considerable justification, the skeptic might say that much of the putative psychic reporting has been little more than fantasy, selective memory, or some other form of self-delusion. Beginning with the founding of the Society for Psychic Research in London in 1882 and the later pioneering efforts of J. B. Rhine at Duke University, scientists have been challenged to determine what, if any, of these remarkable self-reports can be teased into the laboratory and studied according to the rules of the scientific method. Perhaps surprisingly, a great deal has passed that requirement.

As project leader for the research section of Star Gate, Edwin C. May subcontracted nearly one million dollars over the years to qualified researchers in the field. In one of those contracts, he asked Charles Honorton to conduct a detailed meta-analysis of the precognitive "Zener card" (standard ESP card) guessing data. Honorton and Diane Ferrari conducted a meta-analysis to examine all such experiments published from 1935 to 1987. Their assessment of all such experiments between 1935 and 1987 showed a cumulative statistical effect 11.4 standard errors over chance expectation. "In other words, a knock your socks off result," said May. Moreover, they determined that neither selective reporting practices nor variations in study quality could account for the observation that, on average, human subjects were able to correctly guess the symbol of a randomly-determined future stimulus card (slightly but significantly) more often than expected by chance.[3] These results stand to this day.

It is beyond the scope of this chapter to provide an assessment of all the anomalous cognition (a.k.a. ESP) research spanning the last eighty years or so. Perhaps the best evidence for the existence of anomalous cognition arises not from pure academic pursuits, but rather from successful applications. The intelligence community, for example, could not care less about the mechanisms of anomalous cognition. As you'll see by the material in the next two chapters, it certainly worked well enough for them to keep the program alive for two full decades.

We realize, of course, that the cynical reader will simply observe that our stupid government kept many dumb things funded. Hence the Golden Fleece Awards.

The defense May offers against that accusation is simple. There were many people in the government who wanted to shut the program down even from its beginning. If it were not for a handful of heroes who put their considerable weight and reputations on the line supporting the project, these detractors would clearly have been successful. Would they have done so if there were nothing to the application of apparent ESP? Unlikely, given the already controversial nature of any claims of psychic abilities.

Ed May is often asked, "Is the government still involved?" As he has given up all his security clearances long ago in the spy versus spy game, "I simply cannot say for certain. In my opinion, I believe it is not funding further work. Given the state of the world just now in 2012, all I can do is hope that my assessment is incorrect."

In this chapter, we focused on the Star Gate contractor's perspective. There is another side to the story, regarding the formation of the Government's own psychic spy unit at Ft. Meade, in Maryland from the perspective of one of the remote viewers. The project's successes and failures, and thoughts on that of the program, are described in the next two chapters.

NOTES:

1) The essay can be downloaded from www.lfr.org/LFR/csl/library/ PsychicMagArticle.pdf.

2) The program had various names before Star Gate. These included: Gondola Wish, Fish Fry, Sun Streak, Center Lane, Grill Flame and Quantum Leap.

3) Their technical paper can be downloaded from www.lfr.org/LFR/ csl/library/HonortonFerrari.pdf.

CHAPTER 5

REMOTE VIEWING AGENT 001:
JOE McMONEAGLE'S STORY

Joseph W. McMoneagle was officially registered as Agent 001 and became the Star Gate project's most successful psychic. Like Ed May, he is capable of providing a continuous history of the program, in his case from late 1977 through to its closure in late 1995, part of the time with the military unit, the remainder—after retirement from the Army—as a civilian contractor. Specifically, his perspective is that of the remote viewers. No other viewer associated with either the US government's in-house psychic spying effort or the contractor's spying and research activity can make the claim of such longevity. Furthermore, as the most successful agent, McMoneagle's story covering some of the deep nuances of the psychics' work, espionage and the experience of ESP phenomena is very telling.

Even though he made the decision to join the project as a remote viewer under the warning that his career and possibly life outside the military would be jeopardized—something that did play out—Joe McMoneagle's participation was recognized with the highest honor for any intelligence officer for his excellence in providing psychic intelligence. His 1984 Legion of Merit award citation reads in part:

...[McMoneagle] used his talents and expertise in the execution of more than 200 missions, addressing over 150 essential elements of information. These EEI [essential elements of information] contained critical intelligence reported at the highest echelons of our military and government, including such national level agencies as the Joint Chiefs of Staff, DIA, NSA, CIA, DEA, and the Secret Service, producing crucial and vital intelligence unavailable from any other source ..."

The actual certificate is shown below.

THE UNITED STATES OF AMERICA

TO ALL WHO SHALL SEE THESE PRESENTS, GREETING: THIS IS TO CERTIFY THAT THE PRESIDENT OF THE UNITED STATES OF AMERICA AUTHORIZED BY ACT OF CONGRESS 20 JULY 1942 HAS AWARDED

THE LEGION OF MERIT

TO　　　CHIEF WARRANT OFFICER, 2ND JOSEPH W. McMONEAGLE
UNITED STATES ARMY

FOR　　distinguishing himself by exceptionally meritorious conduct in the performance of outstanding services during his Army career, culminating in his assignment as Special Project Intelligence Officer with the 902d Military Intelligence Group from 1 August 1984 to 1 September 1984. He was instrumental in developing a new, revolutionary intelligence project. He successfully supported national-level agencies with critical intelligence, often producing operations single-handedly. Chief Warrant Officer McMoneagle's distinguished performance of duty throughout this period represents outstanding accomplishments in the most cherished traditions of the United States Army and reflects utmost credit upon him and the military service.

GIVEN UNDER MY HAND IN THE CITY OF WASHINGTON
THIS ____ DAY OF ____ 19__

Major General, USA
Commanding

However, one other thing is very important where Joe McMoneagle is concerned: he didn't set out to be a "psychic." He was, however, a career military man. How he discovered his talents and moved into position as the best of the best when it comes to remote viewing is a story worth telling before moving into his experiences within Star Gate and beyond. In fact, in his psychic experiences growing up, Joe shared many commonalities with others around the world, as you'll see.

Since the beginning of his participation in the Star Gate program, many have asked when he first noticed that he had psychic skills. "This is almost an impossible question to answer," said McMoneagle, "because it seems like I've had them as long as I can remember." In this chapter, he tells us about how he found out about his abilities, how and why he got involved with remote viewing, and the early days of the project from the viewers' perspective.

A VIEWER'S CHILDHOOD

ESP abilities among children are quite common, that is until they are essentially educated out of them while growing up. In the West, the cultural perspective is that ESP is weird (meaning not desirable) and even scary to many. In addition, there is a disbelief in the experiences and abilities overtly displayed by academics. Consequently, children often learn to keep their psychic experiences to themselves for fear of ridicule—something that adults do as well—and may lose any aptitude for ESP as they take on the belief that the abilities may be "bad," that they are "not possible," or just plain "different." Most people don't want to be seen as "different" or "weird." In McMoneagle's case, the experiences persisted.

Joseph W. McMoneagle was born in Miami, Florida in 1946. First to arrive of a pair of twins in a difficult birth, he and his sister Margaret were premature by almost two months. Back in those days, the probability for survival for premature infants was rather bleak given that the use of incubators was a brand new idea, and even then they hadn't yet learned that too much oxygen could cause permanent blindness to the child.

Surprisingly, he was home in only a few weeks' time, while his twin spent a much longer period in the hospital, fighting to live. Eventually, she was allowed to join Joe at home. They were inseparable growing up, at least until high school. "It was difficult to separate us. We were at the very least, ultra-sensitive to one another's needs," said McMoneagle. "There were times my mother said that it seemed we had an orchestrated plan to drive her crazy. I suppose we were just reading each other's minds."

As they grew up, they noticed a shared unique ability that others didn't seem to possess, or if they did, weren't using. The twins seemed to know things, and it was so noticeable between them that the teachers always tried to keep them separated in the classrooms. "I'm sure they thought we were cheating. There were many times that we both scored the same on tests—same questions right and same questions wrong."

Telepathy between twins has been studied the world over, and there are studies and many more examples one can find with some minor research. In general, the telepathy is between identical twins, rather than fraternal twins as in the case of Joe and his sister.

Apparently, telepathy with his sister wasn't the only type of early psychic experience he had. McMoneagle recalls one of the most common kinds of experiences with apparitions reported by people the world over. In his case, it was an encounter with a newly deceased loved one:

Once when we were very young and still sleeping in the same bedroom together, we had a visitation from one of our favorite aunts in the middle of the night. It was our father's baby sister, our Aunt Anna whom we dearly loved. She appeared to us one night while we were sleeping. It woke us, because she was fully enveloped in a shimmering light and dressed in white. I had never seen her look so radiant and beautiful. She looked very happy and was smiling as she came over and sat on the edge of my bed. My sister and I huddled together in front of her, while she ran her fingers through our hair and quietly told us that in a short time we would hear some sad news about her, but we shouldn't worry, that she was okay. People would talk about how she had died and gone to heaven, everyone would be sad, and they would cry. But, we shouldn't worry, because she was going to be with the angels and she would watch over us from that point on. She made us happy telling us about this, and we were both happy for her. It was obvious that this was something that she wanted to do very much.

The next morning we decided that I should be the one to tell my father, which I did. I simply told him that Aunt Anna had gone to be with the angels.

Anna was his favorite sister. He worried about her all the time and we didn't know why. But, when I told him this he became very angry and he slapped me hard across the face, knocking me off my feet. He told me to never talk like that again about his sister Anna. I hid under my bed for an hour and cried, but remembered what my Aunt had told me. My sister came and stayed with me under the bed.

That afternoon, my father received a phone call. His youngest sister, Anna, had died from lung cancer during the night. She had just had her twenty-first birthday. She had also never smoked.

There were many times that the siblings knew things before anyone else did. They discussed them together, and for a long time agreed never to tell a grownup. It wasn't safe. Such a feeling—that talking about the experiences or perhaps even the subject in general—is not "safe" for kids is unfortunately a common one in much of our society. Eventually, Joe's sister Margaret forgot their agreement and began discussing these things with their mother. "I think it was around our 15th birthday."

Their mother became concerned, especially when Margaret spoke of the many times they were able to pass information between the two of them in school, or know things before they would happen. But, what disturbed her most of all apparently was Margaret describing how she could talk to those who were no longer with us.

As a result, Joe's mother started taking his sister to see a psychiatrist. Margaret asked Joe to back her up on some of the issues that she argued with their mother over, "but I was afraid and refused." Over time, the doctors ordered Margaret to take medications in order to control some of her illusions.

"I know that she fought them for some time, but eventually had to give up," said Joe. "Over the years, it became more and more difficult to communicate with my twin. Her mind seemed to be too confused, and I couldn't understand it. Eventually, we could only communicate when she was in great pain, fear, or needed me desperately for something. I probably should have been there for her, but as a small child I was afraid. I hid my abilities and used them in self-defense."

It would be many years until Joe McMoneagle would feel comfortable talking about the experiences with anyone, and that person turned out to be another favorite aunt. He explained that he continued to use his skills to stay out of the way of his parents when they were drinking, to stay out of trouble in school, and maintain near perfect test scores for all his subjects. "No one ever could figure out why I never carried school books home from school to study. ESP served as my silent partner, and my life was saved several times when I used extrasensory powers in times of danger, especially as a soldier during the Vietnam War."

AN EXPERIENCE IN VIETNAM, 1967

In Vietnam in the 1960s, McMoneagle found his abilities as much survival-centered as anything else. In one experience in 1967 he related, his life and the lives of his comrades in arms were saved by his ESP.

Just east of Ahn Khe, a convoy McMoneagle was part of formed up on the main highway, Route 19, for the run through the mountains to Qui Nhon. There had been considerable troop movement in the mountain areas just north of Route 19 between the villages of Tay So'n and Nam Tu'o'ng, and their mission was to move into the area for a number of days with some sensitive sensor equipment to see if they could pinpoint the main body of this North Vietnamese Army (NVA) movement. All of their equipment was supposed to be able to be carried in their packs, but since the batteries were heavy and much of the equipment was delicate in nature, they preferred to carry it by jeep to as close as they could to its area of operation. "We had learned the hard way that the less exposure the equipment had to the jungles of Southeast Asia, the more likely it was to operate effectively and the longer it would last. Under a triple canopy of leaves, with no air movement at all, and a constant temperature of 107-109 F and 100% humidity, the heat and moisture was oppressive to humans and totally destructive to electronics."

It was necessary to travel in convoy, because a single vehicle, especially a jeep that might be carrying non-commissioned officers and/or officers would be too great a target for an ambush. Convoys travelling with armored vehicles and heavy guns guaranteed protection to lone vehicles such as theirs. There was also a greater possibility that a single vehicle traveling the road alone might trigger a mine and leave the occupants stranded and vulnerable to attack by an overwhelming force, or death from lack of immediate medical support.

The men had been sitting in the sun almost an hour, waiting on the other trucks to assemble. McMoneagle's stomach had been turning over the entire time. "Every small voice in my mind that morning was screaming at me to just take off, leave, to drive it alone, and not to spend another minute waiting on the convoy that morning. I told the other two men in my team what I was thinking and they knew me well enough not to argue."

McMoneagle started the jeep, pulled out of the line, and rocketed to the barriers where they were stopped by the Military Police. He showed them their Intelligence orders and ordered the barriers lifted. They headed down Route 19 in a cloud of dust a full twenty minutes ahead of the convoy.

"I'd like to say nothing happened that day and it didn't to us." However, approximately 13-14 kilometers just east of An Khe, there were a number of switch-backs in the road which are severe enough that all vehicles, especially large trucks, had to slow to 10 km/hr. or less in order to negotiate the turns. The road also dropped precipitously for a long stretch just before the turns and then climbed a long distance immediately following this stretch of turns.

The North Vietnamese soldiers set up four heavy mortars in the mountain directly overlooking these switchback turns and bracketed the top and bottom of the road with heavy machinegun emplacements. When McMoneagle and company drove through with their single jeep, the enemy apparently did not want to waste their ambush on a single vehicle with only three riders. Instead, they waited for the entire convoy, which came along twenty minutes behind. They allowed the convoy to drive down through the switch back turns and begin its accent up the steep climb. Just before it reached the top of the climb, they hit the lead vehicle with numerous rocket propelled grenades, while simultaneously hitting the rear vehicles, trapping the convoy in the middle, which they then raked heavily with mortar fire.

Needless to say, the electronics they carried were not needed to indicate where the bulk of the NVA was located. "We only had to look over our shoulders to see the columns of black smoke. It was an ugly ambush and one we might have been caught in if it hadn't been for the voices in my head. This was one example of so many instances of knowing that led to many of my closer friends starting to mimic me in my actions. While in the base camp, if I chose to move into a bunker for a couple of nights, it would soon become extraordinarily crowded inside within just a few hours."

A WARNING OF DEATH?

Just before he arrived in Southeast Asia, McMoneagle had a lucid dream in which he envisioned himself dying. In the dream, "at the very moment of my death, there was a brilliant white flash of light and I knew that I was dead, that I had been killed. But my death was okay. I had died doing my duty and with honor. Somehow, that made it right. I interpreted the dream as meaning a short round from a large American cannon would probably get me, or a large mortar from an enemy tube would come down at my feet and I'd die in the ensuing blast. Also, because of this dream I felt it was only right that I tell those around me that death as a soldier wasn't so bad and I actually had good feelings about it. I was telling people for almost a month that I wasn't going to survive."

McMoneagle shared this dream with his closest friends and colleagues. It wasn't well received. On numerous occasions—often in the middle of firefights—he'd walk around giving orders standing up, while everyone else was on the ground. Everyone looked at this as either brave or utterly crazy. It was neither since he already knew he wasn't going die by a bullet.

During the Tet Offensive of 1968, one of his friends was hit trying to cross an open field. McMoneagle stopped to cover him with his flak vest and then pulled him behind an Armored Personnel Carrier (APC). "It sounded like I was working inside a beehive. There is nothing brave about this. I already knew how I was going to die. But if the enemy shelled us with mortars or 122mm rockets and RPGs, you'd usually find me standing alone! No one wanted to be standing next to me."

The dream clearly did not come true as originally interpreted, as McMoneagle survived the Vietnam War. "I was never hit with an artillery round, and although I got metal fragments from many mortar rounds, I was never seriously injured by one." However, it turned out to be a premonition of another close call with death, which we'll discuss shortly.

He did have another rather odd vision that did come to pass. "When I got to Vietnam and left the airplane, as my feet hit the tarmac I had a vision of myself turning around and waving to friends as I climbed the ladder to the plane to leave. Only the plane wasn't a military plane that I was boarding, it was a civilian aircraft and it was painted all yellow. And on the side it said 'Canary Bird.' Of course this was absurd, because no planes were yellow and all planes in and out of Vietnam were military. When I was ordered to report to the repo-depot in Saigon for departure home, I ended up flying home on a brand new airline called Braniff, and all of their planes were pastel colors. My plane was a very pale yellow and on the side of the plane it said 'Yellow Bird.' I left Vietnam on the 28th of August, 1968."

NEAR-DEATH EXPERIENCE

The dream McMoneagle had led him to be arguably a bit reckless on the battlefield when bullets (not mortars) were flying, so perhaps it was luck alone that kept him out of harm. "After coming home from Vietnam, it was obvious that the dream was wrong," since he was still alive, "so, I figured it must not be important." He was wrong on that front. As he learned in the following experience, "I had gotten the information exactly correct, but had interpreted it badly."

As part of his military service in 1970, Joe McMoneagle was sent to Braunau Am Inn, Austria. It was here that he had a heart attack and subsequent out-of-body experience that would eventually alert certain military leaders to his abilities.

On one of his missions in Europe, Joe was meeting with his first wife for a weekend retreat at a guesthouse in Braunau Am Inn. He recalls the time of year as being wet and cold, mostly rainy with lots of fog in the early morning hours. He and his wife were going to be staying at the small guesthouse across the German-Austrian border for a weekend, after which he would continue with his mission. Also present was one of his closest friends at the time, who was going to stay for dinner at the guesthouse and then leave. They had entered the restaurant of the guesthouse, sat down towards the rear of the room and ordered drinks before dinner. McMoneagle had just taken a few sips of his drink once they ordered their meals when he began to feel very ill. Not wanting to become violently sick in front of the other patrons who were eating inside the restaurant, Joe excused himself from the table. He told his wife that he needed some fresh air and that he would return in a moment.

He couldn't find the men's room, so he headed directly to the glass door at the front of the guesthouse restaurant. "I remember as I pushed on the glass door with my hand, it swung outward, and as my body passed through it, there was a popping noise, very much like someone snapping their fingers. The next thing I noticed was that I was suddenly standing on the cobblestones of the road outside the building." He recalled that it was raining and that the rain was warm and felt good to him. "I held out my hands to collect the rain in them to see how hard it was raining and was surprised to see the rain drops were passing right through my palms. This amazed me. I watched this happening for a few seconds, until I noticed a small commotion near the front door of the building in front of me. There was a crowd gathering there, so I moved in that direction. What I saw sent a shock wave through my being."

Lying on the sidewalk in front of the building was the body of Joe McMoneagle. His wife was standing there with her hands over her mouth and she was crying. His friend sat down on the wet pavement and pulled Joe's body up into his lap and began striking him in the chest. "Each time he struck me in the chest, I found myself back inside my body staring up at him and feeling intense burning pain all through my body. I wanted to scream out at him to stop doing what he was doing. But, every time I started to yell, I'd find myself back outside of my body looking down at him raising his fist again to strike me in the chest."

Joe tried to yell at him. "No! Don't do that!" But with Joe experiencing being out of his physical body, his friend couldn't hear him. The friend would strike again, and McMoneagle would "suddenly be back inside my body looking up at him again. In my mind I'd be screaming, no, no, you must stop this, it hurts too much. And finally I stopped going in and out of my body. I just stayed out, sort of hovering there and watching."

After a few moments, a Volkswagen Beetle pulled up and Joe watched as they loaded his body into the back seat and drove away. He panicked and began flying off trying to catch them. "I flew along beside the car, yelling at them to wait. I watched as they never slowed down for the border crossing at the Austrian-German check point, they just drove right through. I flew along beside the car all the way to the hospital in Passau, Germany."

Once there, the still out-of-body McMoneagle watched as his friend pulled Joe's body from the car and carried him over the shoulder to the emergency room door and tried to enter. It was locked—German hospitals always locked their doors at 8 PM back then. The friend began kicking the glass doors with his foot, until a nurse came and unlocked the doors. He carried Joe into the emergency room and laid him on a table, where they began to cut off his clothing and insert needles into his arms.

Joe recalled that he became very bored by the process and felt as though he was becoming sleepy. He drifted up towards the ceiling and felt intense heat against the back of his neck, thinking this might be from the bright lights they install in the emergency rooms. He turned to see if that were true and suddenly found himself falling backward through a dark tunnel. Thus began a part of the experience that is fairly stereotypical of the Near Death Experiences (NDE) reported by so many over the last several decades. Said McMoneagle:

The tunnel was filled with the faces of people. Many of these faces were familiar to me. They were people I had known or met during my lifetime. Some were totally unfamiliar, people I didn't remember. Many reached out to me, grabbed at me. Some were crying, some were moaning, and some were smiling and laughing. It was sometimes terrifying and sometimes comforting, but it constantly changed. I closed my eyes and found that I was reviewing my whole life. It was passing before my eyes instantaneously, every action, every item, from birth to death. It wasn't judgmental however. It was more of an assessment, a review of "what if?" What if I had only been paying more attention here? What if I had only spent a bit more time on this? What if I had only given this person a little bit more respect? It had to do with being more aware of my actions and how they impacted others—how my actions impacted on myself.

I soon began to see light coming towards me from the end of the tunnel. I instantly recognized it as being identical to my old lucid dream, which up until that point had not happened. Faint at first, the light brought hope. It encouraged me. I moved faster toward it. Suddenly I popped out of the end of the tunnel into a very bright and warm light, which completely enveloped me. At that point, I felt complete. I felt whole. I knew all the answers to all the questions that I had ever carried within my mind. I was totally at peace with myself. I knew that I was at home. I wanted to be nowhere else and I needed nothing else to exist. I thought this must be what God means.

A voice in my head said; "You are too early. You must go back." And I said "No," which made no difference whatsoever. There was another pop, like someone snapping their fingers and I was suddenly conscious. I opened my eyes and sat bolt upright. I was

naked and lying under a sheet in a bed next to another patient. He
was startled by my sudden and unexpected movement.

Up until this point, McMoneagle says he wasn't really conscious
of all that happened. When he exited the restaurant on that fateful
evening, he made it to the front and collapsed through the door and
onto the sidewalk as he pushed on the glass panel. He went into
violent convulsions, which resulted in him swallowing his tongue
at some point before he got to the hospital. No one knew that he
had done that. When someone swallows their tongue, they can't
breathe. How soon this happened after he collapsed is unknown,
but it was likely it was closer to the time he was treated.

In 1970, the knowledge concerning Cardio Pulmonary
Resuscitation (CPR) was minimal compared to today. The natural
reaction was to just beat on someone's chest with a fist or the palm
of one's hand. That's what Joe's friend did, yelling at him to breathe.
But as Joe had swallowed his tongue, he couldn't really breathe. It
took Joe's wife and friend somewhere between 30 and 45 minutes to
drive the approximately 60 plus kilometers distance to the hospital
in Passau, Germany. As a result, Joe was delivered to the emergency
room Dead on Arrival (DOA). The German Doctor was extremely
skilled and was able to restart Joe's heart and breathing. After that,
he was in a coma for more than 24 hours, after which he finally
regained consciousness sometime in the early morning hours on
the beginning of the third day.

McMoneagle looked at the German patient lying in the bed
next to his and began telling him in a mix of broken German and
English, "I think I met God, and it's a white light. You can never die.
Your identity lives on, but you don't care. We needed to understand
that we were all part of one another, and what you actually did to
others you most assuredly were doing to yourself. "

And as he rambled on, the other patient quickly ran out of the
room and soon returned with the doctor and a nurse who injected
his IV-line with something that promptly made Joe "feel all warm
all over and put me back to sleep. I found out much later that when
the doctor came into the room, he said that my eyes were wide
open and had an almost blue aura in them. He said they had an
appearance as though they were glowing, almost radiating light."
Joe thought that was very strange since his eyes have always been

green. He probably did scare that poor German patient out of his mind, suddenly sitting bolt upright after lying there totally comatose for over twenty-four hours!

The next time McMoneagle regained consciousness, it was early morning and he was strapped tightly to a gurney. He had an oxygen mask strapped tightly to his face and the gurney was being loaded into the back end of a limousine. A First Lieutenant was walking beside Joe and whispering in his ear. "He said, 'We're taking you to Munich. You're being replaced as the Detachment Commander at the unit, and we're going to leave things as they are for the moment. People there will think that you are dead, at least until we can sort all this out. Just relax and enjoy the trip.'" Joe was given another shot in his IV-line and remembers nothing of the long drive to Munich in the back of the limousine—only that the windows were covered with tinfoil.

His next awakening was in "a small but comfortable bed, in a small and comfortable room of what felt like a very nice hospital." Joe was too weak to climb out of the bed, but he said he had a nice view of an interior garden the wing itself wrapped around. It was actually a room in the empty wing of a rest home on the outskirts of Munich. "My head was spinning and felt as though it had been exploded all over the place. My mind felt as though it was spread, like peanut butter or jam, all over the walls of the entire building. I could sense all the rooms and all the people in them and it felt like everyone was talking to me, all at the same time. My head was filled with voices and I couldn't shut any of them out. I knew I was probably going crazy."

In a small percentage of NDEs, on recovery the individual has reported an expanded feeling of consciousness or some other psychic perceptions, and even full blown psychic abilities. It seems McMoneagle was in that small group. His extended perceptions continued. "I envisioned a large man, wearing a US Army medical uniform walking into the room and asking me how I was doing. And I could hear myself telling him that I wasn't doing well because I had already told him twice that I wasn't doing well. I had a headache, I felt nausea, and needed sleep, but I couldn't turn the voices off. The vision then repeated itself a few more times until I dozed off."

He was awakened from his nap by a knock at the door. Standing in the doorway was a large man wearing a US Army medical uniform. This was the man who had been in Joe's vision. The man asked if he could come in, and how Joe was feeling. "I didn't answer as he went through the entire vision of pre-questions I had already rehearsed four or five times before I ever met him. My headache came back with a vengeance. I wished I could be somewhere else, anywhere but in the room, and suddenly I was."

McMoneagle found himself out of body again, in the garden outside the windows, peering inside and watching this man addressing someone who looked like himself sitting up in a bed wearing a white medical gown. He couldn't hear their voices through the glass. "I watched as he walked over to the 'me' sitting up in the bed, bent over, lifted 'my' left eyelid and pointed a small bright light into the eye. The sudden flash of light in 'my' left eye had me instantly back inside my body within the room."

"Ouch!" said Joe as he jerked his head away.

"I knew you were in there somewhere," the medical doctor responded. "You weren't responsive for some reason. What do you think is going on?"

Instinctively Joe knew that if he told this man exactly what was going on inside his mind at that point, he would think Joe was totally insane. He had to try and act normal. "The problem was I no longer knew what normal was," said Joe.

Over the course of the next few weeks, McMoneagle came to understand that their primary concerns centered on the fact that he had been delivered to the hospital in Passau DOA. They estimated from the circumstances that his brain had gone without oxygen for approximately 8-10 minutes (minimum), which meant that he must have suffered irreparable brain damage. Because of his security clearances and accesses, they were very concerned about what that meant. Exactly how much did he still know, how much did he remember about what he knew, and how much of a security risk was he after the experience? Could he be trusted once he walked out of the ward and their control?

They were also concerned about all the "crazy talk" he'd been doing. The statements about God, that you can't die, and that you can know things without knowing them—what was that all about?

None of it made any sense to them. They were absolutely sure that Joe had suffered severe brain damage and they were not going to let him go until they had determined exactly how much and how serious it might threaten the system within which he was assigned.

"My difficulty was that my mind was spread half way across Munich and then some. I couldn't remember what normal was like. I had trouble deciding what images were real and not real, what conversations I remembered that were things that I imagined and which were recall of actual events."

He would slip into daydreams and hear exchanges of discussions that wouldn't happen for two days. Then when they actually happened, he would know the answers before any questions were asked. To Joe, it was like being caught in the middle of a self-made nightmare. Slowly, over time, he began to heal. "The staff psychiatrist was actually very helpful. I think he believed many of the things I told him, since sometimes I observed that he didn't write anything down. He listened very intently and he asked serious questions about what I was telling him, and then he would close the notebook and discuss them with me. Instinctively, I grew to trust him. If it were not for him I'm not sure I would have been able to piece myself back together again."

Eventually, Joe started to feel somewhat normal. Many of the tests they did with scanning equipment and the EEG's came back as negative. There was absolutely no sign of serious damage or effects from the experience. They did find some scarring from his previous tour in Vietnam, but that was considered to be a normal effect from proximity to explosive detonations. After many weeks, they finally released him for duty, though a decision was made at the time of his release not to send him back to his original unit.

They still could not determine the unusual cause for his incident that resulted in his emergency hospitalization. This would always remain a mystery. Instead, he was moved to another installation where he assumed full responsibilities as an Operational Supervisor until his next assignment. Joe quickly gained attention as someone who no longer feared death and who had a somewhat humorous outlook on life—something common with people who have experienced an NDE. "Unfortunately, this was an outlook not shared by the majority who would now no longer work with me.

So I quickly became the man no one else would hang out with—the loner, who always seemed to get the job done. I was the guy who always got the stuff no one else wanted to touch. 'Give it to Joe. He'll do it. He'll do anything.'" That kept Joe McMoneagle overseas seven more years.

GRILL FLAME TO STAR GATE

As a Chief Warrant Officer Two in the United States Army McMoneagle was assigned to the Headquarters, Intelligence and Security Command (INSCOM) in Arlington, Virginia, after serving overseas for more than a decade. His various tours took him to Europe, the Far East, and a 27-month tour in Southeast Asia. A decision had been made by the Commanding General of INSCOM to bring him to the HQ where Joe was serving both as a technical consultant to his office as well as assuming responsibility for Joe's Military Occupational Specialty (MOS) worldwide. This included management of manned and unmanned intelligence collection sites within the Continental United States as well as overseas in Europe and the Far East.

In such a position, McMoneagle was responsible for all tactical and strategic equipment, including aircraft and vehicles, development of new and future technology as well as current technology, planning, support and maintenance, funding, training, and personnel. In addition, he was asked to perform responsibilities as a primary in international and intra-service negotiations and agreements in support of six national-level intelligence agencies, and act as a direct consult to the Army Chief of Staff for Intelligence at the Pentagon. It was an awesome responsibility and one that far exceeded his background experiences—or at least Joe thought so.

Before this assignment, he had been assistant to the Security Office for one of the largest overseas intelligence facilities in the world. He served in counter-terrorist and counter-intelligence operations at home and abroad. He was Detachment Commander at two remote intelligence collection sites, served in Air and Sea Rescue, in Long Range Reconnaissance, as a Quick Reaction Strike Force Team Leader, and as a Rifleman in a war zone. "But I didn't feel it was enough."

Then something different occurred.

It was the middle of the Cold War, and McMoneagle had just returned from an overseas inspection tour of a number of his collection sites. He was buried in work when he received a message asking him to report to a private office on the third floor of HQ. It came at a bad time, as he had a budget meeting scheduled four hours later and he wasn't completely prepared for it.

When he entered the room, he found two men waiting dressed in civilian clothes. They displayed Counter-Intelligence Credentials and asked Joe to take a seat. This usually means trouble, "So, I was instantly on my guard as I took a seat. They were friendly which increased my guard against any possible threat." They said they were taking a survey and interviewing selected people from the HQ. McMoneagle's name had been given to them by the Commanding General and his immediate superior as someone who was both open minded as well as someone who was not afraid to speak his mind. "I just nodded in the affirmative. I remember wondering if there might not be a tape machine hidden somewhere in the room.

"One of them asked me how I felt about a subject called 'the paranormal?' I remember at the time that I began to sweat. My mind began to flash back to many instances in my life when a number of events had occurred that I had hoped were long forgotten, especially by the military. No one had ever called them paranormal, but clearly, that's what they were. Was this what this interview was all about?"

Thinking back on his experiences growing up, he recalled that as a very young child, his grandmother told him it was called "bug sense. She would say, "That's how bugs find water and food. That's how bugs find you in the dark."

"My mother, on the other hand, would say, 'Don't listen to your Grandmother. That's silly talk. If people hear you talking about the voices in your head, they'll think you're crazy.' That's what was making me break out in a huge sweat now sitting in the room with the two men from the Counter-Intelligence Division of INSCOM."

Joe nodded his head in the affirmative when they asked if he knew what the word paranormal meant. This made one of them smile a little bit, and it made him even more nervous. He wondered just how much they knew about his background and history.

One of the men, Frederick Atwater (a First Lieutenant), opened his briefcase and turned it upside down, dumping a pile of material onto the table and pushing the material around in front of him. Some of it was classified, having originated from many of the satellite communist-bloc countries. Many of the materials were news clippings taken from magazines, newspapers, and machine copies of articles from books. This array of materials covered every conceivable topic of the paranormal from Big Foot reported in the American Northwest to telepathy.

The other man, who called himself Scotty Watt (a Major), acted outwardly derisive toward the subject and seemed openly hostile to McMoneagle. He snickered when he asked, "You can't possibly believe in this stuff, can you?" Joe gave him an honest response; that he didn't know because he didn't know that much about it. So, Watt suggested that Joe take a little bit of time to get to know some of it better while they went and got a cup of coffee.

Once they left the room he looked the material over carefully, noting it was very outdated. The first article he picked up was one on Karl Nikolayev, from an experiment that was run in Russia. The "sender" was located in Moscow when Nikolayev himself was the "receiver" located in Novosibirsk, almost three thousand kilometers away. This started a series of experiments that ranged in distances of a few kilometers up to thousands, and eventually it seems, perpetuated a huge leap in interest in parapsychology within the Soviet Union. Nikolayev claimed to get his powers from very strenuous training, and he was apparently good enough at his talent to receive very special privileges from the Communist Party—a private home, large salary, car, clothing, and other perks not available to the average citizen. Of course, because of that last bit, this document was classified.

He spent quite a bit of time reading many of the shorter articles and poked around at the larger documents. They returned after about 45-minutes, coffee in hand. "I noticed they were not carrying one for me. Atwater, if not directly supportive, at least was not outwardly hostile. He asked if I thought there might be some degree of threat contained within the materials lying on the table in front of me. This took me totally by surprise. I took it as a serious question, and therefore thought about it seriously and didn't answer right away. Watt pushed me for an answer." He was clearly hostile and not supportive to any of the ideas contained within the material. Apparently, it was nothing but a load of cow manure to him.

After considerable thought, McMoneagle said, "Yes. I do think there might be a threat there. I'm not sure what it is, or how severe it might be. But, I think someone should study it and try to understand at least the severity of the threat, and maybe how vulnerable we might be to it."

His sense at the time was that neither of them believed Joe. "My feeling was that they thought I was out of my mind or somewhat crazy. They thanked me for my time and nodded to the door, which was clearly giving me permission to leave." On the way to the door, Watt cleared his throat and reminded Joe that he had signed a non-disclosure agreement and was not to discuss the interview with anyone outside the room. "As he said it, he had the beginnings of one of those smiles of knowing on his face. Those kinds of smiles you see on someone's face when they are dealing with someone they believe might be putting them on, or joking with them." McMoneagle left as mystified as he was when he first entered the room.

Almost three weeks later, he received a call from Major Watt. "Looks like you said all the right words," said Watt. "You'll be receiving orders to come over for a second interview from the General. Don't discuss this with anyone." An hour later, McMoneagle's immediate superior informed him that his Commander, Brigadier General Rolya, requested he report to the 902nd Military Intelligence Group, Fort Meade, Maryland, the next day at 0900 hours.

The following morning as McMoneagle entered the small office at Ft. Meade, he was again met by Atwater and Watt, still in civilian clothes. This time they were very cordial and less formal. They smiled, shook his hand, offered him coffee and a comfortable seat. Joe was asked to sign a much more formal non-disclosure agreement regarding the material that he was to be shown. They told him that it was the belief of US Military Intelligence that there was a strong possibility that the Soviet Union and many of the Communist Bloc nations might be using psychics to spy on the United States and its allies. They asked Joe if he believed that was possible. Joe responded that he didn't know the answer to that question, but if it were at all possible, "We should know about it and counter it. In my own mind,

I think I knew that it was probably true, but I was afraid to simply state that. I thought that if I said it outright, no one would actually believe me." Watt and Atwater looked at each other, smiled, and agreed. They too viewed it as a threat—that's why they'd brought McMoneagle in.

Watt left the room and Joe spent about an hour talking with Atwater about the paranormal and his personal background and experiences. When Watt returned to the office, he was carrying McMoneagle's personnel file, which he handed to Atwater. As Atwater paged down through the thick folder, he came to a small brown envelope fastened to the inside edge of the folder. It was sealed with brown paper tape and had a diagonal red stripe across it and a warning that said, "To be opened only by the Commanding General INSCOM."

Joe found that his earlier nervousness had returned and "all my lightheartedness had drained from my body." Atwater fingered the brown envelope and then suddenly ripped it from the folder. "Please don't open that, I asked. Only the Commander is supposed to read the contents."

Atwater looked at Watt, who nodded, smiling, and he quickly ripped the end from the envelope. It was obvious that they wanted to know everything about Joe McMoneagle and were not going to let a warning note stop them. Inside were papers relating to the Near Death Experience that had happened to Joe many years ago that had almost ended his career when it occurred. For Joe, to suddenly revisit it again at that precise point in time was not something he looked forward to. "Now in retrospect, it sure seems to be key and synchronistic to all that eventually transpired, at least within my life and for all that followed," said Joe.

For his third interview, which also occurred at Ft. Meade, there were about thirty other men in the room with Joe. They had been sitting around a large room for nearly an hour. There were classified paranormal booklets from all over the world piled all over the table in the center of the room, and the men had been reading them while they waited. A few of the men had been joking about the contents of the booklets, which made some uncomfortable.

Someone once said history is always written by the winners, but this isn't always true when history is being written by a soldier.

Soldiers understand that within the nature of their business, it sometimes isn't about winning or losing, it's about doing what is necessary or what is the right thing to do within the circumstance. Soldiers sometimes make a decision, which at the time might not appear to be appropriate within the circumstance, but based on their experience and knowledge garnered from years of being at risk and taking risks, they know it to be the right thing to do. So they just do it. Joe McMoneagle was asked to make that kind of decision back in late 1977.

Watt finally came into the room and made a short speech. He said that in five minutes everyone would be leaving the room and moving to another room where they would be given a briefing on a project that they'd probably be asked to join. Once they got that briefing, they would not be allowed to back out. "So, if any of us were uncomfortable in the least bit with the material we had been reading, or with any of the subject material we had been handling over the past couple of months during our interviews, we should make it known now." There was silence in the room.

Watt went on by stating that once the men left the room and entered the other room, there would be a good chance—in fact a better than 50 to 50 chance—that they'd never see another promotion during their careers because of the top-secret nature of the work that lay ahead. But, it would be for a good cause—the defense of our nation.

Again, there was silence in the room.

Watt spoke again, saying that what he was exposing the men to would probably end marriages and some would probably stop going to their churches before they were finished with the project.

Again, silence, at which point Watt said to move to the other room.

"I was surprised when only about twelve people got up and actually moved to the other room," said Joe. "Stunned would be more the word I suppose. I don't know if it scared or frightened me as much as it bothered me that so many men wouldn't lay their life on the line for their nation."

"Initially, I was skeptical of the project but decided to take part it because it seemed 'the right thing to do' in the service of my country. In any event, I look back on my decision now and I guess I would still do it again, even if in retrospect I can see that everything he said was absolutely true; that it was going to cost marriages, health, cause death, and the loss of all one's friends both in and out of the military. Yes, I would still do it again. It was that important."

When they entered the other room, they signed more papers and received briefing certificates for Project Grill Flame (an earlier name for Project Star Gate). It was the beginning of McMoneagle's introduction to the US Army's psychic spy program. Physicists Hal Puthoff and Russell Targ gave a presentation on "something called 'remote viewing,'" which had been under a CIA sponsored study for about five years at Stanford Research Institute in Menlo Park, California. They showed a film of Ingo Swann who was able to describe with considerable accuracy a location to which Puthoff had gone without Ingo's knowledge. The location had been chosen randomly after Ingo had been locked up in a secluded location with Targ. Ingo had drawn the location on paper while being secured in a windowless room. After Puthoff returned to Ingo's location, another person was able to match Ingo's drawing immediately to the photograph of where Puthoff had been by choosing the photo from a group of five photos placed in front of him. "It was an impressive demonstration, but still I was skeptical. How many times had this been demonstrated?" McMoneagle wondered.

Following the film, the men were again interviewed, only this time in private by Puthoff and Targ. They were told that they were being interviewed for the selection of three of them for possible exposure to and training in Remote Viewing at SRI, for use within Project Grill Flame. Once trained, they would train the others back at Ft. Meade.

"Unknown to us at the time, there was a well-orchestrated plan, in which we would be spending at least a year to train as remote viewers, after which we would be running a counter-espionage effort against specially selected targets within the US Army." These targets were to be selected based on a broad spread of type, materials, and depth of security protection. Once the viewers had used their psychic abilities to acquire information on these targets for which they had access to all known information, the information they perceived would be turned over to an independent agency for analysis and evaluation to determine just how effective the collection effort had been. "In other words, we were going to mimic exactly what the Soviet Bloc operationally might be capable of. Only in the end, we'd be able to evaluate exactly how capable they just might be and the degree to which they might constitute a threat."

During McMoneagle's evaluation with Puthoff and Targ, Atwater discussed all of the previous items uncovered within Joe's previous interviews. Atwater talked about Joe's NDE in Austria, as well as the out-of-body experiences that Joe had as a result. This thoroughly interested both Puthoff and Targ during the interview and as a result, McMoneagle was placed high on their list of possible candidates.

The interviews took most of the day. While they went on, those not in the individual interview spent the afternoon reading the documents brought into the room for them. Eventually it was announced that a change had been made. The long, involved selection process had been so successful that they couldn't reduce the twelve participants to only three. They chose six, and Joe was to be the first to travel out to the west coast for remote viewing.

SRI, MENLO PARK, CALIFORNIA: FIRST REMOTE VIEWING

McMoneagle's trip to SRI was difficult. "Even though I was traveling on the orders of the Commander of INSCOM, the Brigadier General, my immediate superior was a Civilian-GS14 (roughly equivalent to half way between a Lieutenant Colonel and Colonel) and he wasn't very happy at all. He had no idea what I was doing, who I was working for, or why I wasn't in the office. My work was falling farther and farther behind, and most of what was getting done, he was doing. It was one of the first trips I had taken that I wasn't able to tell my wife anything about as well. Since I couldn't really explain what the purpose was for this trip, there was no one to talk to, and I was beginning to re-think my commitment. The only good thing about it had been civilian clothing and the extra money for my meal allotments."

McMoneagle went in expecting to immediately start an aggressive two weeks of training, but to his surprise, that isn't what happened. He was left to relax by the motel pool, and by the second day was already bored. Fortunately, they rescued him from that relaxation, brought him to the top floor of the laboratory, and walked him into a windowless room that looked more like a lounge with a large soft couch and a pleasant atmosphere.

McMoneagle and Russell Targ made themselves comfortable, sitting directly across from each other. Joe was given a small drawing pad along with some pens and pencils. Puthoff then explained that in one hour another researcher, Beverly Humphrey, would be arriving at a randomly chosen site somewhere in the San Francisco Bay area. It would be Joe's job to try to describe exactly where she was standing at that site. Humphrey would interact with the site location for exactly fifteen minutes and then return to the lab. She would pick up Russell and McMoneagle and they would all return to the actual site for feedback. Later there would be an independent judging of the results by someone who wasn't involved in the actual remote viewing problem. Puthoff asked if Joe had any questions.

"Exactly how do I do this kind of thing?"

Puthoff explained that there really was no basic way of "doing it." It was up to the viewer to just kind of empty his mind and then when he felt ready, open it to whatever information was there for him to "see." Joe was told not to worry, that there would be stuff there that was pertinent to the site location. The viewer had to trust in the system to work. Then Puthoff left.

Targ unhooked the phone and locked the doors so that they wouldn't be disturbed. He then suggested Joe might want to try to relax, since they had approximately forty-five minutes until Puthoff reached the random location. He explained that Humphrey would go down to another office and use a random number generator to produce a five-digit number, using the last three digits to select a file from the safe. Taking the file out to the car, she would drive away from the building. After she had been driving around for about ten or fifteen minutes, she would pull over and open the sealed envelope inside the file. Inside the envelope were directions and photos of a target location that she was supposed to drive to. As Puthoff and Targ had previously explained–and perhaps to further reinforce what was happening–Targ said that once the other researcher got to the target location, she would enter the site at precisely the correct target time and then interact with the target for fifteen minutes. During that period, Joe would have to try to draw where Humphrey was. At the completion of that time, Humphrey would drive back to the lab and get Targ and McMoneagle, then drive the three back to the actual location. "I was told this so when we got to the site, I would see if that was indeed what I was seeing earlier with my mind's eye." Such positive feedback would reinforce the viewer's ability, or so it was believed (and confirmed by research over the years after).

Perhaps Joe's greatest surprise was how fast forty-five minutes goes by when one is trying to relax and empty one's mind. He also realized how hard it was to consciously stop his mind from thinking. "As hard as I tried, my head filled with more junk mail than the average modern computer gets in a lifetime, not the least of which is all the possible places that Beverly Humphrey could have traveled to within a forty-five minute drive of the laboratory in Menlo Park. I felt this task was going to be impossible."

He was fighting all the "junk" in his mind when he was suddenly startled by Russell Targ's voice saying, "Okay, Joe. Tell me where you think Beverly might be standing at this moment in time" at which point McMoneagle's entire mind went totally blank.

"After wondering what I was supposed to do, I asked Targ if he could give me a hint, to which he responded 'no.'" How could he? Targ had no idea where Humphrey was! Joe asked him if he could provide an idea how to do it. "He suggested that I just try and relax and let the information just come to me. I tried, but there wasn't anything there. Every time I relaxed and searched my head for information, my mind just filled up with nonsense, junk, so much stuff that I couldn't pick one thing important from it."

Time was passing by and Joe's pad of paper was as clean as when he'd entered the room. Targ spoke up and said they had about ten minutes until Humphrey would be leaving the target area. Joe closed his eyes in frustration and shook his head. "I was going to fail."

Just then he caught what he thought might have been just a glimpse of something, a small flash. It was a very short and quick sighting or vision of something coming quickly that it seemed to flicker across the back of his eyelids. "Wait! There it was again.

It looked like shadows of something, like darkness or shadows behind large stanchions or poles, like support columns in Greek Temples." Joe quickly began to sketch. There were flashes of other things as well–a barbell kind of object, statues, bicycles, or at least a bicycle stand made of metal standing off to the side. "There to the front were two round planters with short trees planted inside them. Oh yes, and more…and I quickly began sketching stuff onto the pad."

By the time Targ called "time," Joe had filled the entire page with bits and pieces of items he felt were relevant to the target. As soon as Targ took the pad from Joe's hands, he felt as though a sudden break had been made. "I felt energy suddenly drain from my body. I was suddenly lost, momentarily adrift. I felt as though I had suddenly lost all contact with the target and had failed completely in the effort. I told him that I thought I probably screwed the whole thing up."

Targ looked at his drawings and smiled. Based on Joe's notes and drawings, Targ said he already knew where they were going. Half an hour later, Humphrey returned to the lab and the three piled into the car and drove to the target. On the way, McMoneagle saw a few things that seemed to resemble some of the items that he had drawn, but not many. They entered the Stanford University main drive and made a few turns. Joe had never been on the campus so he had no idea where we were going. "When Beverly made a sharp left turn, I immediately saw a building coming up on the right side of the car and knew it was my target building—the Stanford University Art Museum." Humphrey pulled up and stopped. The large columns in the front of the building were unmistakable, especially framed by the small trees in the circular pits to the front. There was even an iron bicycle stand exactly where Joe had seen it in his partial vision. "I turned around in the front seat of the car and looked at Russell Targ. He was grinning from ear to ear."

"Not bad for your first remote viewing, Joe," Targ said.

After several more such trials, McMoneagle received a first place match in the independent judging for his first remote viewing, and three of the remaining six. His fifth and sixth were a second place match. Hal Puthoff told Joe it was the best series they had ever demonstrated at SRI.

When McMoneagle returned to Ft. Meade and the 902nd MI Group with the final results, they were entered into a brand new file under the title REMOTE VIEWER #001. He was taken into the front office and asked to volunteer for the remote viewing program with the full understanding that he would be giving up his career, future promotions, and probably walking into nothing but ridicule for such an action. After what Joe had experienced at SRI, what he'd read in the documents over the past number of weeks, and what he perceived to be a new threat to the nation, he was left with very little choice.

"It was something that needed to be done, and I was the one to do it."

PROJECT GRILL FLAME AT FT. MEADE

Work on Project Grill Flame in Maryland was extremely difficult, not only from a very basic "how to," but also from a military and political viewpoint. Fundamentally, in the area of using remote viewing for military purposes, no one had ever attempted to do what they were trying to accomplish. The building that housed the psychic spying unit at Ft. Meade was both SECRET, unpretentious and inconspicuous.

The inflexible hierarchy typical of military systems accommodated the ESP program only with great difficulty. It suffered from automatic ridicule if it was even brought up as a subject and therefore had to be kept hidden even from those who were required to support it within the command. In effect, it was a "Black Project" being run within a Black Project. There were multiple levels of security, and only those with topmost security and the Commanding General's permission were allowed to know of the project's existence. Those who had to support McMoneagle and company directly were allowed to know the project existed but not know exactly what was being done. They thought all kinds of things (and were encouraged to think others), but never knew what exactly the folks in the project were up to. Only a handful of people were ever allowed actual entry into the building.

The Ft. Meade building that was home to the psychic spying unit

"Because of the natural animosity towards the subject by those with certain religious beliefs, we had to be exceptionally careful in how we vested those who we allowed into our network, including secretarial personnel and others who worked as trainers, analysts, and so on," said McMoneagle. Support personnel were kept to the absolute minimum. Since initially all of the remote viewing personnel were officers and ranking civilians, except for one man (a senior non-commissioned officer), this necessitated officers having to pull duty cleaning floors, washing windows, scraping walls, painting, procuring furniture (sometimes procuring meant "borrowing" in the looser sense of the word), and even cleaning out the toilets on occasion.

In the beginning, the viewers trained very hard. They started early in the morning at 7:30 AM doing practice remote viewings and switched up their roles of who would travel to the randomly chosen target locations and who would do the remote viewing. They excluded the judging procedures because they didn't require additional protocol, which was more designed for independent support of remote viewing. They only wanted to improve their capabilities. As the next five remote viewers visited and returned from SRI, the extent of their abilities improved. The original six viewers were eventually assigned full time to the project, and the other six volunteered to come in as viewers and train part-time in order to participate on a part-time basis.

The idea remained to see if psychic functioning was a threat by targeting US Army resources against known US Army targets; however, the project was never supposed to be a fully operational unit. The original function of the project was to ascertain what the Soviets knew about the US through ESP, and then determine the value of this information. The entire effort was never formally authorized, and therefore was being run on very little funds. About six months into the project, this was all to change.

JOE MCMONEAGLE'S FIRST US ARMY TARGET

Towards the end of 1978, McMoneagle reached a pivotal point in his practice training. Fred Atwater notified Joe that he would be attempting his first real target at 0900 hours the following morning. He arrived prepared for the challenge, with a good night's sleep and an attitude of anticipation. "I couldn't wait to see how well I could do against a real world target."

Once situated inside the room they had been using for practice remote viewings, Atwater pulled an envelope from his briefcase and extracted a photograph from it. Joe was surprised to see a picture of an aircraft hangar. The photo had been taken from the air at approximately three thousand feet. It was an oblique photograph from the front right side of the hangar and showed the hangar with its doors slid shut. There were a number of small aircraft parked all around the hangar. Most were single and twin engine aircraft, both civilian and military. None were jets. It was clearly a military airfield, however.

McMoneagle knew that this was not protocol. The act of showing a psychic images before the viewing is called "front loading" and often causes the subject to lose focus and lose useful information. It's difficult enough trying to open to what the target might be when you are totally blind and have no idea what the information might relate to, but now that Atwater had showed him a photograph of an aircraft hangar, his mind had filled with all the possibilities that this entailed. Joe became a bit angry and asked the other man what he was doing. Atwater said he was sorry, but those in charge had directed that it had to be this way. He was ordered to show Joe the photograph before the session, and to tell him that the target was located inside the aircraft hangar. He didn't know why he was supposed to do that, but those were his orders. He handed Joe the photograph and repeated his orders. All McMoneagle could do was go along with what he was told.

Joe looked at the photograph, but didn't study it. He felt the less he knew the better. He thanked Atwater and placed it on the small table between the two of them. He chose to lie back on the leather couch and close he eyes and try to forget that he had ever seen it. "I couldn't do it," said McMoneagle, "but, I tried. I kept telling myself they were only interested in the target inside the building, not the building, only what was inside, not the building. I kept repeating this over and over to myself."

Apparently, something did shift inside him, as his focus and mental imagery did indeed make a dramatic shift. Joe continued:

I soon felt as though I had drifted off momentarily into a fine mist or a partial day dream-like state, but then I suddenly felt like I was coming back into reality—remembering that I had a target to focus on. I instantly had a vision of a stovepipe, or a long periscope type of device of some kind that snapped suddenly into my vision. I held onto that view and fought to control it. The periscope slid down into some kind of an optical sighting device, with a soft rubber cup and eyepiece, supported directly over a console.

I opened my eyes, picked up paper and pencil, and began to rapidly sketch what I was fighting to hold onto with my mind's eye. These things faded quickly into what seemed like two layers of some kind of a vehicle. There was an upper layer and a lower, more forward layer. There were seats in both layers. The upper and lower layers had different functions and different layouts with different armoring and protection. I suddenly saw a very hardened military type computer, with a keyboard and sketched its layout. It was difficult, but I was able to sketch the layout of the keys and where the different pads were.

I began getting images of bullet points, which quickly turned into large gun shells and then rolled over onto their sides, falling into sliding trays that curved back into the rear of the vehicle. This curved area became an automated feed segment and armored holding feed area, with auto feed arrangement. Details really started flowing then as I sketched in the details between all these points and the interior of the vehicle began to fill out even more in a three dimension way. Eventually I ran out of material in my mind's eye and stopped drawing. I passed the drawings to Fred and told him that it was about all that I was going to be getting on the target inside the aircraft hangar.

Fred Atwater was pleased. The two discussed the target a little bit before they turned in the materials. He said he had no idea what the target was, since even the project manager at Grill Flame had no idea what the target was. It was a test of the entire project to see how they were doing. But he said that almost anyone would have drawn a plane given the front loading. Joe didn't, which apparently was good. He also didn't draw the inside of the building which meant that he probably had made actual contact with the target that was inside the building, and that was also good, Atwater said. Joe told Atwater that he knew he was in full contact with the target the entire time. "I knew it was good and I felt that it might not be the best that I could do, but I knew that I hadn't failed either."

It turned out they were both right. The target was the Abrams XM-1 Tank, one of the US Army's newest and still SECRET Tank prototypes, of which there were only three in existence at the time. They had deliberately parked one of them inside the aircraft hangar to test whether or not it could be described as a target. They thought that at best, a viewer would only be able to guess at the existence of an aircraft and totally miss the tank. "However, they were surprised that we not only identified the target as being a tank, but were able to draw the outside of the Abrams in profile and the inside, to include its automated loading system, its new optical targeting system, its computer system to include keyboard setup and pads, and the general layout of the interior." They were especially impressed that this was done double blind from a very long distance away, and after being front-loaded with false information. It was an impressive start to McMoneagle's remote viewing effort within Project Grill Flame.

At the same time his career was taking off as a psychic within the newly developing intelligence project at the 902nd MI Group, McMoneagle's superior at the HQ back in Arlington, Virginia, was pressing the administrators at Branch Division, Department of the Army, for a replacement to fill his position. The General had moved Joe from the very important position he had previously filled. This was a position that occupied an identified requirement and slot number at the Department of the Army in one of the twenty-nine very special Chief Warrant Officer Intelligence requirements in his field of expertise worldwide. Joe was moved to an "excess/non-required" slot on the 902nd MI Group books. This did not set well with Department of the Army, especially since they had only a 79% fill percentage (23 Chief Warrant Officers qualified to fill 29 requirements world-wide), and over half of those requirements were in either hazardous duty areas or hardship tour areas.

In actuality, the average time overseas for anyone of those Warrant Officers was approximately five years. Accumulated time overseas as both a Warrant Officer and Non-Commissioned Officer for any one of those Warrant Officers did not exceed eight years. McMoneagle had already served more than 12 years overseas and more than a year in the number one job for his MOS. He was due at least nine years of stateside tours before any one of them could rightfully complain. But two of those Warrant Officers complained to the Department of the Army about Joe's assignment to 902nd MI Group as Excess/No Requirement as soon as they received assignment orders for their first hardship tour overseas. "They identified me by name in their complaint, stating that I should fill the hardship tour since I was excess and they were not."

To understand how this affected him politically as a Warrant Officer, McMoneagle quotes his personnel representative at Department of the Army—the man who is directly responsible for looking out for Joe's promotions and protecting his interests in the Army: "If you persist in working outside your MOS (Military Occupational Specialty), I will no longer protect your interests. In fact, I will do what I can to remove you as a Chief Warrant Officer from the Roles of the Department of the Army."

Joe took this comment to his Commanding General. While he remained assigned in excess/no requirement, he never again saw a promotion board or other benefit, exactly as discussed with him during the beginnings of his involvement with the remote viewing project.

In addition, since it was a temporary project, they were not authorized for housing at Ft. Meade, Maryland. Therefore, Joe was required to drive from his quarters in Reston, Virginia, on the other side of the Beltway about as far from Ft. Meade, Maryland as one could get in terms of heavy Washington D.C. rush hour traffic. Since they started work at 7:30 AM, he was required to be on the road by 4:30 AM each morning in order to be at work by 7:30. Fighting almost three hours of murderous traffic was not very supportive to remote viewing, given the stress such a situation creates.

During the winter it was worse, especially if it snowed or the roads were glazed with ice. There were more than one or two nights that it took Joe eight to nine hours of bumper to bumper traffic only to return home, just in time to fall into bed, sleep four hours, rise, and then begin the whole routine again. There were times he missed five or six car pile-ups on the beltway only by the narrowest of circumstances. Only the very best of psychics could have survived the years of combat driving he was required to do! "In fact, I would suggest this as a perfect way to select future psychics for any such a project. Anyone who commutes more than fifty miles on the Washington D.C. Beltway for four years and turns in their lease vehicle without a ding is absolutely psychic!"

THE SWITCH TO OPERATIONS

With successes in the research phase, it was clear that the time had come for the remote viewing unit to start getting tasks that were of a more applicable to actual intelligence work. Project Grill Flame would take an operational hand with some difficult missions.

HOSTAGES IN IRAN

In 1979, the US had its first significant connection to terrorism with the Middle East with the hostage crisis, and Project Grill Flame and Joe McMoneagle were once again to see action.

In early November of that year, the American Embassy in Tehran, Iran was invaded by Iranian revolutionaries and hostages were taken. McMoneagle and the rest of the remote viewers were called from their beds in the very early hours of the morning and ordered to report to the Project office. They were asked not to listen to any radio broadcasts en route, or look at any television broadcasts prior to leaving their quarters. This requirement turned out not to be a problem, because no one in America knew of the takeover until much later that morning.

It was still dark when they arrived at the Project along with Fred

Atwater and Major Watt. "We were given a very strange request," said McMoneagle. "We were told that one of our embassies had been taken somewhere in the world and hostages had been taken."

Atwater then threw over a hundred photographs onto the conference table and asked the viewers to identify only those photographs that belonged to people who were positively hostages. Thus began a year-long problem involving hundreds of individual remote viewings that drove just about all of them as far as one can go as a remote viewer while remaining sane. "It is impossible to describe how difficult it is to target the same thing over and over again, day in and day out, for months on end, while dealing with the front loading problems in looking at the same people, buildings, rooms, areas, items, schedules, equipment, colors, attitudes, etc., with only the smallest of changes under the most stressful circumstances." For the viewers, the difference between reality and imagination quickly becomes blurred, time today, versus yesterday or tomorrow all runs together. "Who you're working for, whether it's the CIA, National Security Council (NSC), National Security Agency (NSA), or INSCOM, quickly seems to all run together. On top of which we also inadvertently made enemies."

Because the intelligence community wanted everything, that's what the group attempted to provide. "Every building, room, person, what everyone was doing, what they were wearing, carrying, eating, their health, what they carried, what the furniture looked like, what kind of paint or pictures were on the walls and rugs were on the floors. Even how long the grass had been growing between the quadrangles, and how many cars were parked, where they were parked, what kind they were, and whether they were parked nose in or out." As a result, they began to get information on hostages that weren't hostages, US Military exercises, and other things in and around downtown Tehran that appeared to be somewhat sensitive, mysterious, or out of place that involved people the viewers were sure were Americans, or at least people allied to the American cause.

At one point, they had inadvertently stumbled onto the very tightly controlled and secret operational plan for rescuing the hostages. "As a result there was a sudden and unexplained influx of Operational Security personnel that descended upon some of our people, snatching them up for interrogation, demanding to know who was leaking information to them regarding the Operation that was to take place at 'Desert One' and a number of other locations within the city." This resulted in considerable embarrassment to some of the tasking agencies, especially within Special Operations of the NSC.

SOVIET ELECTRONIC RECONNAISSANCE AIRCRAFT, AFRICAN CONGO, ZAIRE

A secret Soviet Electronic Reconnaissance Aircraft went down somewhere in Central Africa during the 1979 time frame and many people were looking for it for obvious reasons. Its intelligence value was inestimable. There was reason to believe that it had probably crashed somewhere over the Central Congo, in Zaire. Because of the vastness of the search area and the density of the terrain, even the use of overhead surveillance had provided no useful intelligence to find the wreckage or any evidence of its location. It was a perfect test for the now operational Grill Flame project. If no one else could find it, it would take some extraordinary means to locate and extract the nuggets of value from such a target.

McMoneagle and two other viewers worked on the problem within the Grill Flame project, as well as a number of people from SRI, and a viewer from another location within a study group associated with SRI. Their effort produced three independent locations within Zaire, all of which overlapped within a circle of approximately 13 kilometers. The locations produced by the viewers at SRI and the additional study group put the crash site within the 13-kilometer circle. Search teams were sent into the area and the plane was located within a kilometer of the location provided by the SRI remote viewer. All the locations that had been provided were within eight kilometers of the actual crash site. When the search teams first arrived on the ground, they said that as soon as they entered the circled area on the map, they began to encounter natives on the trails carrying pieces of the wreckage, which they were taking back to their villages to use to reinforce their village huts and buildings.

President Jimmy Carter formally briefed this incident to

newspaper and television reporters while discussing the incident with college students in 1979. He talked about the missing secret Soviet aircraft that was thought to have carried nuclear materials and other technology, which would prove beneficial to anyone who could locate it, not only the intelligence agencies of the US and other countries, but terrorist organizations as well. When asked how the US had been able to find it first, Carter said that it was located "using a female psychic."

Unfortunately, while he was making these comments, he was also holding a folder in his arms which had "Grill Flame" embossed on the edge. As a result of President Carter's comments on national television, the code name was quickly changed to Project Center Lane, and the Grill Flame title was retired.

TK208, TYPHOON CLASS SUBMARINE, SEVERODVINSK SHIPYARD, SOVIET UNION

[Authors' Note: Portions of transcripts of Joe McMoneagle's remote viewing sessions of this particular target are reprinted in this book's Appendix B.]

During the month of September of 1979, a Naval Officer working for the NSC brought one of the most important targets ever worked by the project to the office. It was one of the first operational intelligence targets McMoneagle worked on and certainly one of the most significant. But, in the beginning, no one had any idea as to the importance of the target or the impact it would have on the project either politically, or militarily.

The Soviet target in the black and white photograph was a very large industrial building sitting some distance from the water at the Severodvinsk Shipyard facility, on the White Sea, near the Arctic Circle. During the long winter it was a port totally frozen in with a thick and impenetrable sheet of ice. The exterior of the building had industrialized materials stacked beside it, and it also had railroad tracks running in one end and out the other. For many months materials had been delivered into the building, and the cars had been leaving empty from the other side, but nothing had come out. The materials were general in nature and gave no hint as to what they might be used for. The structure itself was huge. It was probably one of the largest, if not the largest building under a single roof in the world at that time. It was labeled 'Building Number 402' and otherwise had no other spectacular feature or significance about it. Numerous agencies had been tasked to determine what was going on inside this facility for many months, but up until the remote viewers had been tasked, no one had been able to determine anything specific in nature about the building or what might be happening inside. Joe drew the remote viewing mission to target the structure.

On his first remote viewing effort for this target, Joe was only given a set of geographic coordinates for the location of the facility, "which in my mind was somewhere obviously in the extreme north. I knew that it was at least as far north as Finland, and somewhere to the east. But, in my own mind as I focused on the target, all I could sense was a total wasteland of cold, ice and rock." Within that wasteland he reported seeing a very large industrial building of some sort, with large smokestacks, and somewhere in the distance a harbor or sea covered with ice caps.

Seeing that McMoneagle was clearly in the right place and on target, Fred Atwater opened the brown envelope and showed him the high altitude photograph of the building itself. It looked to me like a very large shed-like building of gigantic proportions, with an unremarkable and flat roof line. Atwater then asked Joe what he thought might be going on inside the building. According to McMoneagle:

Spending a considerable amount of time relaxing and trying to empty my mind, I imagined myself drifting down and slowly passing through the shed-like roof to the inside of the structure. What suddenly greeted my vision was completely mind blowing. I felt as though I was hovering inside a building that was the size of two and a half to three shopping centers, all under one roof. I had completely misconstrued the size of the building. It really was larger than I could imagine. I could just make out two internal walls that ran the length of the building end to end. They appeared to be structural support walls—primary to the support of the building and roof itself. These were open in segments along their length. I felt as though I was hovering and seeing with my own eyes inside the building. This rarely happens when remote viewing. My vision of the target was so precise that it almost seemed unreal.

In the giant bay areas between the walls there appeared to be what looked like large sections of cut away cigar shapes, or sections of cigar shapes that were being individually constructed. There were thick masses of scaffolding everywhere, all arranged around these shapes. Parts and sections of these shapes were being welded together side-to-side, as though two cigar shapes were being constructed together in a twin-pair. It looked like a colossal submarine of enormous proportions was being constructed unlike any I had ever seen before. It was actually two submarines being brought together side-by-side, and they were longer, higher, and larger than any I'd ever seen before. Together, they were at least the size of a WWII aircraft carrier.

The entire area was filled with nothing but the noise of construction—hammering, grinding, and the sounds of high energy electronics, generating powerful beams of light, welding half meter thick walls of steel. Thick blue and purple smoke filled the air from the bright arcs of light dancing off the beams of light striking the steel. Showers of hot metal were splashing in an arc across the concrete flooring. I was totally overwhelmed by the details. There was so much detail in fact, my brain shut down. I spent hours trying to draw all the detail I collected in the few minutes I spent inside Building 402.

They passed the results of the first remote viewing to the NSC. It created quite a bit of controversy. A number of the agencies had already become wedded to their own theories about what was going on inside Building 402. As a result, McMoneagle's remote viewing of the interior of the building drove them to defend their positions of belief, even though their analysis had been made on as much thin air as they believed Joe's was. The almost unanimous decision was the Soviets were building a brand-new type of assault ship—a troop carrier, possibly one with helicopter capability—but a submarine? That was completely out of the question.

"There were many other things I provided at the time, but since it is now nearly two decades after the event I can no longer recall much detail." What is important to note is that much of this material was validated in subsequent remote viewing by one of the other remote viewers, Hartleigh Trent. All of this material, typed transcripts and sketches, were forwarded to the NSC.

They were told sometime later that the material was summarily rejected out of hand by the others working at the NSC, one of whom was Robert Gates who would later become the Deputy Director of the CIA, and eventually the Secretary of Defense under Presidents Bush and Obama.

Upon hearing that the material was rejected, McMoneagle did another viewing and revisited the site a last time. Based on a personal estimate as to the speed of construction taking place and the differences in the condition of the submarine from one session date to the next, he estimated a probable launch date of four months later, which put the date of launch in the middle of September 1980.

Overhead satellite photographs taken of the facility on September 28, 1980, showed a new canal running alongside the building and out to the sea. Standing at dockside was a huge new submarine, the likes of which had never been seen before in the west. Tied up along beside it rested a somewhat dwarfed Oscar Class attack sub, which had been in for repairs. Very clearly seen in the photograph with their doors open for loading were twenty canted missile tubes. The completely new submarine was appropriately named Typhoon Class, a tribute to the mammoth amount of water it displaced within the harbor—water now exposed by two of the largest Soviet icebreakers in the fleet. A modern picture of the sub is shown above.

Typhoon Class submarine. Notice the people amid ship for scale.

It was due to McMoneagle's predictions that a US Naval Admiral who worked in the NSC—and who admired the Project's ability to produce such detailed and intriguing drawings—had the foresight to arrange for overhead surveillance of Severodvinsk Shipyard the week of the Typhoon launching. As a result, more intelligence was collected on the Typhoon Class Submarine than on any other submarine in history, at a time when the US otherwise might have not noticed its existence.

The preceding are just a few examples of the operational use of remote viewing for intelligence gathering that went on within the project that eventually became known as Star Gate. Joseph McMoneagle, Viewer #001, has written his own accounts of many other such missions, and covering all of his years as a remote viewer in his book, *The Stargate Chronicles: Memoirs of a Psychic Spy* (Hampton Roads, 2000).

The intent of this chapter was to give you some idea of the experience of one of the main viewers in the project, especially how an army officer was pulled in to work as a "psychic." It was also to illustrate how the American program worked, which you, our readers, will be able to compare against that of the Russians as you progress through this book. In our next chapter, we'll discuss the pros and cons, successes and failures, and an assessment of the project that was renamed Star Gate.

CHAPTER 6

THE AMERICAN MILITARY ESP PROGRAM: WHAT WORKED & WHAT DIDN'T

Any intelligence project such as Star Gate comes with pros and cons as far as running studies, applying science, assessing the validity and usefulness of the information, and deciding the overall efficacy of the project. There are bureaucratic and belief-centered issues that arise, especially with programs dealing with phenomena and processes that are themselves not understood, in this case the military and intelligence communities' in-house efforts to research ESP.

Some question whether an in-house—meaning inside the US Government—program was necessary or even appropriate. Many question whether it actually worked. This is an easy question to ask, but the answer is quite complex. "I suppose if I had to do it all over again and it was up to me, I would not have established such a unit," said Ed May. On the other hand, as we demonstrate in this chapter, there were some stunning successes, despite the crushing administrative, scientific, and personnel problems that emerged. Another indicator of its success in the broadest possible sense is that the in-house psychic spying unit lasted from 1978 until the whole program was closed down in 1995. It is all too easy to criticize the government and suggest that it lasted so long merely because of incompetence or because the project personnel had somehow pulled a con job on their superiors, but given the substantial number of powerful naysayers, its longevity can be considered quite a testimony to the unit's overall value.

As mentioned earlier, prior to 1978, SRI had total responsibility for the psychic spying program. In those early days, there was very little funding support for any kind of research, but it was accomplished to some extent under the general heading of foreign assessment. Here's an example.

Professor I. M. Kogan, a serious and accomplished information theorist in the Soviet Union, wrote an article entitled, "Is Telepathy Possible?" in 1971. The article was passed on to May and the project personnel by the Foreign Technology Division of the Wright-Patterson Air Force base in Ohio. In that paper, Kogan suggested that the way ESP works is similar to a radio transmitter/receiver pairing. According to his hypothesis, while the sender in a telepathy experiment is thinking about the target, his or her brain gives off radio waves that are received by the brain of the psychic telepathic receiver. As it happens, the concept that telepathy works similar to radio is an old one in the West, possibly because the early concepts of ESP in the 19th century evolved at the same time as other distance and invisible signal transmission—telegraphy and radio itself. Kogan's paper deeply looked at this concept.

To test Kogan's idea, the SRI folks piggybacked a then-classified extra task onto the Deep Quest project led by Stephan Schwartz of the Möbius Group in Los Angeles. Deep Quest was a psychic archeology project involving using remote viewing to find previously unknown sunken ships in the waters around Santa Catalina Island. Remote viewers Ingo Swann and Hella Hammid were part of the project. While Schwartz and his people were aware there was something additional going on, they were not privy to the actual study being done, though Swann and Hammid were. No mention of Ed May's presence is included in any of the write-ups or television coverage of Deep Quest, and May is nowhere to be seen in the footage though he was actually present.

The added study was to consider whether or not radio waves could account for the information gathered via ESP. Given the undersea exploration that was part of Deep Quest, they were able to surround a psychic with a thick slab of seawater as a shield against brain-generated radio waves. As it turned out, the remote viewing test under such conditions showed that Kogan's idea was not valid, due to the viewing being successful in spite of the shielding seawater.

As an aside, in 1992 Ed May had the honor of meeting Professor

Kogan in person and after pleasantries, told him that there was bad news about Kogan's seminal telepathy paper, that his radio theory of ESP was not correct. Kogan smiled and said he, too, had come to that same way of thinking and was glad to see the hypothesis had been properly tested. The photo below was taking in Moscow in 1996.

Even though the program at SRI was highly classified, word began to spread within the intelligence community that if they had an intractable problem that could not be solved using traditional methods of intelligence collection, they could, as an act of desperation, try those "far-out" psychics in California. Fortunately for the project and for the academic discipline of psychic research, the project's success rate, while not great, was good enough to help solve a handful of these seemingly intractable problems. Or, as one CIA agent remarked on ABC-TV's Nightline, these were three-martini moments!

L to R: I.M. Kogan, Edwin May, Joe McMoneagle

It became clear both to the project's sponsors and to the folks working at SRI, that that they were facing a long-term problem. They simply could not rely on a small handful of psychics to continue to conduct intelligence collection via psychic means. There was a fairly obvious two-part solution to this problem: find people with some ESP talent then guide them in the development of their innate expertise.

This happens every day in sports. A recruitment scout sees a young person who, for example, is terrific at playing golf. Then that young person goes to golf camp, and if improvement is seen, she or he may acquire a golf pro to train with individually. Eventually, you might end up with someone like Tiger Woods. Why not follow the same path with remote viewers?

However, the solution creates two questions: how does one find the people with an innate skill, and then how does one train them to improve their psychic ability? These two problems, probably more than anything else, plagued the research team throughout the entire history of the US Government's activity with ESP.

As described in Puthoff and Targ's Mind Reach, substantial resources were expended in the early days at SRI to examine a handful of individuals from every possible perspective, in order to determine what makes these people special. In fact, research in parapsychology has looked at the same question, considering whether there were all sorts of common traits for people who did better at psychic tasks. Research has looked at all sorts of individual characteristics, from personality variables to family history, from altered states to belief factors (belief in psi, religious and cultural beliefs), covering both the psychology and physiology of the subjects. Correlations to a variety of factors have been found in parapsychology, but these weren't necessarily important to remote viewing.

So what did Targ and Puthoff find in their own consideration of the question? The short answer is ... nothing! The ESP performers did have a tendency to possess IQs that were slightly higher than those of the population at large, but this was attributed to an artifact of the selection process, rather than something innate to ESP. During the entire 20-year program, this question was never answered effectively. The research reports, first at SRI and later at Science Applications International Corporation (SAIC), are full of attempts to isolate some external factor that might correlate with an individual's fundamental ESP skill. Over time, they did look at behavioral questions such as "does an individual physically do something different during a session when they are correct, compared to when they are not?" They also examined the viewers from neuropsychological and personality perspectives and even susceptibility to being hypnotized, but ultimately were unable to define a "psychic" type of individual.

Failing this, the best May and company could do was conclude that if you wanted to find psychics, you should ask large groups of people to try to function as psychics, and then select the ones that actually could.

At SRI, one of the formal government-directed tasks was to screen for psychic ability in a number of populations which included SRI employees across the Institute, a group from the United States Geological Survey, two different Stanford University alumni groups, and the San Francisco Bay Area MENSA society—an organization of individuals with exceptionally high IQs. Of approximately 600 people, only a small handful met a predefined criterion of being psychic according to strict laboratory conditions.

As to the other problem, bringing out the innate ESP that some people had, the Army wanted the project personnel to learn how to train the "average" soldier. During the early years at SRI, the project was funded by the CIA. After that, it was funded by the US Air Force, via the Foreign Technology Division of the Wright-Patterson Air Force base in Ohio. Two elements of the US Army became interested in the project a bit later. The first of these was the US Army Material Systems Analysis Activity, which was under the direction of John W. Kramar, attempted to establish a small remote viewing group at the Army's Edgewood Arsenal in Maryland. This group never became formally established, but they conducted some traditional remote viewing trials against locations within a few kilometers of the post. "Having acted as an analyst for some of those trials," said May, "I can attest that there was little evidence of psychic functioning."

In parallel with all this work, Ingo Swann, that highly accomplished artist from New York City with substantial psychic ability who had befriended Ed May, was attempting to design a training system for remote viewing. Ingo was not a scientist, but he had a brilliant mind, and May can only praise his efforts. He worked 12 to 14 hours each day for years, much of this time being spent in the libraries at Stanford University.

In the meantime, an Army group at the Intelligence and Security Command (INSCOM) became vitally interested in psychic research. Much of this story can be found in Joseph McMoneagle's book, The Stargate Chronicles: Memoirs of a Psychic Spy. But the bottom line is that approximately 3,000 intelligence personnel worldwide were screened with regard to their potential participation as putative psychics in the Grill Flame activity.[1] This screening involved their psychology, general interest in the topic, mental stability, and whether or not their records indicated a higher than normal success rate within their job categories. As described in the previous chapter, ultimately six individuals were selected to come to SRI for what was labeled "Technology Transfer." That is, it was agreed to conduct six remote viewing sessions with each of the six army individuals, one of them being Joe McMoneagle.

This new project was highly sensitive, but it seemed to the folks at SRI that the Army was overly paranoid. Each person arriving at SRI for the six remote viewing sessions were signed in at the control desk using the name of Scotty Watt, the recently assigned commander of the group. That became an SRI joke, especially when the one female remote viewer signed in under that same name! In fact, the SRI people all considered the military intelligence experts to be gross amateurs. "Joe McMoneagle told me that the intelligence professionals at the working level in the Unit had also seen this as amateurish pseudo-security," said May.

When the Army personnel flew out from the East to SRI for technology transfer, the original concern was that people on the West Coast might learn, and possibly leak, the names of those involved as psychics within the Ft. Meade unit. Most clandestine collection units go to extremes to protect the real names of those involved, especially in the collection—i.e., spying—side of a unit. Their military unit was supposed to be treated no differently. However, rather than regard these measures at all seriously, everyone treated them like a joke initially, because they involved "psychics" and not "real field agents." That's what was particularly annoying to the original six participants.

This group of six people proved to be quite psychic, under the strict laboratory conditions enforced at that time.

At about the same time, May landed a $495,000 contract with the US Army Missile Development Command located at the Redstone Army Arsenal in Huntsville, Alabama. They worked with Randi Clinton, a senior official there who, incidentally, occupied the former office of Dr. Werner von Braun, the brilliant ex-Nazi rocket scientist.

As May states, "My day-to-day contact there was with one of the most gifted scientists I had ever met in government service, Dr. Billy Jenkins. Our joint effort was to build from scratch a duplicate set of carefully designed hardware random number generators, similar to an electronic coin flipper, to see if previously published results could be replicated under exquisite engineering and laboratory controls." SRI did its part with a successful replication, but the Army group never built their system. As part of this work, Jenkins was asked to provide a briefing on the progress of the project as part of an overall assessment of the Grill Flame project.

The proposed, but never shown Grill Flame cover slide

Since this was in the days before personal computers, Jenkins went to his Army graphic arts department and told them he needed a cover slide for his upcoming presentation that involved Project Grill Flame. He explained to them that it involved remote viewing, and told them a little about what that was. "Fortunately for all concerned, Jenkins showed me the cover slide before he gave his presentation," said May, "so I was able to keep it from being shown!"

Does May think it was a good idea for the Army, or any other government organization for that matter, to set up their own operational unit to use psychics to collect intelligence information? "My answer would be 'no' if it were to be set up and run the way it previously had been done. Circumstances dictated what occurred back in 1978, but in retrospect, considering the requirements of science in concert with the performance of remote viewing, the seriousness with which it must be managed, and the structure within which it must operate—politically, socially, militarily, and otherwise—it was destined to turn out the way it did. That is, disastrously."

Before we can start a discussion about success or failure, one must consider the meaning of these concepts in an intelligence environment and in light of the application of ESP.

In a very real sense, the Grill Flame / Star Gate project personnel were developing a new tool for the intelligence community. However, unlike an academic test where the parameters and analyses are easily set in advance, the intelligence value of any data, regardless of its origin, is often problematic. In general, intelligence gathering suffers from a major problem—the quality of the data is often separated from its intelligence value.

Let us illustrate with a hypothetical situation: Suppose a spy satellite captures a high-resolution photograph of a new Soviet tank in production. Perhaps it is possible to learn many details about the tank from the photograph, and even count the rivets in the armor— high quality data, indeed. But, unknown to the satellite team, a US military special operations unit has actually stolen one of these tanks and is keeping it in a secure location. Thus, everything that can possibly be known about this tank is already known. So this very high-quality satellite photograph (the data) is worthless from an intelligence point of view.

The inverse might also be true. Suppose a high-resolution satellite photograph taken during a huge dust storm shows a very hazy outline that cannot be identified easily. Yet, an intelligence analyst who is working on a separate problem altogether sees the photograph and is inspired even by the low quality image to re-check some other data that ends up solving a long-standing intelligence problem. In this hypothetical example, low-quality data turns out to have extremely high intelligence value.

The separating of data quality from intelligence value is a general problem, which also applies to traditional human spies as well as to ESP sources of data. This is best illustrated by the CIA's own analysis of Star Gate.

In 1995, as part of an activity directed by Congress, the CIA was tasked to conduct a twenty-year retrospective review of the Star Gate program and report their findings back to Congress. In a release of many of the Star Gate documents in 2000, the CIA published a report entitled, "Summary Report: Star Gate Operational Tasking and Evaluation" in which they conducted a detailed analysis of forty ESP operations. Quoting from this report:

From 1986 to the first quarter of FY 1995, the DoD paranormal psychology program received more than 200 tasks from operational military organizations requesting to attain information unavailable from other sources. The operational tasking comprised "targets" identified with as little specificity as possible to avoid "telegraphing" the desired response.

In 1994, the DIA Star Gate program office created a methodology for obtaining numerical evaluations from the operational tasking organizations of the accuracy and value of the products provided by the Star Gate program. By May 1, 1995, the three remote viewers assigned to the program office had responded, i.e. provided RV product, to 40 tasks from five operational organizations. Normally, RV product was provided by at least two viewers for each task.

Data from these 40 operational tasks were evaluated by the tasking organization (not by the ESP team members) along two separate dimensions. About 70 percent of the 100 separate evaluations of these data were deemed to be possibly true or better. However, only 50 percent were deemed to be of some value, however minimal.

Before we jump to conclusions that the spying unit was worthless, there are a number of major problems not mentioned in this particular CIA report that we must consider. First, the evaluations shown above were all gathered "after the fact." That is, they were gathered when some form of "ground truth" was eventually determined. In all the years of research effort under the Star Gate program, they were never able to identify in advance a reliable indicator of the value of the data in a particular response, in total or in part. Thus, it would be considered a major risk to assign scarce resources to intelligence gathered by ESP without having confirmatory data from other independent sources and methods.

The conclusion was that ESP was not particularly useful, so the CIA eventually decided not to assume responsibility for the Star Gate program in 1995, although they did suggest that the academic community continue to look into ESP. Thus, the Government sponsorship of ESP activity came to a close. More on the closure, additional politics behind it, and the various reports analyzing/ evaluating the project will be discussed in Chapter 10.

It was clearly a mistake to curtail the operations, based on their analysis. By the CIA's own admission, they only evaluated forty sessions out of many hundreds, and only looked at data from 1994 onward. Even though they were requested to do so, they did not interview Joseph W. McMoneagle or any of the individuals who were responsible for McMoneagle receiving a Legion of Merit award—the highest honor for any intelligence officer—for his excellent contribution to intelligence collection.

This "inconvenient" citation was never considered in the CIA decision, nor was it part of the overall investigation ordered by the US Congress to evaluate a twenty-year-long program. So, the issue of whether the unit was pulling its own weight in the intelligence community remains murky.

According to McMoneagle's assessment, during his time at Ft. Meade from 1978 to when he retired from the Army in 1984, approximately 15-20 percent of the cases of psychic espionage were resolved successfully. This sounds terrible—but one must remember that the program, first at SRI and later at Ft. Meade always seemed to be a court of last resort. Only the "impossible" problems were tasked: those problems that did not yield to traditional methods of intelligence collection. From that perspective, a 15-20 percent success rate is as close as one could get to a miracle. Many of those successes remain classified, along with the few that had been gained since. McMoneagle did continue with his remote viewing and his participation in Star Gate, though after his retirement from the Army he did so by being hired back into the program as a civilian contractor, working with May and his group at SRI and SAIC.

With permission from DIA, Ed May was able to interview a retired employee by the name of Angela D. Ford, who was part of the Star Gate Unit at Ft. Meade after McMoneagle had retired. From the interview, and with additional information, we're able to describe one of her many intelligence collection successes that has also appeared on US television. One can pretty much say that with this book, as the spy novels are fond of saying, Angela has "come in from the cold."

During a portion of her thirty years of government service, Angela Ford served as a very successful psychic for DIA. She had been trained in two types of remote viewing, called coordinate and extended, and Ford's managers told her that she did wonderful work using both techniques. In a coordinate remote viewing session, the psychic is tasked only with locating the geographical coordinates of the intended site and uses a predefined and quite structured response method. In an extended viewing session, the psychic relaxes and free-associates, similar to the approach in the early days of SRI. In addition, we are also able to attribute to her psychic ability an amazing solution to a law enforcement case within the US Customs Department.

The case involved a Drug Enforcement Agency agent, Charles Jordan, who had turned criminal and was cooperating with drug smugglers. When the Customs agents moved in to make an arrest, he fled, which resulted in a nationwide manhunt that had failed to locate him. Most of the FBI and Customs agents involved in the manhunt assumed that Jordan would be near one of the coasts, because of his love of the sea. This turned out to be one of those examples of "when all else fails, ask a psychic."

In the following description, we include many details of this specific case to give a better idea how an operational remote viewing is conducted, used, and its political ramifications. The names of Ft. Meade personnel have been changed to protect their identities. Here's what Angela Ford revealed in her interview:

I didn't know what we were doing. David (the session monitor), Carolyn (a colleague), and I went over and we worked. I wasn't even sitting down when David said, 'where is Charles Jordan?' So I sat down for one second or anyway less than one minute, for sure. I looked at David and said, Lowell, Wyoming.

Okay, so David said he never heard of a Lowell, Wyoming but he had heard of Lowell, Massachusetts, because that is where he was born.

This is a good example of a violation of a well-known protocol—NEVER allow a session monitor put his or her impressions into the record. Ford continues:

I said NO, it's Wyoming. I just kept saying that over and over again. Carolyn started to jump up and down stamping on the floor, saying, 'She said Wyoming—she didn't say Massachusetts!' David grabbed an atlas and started looking at Wyoming. There is a Lovell there, and I said, close enough. Everyone thought I was crazy for saying such a thing. Even the people at the Customs Department assigned to this case thought that there was no way this could be correct.

Later, David pulled me back into the session, and I said something to the effect of 'I'm not sure, but you better act now because he is going to be moving,' and I described a tomb, an Indian burial ground ... go get him now ... I was describing the Indian burial ground; he was going to be moving; and you have to go get him now.

David kept telling DIA authorities 'you've got an isolated area up there, surely couldn't Customs or FBI agents just go up and act on it?' Well, they wouldn't. Years later I learned that apparently Charlie Jordan sent a picture of himself to his mother to let her know that he was doing well. When she received the picture, she must have called the Customs Department or FBI, but when they looked at the picture they saw a car with Wyoming license plates.

As it turned out, the DIA authorities were told that Charles Jordan was being apprehended 100 miles west of Lovell, Wyoming."

William Green, a Customs Department official, commented on Angela's data on television in 1995 as part of a lead-in for an ABC Nightline episode:

The collective wisdom at the time, including from everybody I talked to, was that he was probably in the Caribbean.

Jordan was finally caught in Wyoming near a National Park, near the Grand Tetons, near Yellowstone, next to an Indian reservation, next to an Indian grave site. It was almost ... I hate to use the word spooky, but here is the guy next to a famous grave site, next to a reservation. It couldn't be much more accurate than that.

Shortly after Jordan was apprehended, Mr. Green called Ed May at SAIC and told him about the case, and partly in jest asked for a job. He said that the work was most fascinating, indeed!

Even with successes like this one, the internal problems of inappropriate monitor comments in the session, the overall poor management of the Ft. Meade Unit and the lax and mostly inappropriate protocols, has led May to conclude that the US Government's and military's foray into the psychic business was a failure.

One problem was infrastructural. Being assigned as a commander for this special unit at Ft. Meade was a career-ender for many officers. An exception to this rule was Scotty Watt, who was the first to be assigned the role of commander because he had been passed over twice for promotion to Lieutenant Colonel. That would normally mean he was looking at retirement, because he would never reach that rank. But, as a result of his work with the original six viewers, he was promoted on his third try, which almost never happens. He made Lieutenant Colonel while assigned to the unit, the sole exception with regard to unit managers.

Assignment of uninterested or incompetent commanders of the Unit generally led to bad protocols. More importantly, this led to a downward spiral of Unit morale, which was so poor that every time May visited the Unit at Ft. Meade, military and civilian members would take him out to lunch to complain about their boss, begging him to intervene back at DIA headquarters. "I did just that," said May, "and while in the office of the DIA person responsible for the Ft. Meade Unit, I was offered deep appreciation for my inside information and a promise to fix things. However, no improvements were ever made. I can make an educated guess regarding why this might be the case. It has to do with how funding is handled."

During the transition time between the closing of the SRI project and the startup at SAIC, a strange thing happened. One way in which the US Government funds things is through what is called 'supplemental appropriations'. Normally government agencies are asked two years in advance to submit their budget request. Of course, responsible budgeting cannot do this perfectly, so the supplemental approach was designed to cover unforeseen requirements.

Government funding always runs through two or three steps. First, the funds must be authorized. Then they are appropriated, after which a joint conference between the House and Senate determines the final level of funding. Over the years, this was the way the remote viewing program was funded.

Once money is appropriated, it cannot be transferred to any entity other than some Government agency. That agency, in turn, may decide to contract the work to the private sector. Thus in 1990, a $2 million appropriation made it through Congress that was earmarked to support the Ft. Meade Unit conducting ESP research. There were two major problems. No agency had been defined to receive the funds, nor did any contractor exist. At the time, Ed May was between jobs at SRI and SAIC.

The obvious place for Congress to target that funding was the Defense Intelligence Agency, but its commander at the time, Lt. General Harry E. Soyster, refused to accept the money for a program he had no appreciation for in the first place. So here is the crux of the problem. As May remarks, "I saw a letter from the Senate Select Committee for Intelligence, the Congressional committee that put in an authorization request for the funding, giving General Soyster twenty-four hours to show why he was not in contempt of Congress for not accepting this $2 million appropriation."

This kind of macho 'I'm-bigger-than-you-are' approach may appeal to the fighter in us all, but it is a disaster as a management approach. It forced a controversial program down the throat of an uncooperative Defense Department agency. As you can imagine, this angered the military management at DIA. "So, yes, we got the funding, but at every turn DIA successfully created conditions that would make the Unit ineffective—for example, assigning generally incompetent dead-enders as Unit commanders. However, this is just my guess as regards one of our core problems."

There was also the notion that the problem lay with Ingo Swann's training idea (not with Ingo personally), and may be easier to defend. May blames the SRI project management team for not putting the required scientific discipline into operation, to determine the degree to which Ingo's idea was or was not sound. This had the effect of injecting two inappropriate attitudes into the Ft. Meade Unit, the negative results of which last through today. During this time, May was not part of the project management but a senior research physicist assigned to the project.

The concept behind Ingo's remote viewing training idea was based upon one very sound scientific principle and, in addition, an often-heard anecdotal concept. Many people are aware of B. F. Skinner and his behavioral ideas in psychology. As an example, a pigeon can be trained to press a lever to get food by rewarding it with food pellets every time it may have randomly bumped into the lever. Over time, the bird recognizes what is necessary to do to get the food. An extension to this basic idea is called operant conditioning, which Wikipedia (admittedly not the best source) defines as follows:

Operant conditioning is the use of consequences to modify the occurrence and form of behavior. Operant conditioning is distinguished from classical conditioning (also called respondent conditioning, or Pavlovian conditioning) in that operant conditioning deals with the modification of 'voluntary behavior' or operant behavior....

One necessary aspect of operant conditioning in biofeedback is that the reward follows rapidly after the desired behavior. Ingo latched on to this idea first by breaking the well-known and sacrosanct requirement when doing experiments that they must be conducted under double-blind conditions. In the context of an ESP trial, no one who knows anything about the ESP target may have any interaction whatsoever with the psychic. This idea is true for all laboratory studies and for the beginning of all operational uses of ESP—though depending upon the circumstances, it may be useful to begin to break this rule in operations, but for very proscribed reasons. Ingo, of course, knew this as well as did the SRI project management.

However, they made the decision to violate the double-blind requirement with a variation of the tired and false argument that "the end justifies the means." So, in the vast majority of training sessions where Ingo took on the role of trainer, he was looking at the target photograph and the trainee was sitting across a table from him. Professor (Emeritus) Robert Rosenthal, the renowned psychologist from Harvard University, and others have amply demonstrated the power of nonverbal communication. In fact, if someone who effectively expresses ideas nonverbally is paired with someone who is equally good at understanding others who communicate that way, then that form of communication may surpass normal verbal communications. It can certainly seem psychic.

To illustrate how this might work in an actual ESP training session, imagine you are the trainee. The trainer is sitting opposite you, and is looking at a picture of a waterfall. Let's further assume that you possess absolutely no psychic ability at all, so you just report out loud whatever random impressions come to your mind. The trainer properly remains silent through your two-minute discourse on your guess about the target photograph. However, unconsciously, the trainer leans slightly forward when you mention water and slightly backward when you mention desert, while cliffs and trees in your discourse result in other forms of unconscious behavioral feedback. As Rosenthal's research clearly demonstrates, you will begin to talk more about a cliff, trees, and water, and arrive quickly at the idea of a waterfall. This would appear as if you were doing remote viewing, when you actually had no such ability.

Although May emphatically pointed out the influence of unconscious nonverbal behavior in this training format, his strong objections went unheeded. As bad as breaking the double-blind rule was, "It was only the first of two fatal mistakes Ingo was allowed to commit," said May. Misunderstanding the rules of operant conditioning, Ingo thought that he could reinforce good remote viewing by giving quick and immediate feedback, in session, when a trainee mentioned something. At first glance, this sounds perfectly reasonable—in proper training sessions, the trainer rewards real trainees as having done excellently in psychically accessing the target. But it's the timing of the feedback that's important.

Going the way Ingo proceeded makes it a major disaster. When Ingo gave the feedback, the trainee marked the appropriate element with a feedback symbol. To be precise, we quote from a formerly secret memorandum from an official of the special access ESP spying program[2] called SUN STREAK to the then Deputy Director for Science and Technical Intelligence at the DIA. The description in the memorandum that follows is quoted verbatim from the appropriate SRI report.

(S/SK/WNINTEL)[3] CLASS C: The majority of the training sessions for novice trainees are Class C. During this phase, the source trainee must learn to differentiate between emerging target-relevant perceptions and imaginative overlay. To assist the trainee in this learning, immediate feedback is provided during the session. The interviewer is provided with a feedback package which may contain a map, photographs, and/or a narrative description of the target. During Class C sessions, the interviewer provides the trainee with immediate feedback for each element of data he provides. No negative feedback is given. Should the trainee state an element of information that appears incorrect, the interviewer remains silent. Feedback, in order to prevent inadvertent cuing (interviewer overlay), is in the form of very specific statements made by the interviewer. These statements and their definitions are as follows:

Correct (C)—The information is Correct in context with the site location, but is not sufficient to end the session.

Probably Correct (PC)—The interviewer, having limited information about the target, although he cannot be absolutely sure, believes that the information provided is correct.

Near (N)—The information provided is not an element of the specific site, but is correct for the immediately surrounding area.

Can't Feedback (CFB)—Due to limited information about the target, the interviewer cannot make a judgment as to the correctness of the data. It means neither correct nor incorrect.

Site (S)—The site has been correctly named for the specific stage being trained (man-made structure for Stage I, bridge for Stage III, etc.). "Site" indicates that the session is complete."

At first glance, all this seems entirely reasonable. Then as now, it seemed reasonable to Ingo as well as to a plethora of would-be remote viewing trainers on the Internet, who since have naively adopted Ingo's methods. However, this putative training approach is utterly incorrect. Leaving aside the problems of inadvertent cuing by nonverbal communication, which is certainly bad enough, a host of fatal flaws can be found in this approach.

First, a trivial example: Ingo never wanted to provide negative feedback like "you missed," "you're wrong," or "incorrect." So as the quote above clearly states, if the trainee hears no feedback after he or she has given an element in the psychic impression, it is, by definition, wrong, and she or he clearly has received a form of negative feedback—which violated Ingo's idea of no negative feedback in the first place.

The major flaw is likened to a popular game that was also a radio quiz show in the US in the 1940s and 1950s, Twenty Questions. In that show, a contestant was told that the hidden topic was "animal, vegetable, or mineral." The contestant then asked up to twenty questions that could only be answered by "yes" or "no." The challenge lay in whether or not, within those twenty questions, the contestant could find the right answer, in which case he or she was rewarded with a prize. Of course, many contestants were successful, which added to the show's popularity, and we're sure our readers have likely played a version of that. In fact, there is an electronic toy called 20Q and associated website (20Q.com) where you can think of something, someone, or someplace and have the device/program ask you questions. It's an uncanny thing.

Ingo's training feedback approach was and is a variant of the Twenty Questions game. Assuming no psychic ability whatsoever, a person could arrive at the correct site via clever responses, conscious or unconscious. This problem was immediately clear to those who were on the SRI team, and to Dale Graff, a civilian working at DIA. Yet, it was allowed to stand.

What is so terribly wrong with this approach?

Answer: you have no idea whether or not you are training remote viewing, training sensitivity to nonverbal communication, simply playing the game of Twenty Questions, or perhaps a combination of the above. And yet the intelligence community might waste resources or even lives by acting on such ambiguous information from individuals "trained" by this flawed technique. And if the US Government was giving SRI many hundreds of thousands of dollars to develop a training methodology for the Army, one can say this borders upon noncompliance of contract at best and outright fraud at worst.

As a scientist, Ed May voiced strenuous objection to this approach—not only to the project management at the time but also to an on-site DIA representative, Jim Salyer, as well as to Ingo himself. "I was frustrated, because I thought the basics of Ingo's idea deserved much better treatment than it was being given. Ingo was not a scientist, and because of this, the responsibility of determining the validity of his creative ideals was our responsibility and not his."

Another area where May thinks a mistake was made with Ingo's training idea is a sort of a one-size-fits-all mentality. "While I did not know it at the time, I have since learned from very high-ranking Army officers that part of the psychology of Army culture is this mentality of not recognizing individual differences, something well-understood in the field of psychology. The Army appears to think that any well-trained soldier who is given a stimulus will respond exactly the same way every time, and every soldier will also respond exactly the same. Of course, this is not even close to being true."

When Ingo was developing his training method at SRI and trying it out on local people with natural psychic abilities, "we nearly had riots on our hands!" said May. "Ingo set the rules, and they applied to everyone. In fact, one such rule was 'Content be Damned—Structure is All that Matters!' This related to Ingo's training procedure and the actual structure of what to do with the perceptions as they came to the viewers, such as how the folks needed to put their data down on paper (even where on the paper to put the perceptions as they happened). The rule meant that it didn't matter as much what the viewers perceived (content) as how they recorded it (structure), which seems somewhat counter-intuitive. Ingo enforced this rule with an iron fist, and made people contribute money to a kitty each time it was violated. Some of these talented 'guinea pigs' quit the training in fear it would harm their natural ability."

Although Ingo and May were good friends, somehow his criticism disturbed Ingo deeply. He was further upset as May voiced a strong opinion that, while recognizing that training Army personnel in New York City would be very convenient for Ingo since he lived there, May felt it was terribly inappropriate for him to do so unsupervised. "In addition, I had explained to him that the training methodology was fatally flawed," which certainly couldn't have made the psychic happy.

Once again, May's concerns were ignored. Ingo worked, unsupervised, in SRI's New York office with a number of personnel from the newly established Unit at Ft. Meade. Because he was angry at egghead scientists in general and Ed May in particular, he instilled bogus thinking in his trainees which has endured to this day. This "poisoning of the well" took the form that protocols and science are perhaps good for the laboratory, but the "real-world people" who were saving the world against communism did not need to pay any attention at all to the scientists. When May became the project director in the fall of 1985, this negative attitude was palpable during his many visits to Ft. Meade.

But the proof was in the pudding. Regardless of the obvious flaws, if individuals who were trained by this method could produce actionable intelligence, then one can say May's supposition is wrong.

Until Joe McMoneagle retired in 1984, all the intelligence success came from him or one of the other original six remote viewers. Very few, if any, of the successes came from Ingo-trained people. Since McMoneagle was the last of the original six psychics who left the Unit, the success rate plummeted and the successes were highly concentrated with people such as Angela Ford, who were never trained by Ingo. McMoneagle's decision to retire from the Army and leave the Unit was totally predicated on the erroneous and bogus training method pushed by Ingo and his trainees. The fact was that the methodology wasn't working in early testing within the Unit. There was the further obvious problem that there were going to be no other attempts to recruit people with natural psychic ability. This could only result in eventual failure with the Unit and Joe's burning out completely as the only remote viewer.

There were a number of consequences that resulted from the anti-science attitude in the Ft. Meade Unit. After the Unit was established, the Army, and later the DIA, paid the personnel at SRI and later at SAIC millions of dollars to conduct research with the primary goal of improving the quality of the psychic output at Ft. Meade. The civilian project personnel did just that and, from an academic perspective, gained significant progress towards the understanding of ESP. But, there was an uneasy relationship between Ft. Meade and SRI/SAIC, As a result of the anti-science bias, the DIA eschewed much of the data from SRI/SAIC, which helped lead to the eventual closure of the program.

Beginning in 1986, the Air Force was exceptionally interested in learning the degree to which remote viewing could provide useful information on directed-energy weapon systems. To test this idea, they awarded May and company a contract to examine this question in three trials—one per year, for three years.

As always, they used a double-blind protocol, meaning that no one who interacted with the psychics knew anything about the potential target, or even in this case, the identity of the client.

As discussed in Chapter 3, a session would involve the Social Security number of an individual none of them had met, that on a specific date this person would be somewhere in the continental United States, and May having knowledge that the targets would be directed-energy systems of some kind, but no specifics beyond that. The analysis of the result was a breakthrough, with implications beyond laboratory studies.

For the results and the analysis, the way to obtain a high figure of merit—again, the product of accuracy and reliability of the information—was for the psychic to describe as much of the intended target as possible, but in as simple and minimal a way as possible and not to include many incorrect aspects. To get a hint of what a random response could be like in the absence of any psychic ability, they had determined in the laboratory that using a rough rule of thumb, about a third of any site can be described by about a third of any response—sort of like the 100th monkey on a typewriter analogy.

One of the best examples was discussed in Chapter 3, the target being Project Rose, a high-frequency, high-power microwave device in the New Mexico desert at Sandia National Laboratory.

The point in all this detail bears repeating: their system of analysis had the potential to allow an operations analyst looking at real psychic spying data to evaluate the results quantitatively. Combining that analysis with more traditional methods of intelligence collection, the military could more accurately assess whether or not it made sense to invest further resources.

Another excellent example involved three targets at or around Lawrence Livermore Laboratory (now Lawrence Livermore National Laboratory—LLNL) in Livermore, CA, about 50 miles east of San Francisco. The primary target system was the Advanced Technology Accelerator located approximately 10 miles from the lab. A secondary target was the windmill farm at the Altamont pass through the hills east of Livermore, and a tertiary target was the West gate of LLNL.

The following are examples of visual correspondences in the remote viewing. The accelerator response is shown as a partial drawing, but the remaining responses are the complete drawings for the targets.

The partial response to the electron accelerator shown below describes a beam being labeled as three feet in diameter whereas the actual electron beam is about 0.3 mm. But for McMoneagle to even recognize there is a beam involved is not only a testimony for his skill but for ESP in general. The other targets are near-perfect in depiction by what was drawn in the remote viewing.

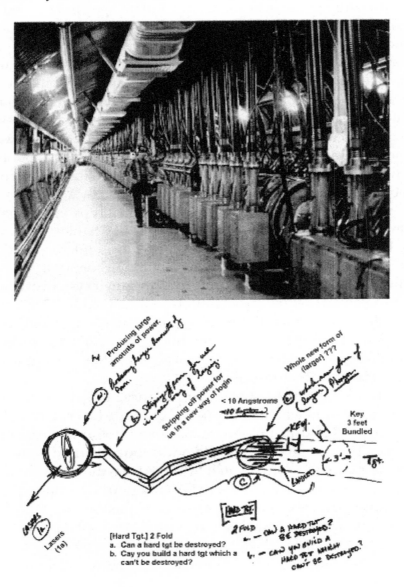

The electron accelerator and a partial response (annotated for clarity)

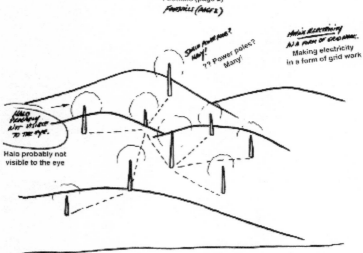

Foothills (page 2)

The secondary target windmill farm and the complete RV response

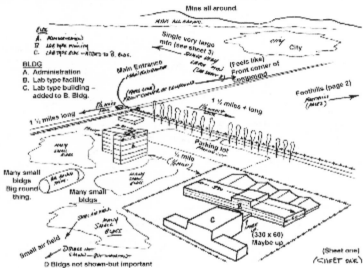

*The tertiary target of the West Gate of Lawrence Livermore Laboratory
and the complete RV response*

As mentioned previously, the experimental team had no information as to what the specific target or its location might be. As can be plainly seen by the above images, the visual correspondences were stunning.

May's group had numerous examples of laboratory-verified

studies that, if used, would have increased the effectiveness of the Ft. Meade psychic spying unit. But sadly, the group was considered to be composed of "just those scientific eggheads in California," said May. "What did we know about the real world of intelligence collection? It seems an abhorrence of science, and the unscientific attitude won out."

Shortly after the government closed the Ft. Meade Unit, Congress required them to send all their records to the CIA. They sent approximately thirty-five sealed boxes so that the Agency could conduct their Congressionally directed evaluation of the Star Gate program. In both the classified and unclassified versions of their report to Congress, they implied that the result of their careful examination of the record showed that further military or intelligence community support was not warranted.

Two years later, after the CIA program evaluation reports had been published, two colleagues, one from DIA and one from the Pentagon, officially had access to the room at the CIA in which all the boxes were stored. What they found was a bit disturbing: Not a single one of the boxes had ever been opened! So much for a careful and in-depth review of the material as required by the US Congress. This is one terrible consequence of self-defeatism and of a well that was poisoned against scientific inquiry.

Since the DIA person had helped pack the boxes, and could identify which ones to open, in a matter of minutes they were able to find incontrovertible proof of intelligence collection examples that were not only successful, but constituted a valuable contribution to solving the problem at hand. Thus, one must question the veracity— or ignorance—of former CIA Director Robert Gates when, on the news television program Nightline in 1995, he said:

Well, I can say is that in the 20 years or 25 years where I was in a position perhaps to be aware, I don't know of a single instance where it is documented where this kind of activity contributed in any significant way to a policy decision or even informing policymakers about important information.

This statement is either blatantly false, or a result of ignorance or a conveniently faulty memory not worthy of a former Director of the CIA. "Director Gates knew that I knew he had been briefed on specific examples to the contrary," said May. "In fact, my role on this episode of Nightline was simply to act as a foil to Director Gates. Many of my comments contradicting him were edited out in the final aired version. I chose to go on this program, even though my managers at SAIC ordered me not to, and I was threatened, by implication, that both CIA and SAIC lawyers were going to watch the show for any transgressions I might commit. My only alternative was to resign my post at SAIC effective immediately." The full story of this and more on the Nightline appearance and its fallout is discussed in Chapter 10.

May went on to say, "I am saddened that the picture I have painted had to reveal such bias, ignorance, and mismanagement of what could have been a valuable asset in the arsenal of intelligence collection tools. I suppose my main disappointment, however, lies in the consequences that continue today."

One relatively small consequence is the explosion of ethically challenged remote viewing courses being hawked on the internet by former low-level, scientifically untrained military and civilian personnel from the Ft. Meade Unit, which cost unsuspecting clients substantial amounts of money. These courses promise that their operant conditioning-derived training methods will turn their customers into expert remote viewers. But their training suffers from the "fatal flaws" we described above. In addition, said May, "Joe McMoneagle, and to a lesser extent I myself, have received painful phone calls from former customers of these near-fraudulent training courses complaining that they could not perform remote viewing at all when they tried to conduct sessions on their own at home in front of their families and friends."

A much more important consequence, however, is the fact that the US Government is apparently not using psychic intelligence as an additional aid in the required intelligence collection in our time of terrorism. Three reasons come to mind regarding why this is the case.

The first and probably the most important one is that the diehard "believers" in the Ft. Meade Unit set up expectations for the veracity of psychic-derived intelligence that not only weren't credible but, in fact, could never be met. This attitude can be traced directly back to Swann and his unsupervised indoctrination of Army and DIA personnel. The fault for this lies directly with the SRI management of the program. Failed expectations based on irrationally high expectations and unattainable results are a sure way of killing any project. Unfortunately, they killed this one.

Another contributor to the lack of use of psychics today is the fact that from 1972 to 1995, we had benefited from a limited number of very brave and dedicated US Government officials, including Senators, Congresspersons, Congressional staffers, and agency directors and deputy directors. These persons, in many cases, put their jobs and reputations on the line to protect the project's very fragile activity. Now, many of them have retired.

Finally, counterterrorism is both a tactical as well as a strategic problem. Although psi is significantly better when applied to strategic problems, nonetheless the proper use of psi can assist in planning for military operations in the future. The shift of terrorism to unconventional and transcendent warfare opens the door to psychic collection methodologies being used even more effectively.

Joe McMoneagle and Ed May, even with total cooperation by the top management as well as that of General Alexei Savin of the on-going Russian remote viewing program, were unable to convince a number of elements within our intelligence community of the worthiness of even a baby step in this direction. With Savin's blessing, May created a detailed intelligence contact report after a visit to Russia in 2000. Later he was able to hand this stunning report to the DIA director, Admiral Thomas R. Wilson. It described in detail the major management players of the Russian psychic program by name and by their positions in the reporting chain within the Russian military, and it included information about some of the psychics and their abilities and achievements. Lastly, May was able to emphasize to Admiral Wilson that General Savin wanted to create a joint American/Russian program to use psychics to deal with the common challenge of counterterrorism.

Nothing ever came of it. How tragic.

There's more to this part of the story, of the final days of Star Gate, why it was not picked up by another agency, and how the results were buried amidst incorrect assessments of the project's results. We'll get to all of that after we take a slight detour in space and time to consider what our Soviet/Russian counterparts were doing all this time.

NOTES:

1) Grill Flame was the second cover name for the group at Meade. The first one was Gondola Wish. These cover names were especially handy in that they could be used in an unclassified environment, like the telephone without the worry of compromising the secret nature of the work.

2) A special access program, or SAP for short, is a highly classified project that only specified individuals who had been read-on and signed legal documents could have access to the material regardless of the clearance level they may have possessed.

3) This is called portion marking wherein each paragraph in a classified document must indicate the level of classification for that paragraph. Here, the S means secret; the SK means SUN STREAK, and the WNINTEL means Warning Notice—Intelligence Sources & Methods Involved.

ESP IN THE MILITARY

THE EAST

AN INTRODUCTORY NOTE
FROM THE AUTHORS

The material in this section came about through interviews with the individuals who are the subjects of these chapters. The narrative and commentary are from the authors, based on what came directly from the subjects either in interview or direct contribution (or both). In our narrative, we've tried to tell the story as much from the Russian perspective as possible and we've quoted our sources where most appropriate, and where their words best relate their perspective on and memories of the events, experiences and other individuals taking part.

It's important to point out that the Russian cultural beliefs and the language itself (as translated into English) provide filters and biases that leave us with a story that may not be what westerners have come to expect of the Russians where psychic spying (and possible psychotronic "weaponry") is concerned. Additionally, some of the personal comments and stories may leave our western readers with strained credulity, given decades of the US government, politicians, media and others giving us a perspective of the Russians during the Cold War (when they were Soviets) as the "godless Communists" we were so concerned with, starting not long after the end of World War II.

A good portion of how Americans viewed the Soviets came from the fiction that erupted out of the 50s. Over the years, many authors such as Ian Fleming and Robert Ludlum provided us with enemy agents, sometimes thinly disguised Soviets, sometimes KGB agents. In other words, spy novels gave us the "us vs. them" mentality. Other broadcast mediums, including radio dramas ("I Was a Communist for the FBI") and certainly television, coupled with motion pictures, truly cemented the image of the trench coat-wearing Russian spy in American minds.

Would it surprise you to learn that the "godless" label was quite far from the actual truth? That it was likely simply a way for the US government to further distance Americans from Soviets? In other words, it was a bit of propaganda though this is not to say they were not "enemies" per se.

While the Communist State may have had more of a very clear separation of Church and State in the USSR, the peoples of the many countries making up the Union of Soviet Socialist Republics did not suddenly give up their religious beliefs—or even practices—because their country suddenly went Communist. Even in Moscow, a short way from Red Square and the Kremlin, there are many old churches that continued with worship through the existence of the Soviet Union, with even high party members attending on a regular basis. Yes, there were persecution and killings of members of certain religious groups during the Stalinist era, especially the Jews, but the Russian forms of Christianity continued with only minor non-State-related disruption.

As a reminder of some of the material in our first chapter, the religious and mystical beliefs of the Russian people have strong roots in shamanic tradition, though merged with Russian Orthodox/ Christian beliefs. Western New Age beliefs and practices—and there is a spectrum of them—have often co-opted various shamanic traditions. In addition, the Russians seem to have developed their own psi zeitgeist involving bioenergetic fields (subtle energy fields), information fields and more. Consequently, some of what you will read in the following section may seem a little on the "New Age" side, though this is hardly the way the Russians would see it. The descriptions of psychic practices and activities are as much based in the ingrained shamanic beliefs that are part of the Russian identity as anything else. However, while similar views are held in the West, they were hardly a part of Star Gate or associated programs.

We've tried to remain true to the way the Russians perceive psi and the ESP Wars, as to do anything else would be to do their beliefs an injustice. So, as you read the narrative based on the Russian sources and their own words, do keep in mind that the American perspective on ESP may seem as odd (or even "New Age") to them as some of the following might seem to us.

CHAPTER 7

BEFORE THE FALL: THE KGB AND ESP

Authors' Note: Much of the following is based on interviews with and direct contributions from those described and quoted, with an eye towards keeping even the narrative in context with the quoted material.

The Soviet secret service, the KGB, has been the fodder of numerous espionage and political movies, novels and TV shows for decades in the West. However, they were hardly portrayed as being involved with psychic spies. What we in the West typically heard about psychic (psychotronic) weaponry was usually connected to the Soviet Military, rather than the KGB. Then again, American espionage agencies were also not portrayed as having parapsychological involvement.

As you've already read, the US military psychic programs did have some relationship to what was going on in the Soviet Union, even if it was to "keep up with the Joneses." It's hard to imagine that the Soviets were not doing the same with some kind of military program(s). Given western stereotypes of the KGB, it's also difficult to imagine that the agency was not at least somewhat involved with applications of parapsychology.

So, what was happening with ESP in the Soviet Union during the 1970s and 1980s? Was the KGB using psychics to spy on the West? Were they trying to use psi for mind control, or to physically harm people, as was suggested in the popular media and amongst conspiracy theorists?

The KGB did indeed work with psychics from time to time, but no distinct grouping of psychics was ever established within the KGB itself. Even if the idea of creating such a group had occurred to anyone at the higher administrative levels of the KGB, no one would have dared to endanger their career by officially proposing such a program due to its obvious spiritualistic bias. In addition, Soviet-Communist dogma required a strong "materialistic" base—something more "physical"—for the research and practical work. Violating this concept would be considered nearly treasonous. For this reason, the work that the KGB did with psychics was always more or less sporadic in nature through the end of the 1980s, with individual chiefs taking the initiative only when it was necessary for certain specific operations, more often than not to detect crime rather than for military operations or espionage.

Contrary to what may have been believed in the West, the KGB was only indirectly involved with the development of psychotronic weapons and military ESP research. The agency was only related to it by nature of their charge by ensuring that the necessary secrecy of this work was guaranteed, as they did with so much other Soviet government work.

As a quick aside, a psychotronic weapon would be one that ostensibly utilizes psychic energy (or other mental or life energies) stored in batteries often referred to as psychotronic generators. They were hardware devices—often with nothing inside the shell—that were seemingly necessary given the Soviet materialistic outlook. Psychotronic weapons were to affect, influence or control the minds of their targets, potentially affect a target's health (for example, to give the target a headache or stomach ache to distract him from some task), or perhaps even drive them to suicide or accidental death. The latter notwithstanding, had they actually worked as designed, most psychotronic devices were designed as non-lethal weaponry.

Research and development work was conducted in secret institutes affiliated with various establishments, most often the Ministry of Defense Industry. Decisions about any ESP R&D were made by the Directors or General Directors of these enterprises, sometimes with the support of division managers at the appropriate ministry. But a program of integrated ESP research and psychotronic weapons creation did not exist in the USSR, nor could it exist. Such a program would have required authorization from the top ideologues of the Central Committee of the Communist Party, which was absolutely impossible because parapsychology was considered inconsistent with ideological dogma. The following quote from a special interview conducted with Colonel Vyacheslav Zvonikov M.D. for this book is a good example of this. Zvonikov worked in those years at the Institute of Aviation and Space Medicine. From Zvonikov:

I remember a time in the early 1980s when we tested a psychotronic generator. A scientist brought a team together for this purpose, and they created a generator. Their goal was to test it in an established strict scientific setting.

Finding a good laboratory was not an easy task. This scientist came to our Institute seeking one, because he knew we had good training facilities there. We looked at his device and decided to assist him, but not openly, of course. We found a test pilot-operator to conduct trials and paid him under the table. He was given the tasks for a standard training flight. This training apparatus was especially appropriate because it measured physiological indicators on the subject and recorded them during the virtual takeoff, aerobatics operations, and landing.

Everything was registered and all parameters noted. In addition, we examined the tester's blood before and after the "flight." Following the experiment, we analyzed all the results. There were no deviations in the behavior of the test pilot, even though the psychotronic generator was running. A conclusion could have been drawn that if a pilot's skills are good, generators of that type will not affect an experiment's results.

However, there was more to it than just that. While there were no behavioral changes in the test subject, in fact there were internal variations: Voll's electro-acupuncture diagnostics equipment[1] had responded to the psychotronic generator. But the most interesting thing was that the test subject's blood had also been affected. Indeed, there were dramatic changes: the leukocyte level had increased threefold. I think if we had waited and exposed the operator for a longer "flight" time under the influence of the generator, there would have been deviations in his piloting behavior.

Unfortunately, we were not able to keep this experiment a secret from the Institute's higher management, and they ordered us to write up our conclusions from the tests. We asked that information regarding our experiments not leave the Institute, and this was promised to us. News of the experiment, however, was leaked to the CPSU's [Communist Party of the Soviet Union] Central Committee, and the illegal tests of the psychotronic generator were denounced. Everyone in the department was punished: one person lost his job, another lost her award, and yet another lost a place in line for an apartment. Our bosses received censure, and we were reprimanded no less.

The lack of an integrated program did not prevent the invention of an immense number of psychotronic weapons—whose efficacy is quite questionable—and seemed to encourage an expansion of research and development. Many scientists had already realized the existence of ESP phenomena, and as a result, many secret enterprises and laboratories partly worked on psychotronic gadgetry because it was relatively easy to hide this work from the CPSU political authorities.

Edward Naumov (1932-1997)

To give the reader a sense of the state of military ESP in the USSR, we'll describe the general atmosphere of parapsychology there during the 1970s and 1980s.

It should be no surprise that the KGB kept tabs on psychics. The KGB determined who they were and made them agree not to influence people in negative ways. Psychics were "allowed" to conduct their own research and to do healing work, but they were warned that if they went beyond permissible limits, they would be subjected to disciplinary action. These were Soviet times and the following activities were not permitted: individual entrepreneurship (receiving money for doing work privately), folk healing practices (considered illegal medical activity), distribution of illegal literature (any literature which was not published officially, which included practically all literature about ESP-related subjects), public lectures given by private individuals, and many other activities. The lives of psychics and research parapsychologists were difficult during those times. There were too many prohibitions, and it was too easy to make a false step and run afoul of the KGB and the authorities. Unfortunately, this did happen to a majority of them.

The case of Edward Naumov, one of the first activists in the parapsychology revival in the USSR during the 1960s, is one such example. He was one of the pioneering individuals who worked very hard to conduct ESP research on a volunteer basis, to get permission from officials to lecture on the subject, to make films about the authenticity of ESP "miracles," and to establish contact with foreign scientists. A photo of Naumov is shown on the previous page.

The authorities were suspicious of his activities and with his unauthorized contact with foreigners something that especially annoyed the KGB. In 1974, Naumov was arrested and condemned to two years in a prison camp. His case evoked a broad public response at home and in the West, perhaps especially because Naumov was not a political or social dissident. He did not criticize the system or sign protest letters. Many Soviet scientists and the cultural intelligentsia noted that he was actually subjected to repression for lecturing about ESP and for meeting with foreign scientists. On November 18, 1974, the London Times ran a letter signed by world-renowned writers and scientists J. B. Priestley, Francis Huxley, and Robert Harvey among others, who openly stated that Naumov was condemned because he called for the free and open study of parapsychological phenomena in the USSR with collaboration from non-Soviet scientists. The English scientists and writers urged Moscow to reconsider the charges that were brought against Naumov and to release him from detention.

It is difficult to tell whether the protests of these foreign luminaries played a role in his release or whether the reason was some internal political mechanism at work in the USSR. On April 9, 1975, the Supreme Court of the Russian Federative Republic made the decision to dismiss Naumov's case for lack of any criminal offense in his actions. Naumov continued to connect with foreign scientists, and in 1992 he hosted Larissa Vilenskaya and Ed May when they visited Russia and, much to their delight, took them to the renowned Moscow Circus, among other activities.

The prosecution and persecution of amateur parapsychologists and psychics was not limited to Naumov. During this same period, psychic practitioner Varvara Ivanova was fired from her position "for charlatanism and lecturing incompatible with the rank of teacher." She taught at the very prestigious Moscow Institute of International Relations and did research at the public Bio-Information Laboratory in her spare time. This list of psychics and researchers who suffered from the State for their work with ESP is quite extensive.

It was also during the same time that the Bio-Information Laboratory and the section dealing with ESP research in the A.S. Popov Scientific and Technical Society of Radio Engineering, Electronics and Communication (NTORES) was also closed. In subsequent years this section would be re-opened and closed and re-opened again under different names and different directors. Research on ESP was also conducted in the Commission on Bio-Energetics at the All-Union Association of Science and Technology Societies (VSNTO), in the NTO Priborprom (a huge military industrial company, a manufacturer of many military hi-tech devices), and the Moscow Society of Nature Explorers. Scientists did in-depth studies of well-known Russian psychics Rosa Kuleshova, Nina Kulagina and many others. This research was purely civilian, and we won't dwell on it here except to describe one of the programs in which the top leadership of the USSR was involved.

Larissa Vilenskaya a.k.a. Laura V. Faith (1948-2001)

At the end of the 1970s, Leonid Brezhnev, the General Secretary of the Central Committee of the CPSU, was very ill. Not only was he beginning to feel his age, but Brezhnev had also become addicted to medications containing narcotics. This began with a "harmless" sleeping pill and ended with Brezhnev terrorizing doctors and forcing them to give him a "dose." This addiction quickly pushed him towards senility. Not only could Brezhnev no longer work normally, but he couldn't even think or speak normally. However, in no way did his "loyal companions" wish to let the old man retire. His departure would have disturbed the established power structure, and the higher party and state bigwigs feared for their positions. Doctors could no longer help him, and a miracle worker was needed.

That miracle worker actually appeared—Djuna Davitashvilli, a nurse from Georgia. She had gained a reputation in the Tbilisi region where she lived, for healing people by using her psychic ability; she was sent from there to Moscow. Davitashvilli began treating the leader, and it seemed to help him. In spite of the wholly "idealistic" nature of the treatments, Brezhnev felt better.

Whether directly or indirectly, this seemed to lead to a retreat of Marxist-Leninist doctrine in such matters. Orders came down from the Central Committee, enormous resources were allocated, and the Institute of Radio-engineering and Electronics (IRE), one of the leading institutes of the Academy of Sciences, was instructed to determine the mechanism of Davitashvilli's healing influence, and to simultaneously study the entire field of ESP as well.

The top IRE scientists were not very happy with this assignment, but there was no getting out of it. They had to carry out party orders. For the IRE, there was a gigantic silver lining in what these scientists might have believed was a very dark cloud: funding. The government allocated a princely sum to the Institute for this research.

A special laboratory to study psychics was established with Eduard Emmanuilovich Godik, a Ph.D. in physical and mathematical sciences, appointed as its director. Academician Yuri Vasilievich Gulyaev became head of the entire program. Gulyaev was a corresponding member of the Academy of Sciences and Deputy Director of IRE at that time. The renowned academician Yuri Borisovich Kobzarev also became interested in ESP. (Later Gulyaev became head of the Russian Academy Sciences and the director of IRE. Below is a photo taken in Moscow in 2009.)

Research work into psychics had hardly ever been conducted at such a high scientific level in the USSR. Gulyaev had founded an entirely new area in science—acoustic electronics—and was subsequently nominated for the Nobel Prize over ten times. Devices based on his discovery and patents are used in every TV and every mobile phone in the world today. Kobzarev was the founder of Soviet radiolocation and radar technology. Graduates of the Moscow Institute of Physics and Technology, the Soviet counterpart of the Massachusetts Institute of Technology, worked at the laboratory.

Parapsychologists—in fact, any good scientist looking at psi—consistently try to find alternative explanations for ESP in specific instances of the phenomena and in general. In the course of their research, the physicists discovered several very ordinary mechanisms that had initially appeared to be ESP phenomena. In Nina Kulagina's case, it turned out her palms emitted a spray of small droplets of histamine, which formed an electrically charged aerosol in the air. These micro drops of histamine then settled on the objects nearby, and the greater the concentration of the electrostatically-charged forces, the greater the attraction between the surfaces of objects. This is what explained Kulagina's ability to move small subjects without touching them. There was no telekinesis (influence of mind over matter) involved, at least in the form of some unexplained mental or physical energy or force.

Djuna Davitashvili's work apparently did not contain any psi elements either. The researchers gave a rather convincing explanation that the healing was a result of the heat from her hands. However, there were also other psychics like Yuri Kharitonov, whose powers the physicists were unable to explain definitively. On the whole, the question of how ESP worked remained an open one.

Academician Y. V. Gulyaev and Dr. May in Moscow 2009

What did this have to do with military ESP? As with the situation in the West at SRI, where some of the research was conducted in a more public fashion and a good deal under military contract, some of the research at the Laboratory was also secret. On the one hand, people knew "all" about it and there was constant talk about Djuna and Gulyaev not only in the student hostels, but in all the circles of Moscow intellectuals as well. On the other hand, all the reports about their work were being classified.

As a result, people in the West knew about Gulyaev-Godik Laboratory, but not what was actually being done. They suspected that military ESP research work was being conducted there. Suspicions were heightened by the fact that there really were a lot of other kinds of classified research being done at the IRE, which had a secret branch in the closed city of Fryazino on the outskirts of

Moscow. This was similar to the work of government-funded think tanks in the US like SRI, where a variety of different topics were being researched, including classified and non-classified work.

In fact, there wasn't any military ESP research going on at IRE. It was simply a matter of the Soviet habit of classifying everything—whether it was necessary or not. However, this did result in the next ramp-up in the ESP arms race: the Gulyaev-Godik Laboratory was one of the main reasons for a new round of financing in the Star Gate program, even though the KGB was not involved with the Soviet work.

One genuinely collaborative work by the KGB with psychics revolved around Tofik Dadashev, a young talented psychic, who began gaining public recognition in 1967. In 1973, as a member of a delegation of the USSR Academy of Sciences, Dadashev took part in the First International Congress on Psychotronic Research in Prague, where many of the scientists in attendance recognized him as "the most powerful medium in the world." The KGB took notice of him and immediately tried to get him involved in working with them. Dadashev agreed, but on condition that his help would not be used against his fellow citizens who were not involved in criminal activity.

Among his many tasks over the years, Dadashev described a unique anti-terrorist operation in which 50 hostages were freed. We include it here in full detail even though it is from a later period because it does illustrate his abilities as well as a real application of ESP quite dramatically. It may be, in fact, the first time in history when a psychic's ESP abilities were used by security services to seize a hijacker with such sensational success.

On March 30, 1989, a TU-134A airplane en route from Voronezh to Baku was hijacked by a terrorist. When it landed in Baku, the terrorist, who was later identified as Stanislav Skok, held all 50 passengers and crew members on board hostage. He stated that he had two accomplices and an explosive device on board and demanded a half a million dollars (a considerable sum of money at that time), a refueling of the plane, and the chance to escape to Pakistan. Viktor Barannikov (Deputy Minister of Internal Affairs of Azerbaijan and subsequently the Director of the FSB of the Russian

Federation), Ivan Gorelovsky (Chairman of the Azerbaijan KGB), and a special Alfa detachment swiftly arrived at the airport. The following is a quote from the accounts of two high-ranking KGB officers who took part in this operation:

Lt. Colonel Guseinov's Account:

At that time, I, KGB Lieutenant Colonel Elshad Bakhabogli Guseinov, served as the head of the KGB aviation security unit of the Azerbaijan Republic of the USSR and was directly involved in the anti-terrorist defense of air-passenger transport in the republic. In those years, I trained and headed a special anti-terrorist response team for air transport. I am emphasizing this only to show that I am writing all this as a direct participant in these events, not from hearsay...

The criminal claimed that he was not alone, that he had accomplices, and that there was an explosive device in the cargo hold of the plane, which would automatically detonate unless the alarm he had set on his watch was disabled in time. He said that he had a remote control device in the bag slung across his chest and that he was keeping his hands in the bag all the time, ostensibly to control the remote. One of the officers in the operations team, namely Aleksandr Valentinovich Izmodenov, who then worked in the transportation section of the KGB of the Azerbaijan Soviet Socialist Republic (and who is currently a lieutenant general in the FSB of Russia), proposed that they utilize the ESP powers of the well-known psychic Tofik Gasanovich Dadashev, who was in Baku at the time. Tofik Dadashev arrived at the airport with Azerbaijan SSR KGB Major A. Kuryanov...

Lt. Colonel Kuryanov's Account:

I, Aleksandr Alekseyevich Kuryanov, now a retired KGB lieutenant colonel, directly witnessed Tofik Dadashev's participation in this operation. At that time, I was the head of a personal security group in the KGB of the Azerbaijan Republic. At about 10pm on March 30, 1989, a duty officer of the Azerbaijan KGB called and informed me that there was a plane at the airport which had been seized by an unknown individual, and that the Azerbaijan KGB leadership had decided to bring T. Dadashev into the operation to free the hostages. Early the next morning, a car came to pick us up. Deputy Chairman of the KGB of the Azerbaijan Republic of the

USSR Rafik Alieyevich Sadykhov met us at the airport and told us that was very little time left—literally a few minutes. In the airport building, the head of the operations group along with Alfa group commander Major General Viktor Fedorovich Karpukhin, Hero of the Soviet Union, asked T. Dadashev to convince the terrorist to wait until 11:00 am, insofar as he was very agitated, he was on the verge of a breakdown, and threatened to blow up the airplane. At the same time he showed the bag slung across his shoulder and kept his right hand on his watch, into which, according to him, the detonating fuse was wired. His conditions were that the plane be refueled and that a substantial amount of hard currency in US dollars and German marks be delivered. Such a large sum of cash was not available at the local state bank at that time, and the money had to be delivered from Moscow by 11:00 am. Tofik Dadashev offered to initiate a dialogue with the terrorist under the guise of an official from the Ministry of Foreign Affairs of Azerbaijan.

The airplane had been parked far from the airport building, so I drove T. Dadashev to the tail end of the hijacked airplane in an official car. I then got out of the car, unbuttoned my raincoat, raised my arms above my head to show that I was unarmed, and I remained close to the car. He then specified that the "MFA official" stand several meters from the airplane-boarding ramp so that he could remain inaccessible inside. He peeked out of the airplane door for a moment.

T. Dadashev walked toward the airplane walkway and began talking to the terrorist. I couldn't hear their conversation because the wind was blowing at my back. All of a sudden, a minute or two later, Tofik shook his finger at him. I tensed up, because any careless movements could have aggravated the situation, but everything worked out. Then Tofik got into the car and exclaimed, "Sasha! Your men told me that he has a bomb and accomplices, but I can see that he's bluffing. He doesn't have a bomb or accomplices!"

In spite of our decade-long friendship and close relationship, I replied (perhaps in too official a manner) at that time that we would relate everything that he picked up to leaders of the operations team, because only they had the right to make a decision about how to conduct the operation. The leaders of the operations team surrounded us in the airport building when we gave our report. T.

Dadashev briefly reported that the terrorist was bluffing, and that he didn't have explosives or weapons.

Viktor Karpukhin expressed his misgivings about Skok keeping his hand on his watch all the time. What to do? Dadashev thought it over for a few seconds and recommended starting a dialogue with Skok. Dadashev foresaw that Skok would pause to think, ask for a cigarette, take his hand off the watch, and that this would be the moment to seize him (even though Dadashev did not know that Skok was a smoker).

Everything took place exactly as Dadashev had predicted. At the end of the operation, the excited and flushed leaders and members of the Alfa group came up to Dadashev and sincerely thanked him.

The leadership of the Azerbaijan KGB wrote recommendations to the Presidium of the Supreme Soviet of the Azerbaijan Republic. By a decree on December 13, 1989, Tofik Dadashev was decorated with the highest award, a Letter of Commendation from the Presidium of the Supreme Soviet of the Azerbaijan Soviet Socialist Republic for the successful completion of an operation to intercept the hijacking of an airplane, secure the safety of the passengers and capture the criminal.

Tofik Dadashev who, in a special interview for this book, added with a smile:

I was standing at a considerable distance—more than 25 meters away—when I talked with Skok. We spoke for literally just a few minutes, and all I saw was the criminal's silhouette and his beard. But I did the job, I saw the terrorist and was able to "attune myself to him." And most importantly, I greatly appreciate the courage of the KGB officers who believed and accepted my suggestion, even though from their standpoint it could have cost some of them their careers or lives. Then everything moved at lightning speed. At 11 AM the terrorist was still threatening to blow up the plane, and at 11:10 he was already being brought into the airport. General Karpukhin, commander of the Alfa group, addressed me and said, "I'm reporting that I did everything that you told me to do. He allowed me to approach him, and he asked me for a cigarette, and we seized him right at the moment when he was lighting up."

Dadashev also participated in earlier counter-espionage KGB operations. He continues:

The KGB engaged me time and again in work exposing foreign agents. I was once asked in 1978 to determine whether a tourist who had arrived in Moscow was an English spy. The KGB officers drove me to the hotel Rossiya. There was already a large group of foreign tourists in the lobby, about 150 people. My escorts did not know who the suspect was, and we simply went to the bar to wait for another officer who would point the person out to me. While we were walking through the lobby, my attention was immediately drawn to a male with a red moustache, who was sitting some distance away. The officer we were waiting for appeared and, before he had a chance to say anything, I said to him right then and there, "Yes, you're right. He is a spy. He's sitting over there on a couch in the lobby, he has a red mustache, and he's wearing a light-colored raincoat."

The KGB officers burst out laughing, "We were planning a lengthy operation, we were getting prepared for it, but you, Tofik, you're going to put all of us out of business!"

I recall another curious story from the mid-1980s when I was working in Baku and staying at a hotel there with my assistant, Valentin Sablin.

One day while I was seeing people at the office, Valentin got acquainted with two gas industry workers from Siberia. They quickly fell to "splitting one bottle three ways" and then had fun emptying several more bottles. When I returned to the hotel, Valentin introduced me to them, assuring me that they were "first-rate guys and totally one of us". While I was shaking their hands, I said, "I know that one of you is a legal advisor in "deep drilling," and the other is just a simple gas worker who happens to be fluent in several foreign languages."

Our new buddies were very surprised at first, then broke out laughing. "Yes, Tofik, actually, we're KGB officers. And one of us really is an attorney, and the other is a foreign language specialist."

Valentin instantly sobered up and turned pale. "Oh my God, and here I've been spinning off political jokes for several hours!"

We later became friends with the attorney (whose name was Sasha.) Once, we were in a hotel restaurant and I had to go to the bathroom. I walked out into the hallway and was taken aback at the sight of two people there. They were walking toward a hotel room, and I followed to see which room, then quickly returned to our table. I told Sasha, "I just saw two people—one of them is a KGB officer and the other is a German spy!"

Sasha immediately called the KGB overseer of the hotel, who said: "Yes, yes, we know. Our task is to recruit this spy, and our agent is carrying it out. So everything's fine, but thank you for the alert! But... it's still hard to take in that Tofik Dadashev identified this by just looking at them!"

I must say that I have had the chance not only to catch spies, but also save individuals who were falsely accused of being spies.

In the early 1980s, a physicist in Dubna contacted the KGB alleging that a journalist from South Korea was attempting to recruit him. I was asked to check him out. A meeting between this physicist and the journalist (the purported spy) was set up near the hotel Moskva. During the time of the meeting, I was driven in a car past the hotel. I instantly told the KGB officers accompanying me, "The Korean journalist is not a spy! This physicist is just doing a number on you, hoping that you'll notice him and hire him or because he wanted some more material goods"

My words were later confirmed by a simultaneous operations check. I think that the KGB undertook the appropriate measures and that this physicist then lost his desire to bring false accusations against people to aggrandize himself.

In the period of the 1970s into the 1980s, intelligence services tried to enlist or consult with almost all famous psychics in the Soviet Block, at least on a sporadic basis. One example was Vanga Dimitrova, a Bulgarian clairvoyant who was possibly the best known forecaster of the future behind the Iron Curtain in the 20th century. It was primarily the Bulgarian intelligence services who employed her and consulted with her quite often, while the KBG was only occasionally interested in her services in certain situations. Dimitrova focused on predictions of political situations, which she did correctly. For example, she named the winners in future presidential elections in the US. When a question was incompatible with her moral values, Dimitrova simply sidestepped the question and used allegorical language.

Two other famous psychics, Sergei Vronsky and Vladimir Safonov, also worked with KGB at that time. Their interesting work with the KGB was recounted by Major General Georgii Georgievich Rogozin, a KGB officer in the 1970s, who rose to become the first Deputy Chief of the President's Security Service in 1990. With a name familiar to Russians, General Rogozin has become famous as "the astrologer and psychic No.1" of the Russian Secret Services. The Eastern press also likes to call him "the grey cardinal" or "the governmental magician."

General Georgii Georgievich Rogozin provided us with his recollection:

I met Sergei Alekseyevich Vronsky in the early 1970s. At that time, I was a young KGB officer, and several officers and I would come to see the well-known psychic Vladimir Ivanovich Safonov to solve special problems related to our professional work. It was there that we first met. Safonov introduced Vronsky in a rather mysterious way. I already knew from his hints when Safonov greeted us at the door that we would see his teacher.

Kindness radiated from Vronsky, from his words, and from his gaze. We were introduced, and I asked him to help us. He burst out laughing, saying, "I thought that we would be talking about the mysteries of the Universe, while you keep bothering me with your special missions." In general, he approached everything with humor. After our first friendly meeting with Vronsky, we began to ask him frequent questions related to secret service operations. He would help us very simply, quickly and easily.

One amazing situation comes to mind, when a person who was searching for his lost nephew came to see Vronsky while we were with him. We were already on our way out, but Vronsky suddenly became agitated, and asked us to stay. The visitor's eyes were more shifty than inquisitive. Vronsky listened attentively to his story about the boy who disappeared, and how they, his relatives, were all concerned and searching for him. The visitor left the room about 15-20 minutes later, and Vronsky turned to us and said with sadness, "He's the one who murdered the boy." He explained to us that the visitor had come with one goal—to find out whether he was in danger of being found out. The case was then closed by the KGB. The individual was arrested, and a judicial investigation was held. Vronsky turned out to be right: this man was the murderer.

My interest in ESP and acquaintance with Vronsky originally arose from practical operations interests, and it was only later that mundane considerations entered the picture. We often contacted him to ask for medical diagnoses when one of us or members of our families experienced health problems. We gave him the home telephone numbers of relatives whose health was causing us concern so that he would speak directly to them. After a short conversation, Vronsky could not only diagnose the wife or child of a staff member, but he would also give them specific recommendations and bring harmony into their situations, work on their internal organs and systems at the cellular level, and also tune up the functioning of their physical energy systems using ESP methods.

Sometime later, I learned about Vronsky's amazing life. Not all of its details can be revealed even at the present time, but Vronsky played an indisputable role in many confrontations in Soviet-German relations before and during World War II, and in the lives of Hess and Rommel. He worked for the top German leadership and was directly connected with the "Ahnenerbe" group. Vronsky evaluated the capabilities of the Tibetan monks who were being recruited by the SS. Vronsky's opinion was very important to Hitler's staff, at the same time as he was working for the Soviet Union!

I will not comment about Sergei Vronsky as a General in the GRU [Main Intelligence Directorate]. Official GRU representatives can do this. But it is impossible to deny the fact that he was a very powerful individual who possessed phenomenal abilities.

But how was it that Vronsky—with all his unique abilities and achievements as an agent—was unable to escape the meat grinder of the Stalinist camps? After all, the top Soviet leadership needed his gift! The answer is obvious: they became frightened of Vronsky's abilities, and of the fact that he could use these abilities against them, so they put him in a Stalinist camp, and thank God that they didn't kill him. As a result, Vronsky became rather reserved and unwilling to allow the outside world to come too close. Naturally, Vronsky felt anguished by many of the events taking place in our nation, but at the same time, he didn't allow what was around him to destroy him.

Vronsky tried to be more involved in astrology than in ESP, because criminal elements were already meddling in ESP in those days, and he realized how dangerous it could be. There was no modern equipment then, no astrological software. Nothing was automatic—he did everything manually. Vronsky would get the details of the placidus [an astrological house system], ephemeris [astronomical data], degrees, minutes, seconds, and draw each horoscope to order. It wasn't for money, it was for his internal self-realization. He was affirming himself, proving that he was on the right path, even though everyone around him was calling astrology obscurantism and a pseudo-science.

Vronsky was under rather powerful pressure from state structures. This was understandable, considering his background and unusual abilities. He was a very high-level expert and could give interesting evaluations, arrive at unconventional solutions and develop independent and rather sincere forecasts.

People like Vronsky, who have attained certain thresholds, were passing on their knowledge, but only to people whom they knew well and whom they trusted completely. Somewhat later, I also began studying with him. As a teacher, Vronsky always explained everything in detail. He did not skate on the surface of knowledge, but went deeply into issues.

He trained us primarily in astrology. But once, when we were sitting with him, I asked him to teach me some ESP. Vronsky gave me a problem specifically pertaining to ESP. I wasn't able to solve it in any way and was tuning out, contemplatively staring into the space in front of me. I still remember our conversation:

"Why the meditative look?" Vronsky asked.

"I don't have the abilities that you have," I replied.

He put his hand on my head as if he were stroking me and said, "Now you do."

Suddenly, something inexplicable happened: I actually saw a situation—images began to appear, and pictures came. That's how I became a psychic myself.

Dr. May and General Georgii Georgievich Rogozin

While research was going on outside of the KGB, the use of psychics by the agency during those years was sporadic. It is difficult to say whether the Soviets had a version of Star Gate, aside from stating that it wasn't a KGB operation. A similar remote viewing program directed by Boris Timofeevich Litunenko was conducted on Dickson Island in the Kara Sea (Russian Arctic), where psychics studied the American military satellites by means of remote viewing, even to the details of their designs.

They used technology (radar) to point to a specific satellite before the psychics would start, as described by General Sham later in this chapter. This procedure, they claimed, gave the correct correlation of the ESP-derived information to the specific satellite. This approach would seem utterly strange and inexplicable to the remote viewers in the Star Gate program, as the added aiming mechanism of the technology was unnecessary to the Americans. However, the results of Litunenko's ESP program were very convincing and independent data gathered by conventional intelligence proved that they were valid. Perhaps the Soviet mentality was in play here, demanding some "material" data. It is possible, however, that the project director, Litunenko, simply used the radar locators as a cover, to avoid ideological objections.

Getting back to our KGB/ESP connection, the following story is from KGB Major General Nikolai Alekseevich Sham, who was head of the industrial and scientific counterespionage department at that time and later headed all new technologies and ESP-oriented work in the KGB. In an interview specifically for this book, he shared a bit more on the KGB's collaboration with psychics:

Major General Nikolai Alekseevich Sham:

Working in the KGB put me virtually at the cutting edge of all the new and advanced subjects. As it turned out, the most interesting area in which I was involved was related to people's extraordinary abilities, their capacities that went beyond the general understanding of human possibilities. My interest in these questions developed in the latter part of the 1970s, and strange as it might seem, I came into contact with this field outside my basic work.

Once, at a party given by my friends, I happened to meet a computer engineer who worked in Novosibirsk, Yuri Vladimirovich Noskov. During our conversation, he told me about his ability to do medical diagnoses. He proceeded to demonstrate his skill, accurately determining the medical conditions of the guests at the party. He also possessed powerful healing abilities. He treated many illnesses and worked with healing herbs and tinctures, and his hypnotic passes alleviated heart attacks. I decided to bring him into the space and rocket field and introduced him to Valentin Petrovich Glushko, the head of NPO "Energiya," a huge scientific-industrial conglomerate, which builds our space ships.

Glushko hired him, and Noskov began working as a diagnostician who supervised the health services of the employees. The results were so impressive that Glushko began thinking about using extrasensory energies for defense purposes and decided to create a special laboratory to develop a new high-quality space weapon. The idea was to launch special generators in space to amplify extrasensory energies and their effect on certain regions of the Earth. But another psychic became head of this project due to some internal intrigues at "Energiya" and Noskov found himself out of work.

He left the program and became involved in the "Triad" project, which involved communication by means of space re-transmitters capable of handling up to 12 million pairs of conversations per minute. With Noskov gone, Glushko lost the person who had so carefully supervised his health, and he soon died of an unexpected heart attack.

In the mid-1980s, I was transferred to the 6th Department where

I was involved in industrial counter-espionage—battling against espionage in technical and scientific fields. During my work there, I met increasing numbers of people who were engaged in non-traditional activities. I witnessed many experiments that convinced me of the existence of physical fields and principles that modern science has not yet studied, but which are quite real and suitable for practical use. These fields and principles are connected both to the physical world and to the psyche, and they can work co-operatively with both.

At this time, I met the psychic Valery Valentinovich Kustov. This time the meeting was due to purely operational necessity.

In 1985-86, there were two accidents in the defense industry, which were very unusual for that time. Two high-ranking officials from that sector were killed within a short period. The first was Igor Berezhnoi, the General Director of NPO in Samara, a military scientific-industrial conglomerate involved in laser weapons design. He was given an explosive disguised as a box of medication. He opened the box in a car on the road to the airport and was killed. All his internal organs were damaged, and he died instantly.

We were to conduct an investigation to find the perpetrators. The murder of such a high-ranking individual who was so well protected was very unusual and totally unexpected. We, in the KGB, had never encountered such a problem in our work before.

We began our investigation but hadn't even had time to figure out a basic scenario when the chief engineer of Astrofizika was unexpectedly killed. Astrofizika was a top-secret KGB engineering enterprise in the Moscow area, and its general director was also involved in work with lasers. He was killed along with his mistress in his own house. What a nightmare!

It seemed natural to assume that one of the foreign intelligence services had begun a series of diversionary actions against the creators of Soviet laser weapons, all of which took place right in the center of the USSR! Moreover, the general director of Astrofizika was the son of Marshal Ustinov, who was the Minister of Defense at that time. The strictest commands came down from on high, enormous resources were allocated, every possible scenario was exhausted, and the most complicated technical means were employed. Various infringements of the law, diamond deals, settling of accounts of properties at illegal factories—all these activities were investigated, but we couldn't find any real thing to go by. In short, we got nowhere—it was a dead end.

At one of our meetings with the staff from the Rostov Department of the KGB, we were unexpectedly informed that they had an individual, Valeri Kustov, who could see the past and predict the future. To maintain secrecy, we met with him in a room especially rented for the occasion at the Rossiya Hotel. And I must say that I was dumbfounded at his powers. I had never seen a demonstration of extrasensory capacities of such a high level until this meeting.

Kustov sat in the far corner of the room and suggested that I sit in the opposite corner. He lifted his hand and said, "I am now starting to exert an influence on you." I felt a powerful stream of energy moving toward my face from five meters away. It felt like a stream of air was hitting me. Kustov moved his hand slightly, and the air stream moved over a little. I felt the radiation coming from his hand. Then he spread his hands, and I clearly saw radiation coming off the tips of his fingers in broad daylight; bright bands of energy were visible.

Another time I spilled boiling water on my foot, causing a first-degree burn. My foot swelled up, terrible blisters formed, and the pain was horrible. After two three-minute sessions, he removed all signs of the intense burn; not a trace of it remained. I went to work after his treatment, and when I removed the bandage from my foot after work, I gasped with surprise—there was no burn!

Incidentally, somewhat later, in the 1990s, the documentary film "The Phenomenon of Engineer Kustov" was produced about this remarkable man and his phenomenal abilities. He now lives in Rostov, where he works in a clinic and treats people.

Kustov began to work on solving the crimes. We were ready for anything and everything: from the actions of foreign intelligence services to internal acts of terror in Stalin's paranoid style. But Kustov said that he saw nothing of the kind. In his opinion, they were domestic crimes. We did not believe him, and so these crimes remained unsolved.

A few years later, I met one of Berezhnoi's friends. We recalled this story, and I told him about our fiasco. He was amazed: "You didn't discover the murderer? But it wasn't a secret to any of us in the headquarters! It was extremely simple: it was jealousy." He said that Berezhnoi was intimately involved with a female secretary and that he had taken advantage, so to speak, of his official position. She had an admirer who was pathologically in love with her, and it was he who had committed the crime.

The KGB simply could not tolerate such a simple explanation. We did not even examine such basic scenarios as domestic ones—the victim was too closely connected to top state secrets. We rejected such explanations, searching for perpetrators such as foreign intelligence or terrorists. But Kustov was correct in his prediction.

The reason for the second crime was simple, too. The Astrofizika enterprise had completed work on the creation of a white laser. An enormous amount of work had achieved remarkable results, but the chief engineer, who in fact had not been involved in the work, received the patent for it. One of the actual creators of the white laser said, "I will never forgive him." And he didn't—he murdered him instead.

ESP proved to be more successful in investigating these crimes than the entire investigative branch of the KGB. Consequently, we began to develop an outline for a system for the use of ESP in our operations. Several psychics worked on an assignment independently of one another. They worked with an integrated analytical center to process the information that they provided. The psychics would enter an information field and obtain data there, all of which would be immediately recorded and sent to an analyst who compared its various segments and looked for correspondences. The information obtained through ESP as well as the pattern of correspondences—the new addresses, phone numbers, and people involved in the case—would be quickly verified.

Thus, step by step, each new round of review yielded a complete cycle, and it became clear whether a problem had been resolved or the crime solved.

We also tried to investigate a technique of moving [mentally] back into the past. But it proved very fragmentary, and we weren't able to organize any serious and systematic research. The technique had enthusiastic supporters, but there were also many skeptics who made it impossible to do systematic research. An atmosphere of alienation emerged, and we could sense the thoughts floating around that judged those who proposed doing research in this area as being completely mad.

In one of the areas that resembled the American Star Gate program's remote viewing experiments, we developed a combined psychophysical technique of collecting information from remote objects by using operational radio-commands as a physical base for remote viewing. Specifically, there were experiments in which a person's image was sent into space. Boris Timofeevich Litunenko was very interested and involved in this idea. Experiments were conducted on Dickson Island in the Russian Arctic.

We would take a remote viewer and pinpoint his position using radar. He would then mentally shift to an object in space—usually, to one of the American military satellites—and describe it. The information that was collected from different remote viewers in different laboratories was compared, and the results were rather interesting. For example, psychics' description of the technical components of the American military satellites in such detail made it possible to understand their functions. We also got some confirmation of the data from the intelligence service sources.

Nonetheless, there was no special permanent division in the KGB that was engaged in ESP research and extrasensory operations work of this type.

In the field of psychotronic weapons, complex programs for the covert manipulation of an enemy's life force using technologies of mental and psychophysical influence were developed on the basis of a great deal of research conducted at our scientific research institutes. New technologies for solving problems through the covert manipulation of national leaders of political or economic adversaries or possible adversaries were experimentally created but never used. However, the effectiveness of these manipulation technologies is still questionable.

An "Electric sleep" installation that can induce semi-consciousness at a distance of a few kilometers has often been described in the media, both in Russia and the West. In reality, research was carried out to develop far more powerful and effective installations, in particular, creating space platforms that could influence entire cities and areas and cause laughter, tears, dreams, diarrhea, etc. at certain frequencies. But perhaps we should stop here because now we are turning to a radio-biological weapon, which is actually an intermediate link between a psychotronic weapon and a purely physical one.

Major General (fmr KGB) Nikolai Alekseevich Sham

We will continue General Sham's story later in Chapter 11, which describes more on activities during the period of global geopolitical changes: the fall of communism, the disintegration of the USSR, the end of the KGB, and the formation of new government and military structures. During this time General Sham became the last Deputy Director of the KGB in the history of this organization. Here, however, is his photograph.

Just a final note here about the KGB in its later days:

On December 8, 1991, the presidents of Russia, Ukraine, and Belarus signed the Belovezh Agreement to withdraw their republics from the USSR, signifying the end of the Soviet Union as a unified nation. Fifteen sovereign nations were created as a result of the breakup of the USSR. There was nothing left for Gorbachev to do but sign a decree on his own retirement from the office of the President of the USSR on December 25, in connection with the termination of the nation's existence.

During the Soviet era, the name KGB had become too repugnant.

The political persecution of dissidents in the USSR had amassed an enormous amount of ill feeling toward the organization. This attitude was expressed in mass protests, the toppling of the Dzerzhinsky monument in the square in front of KGB headquarters and the restitution of the square's historical name—Lyubyanka. But most importantly, the disappearance of the USSR radically changed the balance of power in the world. It also inevitably affected the work of the Special Security Services and their organizational structures.

As a result, the KGB was completely reorganized. On November 28, 1991, USSR President Gorbachev signed a decree on the establishment of an Inter-Republic Security Service on the foundation of the KGB. Vadim Bakatin, the last Chairman of the KGB, automatically became its head. At the same time, Boris Yeltsin, in his capacity as the president of the Russian republic, began creating his own Russian Federal Security Agency. However, this dual authority lasted for only a few weeks.

On January 24, 1992, the Ministry of Security of the Russian Federation was created on the foundation of the aforementioned Special Security Services. On April 3, 1995, the Federal Security Service of the Russian Federation (FSB) became its legal successor. Incidentally, Vladimir Putin, who later became the President of Russia, was the director of the FSB from July 1998 until August 1999.

One section of the KGB called "the 9 Directorate of KGB," which was taking care of the top political figures and was dealing with personal secret service, became the General Directorate of Security. It was later divided into the Presidential Security Service headed by Korzhakov and the Federal Security Service headed by Barsukov.

Major General Boris Ratnikov, one of the contributors to this book, originally was a KGB officer, but later became Deputy Head of the Federal Security Service. Under his supervision were analysis, operations, staff, technical and other services. Most relevant to our topic, he established a special parapsychological department and used many ESP techniques for security and intelligence service.

In the next chapter, we will learn about General Ratnikov's own story, his involvement with the KGB and other organizations in the USSR, and his involvement with parapsychology that extended into the new Russia.

NOTES

1) Reinhold Voll (1909-1989), a German medical doctor, in the early 1950s developed an electronic testing device for finding acupuncture points electrically. He was able to find acupuncture points and demonstrate that these points, known to Chinese acupuncturists for millennia, had a different resistance to a tiny electrical current passed through the body. This persuaded Voll to begin a lifelong search to identify correlations between disease states and changes in the electrical resistance of the various acupuncture points. He got significant success, which led to the beginning of a new area in medicine called the Voll's electro-acupuncture diagnostics.

CHAPTER 8

THE RUSSIAN PRESIDENT'S
PARAPSYCHOLOGICAL SHIELD

Authors' Note: The following is based on interviews with and written material from General Ratnikov. We have attempted to keep the narrative in context with the quoted material. We include much of his biographical background and stories of his place in politics in the USSR and Russia—as we do with General Savin in the next chapter—to provide an understanding of the mindset and political climate in which the modern psychic work existed.

MAJOR GENERAL BORIS KONSTANTINOVICH RATNIKOV'S STORY:

As the Soviet Union fell and the new Russia came into being, Major General Boris Konstantinovich Ratnikov was a key player in applying psychic techniques to security, intelligence gathering, and international politics. He established a parapsychological department in the new Federal Security Service (formerly the KGB) in the early 1990s, and the department's techniques were brought to bear in defending Russian political figures against potential psychic scanning and attacks.

Covering his days with the KGB to the Federal Security Service, Major General Ratnikov provided us with a story that is quite interesting, even without the element of the ESP wars. His experiences before and after the fall of the USSR truly gives us a context in which the East's side of psychic warfare exists. General Ratnikov provided us with his perspective of the political scene, having been a direct participant in several key historical events.

*Dr. Edwin C. May and Major General (KGB ret.) Boris
Konstantinovich Ratnikov*

General Ratnikov speaks of ending up "in charge" of the nation
for a couple of short hours during the attempted coup to take over the
Soviet government. His place in other events shows how involved he
was in different levels of government and the intelligence world. To
give you an idea of how central he was to some of these events, let's
start with what happened during the coup, in this story provided
by Boris Ratnikov.

At home on August 21, 1991, the night before the attempted (and
failed) coup[1] to remove Gorbachev from power and silence Yeltsin,
Boris Ratnikov was awakened by an alarm in the form of a phone
call from a Secret Service officer on duty. The urgent call provided
him with orders to report immediately to the Russian Federation
Government Building (the Parliament Building, locally called the
White House[2]) to protect Boris Yeltsin. Tanks and armored personnel carriers were moving toward the building. The crowds in the
area were beyond indignant and saw this as an act of intimidation,
but they felt no fear because they weren't guilty of anything. They
lay down under the tanks, certain that the army would not dare
fight against its own people, who were reacting to social circumstances. The shelves in shops were bare and everything was being
rationed—a real social explosion was building.

Yeltsin arrived at the Parliament Building from his dacha in
Arkhangelskoye (near Moscow) with a minimum of security. He
met with his activists and began writing decrees, keeping things
moving in a business-as-usual mode, though outside the building
the crowd grew larger and spontaneously began drawing together.

The regular police force was protecting the building, yet there were no cordons, and people were entering the building just by showing their passes. Paul Grachev, commander of the Air Borne Forces, brought his deputy General Alexander Lebed to the Parliament Building, and Lebed assigned several tanks, supposedly to protect the building and people inside. In actuality, the tanks were empty of ammunition, and when the enlisted tank drivers drove up to the building, they abandoned their combat vehicles and fled.

The basements of the Parliament Building were seven floors underground, and were designated for use as a reserve post from which the nation could be governed during wartime or a global nuclear crisis. At the time, the site was inactive and being held in reserve—reactivating it required a decision by the Politburo. The site contained everything essential for emergencies. There were two big rooms, one 30-meters on a side and the other 50-meters (along with two toilets), all behind doors that were one and a half meters thick.

While General Ratnikov and his comrades were waiting for the assault, Alexander Korzhakov—the KGB general who was the head of Boris Yeltsin's Presidential Security Services—said that the wives of the men from the Alpha Group Spetsnaz (Special Forces group) came and told him on their behalf that the Alpha fighters did not want a fratricidal massacre and would not engage in storming the Parliament Building. In addition, there was one more potentially disturbing issue: Yeltsin, Ratnikov and the rest of them were vulnerable to capture from below as a secret Metro line came right up to the bunker.

By two in the morning, they made the decision to go down into the basement bunker so that Yeltsin would be out of danger. The electricity went off as they were descending, leaving only emergency lighting. For Yeltsin's protection against sniper fire, they convinced him to put on a bulletproof vest, a gift to Yeltsin from the chess champion Garry Kasparov. Yeltsin was very dissatisfied that there was no water, the phone didn't work, the toilet was boarded up, and that the air was stuffy. It became even more difficult to breathe especially after Khazbulatov, then Chairman of the Supreme Soviet, arrived and filled the space with his pipe smoke. Below, a wide level passageway led to a station platform on the secret Metro line. To prevent assault from the underground Metro, they placed two trip-wire mines so they wouldn't be caught by surprise in the darkness.

After a discussion with Korzhakov, General Ratnikov returned above ground to see what was happening up there. As he approached the President's Reception Room, he noticed that there wasn't a single policeman on guard there. The telephones were ringing off the hook. The situation was critical, but no one could understand what was going on. The general sat down in the Presidential armchair and began answering calls from all across Russia—from the Far East and the Urals, from Siberia and St. Petersburg. "I did the best I could to calm people down, telling them that everything was under control, the country was being governed, and there was no panic." Suddenly the black telephone that was connected to the bunker rang. General Ratnikov picked up the receiver and heard a gruff bass voice:

"Who are you?" said the voice.

"And who are you?" responded General Ratnikov.

"I'm Yeltsin!"

"And I'm Ratnikov."

"What are you doing there?" asked Yeltsin.

"I'm on duty, Boris Nikolaevich.[3] I'm governing the country."

"What??!"

"I could only imagine the colorful scene at the other end of the line," said Ratnikov. Then a call from the U.S. Embassy came in. The Americans made an offer: they would open their gates to Yeltsin and company and hide them in their Embassy if they escaped through the back door of the Parliament Building. Yeltsin flatly refused the offer. When Korzhakov arrived, Ratnikov reported that, in his opinion, "no assault would take place. It would be real madness to launch an assault with such enormous crowds of people present."

It was after three in the morning when they all came up from the bunker, the situation over. Mstislav Rostropovich, a well-known cellist, arrived and walked around the Parliament Building with a submachine gun. "Of course, no one would have allowed him to endanger his life, and the crowd was pleased at the time that the intellectuals were with them!" said General Ratnikov.

Later, the intelligence services analysts came to the conclusion that this was all done at Gorbachev's instruction.[4] They figured that nobody would have undertaken these measures without the leader's knowledge and approval. The analysts were all afraid and covered their own behinds. Gorbachev wasn't sure how this "comedy" would play out, so he kept aloof to ensure that he would win no matter what happened. But none of the members of the State Emergency Committee had anything like a charismatic personality. The entire nation saw them on TV with their shaking hands, their haunted looks—they all looked as if they wanted to avoid taking part in this farce and were simply carrying out orders. "That is why it all ended so badly: one of them hanged himself, another shot himself. They were weak individuals, unable either to dare to disobey the command of the leadership or to act on their own initiative."

"Gorbachev soon returned to Moscow and squatted on his haunches in the Kremlin like a beaten dog—he had gained nothing," said General Ratnikov. "It was clear to most people in Russia that this whole charade was his doing. Pity the poor besieged President of the USSR under siege. Besieged by whom?! Nothing of the sort! He had armed security forces under his personal command right there, military ships awaiting his signal, and phones that worked— not to mention Security Services communication systems. It was nothing more than a cheap performance."[5]

Most likely, the State Emergency Committee idea was the brainchild of Gorbachev's wife, Raisa Maksimovna. "She was the one capable of analyzing, calculating things and proposing such a plan. She, not Gorbachev, was the one who deployed the staff and wove together the plot."

But times had already changed for the USSR. Since violence inevitably begets violence, popular discontent with the system had steadily grown. The winds of freedom were exhilarating, and fear could no longer be used to hold anything back. "It was no longer possible for the then General Secretary Gorbachev, who was a rather weak-willed person, to continue ruling by fiat, through force and coercion, as had been the case since Stalin's times."

After the stressful days of the August coup, Yeltsin decided to get some medical attention and rest and relaxation at the Palanga resort off the Gulf of Finland. Korzhakov accompanied him, and I stood in for Korzhakov. "At his suggestion, I met with the General Secretary," said General Ratnikov. "I can see the scene before me now: Mikhail Sergeyevich (Gorbachev) in shirtsleeves and suspenders, walked over to a meeting table that seated twelve. Gorbachev greeted me and got right down to business. His business was a proposal to create a new security structure that would function separately from the KGB, because he no longer trusted the KGB's agencies." This was the origin of the General Directorate of Security, which was later divided into the Presidential Security Service headed by Korzhakov and the Federal Security Service headed by Barsukov. Ratnikov became Barsukov's Deputy, responsible for operations and analysis. He also supervised the staff, technical operations service, and other departments.

Having set the foundation of Boris Ratnikov's place in Soviet and Russian political history, and for the subject of this book, it was before the coup that General Ratnikov began his work in parapsychology, though it was in the new post-Soviet Russia that most of his work occurred.

"I came to parapsychology in a rather unexpected and roundabout way. I had nothing to do with it during my years of service as a rank-and-file KGB officer, and it wasn't until I reached the rank of colonel that I came into contact with this field. Although I knew that the KGB kept track of psychics and scrutinized their activities closely, I wasn't aware of any specialized parapsychology programs, probably because they were outside the purview of my responsibilities."

His first encounter with the psychic world came when he wound up serving in the Secret Service, providing security for Boris Yeltsin when he was still Chairman of the Supreme Soviet of the Russian Republic. As an officer-analyst, Ratnikov had always been interested in the circumstances in people's lives that lead them towards a particular situation, and the lure of psychic experiences was one more "circumstance" that directed people's lives to a specific place. It seemed that his life and career up until that point was leading him in that direction. How he got from the KGB to the parapsychological world is a story in itself. It may even seem superfluous to the ESP Wars, but understanding the people involved is always telling—context for what they later do with psi.

Boris Konstantinovich Ratnikov was born on June 11, 1944 in a village not far from Moscow. His father had fought during the war and was the chairman of a collective farm for 25 years. This was the Stalinist era, and as time progressed after the war, everything was in ruins and people were starving. People would occasionally write denunciations against his father, alleging that he was allowing collective farm property to be pilfered, and Ratnikov's father really did look the other way when widows, hard-pressed to feed their children, took home farm milk hidden in hot-water bottles under their clothes. "My father could have been arrested and thrown into the Gulag for this, but somehow things worked out."

Boris Ratnikov graduated from high school in 1964, then left for Moscow and enrolled in the Moscow Aviation Institute. He graduated from the Aviation Institute in 1969 and went to work in the design office of the Scientific Research Institute of Aviation in the town of Zhukovsky. Americans might be surprised by the next statements: "I worked there for three years and realized that this job was not for me. I was more interested in working with people, so I turned in an application to work for the KGB." Most of us would assume that "working with people" was not a reason to work for such an entity, especially given the place of KGB agents in Western spy and crime novels, TV shows and movies. Just as we have overzealous government agents and ones with compassion (and a sense of humor) in our agencies, the KGB did as well.

The KGB checked him out for a year, scrutinizing not only the routine details in his application form, but also the psychological details of his personality profile. Ratnikov received a positive evaluation, and was sent to the KGB Officers School in Minsk. There he and others were trained to be dedicated public servants.

They taught us to look at all political and economic situations; in fact, everything that transpired from the point of view of the State and not from the vantage point of a separate individual. We were expressly required to read all the literature that our citizens were forbidden to read, and we took pride in understanding that we were protecting the interests of our fatherland, not the members of the Politburo. We were taught that working with people required our best human qualities. For example, although the KGB investigated many people, officers were taught that it was important to exercise extreme caution in dealing with people, that is, to conduct investigations without people suspecting it, so that innocent people were not morally traumatized.

All this does not match the image of the KGB that has lingered from Stalinist times and reinforced in the West, but it was precisely the way officers were trained in the KGB during the 1970s.

Ratnikov completed his courses with honors and was assigned as an authorized regional operative in the Municipal Department of the KGB in Ramenskoye, a town near Moscow. He worked there for several years, at various classified aviation enterprises, supervising their operations. It was during that period—"the year 1980 as I recall"—that he had his first encounter with ESP. "We were on duty round the clock, providing security for the Moscow Olympics. Afterwards, I was rewarded with a month-long cruise to Southeast Asia." But of course, this wasn't just a cruise, it was also an official trip. The cruise was expensive and out of reach of the average person, so there were mostly sales people and high-level lawyers on board ship. There were three of them from the KGB. Their mission was to see that nobody embarrassed their nation abroad or defected.

The tour program included a "Miss Cruise" pageant. As if to spite the situation, "all the women in our group could hardly be called young. What could we do?" Ratnikov recalls that he "decided to help my group 'hypnotize' all the tourists. I looked quite young and had a trim figure." So he thought about it and volunteered himself to compete for the title of "Miss Cruise." The ladies present started to giggle, but enthusiastically embraced his idea. Said Ratnikov:

They put lipstick on my lips, squeezed me into a stiff bra, and wrapped towels around my hips. They decked me out in a wig and a hat, and, as a fragrant finishing touch, sprayed me with perfume. They turned this KGB officer into quite a pretty woman! To be more convincing, I began attuning myself to the "archetypal feminine," visualizing an attractive mental image and silently suggesting that I was a woman to my associates.

And it all worked. There I was, walking down the runway! Everyone was amazed—where had this beauty come from, where had she been hiding? The contest began and they posed the question, "How did the weight of our ship change after we stopped in Tokyo? I answered in my pretend female voice that the weight of our ship had decreased, because people lose weight under stress. The passengers rushed out to go shopping onshore but when they saw the high prices, they got very upset and lost weight—and so did our ship. Everyone was delighted by my answer. Then they judged our figure, the way we walked, and our manners. And I placed first again! In short, I won the entire contest, and was declared "Miss Cruise." I was presented with a crown and a big sash. Halfway down the runway to receive the awards, I silently took off my disguise and wig. What a scene!

Whether his success was due to the effect of his "mental suggestion" or because the ladies in his group had done their very best, his debut in the role of a female "hypnotist" was unforgettable. Ratnikov's success was also memorable for another reason that had unforeseen consequences. "I had snatched the beauty contest victory from our cruise ladies, and I couldn't imagine that I would now inevitably confront an enemy that was much more formidable than any terrorist—a woman's jealousy, where hypnosis wouldn't protect me!"

Two tall, powerful women from the Rostov group decided to seek revenge. Ratnikov was quietly swimming in a pool, enjoying life, when he was attacked by these two Amazonian women. One of them squeezed him between her thighs, and the other one forcefully lowered his head under water and held him there. "I began to choke, and tried to free myself with all my might, but no such luck! I could see that things were getting really bad and I'd have to save myself, so I bit one of them in a most tender place. She howled from the pain and savagely shredded my back with her sharp claws. I jumped out of the pool and took off, blood running down my back. These wounds took so long to heal that I couldn't sunbathe for the rest of cruise."

During one of their visits together, Ed May asked Ratnikov "Did you win the contest because you look so pretty in a dress, or was this more a commentary about the other women on the ship?"

"Both," he replied with a smile. KGB agents are people, too.

Things changed for Boris Ratnikov after that. In 1981, he was sent to Afghanistan. During several years of service there, he took part in numerous intelligence and combat operations. He met and negotiated with many Afghani leaders, including the leaders of armed bands. He found a common language with almost all of them, so that there was practically no military action in the extensive area that he oversaw, even though it was near the "hot spot" of Kandahar. As a senior KGB officer involved in intelligence who had an inside view of the Afghan campaign in all its details, Ratnikov understood how profoundly terrible the crime was, perpetrated by the instigators of the war, the top leadership of the USSR. "Afghanistan radically changed my attitude toward the Soviet system, and I was not alone—it impacted other KGB officers as well."

After the return from Afghanistan, he worked in aircraft security at the Moscow department of the KGB for nearly three years. It was in early 1991, and the country was already collapsing. "I could see that no one was going to need our services, so I left the KGB and accepted an invitation from Alexander Korzhakov to serve as his assistant in the Security Department for the Supreme Soviet of the RSFSR, of which Boris Yeltsin had recently become chairman." There were twelve people in the Department; some of them were from the Ministry of Internal Affairs, and some from the KGB.

When the coup broke out, the way was paved for the disintegration of the USSR. The structure of the Security Services changed, and a new interpretation of their mission arose. The 9th Directorate of the KGB of the USSR was reformed, and they conducted a great deal of analytical work on the real and potential threats to President Yeltsin and his entourage, threats to the government and threats against the populace. This was when Ratnikov first learned about psycho-technologies. The KGB recommended using Lt. Colonel Georgi Rogozin, an expert in psi-technologies, to develop mechanisms to neutralize the threat of these technologies. Ratnikov secured Rogozin's transfer from the KGB to serve as an advisor in his service.

In 1991, Ratnikov began working with Rogozin, at which time he introduced Ratnikov to the concepts and details of psi. Rogozin displayed his own extrasensory abilities and showed Ratnikov how it was possible to access information as if from thin air by changing one's state of consciousness. Since Ratnikov had a technical education, he naturally wanted to understand the physical aspects of this process. He soon discovered that science views these phenomena in different ways. "After reading Vernadsky and his theory of the noosphere, Tsiolkovsky, the theories of our cosmologists, psychologists and physicists, and studying the literature from the West, I formed an understanding of this phenomenon based on this knowledge. Academic science is very orthodox. It tries to explain these phenomena from the position of the materialistic world and repeatedly excludes the concept of a higher source. Everything that does not fit into its established system is considered unacceptable."

For this reason, his initial attitude toward psycho-technologies was not very positive, and he considered them akin to spiritism or even charlatanism. However, he gradually opened his mind to the concepts he was being exposed to. He came to understand a bit more about the history of beliefs about psi, shamanic tradition, and practices that would otherwise be called "magical," even though he recognized that in their appropriate context, such things were no more "magical" than many beliefs in Christianity and other major religions. As commentary on this, he said "Those of our ancestors who were initiated into them undermined the authority of the church—primarily the Christian church—which considered that only members of a religious cult would possess these secrets, never ordinary citizens. Thus the Christian Ecumenical Council of 533 declared that initiations into altered states of consciousness were the Devil's instigations, and that they needed to be stopped by any means necessary." History has shown that in the time since, such reaction and doctrine led to the persecutions and eventually massive witch hunts and burnings in the Old World, and accusations and hangings in the New—even though as many (or some say more) of the accusations and executions were actually politically or economically motivated.

As it happened, a new wave of mass immersion in psi and related concepts resurfaced in the USSR. "The stressful conditions of people's lives led to the mass induction into altered states of consciousness in which people met and spoke with their relatives, both dead and alive," said Ratnikov. "This helped people to survive in intolerable conditions of physical and moral degradation. Security guards were unaware of it as prisoners did not openly reveal their meditation activity at all nor even discuss it out loud. But, this is how people received the truth and food for their own spirits, how they evolved."

When Ratnikov understood the basic concept, Rogozin familiarized him with the trance process, and how to enter and maintain it. Since we receive information externally with the help of our sensory organs, there are many different ways of entering into a trance—through tactile sensations, massage, hypnotic passes, fragrances, smoke and beverages with particular flavorings. Music and certain rhythms also facilitate entry into altered states of consciousness. All these methods enhance the ability of one's consciousness to float, so to speak, and "by entering altered states, it is possible to connect with the information field of the Earth."

There are different ways to receive information in an altered state of consciousness. One of them is commonly known as automatic writing, which occurs when one allows one's hand to write (or draw or paint) without conscious control. This can happen while in an altered state, or even in a "normal" state of consciousness, and was a technique also used by some of the US military remote viewers. The hand is under control of the unconscious, which is passing through information either from the unconscious (and often a creative process) or outside sources of information. Ratnikov learned that one can ask questions, go into a trance and write down answers to these questions as if taking dictation. "But this method is fraught with many errors: an individual cannot enter into a state of deep hypnosis by himself, and many external factors in the environment can prove distracting or irritating.

"Another method is that of isolated self-hypnosis, when a person no longer sees or hears anything around him: the information that comes through is purer and more authentic than with automatic writing." The ideal method is immersion in an isolation tank of warm salty water—a sensory deprivation tank—which John Lilly describes so well in his somewhat dated book The Center of the Cyclone and which was central to the plot of the film Altered States (1980).

"I became very interested in the practical application of ESP and these psi-techniques to carry out intelligence missions. Of course, distortions in the information are possible, depending on the time an experiment is conducted, how the psychic felt the night before the experiment, whether he was under stress or drank, in what season the research was conducted, and so on." All these external environmental factors exert particular influences on the information obtained, and point to the perennial problem in psi research for everyone.

Ratnikov and the researchers tried to compensate for these distortions through comparative analysis of the data. They posed questions about real and potential threats, filmed the responses of the psychic operatives and recorded them on tape. After decoding the data, they did an analysis. "If there was logical proof that a threat was real, we wrote a request to Intelligence and other branches of the KGB and Special Services to investigate and 'illuminate' these issues. As a result we had the confirmation of real intelligence data that we could append to the document that we were sending to our superiors so they could take appropriate measures." The following are some early striking examples, the first related to their primary mission: protecting top State officials.

In 1992, Boris Yeltsin traveled to America on an official visit in the capacity of President of Russia for the first time. He was accompanied by Yuri Skokov, Secretary of the State Security Council. Said Ratnikov:

Our service prepared a psychic to supervise security for the visit remotely from Moscow.

In the middle of the visit, the psychic operative suddenly informed us that some kind of technique of psychic influence was being applied to Skokov. It turned out that he was attending a meeting at the country estate of a major American businessman who was connected with the CIA. Naturally, US leaders were very interested in the internal mechanism by which political decisions were being made in Russia. This mechanism constantly shifted due to the rapid changes in the former USSR and Yeltsin's unpredictability, and it was difficult for the CIA to track it. As a result, the CIA could not resist the temptation of using Skokov's presence to try to learn about this mechanism from him through psychic means.

Naturally, we tried to protect Skokov from this psychic influence and to block the leak of information through extrasensory methods. I think we were successful. The truth be told, Skokov felt bad physically at this time and soon left that meeting. When he returned from the visit to the US, I personally verified all our ESP data with him, and he confirmed it completely.

[Authors' note: We should point out that there was no confirmation from the US side that such psychic influence was being directed at Skokov by anyone connected with Star Gate or the related ESP units, or any other US source.]

A second situation happened at the end of 1992, when diplomatic channels were studying the matter of Yeltsin's visit to Japan. According to the State Security Council's data, Yeltsin was preparing to hand over two or three of the Kuril Islands to Japan during his visit to demonstrate his new foreign policy. He was being influenced to take this step by certain members of his inner circle. As the issue of the Kuril Islands was very delicate, there was a need to check out the situation and the possible scenarios of how events might unfold. Ratnikov continued:

We prepared a very skilled psychic to connect with the information field. We conducted a session and received information that indicated that as soon as Yeltsin transferred the islands to Japan, China would lay claim to territories they disputed with Russia. This situation would be favorable to many political forces in the world, so their goal was to steer China's leaders toward a military confrontation with Russia, and have the international community declare China an aggressor. Then the United Nations and a number of countries could apply economic and political sanctions against China as an aggressor that had encroached on the sovereign territory of another state.

This would be very advantageous for China's political and economic competitors. But that wasn't all—the situation would go much further. China could react to the pressure in this case and undertake local military action against Russia, as it had at the end of the 1960s. However, in 1993 it would have resulted in a large-scale war in Southeast Asia.

When Ratnikov and company received this catastrophic prediction, they simply could not believe it. The decision was made to check out whether this information had a solid basis and whether the events might unfold according to the predicted script through the intelligence and counterintelligence agencies and services. "A careful check showed that the proposed situation and its consequences were entirely realistic. So that meant it would be impossible to return the islands to Japan."

After meeting with Barsukov and Korzhakov, he reported on the situation to Yuri Skokov. He supported them completely, immediately went to the President, and insisted that the visit be cancelled. But the answer he got from Yeltsin, in addition to some very unpleasant words, was, "Am I the Tsar or not?! If I want to, I'll give them away! If I don't want to, I won't!"

Ratnikov understood that it was useless to expect Yeltsin to behave reasonably, and made the decision to act on his own. The preliminary schedule of the visit had already been sent to Japan, and it came back with revisions:

Yeltsin must not go out into the streets of Tokyo "to meet the people" because there are a lot of motorcyclists who could throw bottles with explosive compounds.

Yeltsin would not be able to attend a sumo competition because it was impossible to screen all the fans. However, according to etiquette, it was also impossible to seat Yeltsin in the Emperor's box.

Yeltsin must not visit the monument in Kyoto dedicated to the Russian sailors who died rescuing the Japanese during an earthquake, because the cemetery was densely overgrown, and there could be a terrorist hiding in the bushes. If the President were to engage in these activities, the Japanese side would not guarantee the President's safety.

Ratnikov's group decided to use these three prohibitions as a pretext to cancel Yeltsin's trip and not permit him to go to Japan. The next day, Minister of Foreign Affairs Kozyrev was meeting with the Japanese Minister of Foreign Affairs. "I was instructed to talk with Kozyrev. I intercepted him before the negotiations and told him that I had been instructed by the President to have a conversation with him, although the President had not given me any such instructions. I explained that the Japanese side was not providing a 100% guarantee of Yeltsin's safety, and I had been asked to request guarantees once again from the Japanese minister in case Yeltsin failed to observe the three prohibitions stipulated in their protocol. Naturally, the Japanese minister would not assume any additional responsibilities. We immediately wrote up Kozyrev's answer in a memorandum to the State Security Council.

Following this, Ratnikov had to fly to Tokyo. Korzhakov signed a document, granting him special powers. In Tokyo, he met with the Russian Ambassador to Japan and explained to him that it was necessary to prevent the visit. "I think that it terrified him, and he didn't know how to react. Then I met with representatives of the Japanese Security and Secret Services, and we discussed how to organize protection procedures, the formation and the route of the procession, the means of communication. While I was leaving I asked, as if an afterthought, whether they could fully provide for the President's security with regard to the three designated points, because our President allegedly would not agree to any restrictions."

Ratnikov received a negative response and boiled over with feigned righteous indignation: "What? How can you, the Security and Secret Services professionals, not provide 100% guarantee of our President's safety?! Why did you invite him to your country? I will report that the visit was badly planned on your part."

The Japanese were completely bewildered.

That evening, Ratnikov gave an interview to a representative of the Russian TV-program Time. "They asked how the preparations for our President's visit were going, and I replied that the situation was not good, that the Japanese side was not ready, and that our President's security was not being adequately guaranteed." Ratnikov immediately sent off an encrypted message to Moscow. Skokov urgently convened the State Security Council with a single issue on the agenda: whether Yeltsin should go to Japan. All the members of the council were already predisposed by the Time program, and there was also his encrypted message and the memo about Kozyrev's conversation with the Japanese minister. "Well, who would dare vote for the visit after getting such a snow job? Everyone voted against the visit."

Skokov presented Yeltsin with a fait accompli: the Security Council had decided to postpone the President's visit to Japan for security reasons. The mission was accomplished, and we retained the islands. As for the Japanese, they hardly would have been overjoyed to receive these islands if it resulted in a war in this region.

On December 29, 1992, the psychic operative from Ratnikov's group received information relating to a meeting between President

Yeltsin and the first President Bush, scheduled in Sochi three days later. The psychic's information purported that if the meeting of the Presidents was to be held in Sochi, serious problems would arise during the negotiations. Neither Russia nor America needed such complications. This meant that the meeting needed to be moved elsewhere, that is, to Moscow. But how? "Yeltsin did not understand reasonable arguments, and he was already drinking, celebrating the upcoming New Year's holiday early. My rank did not permit me to telephone Bush personally. But there wasn't enough time to develop a complex intrigue like the one in the case of the visit to Japan."

Ratnikov was given instructions to fly immediately to Sochi, where preparations for the visit were going on. As New Year's Eve arrived, it was snowing lightly, and a frost began to set in late in the day. President Bush's plane was scheduled to land at the Sochi airport, but there was a plane ahead of it with the people providing security for his visit. The landing strip was a little slippery and shorter than standard airstrips, and the heavy Boeing taxied almost to the edge of the airport, where some old, broken-down planes were parked. Ratnikov met the delegation at the passenger stairs, and when asked about Bush's security, he pointed to the scrap metal that lay about and said to them: "Look, you nearly wound up in a dump. The landing strip is already iced over, and it'll soon get even worse. Weather like this is unusual for Sochi, and we don't have the equipment to clear the landing strip. Bush's plane could go into a skid. It would be better to fly to Moscow."

The Secretary of State contacted Bush's plane, which was already in the air. Bush agreed to change the route, but the Secretary asked Ratnikov to call Yeltsin. "I had to do this so that it would appear as if changing the venue for the meeting was Bush's idea and not mine, otherwise Yeltsin would not take the call. I pretended that I kept calling on the satellite communication system but couldn't get connected to the President. I suggested to the Americans that they try calling Yeltsin, and that's what they did. It looked as if the American President himself wanted to fly to Moscow and have the meeting there. This was good for both Russia and America, and, as for me, I felt that I had done my duty well and I enjoyed a carefree New Year's in Sochi." In Moscow, everyone was in a major uproar, doing the impossible to prepare a new venue for the Presidential meeting on New Year's Eve. "But I think that it was all worth it. I was now already accustomed to trusting my psychics."[6]

While Ratnikov discussed several cases in which ESP was used successfully, he also cited examples where attempts to put it to use proved unsuccessful, though not because the information was incorrect. One such instance occurred in 1992.

Although the Soviet Union had already disintegrated, Yeltsin decided to play peacemaker between Azerbaijan and Armenia, by force of his old habit as the all-Union arbitrator. War had not broken out yet, but skirmishes were occurring, and a conflict was brewing. Yeltsin believed that the growing conflict could be extinguished if he personally visited Nagorno-Karabakh, an internal political hot spot. Ratnikov's psychic aides stated that Yeltsin's trip to Nagorno-Karabakh would only aggravate the conflict, and that a real war would break out in the Caucasus.

Officially, Ratnikov went to Azerbaijan with the mission of arranging for Yeltsin's visit: to develop their security services procedures and to coordinate the interaction with the KGB of Azerbaijan. When he arrived, he decided to talk to Ayazov Mutalibov, the President of Azerbaijan, about the situation. The President granted Ratnikov an audience at once, and they spoke for about 40 minutes. They reached the decision to persuade Yeltsin not to fly to Karabakh, and Mutalibov promised to do his best.

When Yeltsin's plane landed, Ratnikov rushed on board to report to him that an analysis of this situation predicted that his visit to Nagorno-Karabakh would have extremely negative consequences. "Yeltsin, already tipsy, listened to me and, eyeing me like an angry bull, pushed me away with his hand and silently moved toward the exit. It wasn't until that moment that I understood that the magnificent feast Mutalibov had prepared for the occasion of the Russian President's visit, and all the drinking that would accompany it, was much more important to Yeltsin than the entire Caucasus region and the whole of politics."

The feast began. Mutalibov did not drink, but Yeltsin downed glass after glass. He got roaring drunk. Picture the scene with these two heads of state: Mutalibov trying to convince Yeltsin not to go to Nagorno-Karabakh, Yeltsin obstinately sticking to his position, "I'm going, and that's final! And I won't take you with me!" said Yeltsin to the President of the independent country to which Nagorno-Karabakh belongs!

Following this, Yeltsin phoned Nursaltan Nazarbayev, the President of Kazakhstan, with an invitation to accompany him to Karabakh. A few hours later, Nazarbayev arrived and took a helicopter to Karabakh with Yeltsin. "I assumed personal responsibility at that point," said Ratnikov, "and, at my own peril, asked Mutalibov to board a second helicopter with me, and we flew to Karabakh, too. When the two helicopters landed, Yeltsin and Nazarbayev climbed out of one, Mutalibov and I out of the other. When Yeltsin saw Mutalibov, he told Korzhakov pointedly, 'Make sure that I don't see him here!' I was confused and at a loss as to what to do. And what could I do, if our President was so culturally inept and insensitive?"

Ratnikov sequestered Mutalibov in a nearby building for his protection, and asked him to keep out of Yeltsin's sight. In the meantime, an improvised stage on which Yeltsin was to speak was set up; a truck drove up, ramps were lowered, and security guards were posted. A line of local police was stationed about 30 meters from the truck and behind them, a crowd of local residents, mostly Armenians, had already gathered.

Ratnikov was standing and watching the crowd as Yeltsin began his half-inebriated though fiery speech about how everyone needed to live in peace. Suddenly he noticed a movement that reminded him of something he had seen in Afghanistan. The men moved toward the back, leaving the women and children facing the police line. Ratnikov quickly approached the men from the Special Forces Alpha group and instructed them to close ranks "because a breakthrough was obviously being prepared: first the children would dive under the row of police, and then the women would rush after them." The police line would be breached, and then the men would break through the opening.

That's exactly what happened—or rather what they attempted. The crowd tried to break through, but the Alpha group stood firm, and everyone understood that if something happened, these men would shoot. "People began shouting that the land should be given to the Armenians, and they threw rotten vegetables. Yeltsin quickly withdrew, and they were forced to evacuate him, along with

Nazarbayev, to Gandzha, a small neighboring town."

At the last moment, Ratnikov barely had time to push Mutalibov into a government car. "Yeltsin was terribly angry and got drunk again to improve his mood. Then he fell asleep." The great conciliatory mission had ended.

Just as had been surmised, Yeltsin's visit only aggravated an already critical conflict. A real war broke out soon after his trip to Nagorno-Karabakh. "It turned out that our psychic operatives were completely correct in their predictions," though the information could not be acted upon in a way to prevent Yeltsin from undertaking the visit.

"Yeltsin's actions towards the Chechen Republic resulted in even more catastrophic consequences, and we were unable to prevent them. Our psychic operatives warned us repeatedly about the terrible events that were coming to a head in the Chechen Republic, and that it was essential to demonstrate the maximum mutual understanding, self-control and good will to balance the critical situation. All sober-minded, reasonable people also understood this fact."

Dzhokhar Dudayev, the President of Chechnya, repeatedly tried to have a meeting—or at least a telephone conversation—with Yeltsin, but he failed in all his attempts. Prime Minister Chernomyrdin, Minister of Defense Pavel Grachev, and the President's Assistant Victor Ilyushin exhibited particular enthusiasm for kindling this conflict. Conspiracy was closing around Chechnya and many people wanted to use the military conflict in the Chechen Republic to privatize its oil resources, engage in illegal arms trade, and plunder the money budgeted for that region.

The top management at the Security Services understood this and tried their utmost to prevent the military conflict. Based on intelligence information and the predictions they received from the psychics, Korzhakov and Ratnikov wrote an agency memo stating that sending troops to Chechnya and engaging in combat operations there would lead to disastrous consequences. They cited the example of Afghanistan.

That evening Korzhakov informed the President about the memo, and to their relief, Yeltsin agreed with it on the whole. However, the next morning he made the decision to send troops to Chechnya anyway. "We investigated why Yeltsin had reversed his decision and discovered that, after Korzhakov left that evening, Chernomyrdin visited Yeltsin later and that they had apparently talked with plenty of drinking until midnight. It immediately became clear that vodka bore the most responsibility for starting the Chechen war."

According to Ratnikov, the work with ESP is fraught with a number of limitations as well as "off-limits information" that for some reason cannot be accessed, or at least gotten with any degree of accuracy or depth. "We were continuously interested in how the political situation in Russia would develop in the near future, and thus, in detecting the initial indications of social unrest and preventing civil war," said Ratnikov.

In 1993, they were analyzing the conflict between President Yeltsin and Vice-President Rutskoi, looking a half-year ahead with Rogozin in the role of the psychic operative. What they got was a picture of Rutskoi in prison.

They tried to get more clarity about the situation to ensure that it was reliable, but the answer received was on the order of, "This information is not completely reliable, but you won't get information that is more exact because the world is filled with probable ways in which events can unfold—different versions of the future are possible. Besides, you simply must not be given key information about the future because of your level of spiritual development, otherwise the whole world would go to hell." In other words, according to Ratnikov sometimes someone or something interfered with the information process in order to protect humanity.

"In addition to certain information being essentially off-limits to us, there was also the matter of interpretation." In order for information to be evaluated more precisely, criteria needed to be developed to understand what relates to what. These criteria were developed over time during investigative research as well as through an operative's individual life experience. On countless occasions, the group received information about attempts to assassinate the President: they described the nature of the attempt, the time, and the individual would-be perpetrator who would carry it out.

"We would record it and carefully check it out—but there would be no correlation and no assassination attempt. I would return to the operatives again and again with the question: why was the information erroneous?" The operatives would tell Ratnikov that they had interpreted the symbolic picture they received literally. "One has to be able to separate the symbolic from the real, interpret it skillfully and take into account a great many factors including the operative's mental state and his level of personal interest, the specific techniques being used." This is very difficult to do—only teams of skilled psychics and their monitors can do it. "Using group methods and group consciousness is advisable. In addition, after a careful analysis of the facts, they must be compared with information received from other sources such as traditional intelligence gathering."

As a result of trial and error, they found that it was more effective to ask about the probabilities of a particular threat before it reached the point when it was to happen. They could clarify each probability's significant attributes or indicators ("We called them znakovye priznaki) to track them at the level of reality as benchmarks of the changing likelihood of the event. We asked for advice about what to focus on. We were given the znakovye priznaki, and I would immediately start writing up a card of the indicators of each probability. Then, with the help of my colleagues, I would analyze which of the probabilities was rapidly unfolding and map out a system of its indicators to help us consciously calculate how the probability would develop, and track its consistency. This was how I came to understand where this particular probability could lead in reality." Using this method of tracking probabilities can substantially increase the reliability of information.

This view of precognition lines up with the research of Ed May and a number of other western parapsychologists. It seems precognition works with probable futures, whether or not they actually come to pass. In other words, at the moment of the precognitive perception, the viewer is picking up on the most (or one of the most) probable future outcomes—later events bring that future into being, or change the probabilities so that it does not happen.

According to Ratnikov, "Psychic operatives claim that all predictions are probabilistic by nature. The future contains a spectrum of opportunities rather than one absolutely certain future. The choice depends on us. However, choosing the future involves more than just what we desire—it includes our efforts, our understanding, our ethics, and our own work. Even the most talented psychics, even the saints, cannot make choices for us, not to mention fortunetellers and all the other sorts of charlatans!"

And there are certainly charlatans to spare in this field. Ratnikov recalled meeting with one of them—Grigory Grabovoi. "In 1994, our psychologist and I were invited for consultation by Dmitry Rumyantsev, the head of personnel department for the Russian Federation Presidential Administration. Grabovoi had talked his way into a meeting with Rumyantsev and began to praise his extrasensory abilities, puffing himself up in every possible way. He lived in Tashkent at the time and wanted to be hired by the President's Administration at a salary of no less than two thousand dollars a month, plus a three-room apartment in Moscow."

Both Ratnikov and the psychologist were surprised at Grabovoi's aplomb, his demands, and his obviously unacceptable behavior. It was clear that what they had in front of them was a swindler suffering from pathological megalomania. Nevertheless, to be completely rigorous, they asked Grabovoi to demonstrate his ESP abilities by stopping the elevator between floors. Grabovoi refused, claiming an ability to diagnose mechanisms, not influence them. He probably forgot that he had just assured the two of the total opposite several minutes before; nor could he show off his diagnostic abilities, and so Ratnikov's agency had absolutely no interest in him.

Ratnikov informed Korzhakov about the conversation, and Korzhakov remarked that Moscow had enough swindlers already without adding any more from Tashkent. Ten years later, they learned that Grabovoi was deceiving mothers in Beslan by promising to resurrect their lost children. "I sincerely regretted that our Special Services had not dealt with this swindler effectively when we encountered him in 1994," said Ratnikov. "After all, we could have cleared society of trash like him back then and protected the Beslan mothers and many other people from being defrauded."

When the throne beneath Yeltsin began to wobble in 1993, bureaucrats from the administration came to Ratnikov with their questions about which side they should lean toward and where they should place their bets in order not to lose out in the political intrigues. His answer to all of them was, "Guys, place your bets on the Fatherland, and you'll be respected by both your friends and your opponents. This way you won't lose." He openly pointed out one of the main znakovye priznaki, but they thought that he was hiding extrasensory information about the future and playing political games. However, Ratnikov's group really did not have any authentic psychic information about the shelling of the Parliament and other impending events.

His own disappointment with the political and social course on which their ruling elite had embarked grew steadily. Yeltsin, who was still concerned about the Russian people and still trying to do something for them at the end of the 1980s, had turned into "a reigning petty tyrant. Power had completely corrupted him, and he thought only of his own greatness and vodka. His entire inner circle was primarily engaged in pillaging the nation. I was disgusted of having to take part in this and I refused an elite apartment in the center of Moscow and a summer dacha in the fashionable Moscow suburb of Zarechye, and I absolutely refused to accept bribes or take any part in shady commercial operations. As a result I became a thorn in the Kremlin's side."

Ratnikov tried to do analytical work, studied the probabilities of threats, assessed social probabilities, and submitted his reports to his superiors. They reacted with irritation to his memos, because this would have required that they think about the country and take action, and the higher-ups had other concerns. There were remarkable and honest people among them too, but they had no influence at all. Yeltsin was in charge—he was the only one who mattered. Boris Ratnikov's personal crisis coincided with the crisis of power and authority in Russia and the shelling of the Parliament in October 1993.

He recalled a typical incident from that time when passions had reached boiling point and agitated crowds were gathering in the streets:

The day before the Russian White House initially came under assault, Barsukov ordered me to investigate a new weapon for crowd control that had been recommended to him by a government official. I thought that it might be some psychotronic weapon from the classified research institutes that I had no part developing. When the inventor arrived with the device, we discovered that it was a powerful laser intended for cutting up objects. I immediately sent the inventor and the device away, and told the bosses what I thought about it in no uncertain terms.

I could not endure this any longer. I did not side with Parliament, but after all the blood that had been spilled, after the outrages against human conscience and the Russian Constitution, I could no longer remain in the service. I wrote an official report tending my resignation. But I did not bring it to Barsukov, I had the secretary deliver it.

An hour later, the secretary brought me a decree about my dismissal signed by Yeltsin, with no indication of the reason. For some crafty reasons I was being discharged, not dismissed, and was to be kept in reserve temporarily. I was given verbal instructions to turn over my safe, and told that I would be placed under house arrest. My phone would be tapped, and I would be put under overt surveillance. Because it was understood that I was respected by my colleagues in the KGB-FSB, and could always reach some agreement with them, I was placed under the surveillance of the Ministry of Internal Affairs. The top leadership was in fear over their dark secrets. I knew too much, and they were afraid that I would switch over to the opposition and pass classified information to them. I had no intention of doing this because I understood that the opposition was no better than the central leadership. I did what I had advised others to do: I placed my bet on the Fatherland, which was the only right and honest decision at the time.

I was under overt surveillance round the clock for a few weeks. December was coming to an end, and it was snowing. One day I was sitting at home and looking through the window at the surveillance car. The two young guys sitting in it were totally stiff from the cold. I poured some hot tea into a thermos, made sandwiches and took them to the frozen subordinates guarding me. The next day I went to the Kremlin and shamed my former colleagues about using two brigades of police to watch over me while there were so many criminal groups around.

Ratnikov remained in this situation, under surveillance and out of work from November 1993 until May 1994. Time softened the intensity of the conflict, and the opposition was crushed. His own outlook also changed somewhat, though not in any moral sense as his outlook on and assessment of the situation remained the same throughout. But he no longer considered his own actions to be so correct. If everyone who didn't like the present state of politics stuck their noses up in the air and left, then who would remain? "I thought about it, and came to the conclusion that perhaps it would be truer to remain in my place and try to do whatever was in my power to improve the situation. It might not be much, but I would do it anyway!"

Ratnikov went to the Kremlin in May. He had been dismissed from the Secret Service due to staff cutbacks—his position of deputy chief was eliminated the day before he actually left. He met with Korzhakov in the Kremlin and was offered a shot of vodka and asked to work as Korzhakov's advisor in the President's Secret Service. He thought it over and accepted the offer. "I was given an office, a government switchboard telephone, and a car, and I began working as an analyst again. But now there were obstacles arising constantly in our routine work with psychics. To a large extent, this was due to the ruling clique, who feared that we could read their minds, and almost all of them were guilty of something." One wonders if any in the US Congress worried about this with regard to the US psychic spying efforts.

Nonetheless, they did receive curious data from their psychics from time to time. "For example, when we asked why our leadership did not support new technology, the answer we received was that the leadership's spiritual and moral levels were very low, their interests so mercenary, and their inner worlds so impoverished, that they were incapable of comprehending the higher global tasks of saving our civilization. Spiritual and moral issues were too abstract for them, whereas for the Cosmos ethical questions are primary." Again, one might consider whether such issues were (and are) the same for those in the US Government or even Corporate America.

With regard to Yeltsin, Ratnikov and his group were told that Yeltsin's rise to power was not accidental. The populace supported him at that point, but the time would come when people would be disgusted, remembering what he had done. At the time he needed to be susceptible to the same deficiencies that prevailed in Russian society, and "he must not be different from the majority, because people actually do not want a radiant miracle, and would throw stones at it if it suddenly appeared." Yeltsin was a perfect match to the historical situation and corresponded to the overall intellectual and cultural level of the country at the time. A nation virtually always has the leader it deserves. "It was the same for us—we got what we deserved."

His group also worked on emergency situations and accidents. Several days after the Kursk submarine disaster on August 12, 2000, they were able to obtain information about the reasons for the accident with the help of ESP. The accident occurred because the crew was not trained sufficiently to test a new torpedo. A lack of technical readiness resulted in the explosion—a torpedo blew up inside the submarine. The press wrote a lot about the Kursk colliding with another submarine. There was no such collision—ordinary sloppiness, laziness and just showing off were the causes. "If they had assessed all the probable scenarios, the accident would not have happened," said Ratnikov. "But these are technical details, although they are bound up with organizational issues." The most resonant words in the information their psychic operative received was a signal that the wreck of the Kursk was not an accident, it was a critical warning to all people, "Stop! If you do not stop acting the way you do, technology-based accidents will occur with increasing frequency, and their scale will grow larger and more awful until they reach global magnitude!"

"Simply improving technical control 'somewhere out there' is not enough to prevent such accidents. All of us need to work constantly to raise the level of group consciousness. Ideas are like a virus, they invisibly penetrate into the consciousness of people in our environment according to the concept known as the 'information transfer field.' Even if the person does nothing to disseminate information and simply tries to comprehend it, he is a participant in the process because others will respond to the ideas that arose in his mind."

At the same time Boris Ratnikov's parapsychological program was happening in the Federal Security Service and the Presidential Security Service, a new military ESP program started in Russia. The pressure of dull Marxist-Leninist ideology was no longer applied—the climate for exploring ESP had changed. The creation of this program was not elicited by any particular strategic confrontation, but was the natural manifestation of exciting possibilities that had been reawakened. It was for this very reason that the main objective of the most extensive military ESP program in the world, begun in the 1990s in the General Staff of the Armed Forces of the USSR and Russia, was not ESP in and of itself, but the investigation and development of extraordinary human potential. Psychic studies and military applications of ESP methods in this program were means of developing human potential, creating the human of the future, and cultivating super-geniuses as is normally understood. The program was supported by many major government officials, including Soviet Prime Minister Valentin Pavlov, several chiefs of the General Staff, secretaries of the Security Council of the Russian Federation, and a host of the most eminent Academician scientists of Russia's Academy of Sciences.

The creator and head of this program, General Alexei Savin, tells us about it in the next chapter.

NOTES

1) While the attempted coup may have failed, many point to the attempt as the event that helped along the demise of the Soviet Union.

2) The Russian Parliament Building is called the White House for its color, like the American Presidential Building

3) When Russians use two names, as in "Mikhail Sergeyevich," this is not what westerners would do when using middle names (i.e. Mary Ann). They are using a patronymic, which is a modified name of a father. In the example of Gorbachev's name, Sergeyevich means "son of Sergey." Think of this as an extended first name.

4) This version is universally accepted among the personnel of Russian security services and politicians possessing reliable information, as well as in many social circles. For example, this declaration was made repeatedly by the current head of the Communist Party of the Russian Federation, Gennady Zyuganov: http://www.newsru.com/russia/17Aug2001/zuganov.html. In fact, most Russians see Mikhail Gorbachev as the reason for the demise of the USSR. While few in the West see it this way, many Russians, who know Gorbachev and his politics better, are convinced of it. According to a survey by the Public Opinion Foundation, 44% of Russia's population consider him to be responsible for the Soviet Union's collapse: http://bd.fom.ru/report/cat/societas/image/collapse_FSU/of19953203. More than once, the issue of Gorbachev being prosecuted for his actions during the coup of 1991 has been discussed widely. Thus, in an interview about Gorbachev's guilt, former vice-president of the Military Panel of the Supreme Court of the Russian Federation, Lieutenant General of Justice Anatoly Ukolov stated openly, "I am convinced and truly believe that this issue should be raised as a criminal case." http://www.kp.ru/daily/23758/56414/.

5) Further information on this subject can be found in The Kremlin Plot, whose co-authors are Russia's former public prosecutor-general, Valentin Stepankov, and his deputy, Evgeny Lisov. Another good source can be found in documents from the 1992 hearings conducted by a governmental commission in the Supreme Soviet of the Russian Federation, directed by Representative and Deputy Minister of Security Sergei Stepashin, who is also an expert on the role of the KGB during the events of the coup in August, 1991, and in other documents.

6) This account reached the New York Times. See www.nytimes.com/1993/01/03/world/bush-s-last-hurrah-in-cold-wintry-moscow.html

CHAPTER 9

MILITARY MAGIC AND THE GENERAL STAFF: TOP SECRET MILITARY UNIT 10003

Authors' Note: The following is based on interviews with and written material from Gen. Savin. We've attempted to keep the narrative in context with the quoted material, all based on the interviews with Gen. Savin.

LT. GENERAL ALEXEI SAVIN'S STORY:

Lieutenant General Alexei Yuryevich Savin, Ph.D. was and is a major player in the Russian ESP Wars. General Savin has provided us with his story and perspective, which takes us into the Russian military's psychic program. As with our other players in the ESP Wars, providing a bit of his background will further support the idea that people who are serious about the subject, especially when trying to apply ESP to real world scenarios, are not the "woo woo" types or "flakes" that the pseudo-skeptics and debunkers would have us believe.

Creative thinking can be said to be behind "thinking outside the box," something extremely important in the advancements of Science and Technology. Psi can certainly be considered outside that "box." Parapsychology in the West has found a direct correlation between forms of creativity and psi performance, so, it's no real surprise that Alexei Savin was born into a musical family. His mother was a dramatic actress and singer and his father had perfect pitch and played several instruments. His father was more than that, as he was also gifted in mathematics and physics, trained at the N. A. Zhukovsky Air Force Academy, and became an aviation officer—eventually a Major General of the Soviet Air Forces.

Lt. General Alexei Savin

Because of his father, Savin was well acquainted with the Army from childhood, and dreamed about military duty thanks to the postwar heroism of the Soviet Armed Forces inspiring him. "But, at the same time," he said, "I remained immersed in the world of music, literature, fantasy, and theater, which prepared me psychologically to delve deeply into the world of human ideas, imagination, feelings and experiences."

His childhood was a bit atypical, as he endured an unusual succession of illnesses. At age six, he was pronounced clinically dead after a botched appendectomy. He suffered a second apparent death from pneumonia at age seven, and experienced a near-death experience yet again when he was eight. "I complained to my grandmother about my poor health, and she said, 'Beseech the Lord.'

"I began to address God in my thoughts and immediately felt a response. Not yet realizing what was entering my life, I put my faith in this almighty force. Ever since I was a child, I had wanted to peek beyond the brink separating life and death, and to understand what happens there. And this was how my first ESP experiences began." After the third near-death experience, Savin felt that he could read other people's minds, literally "pick up" on them, and clearly detect the flow of a person's thoughts. "I began to sense new qualities in myself. Information about people's destinies—when and why they would die—began coming to me."

Given the above, it's interesting to consider again how the phrase "Godless Communist" became so associated with American ideas about citizens of the Soviet Union. They may have had an extreme separation of Church and State, but the people were far from godless themselves.

Savin's psychic experiences continued throughout his life. He once predicted the death of a good friend of his, the president of the USSR Sports Federation on Weightlifting. He came to visit at the Savin home, and when they shut the door after he left, Alexei shocked his parents by saying, "It's a pity that 'uncle' Dima will die today, just before he gets home." The words were indeed prophetic, as the man actually did die of a heart attack quite near his own house. Alexei's parents tried to explain to him in every possible way that reading another person's mind is no better than spying through a keyhole and that no one should predict when a person will die because this knowledge could rob him of a complete life by causing him to wait, in mental torment, for death.

Savin began paying more and more attention to what his intuition was telling him, and tried to follow these hunches, "recognizing that a certain force was guiding me in my life. I began to seek the meaning of my own life as well as that of all humanity from about the age of fifteen." He read Plato and studied Plotinus's cosmology. He considered questions like "What makes life worth living? At whose behest was this life granted to me? And what is life, anyway?" He searched for answers to these questions in philosophical treatises and in talks with his grandfather, who was a highly intelligent person and closest to him in character. "He explained to me, 'The source of all that exists including our universe is thought, because all creation is conceived in and begins in thought. That's the place to seek answers.'"

Unlike remote viewers in the US who were kept from harm's way, the Russians viewers were on the front lines in the Chechnya campaign, and as such, required combat training in weapons, hand-to-hand combat and knowledge and skill at handling large military systems. When May asked Savin what about 'remote'—as in remote viewing—did he not understand. From May's perspective there was never a need to put viewers in harm's way and keep them remote from the combat. Savin, however, said he found that it allowed the Russian viewer to focus more sharply! The following set of photographs illustrates the point. They were provided by General Savin.

The first result of his extensive inner work was a shift in attitude towards people." I stopped being irritated by people who I thought behaved improperly, after I realized that if God created us all, each individual has his intended purpose and his path. From age seventeen, I understood that we should not separate people by race or nationality. Categories such as 'good' and 'bad' became relative and diffuse. The fact is the same person can behave differently— either as a villain or a hero—in different situations." Wise thoughts for a teenager.

Various kinds of military training for Russian remote viewers: Upper left. Light weapons; Upper right. Hand to hand combat; Lower left. Tanks familiarization; Lower Right. Submarine familiarization.

In 1964, he enrolled in the Sebastopol Naval School to become a naval aircraft radio operator. He immediately became interested in the physics of electromagnetic wave-particles, and began to look for deeper meaning there. "I could barely fathom what others perceived as axiomatic—how such an enormous amount of information could be transmitted along wires. More than thirty years later, I've come to the conclusion that from the standpoint of the laws of physics, this phenomenon still remains unexplained. It looks to me that the physicist Tesla is the only one who came close to understanding this, but I never did find a definitive answer to this question in those of his writings that I studied."

After graduating from the naval school with the rank of lieutenant engineer, Savin was assigned to one of the best research institutes in Russia, known at that time as the Institute of Theoretical Cybernetics (today it is the Scientific Research Institute of Aviation Systems). The Institute was associated with the defense industry and was top secret. He worked there in military reception office #1054, where the work done at the Institute was inspected for quality assurance. The Institute was a refuge for many talented and unconventional thinkers. For example, cruise missiles were conceived and designed in the scientific research institute in the 1950s, long before similar work was begun in the US. These promising designs were kept on ice by the shortsightedness of the top Soviet military brass. As a result, they had to catch up with the Americans. An entire constellation of veritable science fanatics worked practically without breaks or days off within the walls of the institute. "They perceived science through the prism of systems analysis, the inter-relations and interactions of things, and this holistic worldview became the only one possible for me."

During his 16 years working there, Savin completed his graduate work in systems analysis (probability theory, game theory, operations research, the analysis of large systems, etc.), wrote a number of scientific papers about the development of combat aviation, and worked in areas from designing combat aircraft to working out the smallest details of their performance. He wrote a dissertation but didn't manage to defend it, mainly because he was offered the post of senior officer in the Armaments Directorate of the Defense Ministry of the USSR in 1986. He regretted leaving, but he couldn't turn down such a tempting offer.

"I had the occasion to come across many interesting and unusual designs during my work at the Armaments Directorate. During the 1980s, for instance, I worked with a group that investigated torsion fields." The idea of torsion fields is that a very rapidly rotating object creates a new kind of a field which is neither electromagnetic nor like any other known fields. "This is absolutely unique, and has not yet been studied by science. Many people tried to build flying saucers and generators based on this idea, but they didn't achieve anything in particular." Later on, when a special group of analysts responsible for the nation's military aircraft was formed at the Ministry of Defense, Savin was included.

It was at this point in the history of the formation of the Directorate on the Study and Development of Extraordinary Human Capabilities within the General Staff that Savin's involvement with ESP Wars began.

In the late 1980s, a group of civilian psychics contacted the Minister of Defense with a proposal to collaborate. They claimed that they could find lost ships locate missing persons, diagnose illnesses and treat them. This letter found its way to the Chief of the Armaments Directorate. He gave Savin, in his capacity as analyst, the assignment to investigate the matter and write a report with commentary to the Deputy Minister of Defense and the Chief of the General Staff. He assembled a commission of medical doctors, physicists, and military and civilian scientists. They examined the psychics and determined that 80% of their claims were false, while 20% appeared to be genuine. He came to the conclusion that there were several extraordinarily gifted psychic individuals in this group, and informed the leadership of this.

After this report at the Ministry of Defense, he was sent to the Chief of the General Staff, Army General Mikhail Moiseyev. He listened to Savin carefully and suggested that Savin reorganize the department that worked on advanced and non-conventional technologies formerly directed by Colonel Bazhanov, and establish a sector within the General Staff with an area of focus to develop extraordinary human potential, including psi functioning. He provided Savin a staff of ten people, the rank of acting general, and a location with a communications link to the government. Legally it was formalized as Military Unit 10003, a department under the jurisdiction of the General Staff, and almost immediately people began calling this unit "the one thousand and three nights." This was about the same size and support as the Star Gate project at its height.

Here is a close-up the emblem for Unit 10003. McMoneagle, May & Ruble have been given honorary membership in this military Russian remote viewing group.

Lapel pin of the emblem for the Russian 10003 military remote viewing unit

He was allocated an official apartment near the Kropotkinskaya Metro station, which they later used for meetings, negotiations, and experiments they conducted without the hassle of obtaining clearance permissions for civilians to enter the General Staff building. It was in this building that Ed May and Larissa Vilenskaya would first meet Savin. In the several times that the American researchers met him, Savin was not in uniform, underscoring the the nature of the building as non-military.

"We also had a number of other 'support bases' in various military offices, scientific research institutes, and military and civil establishments. Rather, more precisely, we created these support bases as needed. We named the focus area of our work the 'Hidden Human Potentialities and Super-Capabilities Development Program.'"

The goal they set was to develop extraordinary mental capabilities in students such as the ability to memorize great quantities of data, to work with large numbers and data streams in students, and to manifest exceptional creative potential and extrasensory capabilities. They also hoped to endow people with the maximal capacity for work and their bodies with unique physical capacities, which would enable the body to tolerate extreme conditions and mechanical impact without harm. Their intention was not simply to search for psychics and train them to obtain specific information, but to develop to a phenomenal level the potentialities with which nature endowed human beings.

At the same time, they searched for breakthrough trends in the creation of new types of weapons. "We arranged patent research through the Ministry of Education, gained access to all scientific papers, reports, dissertations, conference materials, and so on. Through the auspices of the Ministry of Foreign Affairs we had priority access to attend all the foreign exhibits taking place in our country, as well as the right to examine the exhibitors' materials in detail."

A very high level of secrecy was established for Savin's department from the outset. All the information was reported only to the Chief of the General Staff (equivalent to the Chairman of the Joint Chiefs in the Pentagon). He, in turn, tried to avoid letting the Minister of Defense in on the details of their activities as the Minister was always involved in a web of political intrigues, and it was important to them that politics not interfere with the work. "Marshal Yazov was the Minister of Defense when the area of focus of my research in Military Unit 10003 was being determined. He listened to a report about our proposals and, unable to hold back, said, 'You can make a person believe in the very devil himself. Get out of my sight!'"[1]

So they followed this order. "We were so successful at disappearing that almost a decade went by before the first vague rumors about our work filtered through to the press. The people and organizations with whom we worked knew only what was specifically related to our interaction. Certainly, the commanders of the service branches and their chiefs of staff were informed about our research in general terms, but even they did not know the details." This parallels the US program, which for some time was not on anyone's radar for similar reasons.

According to unwritten bureaucratic rules in Russia, a person who re-appears amidst the top brass is regarded with some degree of suspicion, "yet surprisingly, I was immediately accepted and given assistance in everything," said Savin. "I was subordinate only to Moiseyev in the General Staff, and in due course got to know him well." A clever, powerful, and talented man, Moiseyev was able to gather outstanding people and strong individuals around him. He generally could grasp situations instantly, and was good at sizing up the new and the unknown.

It was there in the General Staff that in 1989 Savin began to systematically study extraordinary human potential and look for the mechanisms which, when understood, could make an ordinary human into a genius through developing his intellectual, physical and psychical potential. "My reasoning was, 'If an entire spectrum of extraordinary abilities exists, this means that mechanisms of their step-by-step formation also exist.'" History is full of examples of how generals have won battles with much smaller armies than those of their opponents. Thus, it is possible to win any campaign by creating a company of grandmasters: "such men, men with extraordinary minds, will beat their enemies in any battle, even in adverse conditions."

Moiseyev was very pleased with the idea, and he gave Savin's program a green light. At his order, several military organizations as well as one of the administrations of the leading Air Force Institutes were made subordinate to the unit. However, the problem of financing arose immediately. They began to handle it according to the standard model in the military bureaucracy and ran into difficulties at every step. "The accepted bureaucratic system of financing research in our nation was so clumsy and inflexible that it could take months, even years, to arrive at decisions, which cooled the ardor of any enthusiast." To raise his subordinates' spirits, Savin constantly shared his most optimistic plans for the future. "However, I myself felt nagging unease."

Savin had the incredible luck to meet Valentin Pavlov, the Finance Minister of the USSR—the most knowledgeable minister in the Soviet government. He helped Savin's group submit their documents properly and to secure the initial financing for their work. They were very grateful to him and did not expect anything further from him.

Then suddenly Valentin Pavlov became the Prime Minister, the second man in charge in the nation after Gorbachev. "We found out about it in the evening while watching television, and at 8 o'clock the next morning he was already at our office with a crate of vodka." Savin added that there was a campaign against drunkenness in the

Soviet Union at the time, and a decree was issued to outlaw drinking alcoholic beverages at the work place. In spite of this, "Pavlov took a bottle from the crate, put it on the table and said to me, 'Gorbachev won't find out and the Lord will forgive us. Let's break the rule and celebrate my promotion.' It sounded funny coming from the mouth of a Prime Minister. We had a drop to drink, and Pavlov said, 'Give me a couple of months, and all your documents will be signed.'" Pavlov also requested that Savin and his group organize an exhibit of their work so as to visually present the main concepts, methods and means of their work with people. Pavlov was very interested in how to tap additional human potential, especially with regard to the intellect.

Savin put together a small exhibit. Within two months (record time for such a request), the Central Committee of the CPSU and the Council of Ministers of the USSR issued a resolution that granted a special place for his research area within the weapons program, with excellent financing. Moreover, Pavlov created a system that would operate in any future political landscape, because it was included in a special part of the budget, which received financing during any administration and in any economic situation. This would be analogous to the "black budgets" in the US government.

Savin's annual budget (in terms of hard currency) was approximately 4 million dollars and remained at this level all through the 1990s and early 2000s, in spite of inflation and fluctuations in the exchange rate. This money was allocated for research and office overhead only. It was not used to pay for employees' salaries, which continued to be paid by the General Staff. Savin said, "It would have cost tens of millions dollars to establish a similar institution in the US Army." In fact, however, it was approximately the same for Star Gate, which included more overhead for private companies such as SRI International and Science Applications International Corporation.

"'Now, let's create a super-elite, which will pull the nation out of this pile of crap,' the Prime Minister said to me."

Together they formulated the mission of creating a new elite in the nation—super-advisors to the government, the Central Committee of the CPSU, and the Ministry of Defense. It was decided that the process be broken up into stages. At first, they planned to create an elite group of 100 to 120 people and to base their training at the Moscow Institute of Physics and Technology. "Our choice of the MIPT as a base organization was not a random one. This institution had created several successful and remarkable programs, and a number of its staff and most distinguished students had already taken our preliminary super-training course. The scientific directors were Nikolai Karlov, the Director of the Institute, a man of great erudition and an intellectual of the highest caliber, and Professor Igor Petrov, a broad-minded man and brilliant systems analyst." They took up the development and evaluation of the new training programs with great enthusiasm. They chose the most successful students, and began to fine-tune the conceptual part of the program together with these "talented guys," refining it to perfection. "This was mainly what we did during the first stage of our work."

Pavlov recommended many talented men to Savin. "Moiseyev helped, and I also scouted them out around the entire country in institutions of higher learning, in industry and in the army. We met the Prime Minister regularly to discuss our work, and we talked a lot about life and politics." Pavlov always listened carefully, and took many notes. He did not spare himself, he wore himself out working, and tried to do everything better than everyone else. This is why he completely overexerted himself when he became Prime Minister. Once, when he had only half an hour of free time because he had urgent matters coming up, he dropped in at Savin's office. "He looked exhausted, and I suggested that he recline on my office cot to rest. He stretched out and immediately fell asleep, and was so tired that he even began to snore. Exactly half an hour went by, and I was already thinking of waking him up, when he suddenly jumped up and cried out, 'Lena, Lena, bring me hot coffee.' (Lena was the name of my secretary). He had such a remarkable sense of responsibility and timing that his internal alarm clock woke him up precisely within half an hour."

If fate had given him the chance to work longer, he would have accomplished a great deal. "But with the downfall of the Soviet Union and Pavlov's arrest, our undertaking was never realized." Pavlov turned out to be an active member of the coup plotters' group (GKChP), and was incarcerated for several years. Pavlov came out of prison broken psychologically, drastically cutting back on his social life and virtually disappearing from view. "This remarkable man died in 2003."

While the main objective was training grandmasters of military art, the General Staff gave General Savin several military operational tasks, one of which was to investigate what ESP can directly accomplish that would be of benefit to their Armed Forces. "The factors of highest priority were ESP espionage and defenses against it. The area of psychic coercion, that is, psychotronic weapons, was treated separately." Given the rumors running around the Western media that the Soviets/Russians were working on psychic mind control, this is especially interesting.

They trained groups in the Navy and Air Force to deal with the operative surveillance of other nations' military forces. After doing several studies of defenses against psi influence, it was concluded that it is practically impossible to cram a program into a foreign president's head that he would carry out with obedience. "Many conditions that were exceedingly difficult to set up are required for such coercion," said Savin, "including a special relaxed psychological state, special circumstances, and time. A president is usually a powerful, strong-willed person, who is monitored by security guards, and who himself is capable of brainwashing anyone he wishes—after all it's not without reason that he became president. So we stopped working on this matter and transferred it to the President's Secret Service and the Federal Security Service."

Naturally, not everyone believed in or supported Savin's group as Prime Minister Pavlov had. They traveled to Zvyozdnyi Gorodok (Star City) in March 1990 when cosmonaut-pilot Vladimir Shatalov was head of the cosmonaut crew at the time. They began telling Shatalov about ESP, and how it could be applied in training cosmonauts. But Shatalov announced that he didn't believe in it, and suggested that other topics be discussed. "Then one of my students said, 'Please, place a pencil on your open palm and bend your wrist downwards.' Shatalov did, and the pencil slid from his hand in exact conformity with the laws of physics. Then my student stared at Shatalov and said again, 'Quickly put the pencil on your palm, but don't bend your wrist yet ... Now bend it!' And the pencil stuck to his palm—it didn't slide off! Shatalov shook the pencil off his hand fearfully, as if it was a wasp, and then he shouted, 'I believe you! I really do!'" As an aside to our western readers, while this is not a good example of psychic functioning, as there are several other possible explanations, according to Savin, the demonstration convinced Shatalov.

Shatakov never did allow the group to work with cosmonauts as he turned out to be psychologically unprepared to do so. This was in spite of the timing, when the "Energiya" scientific-industrial conglomerate, which built space ships, regarded ESP very favorably, and even though a number of physicians who worked at the cosmonauts' training center were very interested in and enthusiastic about the proposals. But Savin did transfer one of these physicians to his department to study a system of diagnosing ESP abilities using Voll's method of electro-acupuncture diagnosis from the Federal Republic of Germany.

Military hospitals, the Institute of Aviation and Space Medicine, institutes of the Russian Academy of Medical Sciences (primarily the Institute of Normal Physiology), as well as the Institute for Higher Nervous Activity and Neurophysiology, the Brain Institute, and others were powerful allies in supporting and developing their investigations. Savin's department had to increase its medical staff, develop a laboratory base, and create work positions in some clinics and scientific centers. They were able to establish a fairly good methodical and laboratory base at the Institute of Normal Physiology, where detailed studies of the properties of water under various conditions and influences were conducted under the direction of the eminent Academician Sudakov. "In scientific and philosophical terms, the results of this research can only be called groundbreaking," said Savin.

Under Moiseyev, Savin began working with military lawyers, investigators from the Ministry of Internal Affairs, and KGB officers. Working with these people added a colorful dimension to their work, and issues of solving crimes and ensuring national security gained an important place in the work as well as providing an increase in their authority. "We often used ESP in solving crimes, and my own extrasensory abilities were also honed here. In addition to doing analytical and research work, I began to heal people, and to diagnose at a distance. I slept for 2-3 hours a day and worked all the time, because I realized that to become a leader in exploring human potential, you had to attain a certain level yourself."

In all fairness, it should be said that the road to achieving success wasn't easy, and that fate at times presented Savin and his group with such problems that only their team's ability to do the impossible allowed them to ably extricate themselves from the most difficult situations. Mainly these were related to solving crimes, developing prognoses of political and economic conditions, and using non-traditional methods to determine the personal traits of individuals who had come to the attention of the security services and law enforcement agencies. These and many similar tasks were not among the team's direct responsibilities, but the most rigorous demands were made on them since the leadership justly considered that Savin had gathered people endowed with miraculous abilities under his banner. Since the cost of a mistake was very high, such work consumed a great deal of psychic and mental energy.

Many of the situations they found themselves in were complicated. In the fall of 1990, Savin's good friend Valerii Ochirov, a Hero of the Soviet Union and Deputy of the USSR Supreme Soviet, called and suggested a trip to his native Kalmykia. The situation had radically worsened there: mafia bosses, thieves and criminals had surfaced from the underworld, and groups of thugs had begun carving up the republic into spheres of influence. The law enforcement and legislative organizations were in need of serious help.

Savin received a green light from the Chief of the General Staff and had an analysis team, including several psychics, flown down to Elista, the capital city of Kalmykia. Ochirov and Savin drove there and quickly got down to business. After clarifying a few points, Savin's team commenced their work. The precision and correctness with which his team of officers assessed the situation impressed the KGB staff, and they gladly helped the team.

"We worked for two days, and my analysts and psychics penetrated the main criminal network of Kalmykia's capital. Using our ESP techniques my operatives singled out the especially dangerous criminals from the lists of suspects and even from the lists of ordinary residents. They also located on maps the places where these criminals secretly lived, met, and stashed weapons. The local KGB and police immediately arrested several leaders of the organized crime world."

Savin's psychics and the local Elista security officers did a first-rate job. The criminal world of Kalmykia lost its leaders and was smashed to pieces, which were then carefully gathered up by the police and security services. The journey back was quite nerve-wracking for Savin and Valerii—they drove back to Moscow in Valerii's car without an escort, and the criminals set up a real car chase after the two, "just like in the movies," said Savin. "But we survived and everything turned out well: the leadership of the republic restored law and order."

Another memorable case in the early 1990s came somewhat as a result of the Chernobyl disaster. "A very high priority was put on developing ESP techniques to control nuclear installations remotely, and I was involved in this work." Savin was in his office working on testing a new technique, when suddenly information came to him via an extrasensory channel that a nuclear explosion similar to the one in Chernobyl would occur in Great Britain, specifically in Glasgow. "I dismissed this information, attributing it to my fatigue. But the next day I experienced the same feelings of impending disaster in Glasgow. This time I used another technique, a traditional one. I began moving my hand over a map, and my arm was practically forced to the area where Glasgow was located on the map."

There was no time to get this information to the British through the official channels of the Ministry of Defense and the Ministry of Foreign Affairs. These were not quick routes to accomplish this, and bureaucratic delays could cost thousands of lives. "I also had no right to contact the British Embassy due to my top-secret work and loyalty oaths that I had signed. Fortunately, I had a friend who had business connections with the British. I called him and asked him to urgently contact them to tell them that there would be a nuclear catastrophe in Glasgow. It might be an explosion on a submarine or an electric power station might blow up. They needed to check everything and try to prevent it."

Savin received a call from his contact the next day to report that he had gone to the British Embassy and passed on Savin's information. Naturally, he didn't explain that the information was received via ESP, but rather simply cited "sources within the Russian General Staff." Thus, to the British the information seemed like a gesture of goodwill, a present from Russian intelligence. "I think that this compelled the embassy officials to take it seriously and immediately pass it on to the proper agencies in Great Britain."

Some time passed, and Savin was beginning to forget about this incident when his friend called again and told him the most amazing news. "It turned out that he had been invited to a reception at the British Embassy a few days before. They treated him graciously there and gave him an expensive present, without addressing the matter directly, but obviously expressing their gratitude. There could be no other reason for this treatment besides the information we had conveyed, and so we concluded that what we had passed on about the impending explosion was true, and that a disaster had been averted in time." The natural pride that a psychic might feel from picking up correct information "paled in comparison to the joy and enormous relief that I felt. The Chernobyl disaster had brought so much grief and misfortune to our people, God forbid that such a thing should befall anyone else!"

However, his joy was overshadowed by an obsessive thought: "why couldn't our government have conducted work like this earlier and avoided the Chernobyl accident? Was it a case of the Russian proverb 'a muzhik (peasant) doesn't cross himself until after the thunder rolls?' What a pity!"

Sometimes in the course of routinely scheduled everyday affairs, extremely alarming and serious situations would arise seemingly out of nowhere. In one instance, Moiseyev summoned Savin and asked him to investigate the seismic situation on Kamchatka, using the psychics on Savin's team. He needed a prediction in connection with upcoming maneuvers. A little while later, Savin reported to him, indicating where and when earthquakes would occur on Kamchatka and how high on the Richter scale they would be. Moiseyev summoned the general who was responsible for this region, and related this information. The general, instead of passing it on cautiously over the phone, sent an encrypted message to Kamchatka requiring that precautionary measures be taken. The encrypted message was disseminated around the military units. But instead of taking preventive measures, people began to leave the places mentioned in the report in droves. Genuine panic broke out.

This was at the beginning of 1991, and actions like these were considered crimes against the Party and the people. "They called from the office of the Minister of Defense and told me that if there were no earthquakes, I would not only bid farewell to the General Staff, but would be tried as a panic-monger and irresponsible rabble-rouser." The situation was exacerbated even more by phone calls with questions and threats from the Central Committee, the government, the Academy of Sciences, and other established institutions. The General that had sent the encrypted message also called Savin to calm him down a bit, if one can call it that. "He told me: 'Tough it out, Alexei. Things are looking bad for you, they couldn't be worse.'"[2]

Savin understood that being a prophet is a rather dangerous business. If the earthquake did not occur, he would be dealt with severely as a lesson to others. "And so on the appointed day, I stayed at work; I didn't go home. It was already midnight, then one o'clock … by two o'clock I dozed off in an armchair, and then phone call came in on the Kremlin line. I picked up the receiver and heard the General's hysterical voice, 'Everything was exactly as you said, Alexei, it went ka-boom there!'"

He felt genuine relief, but on the other hand, he felt sorry for the people who were affected by the earthquake. Everything happened as he had predicted; earthquakes occurred in the areas (they were off only by several kilometers), at the predicted magnitudes and times. "Then the big brass began to harass me again, practically accusing me of sabotage, saying that I was a saboteur, not a patriot, and that I had concealed a method of determining earthquakes … All told—it was a madhouse. If the Soviet Union had not collapsed at that time, I would have been in serious trouble."

People are interested in their futures, not only the foreseeable future but the distant future as well. The farther ahead we try to look, the more anxiety we feel, and this anxiety is increased by the thought of death. For many—though certainly not all—the older a person is, the more concerned he or she becomes about death. After all, the question, "What will happen to me after I die?" has both disturbed and captivated people since ancient times. "This thought is exceedingly important not only from a general philosophical standpoint," said Savin, "but also from a strictly practical military one. We considered one of our main challenges to be eliminating the fear of death from the minds of people and explaining to them what lies beyond the boundary of earthly life. To achieve this, we conducted an intriguing experiment."

In June 1990, with the help of the KGB, Savin's group tested approximately 100 volunteers and selected about 30 who were good hypnotic subjects. "We put them into a deep trance, and asked them to talk about their past lives. They began describing who they had been in their past lives, when they had lived and in what countries." Their descriptions sometimes went into great detail, down to the names of villages, streets, and house numbers. The data was analyzed and then sent to the appropriate departments of the Ministry of Internal Affairs, the Ministry of Foreign Affairs, and to intelligence agencies, asking them to check out the authenticity of the information. It turned out that more than 10 of the 30 people had provided data that correctly matched old records and birth certificates. They'd provided their exact past given and family names, and correctly described the places and houses where they had lived in previous centuries. "We virtually eliminated any tricks because the questionnaires were carefully thought out. The experiment was carefully controlled by scholars, physicians, and military and security personnel, and all the information about the subjects being tested was examined in detail by the all-powerful KGB."[3]

On the philosophical front, this study brought up a working hypothesis about the transmigration of souls. This strictly conducted scientific experiment became the final point in Savin's reasoning about whether the soul and reincarnation exist. "They certainly do exist. Moreover, the soul evolves as it passes from body to body. This makes it possible to understand that in fact there is no death, and that there is no tragedy in dying. There are only changes in the form of consciousness."

As an aside, while this may have been accepted by Savin and

others as proof of survival of consciousness (or the soul), in the West, parapsychologists and philosophers argue whether or not there may be an ESP explanation (often called "super-ESP" or "super-psi") for such detailed information on ostensible past lives.

In the beginning of the 1990s there was another ESP research and operations center in the Ministry of Internal Affairs, headed by Colonel Vyacheslav Zvonikov, a Ph.D. and professor in the medical sciences. The Ministry of Internal Affairs used psychics to solve crimes, but Savin's techniques of selecting people were different. Savin considered that the less bio-energy a person radiates, the better he can pick up information, and therefore, his pupils did not give themselves away through the bio-energy they radiated. Zvonikov approach was different, as he thought that the greater a psychic's personal bio-energy was, the better the outcome. He tested this experimentally, kept records and made reports. He traveled to Tibet and to South America, and worked in remote areas with people there.

A photograph of Dr. Zvonikov is below

Vyacheslav Zvonikov Ph.D.

There was similar research being conducted in the former KGB (the FSB today) under the direction of Major General Nikolai Sham. They studied parapsychology and sought opportunities to use people with phenomenal abilities in intelligence and counterespionage. General Sham also coordinated the joint work of the three security agencies.

The work of Savin's group was gradually becoming known and at one point, several serious offers from various places came in all at once. There was a proposal to create a training area to cultivate new qualities in pilots and discover their additional potential, and to test methods of working with people at the Flight Academy in Monino. The Academy of Rocket Troops, the Military-Political Academy, and both the Ministry of Internal Affairs and counter-intelligence also became interested in the work. "I started to refine my techniques on these experimental platforms," said Savin.

In the fall of 1991, General Vladimir Lobov replaced Moiseyev as the Chief of the General Staff. His exceptional mind, perceptiveness, and expertise were well known in military circles. "Working with such a man was both interesting and challenging," said Savin. "I came to give him a report about our research, and found myself in an extraordinary situation. After listening to me for about three minutes, Lobov broke in and began to lecture me brilliantly on the subject of my research. His erudition shocked me, and I could not hide my admiration. Lobov saved me several months of work by giving it structure and clearly defining the main areas of research within the context of new circumstances."

In 1991, under Lobov, Savin was awarded the military rank of General and a green uniform in place of a black naval uniform. At the time he found out about the rank assignment, he commissioned an admiral's uniform of the kind seen on navy aircraft, but then he was suddenly informed that he had to go to the presentation in a green general's uniform. There was no time left to make a new uniform, and in order to appear before the Minister of Defense for promotion to a rank, he was obliged to "undress" some of the other generals, borrowing a jacket from one, a shirt from another, and trousers from a third. "Finding a jacket my size proved impossible, and I was presented to the minister in a jacket two sizes larger than my own, with the sleeves hanging down my sides." This newly minted general looked like a recruit who had put on a military uniform for the first time. "Lobov, who attended the presentation, could not suppress a smile and winked at our guys: 'Our so-called clairvoyant could not predict the color of his own uniform—he really slipped up!'" The Chiefs of Staff chuckled amiably.

In 1992 at the request of Marshal Shaposhnikov, the Minister of Defense, Army General Victor Samsonov replaced Lobov. He was a very dry, rigid person, and a great lover of order. Many generals said that the blood in their veins ran cold as they approached his office. When Savin first came to him with a report, Samsonov listened to him without showing any emotion or saying anything, but his opinion was apparent in his eyes. Savin's perception was on the order of "Well done, fella, you're working, you're doing your duty, and not asking for anything. Proceed in this manner." He did, and as before, no one prevented Savin from continuing his work.

One of their military program's main areas of focus was the development of a large-scale program to train service men and the personnel of law enforcement and counter-espionage agencies in the use of "our methodology to develop extrasensory abilities." Specifically, they formed several groups of officers from the Navy and Air Force. Operational Naval surveillance of the locations of missile-carrying submarines of potential enemies is very important for naval intelligence. It is very difficult to detect these boats, as they may lie on the ocean bottom silently, doing their best not to reveal themselves. "We did some experiments, and after our psychics underwent special training, it became apparent that they could locate these boats on a map in real time with extreme precision. We trained several groups for the Navy which continue to work there even today."

The aviation people trained by Savin's group located ground targets both on maps and on-site during flights with about 80% accuracy. The officer-psychics in operational surveillance groups had detailed knowledge of the state of health, personal traits, and even the attitudes toward service of practically every crewmember flying American strategic jets. Using photographs, they could also determine the technical condition of many forms of US combat equipment and the level of readiness of the major types of weapons. "Interestingly, the guys they trained, even after they retired, proved themselves to be equally brilliant in civilian life—for example, they began to diagnose illnesses and to treat people." The Ministry of Defense film production studio shot a couple of documentary films for internal use about this work. These films were later declassified, and several excerpts were shown on central TV (and shown to both May and Vilenskaya on one of their visits to Russia).

In 1992, Savin's group put together a group of "lifers" who were to be discharged in six months. "They were mostly smart-alecky, cynical 'bullies'—in Russian military jargon 'grand-dads.' Half a year after we began working with them, they were unrecognizable," said Savin. "They had begun writing poems, bringing flowers to the woman who was head of the project, and had given up smoking. They began showing some manners, and their reactions to disturbing events mellowed. After six lessons in self-regulation, the boys walked on broken glass and burning coals, and felt no pain at all when their bodies were stuck with needles. Lessons in the martial arts, memory training, speed-reading, and language immersion were conducted on an experimental basis."

Savin went on to say that "everything went off with flying colors, and we were able to streamline our techniques. By this time, I myself had already learned to tune into the data field, and I began to fine-tune this technique with the students. Would a healthy, spiritually and intellectually developed individual ever harm anyone? On the contrary, he will extricate himself from a difficult situation and help others. By the time these men left the service, it was impossible to imagine that they would engage in bullying as their personal cultural and spiritual levels no longer permitted such behavior."

He concluded with the statement, "This is a fine example of how ESP solved the hazing problem in the Army."

Vegetarianism and alcohol-free living were the rule in Savin's groups. "Alcohol and meat block the brain and clog blood vessels. They block the flow of energy, and make tuning into the information field difficult. I myself have not eaten meat for 30 years. It was sometimes necessary to drink alcohol; there was no escaping it. Business negotiations, the conferral of ranks and awards, and much else traditionally require booze. It's an idiotic tradition, but it must be followed for the sake of the cause. You don't have to be a psychic to realize that the sooner we get rid of this tradition, the better for our nation's affairs. And the best place to begin is for everyone to introduce his own reasonable personal limits."

Such beliefs and practices also surround some psychic

development techniques in the West, though there are also techniques and practices that contradict the necessity for dropping meat and alcohol from the diet to bring out ESP experiences and abilities. In some cultures around the world, the consumption of alcohol is part of the ramp up for psychic performance and eating meat is said to "ground" the practitioner. However, for Savin's people, this seems to have worked well according to his reports.

"But let's return to our history," said Savin. General Victor Dubynin, a "very intelligent man and profound thinker," soon replaced Samsonov at the General Staff. Dubynin was able to find a strong feature in every officer's character and to structure things so that each officer showed his strong suit. Unfortunately, he had an advanced case of liver cancer, and it was impossible to save him. "We were stunned—what kind of apparition haunted those who occupied the office of the Chief of the General Staff? If, in the past, people were simply sent off to retirement, now it was a matter of death. This could turn you into a believer in mysticism, even if you had no desire to become one."

According to Savin, "Cancer is essentially a mystical illness. It is often called incurable, even though there are thousands of people in the world who have completely recovered from cancer, including some without any help from physicians. Very often unconventional methods are exactly what heal people of cancer. In any case, cancer is a spiritual test, and a means for a person to revise his views about life and the world."

One of Savin's good friends was Nikolai Yegorov, the President's Chief of Staff in the mid-90s. "He obviously possessed psi abilities. It was apparent that he had special intuition and I think that he had an unconscious intuitive channel of communication with the higher dimensions." He was a very interesting person, loved art, and was a gifted speaker. Savin developed incredible rapport with him. The State Committee on Science and Technology, called the "Council of the Wisest," was created under him at Savin's recommendation. The Committee's objective was to introduce the most progressive ideas to industry, science, and the social spheres. Savin's team specifically proposed a number of these ideas and decisions.

Yegorov had cancer, and he was in severe pain. "We might have cured him, but he did not believe in his own recovery, and this is the most important factor for success. It is a pity to lose such good people, but he had probably fulfilled his duty in this life, and that was why he was taken from us." Savin went on to wonder, how much Yegorov could have accomplished in close contact with the eternally drunk Yeltsin in the eternal swamp of dirty intrigues? "So what happened in the outer world was that cancer stood in the path of positive changes in our nation. Actually, it just wasn't the right time."

In December 1992, General Mikhail Kolesnikov replaced Dubynin as Chief of the General Staff. One curious point worth mentioning in the context of psi functioning is that although Kolesnikov was a smoker, when it came to his olfactory sense, his ability to detect scents rivaled that of a hound. He could determine people's traits purely based on their body odors and had certain associations between odors and human traits that only he understood—most likely, they were linked through images. If he felt that "something was off" with the way a person smelled, he would not get up to greet the person. The man was practically a lie detector and seemingly could even determine a person's mood by his scent. Was there a psi component to his perception? Or was this something similar to the ability of some dogs trained to smell changes in human blood sugar levels ("diabetes dogs") or presence of cancer ("cancer dogs") we've seen of late in the West?

Kolesnikov was informed in the most general terms about the scope of Savin's work and regarded it rather skeptically. During the first report that was delivered to him, Kolesnikov told Savin that the decision had been made that there was no place for him in the General Staff. He recommended that Savin see General-Colonel Stanislav Petrov, who was head of the Chemical Defense Troops. "In a very curt manner, Kolesnikov told me 'Petrov is a Ph.D. in the sciences, you speak the same language. You've already made the rank of general, so you won't lose anything when you leave the General Staff.' I had already turned to leave, but Kolesnikov noticed some videocassettes that I was carrying." The following conversation was described by Gen. Savin.

"What's that?" Kolesnikov asked.

Savin replied, "Films about expanding human potential and working with ESP in the armed forces."

"Are they long?"

"No," said Savin. "The first film is about seven minutes, the second one, twelve." (He used a little guile in that response, as the first film was 15 minutes long, and the second one 35.)

"Well, all right, play the short one," Kolesnikov said reluctantly. He eased himself into an armchair and watched without saying a word.

At the end of the film, Kolesnikov got up, got a bottle of cognac and two glasses from a sideboard and suggested, "Now then, shall we have a drink?"

"I won't refuse," replied Savin.

"I thought that you didn't drink," Kolesnikov teased.

"It's no sin to break with tradition on an occasion like this," Savin countered.

"What's the occasion?" Kolesnikov slyly narrowed his eyes.

"On the occasion of your decision to keep me on in the General Staff."

"Oh, these psychic prophets! What else can you say?"

"That you're going to support us."

"Looks like I'll have to," Kolesnikov broke into a smile, "since it's already in the stars…"

They drank their glasses of cognac, and Savin showed him the second film. Kolesnikov watched the entire film very carefully, and concluded, "I've made my decision. Stay on with me, and train at least five such unusual people for me." He instructed his personal assistant to receive Savin without an appointment at any time, day or night. There were only ten people whom he stood up to greet and with whom he shook hands, and Savin was now one of them. Later they began to understand one and other so well that they spoke in allegorical terms rather than in plain language, so that Savin's reports to Kolesnikov often bewildered those of Savin's associates who were present.

Kolesnikov's position as Chief of the General Staff office was very beneficial for Savin's work. He doubled the staff under Savin and intensively began to refine Savin's techniques of training military personnel. Savin had 25 full-time people who worked in his department and a multitude of people and organizations working on contract with them, which included academies, learning centers, scientific research institutes, troop units, and many civilian educational and scientific institutions. To top it off, there was no getting rid of the increasing number of new people who wanted to participate in this interesting work.

Pilots and missile specialists were among the first groups to begin the training. For example, the head of the Peter the Great Academy of Strategic Missile Forces assigned a group of over seventy people to Savin's department after releasing them from their other studies. "Working with them was not easy at first. Sitting in front of me were the 'children from the outskirts of town,' who had lived poor, boring and often semi-criminal lives in small provincial towns and, as a result, were full of cynicism. To arouse their curiosity and encourage their interest, I chose psychologically appropriate tactics, brought in flamboyant students and displayed their psi powers, and I told stories about unusual research. While I can't say that I achieved it right away, I did manage to tune these suspicious students to the right wavelength. I attuned their brains, so to speak, to the stream of energy coming from the Earth's data field."

The cadets were divided into groups, and Savin's students began to work with them. The initial results stunned even the General, while the head of the Academy, unable to restrain his amazement, impulsively wrote a letter of gratitude to Kolesnikov. "The cadets discarded their cynicism and began thinking about what is bright and good. They began treating their associates humanely, they started going to church and writing decent poetry and prose. The inner source of their creativity had been awakened. Their minds began to work better, their ability to think became more powerful, and their physical health also improved." Many cadets were surprised to find themselves diagnosing illnesses and apparently healing people.

"Something had happened to their brains. 'Hooking up' to the information field added new qualities to their thought process," said Savin. "Many of them stopped drinking and smoking. Nearly all of them became philosophers, reflecting on Russia's destiny, and on the Armed Forces' place and the place of each individual in that destiny. It was very similar to a real-life transformation to a 'new man' to which Marxist-Leninist ideology had aspired, or more accurately, had declared that it aspired to. In a sense, these cadets became missionaries of enlightened ideas, which they then carried to the masses—the soldiers and officers with whom they served. This was my super-mission, and I had fulfilled it."

Savin remembers that during this period Kolesnikov, after seeing the results of the work, once said that" the world would not be won by weapons, but by a qualitatively new human being who would be close to God, a human with cosmic consciousness." It's one thing to hear language and ideas like this from a philosopher or a priest, but quite another thing to hear it from the Chief of the General Staff of the Armed Forces of Russia.

Soon after, Kolesnikov gave Savin and his team permission to meet with their American colleagues, Edwin May and Joe McMoneagle, who Savin now counts as his friends. "Edwin and Joe were involved in ESP research in a joint US military intelligence-CIA program, and until just recently, were still considered our adversaries, practically our enemies. However, Kolesnikov turned out to be capable of transcending the existing leaden stereotypes and coming to a new level of understanding of global problems. It was gradually becoming clear to all of us that if we developed an ideology that corresponded to the highest ideals, on the one hand, we would prevent all wars because people would begin to live according to different set of morals and, on the other hand, that we ourselves would wake up to the meaningful priorities that could unite and 'conquer' the world. And that it was a very good thing that we had these trends in Russia and that they were emanating from Russia, because they represent the philosophy of the future."

In other words, it seems that working to use ESP for war had an impact on the practitioners, pushing them to use such developments to end war. This is an extremely important point to make, that a better understanding of ourselves as human—which some would say would be an "evolved viewpoint"—would lead to peaceful coexistence. We all hope for that.

During this time in the early 1990s, Savin worked with his team to put together a conference on contemporary cosmology at Moscow State University in which about 600 philosophers took part. This conference aroused interest, but he could sense that Russian philosophers were not yet ready for these issues—everyone was still too blinded by Marxist-Leninist philosophy. Seeing the need to shatter these entrenched views, Savin summarized a great deal of material, ranging from Buddhist philosophy and Plato to Tolstoy and the Russian cosmologists, and wrote the book The Foundations of a New Cosmology, which served as a textbook in their studies as well as the basis of his future doctoral dissertation in philosophy.

In 1993, their project was picking up speed and everything looked optimistic, but at that same time, the threatening events overtook the nation, and the realities of daily life forced Savin to alter his plans drastically. The Parliament burned in the autumn of 1993. Law enforcement agencies became overwhelmed searching for thugs of all stripes, weapons and drugs caches, and exposing the secret hideouts of terrorists and the dead drops and transfer sites of the foreign agents who were flooding the nation. Moscow had to be cleaned up. Kolesnikov ordered Savin to set aside his primary work and put all efforts into helping KGB officers and the police. While Savin's men were searching for criminals, arms caches, and terrorists' meeting places, they were training counterspies and criminal investigation personnel, and creating "advanced" teams for each of the security agencies.

General Kvashnin, who held one of the top positions in the General Staff, was entrusted with coordinating the teamwork. "He acknowledged our capabilities and the operational efficiency of our work, while I was impressed by his ability to concentrate during emergencies, his unconventional thinking and capacity for work. This was when we became friends. The police and counter-espionage personnel appreciated our participation and sent laudatory testimonials to Kolesnikov." A little while later, they wound up on the pages of the Moskovskii Komsomolets newspaper and, unexpectedly for Savin's group, many people saw the true magnitude of the work they had done.

Savin spent most of 1994 working on these objectives, and then, in late 1994, the Chechen War began. Savin understood the real reasons for this war. "It was essentially manipulation by the oligarchic elite, which was intent on distracting the public from the newly begun rapacious privatization and on setting up unregulated channels of fraudulent financial and commercial schemes its own benefit. The battle for Chechen oil also played a significant role." Savin recalls that it was, in fact, Prime Minister Chernomyrdin who convinced Yeltsin of the need for the war. Savin's friends in the FSB related how, on the eve of the invasion of troops into the Chechen Republic, Aleksandr Korzhakov, Chief of the President's Security Service, wrote Yeltsin a note in which he cautioned against initiating military action. The Chechen leader Dudayev also requested negotiations. Yeltsin vacillated, but on the eve of the fateful decision, Chernomyrdin visited him in the evening and convinced him to send troops to Chechnya, so that others didn't follow on the separatist path. "Could this have happened without the direct interests of the oligarchic elite?"

The grim horror that began in Chechnya ended in the treacherous Hasavyurt Agreement and was renewed after a short pause in the "Second Chechen War." Savin was summoned by the leadership in early 1995 and given orders to fly to the combat region. His assignment included analyzing the distinctive features of this war, developing new operational and tactical means, including techniques of military ESP, working with the commanders, evaluating the interaction of the troops, and working on the frontline with his staff of psychics. In addition to discharging military tasks in Chechnya, it was essential to continue developing training methods for preparing grand masters of the military arts.

Savin began to implement his program. He spent time at various staff headquarters and on the frontlines. He frequently flew around in helicopters and combat aircraft, attempting to see everything in order to include it all in training top-gun combat aces. After a month of intensive work, he summoned a number of colleagues with psi capabilities from Moscow in order to embed them with the troops and to use their help in fine-tuning several programs under combat conditions.

At first glance, it may seem as if psychics can serenely remain at home and accomplish operational tasks at a distance, using their remote and telepathic capabilities. Ed May had a lengthy discussion with Savin on this point by asking, with a twinkle in his eye, "What about remote in remote viewing do not understand? It should not be necessary to put your viewers in harm's way."

Savin responded that in actuality this applies to tasks of a more general, strategic nature. In active combat operations, where the conditions change with every second, it often becomes impossible to contact a psychic located at headquarters or even in Moscow, assign him a task and wait for his recommendations, which in turn often require clarifications. Both mountainous terrain and electromagnetic interference can serve to impede stable radio communication. "Our experience showed that a psychic operative must be located in the zone of combat operations or in close proximity to it in order to quickly solve tactical combat problems. Energetic factors, related to the emotional tension in the conflict zone, also distract the psychic operatives, but if they're given appropriate training, this emotional tension can help them concentrate on their work."

To Savin's great surprise, he saw his own son Anton among the officers and civilian personnel when they arrived. At that time, Anton Savin was already fully trained in the martial arts and a fairly good marksman, and he possessed psi powers developed with my techniques. Anton was a civilian who had nothing to do with the war in Chechnya. What's more, he had just finished graduate studies and was getting ready to defend his dissertation, so his arrival did not fit into Savin's plans at all. However, given the pressure of the circumstances, the General was forced to agree to his presence in Chechnya. Anton subsequently fought in a detachment and saw action numerous times, conducted operational ESP espionage, and was decorated with several medals.

"In Chechnya, I could test the work of my most talented psychics and instructors, some of whom were women, in the field. The 'gals' conducted operational psi espionage, assisted in interrogating captured militants, evaluated people's characters, distinguished between those who lied from those who told the truth, and tackled many other problems." Daily reports about their work were sent to Kolesnikov, and he later recommended them for government decorations and the Order of Courage. They received insignia of distinction from the Ministry of Internal Affairs and medals for distinguished national service. "Of course, it was tougher for the women than for the men. Everyone understood this and tried to ease their burden at least in some small way. They arrived in Khankala in camouflage uniforms that were specially tailored to their bodies, but with open-toed sandals on their feet. The militia commander, a tough, stern-looking guy, made a trip into Grozny at great risk during a shelling and brought back soft gym shoes so that our gals would not injure their feet and suffer." The women helped everyone there, diagnosing physical ailments, providing soldiers with information about what was happening at home, and how their mothers, wives, or children were doing. "Before they left the region, they were presented with many gifts."

While he was visiting the battle zones, Savin met Sergei Vishnevsky, a well-known martial arts coach. Savin became acquainted with him a few years before, while studying weaponless martial arts systems. Witnesses related that during skirmishes he defeated militants at a distance of 3-4 meters through weaponless bio-energetic manipulations—their inner organs burst, their eardrums split, and their eyes popped out of their sockets. A mystical fear would overtake his enemies to such a degree that they would forget to fire their weapons at Vishnevsky, who was frequently unarmed, and they would flee. "Sometimes I invited General Kvashnin to Vishnevsky's training sessions and demonstrations, and his skill made a big impression on everyone. Unfortunately this Hercules perpetually had a cigarette in his mouth, and he recently died of lung cancer."

Chechnya became a good school for Savin where he addressed special matters of intelligence, evaluating the actions of our forces, and anticipating events through both parapsychological and logical prediction. He studied how the staffs of different levels worked in extreme conditions, how operations were conducted, and how battles and operations were prepared for and analyzed. They searched for camouflaged targets, combat groups, and caches in the mountains, and observed people during periods of psychological pressure and under bombardment. All this helped him to consider the question of the kinds of skills the person he was training should possess. "For example, my men studied how to make a person feel less pain so that fewer of our wounded die from the shock of pain." He explored various types of latent reserves within the men, and helped develop their physical, intellectual and psychological potentialities.

"I must single out the outstanding success of using ESP methods during the war in Chechnya as the results that my psychic staff achieved there were just brilliant." As mentioned, they received medals and other government decorations for psychic intelligence work and for carrying out combat tasks using extrasensory methods. "After the Chechen war, we can now boldly assert that on the whole ESP is a proven and effective tool in the arsenal not only of strategic military means but also tactical operational ones."

The Chechen war was a complete and utter all-around set-up, a partition of oil and financial resources, and a battle for drug and arms trafficking. He recalled a meeting in August 1996 in Khankala at which Doku Zavgayev (President of the Chechen Republic), Sergei Stepashin (Chief of the RF Government Staff), Kvashnin and Savin discussed the possible consequences of the capture of several neighborhoods in Grozny by militants. They were put on guard by the calls from Moscow and the equivocation of the Moscow leadership's position about what was happening. Due to the complete lack of concrete information, they began to realize that something was going on that would change the situation and probably not for the better. "It was clear that the first blow would be delivered to Zavgayev. I felt compassion for him. He was a wise and decent man who was being betrayed in the crudest way imaginable. I heard his conversations with Chernomyrdin and was amazed at the monstrous injustice leveled against Zavgayev and marveled at the forbearance of this remarkable man, who literally fought until his final days as a leader for the true interests of his people."

The most absurd orders were coming from above. Businessman Boris Berezovsky, who had been accepted into Yeltsin's "family," constantly interfered in government affairs. The sale of everything and everyone at both the wholesale and retail level was proceeding with the government's silent assent, and Berezovsky appeared wherever he could pick up the smell of money. In 1996 General Lebed, who was appointed by President Yeltsin as secretary of the Security Council, began portraying himself as a peacemaker. To create this image he had to establish peace at any price, even at the cost of Russia's political and military ruin. In the summer of 1996 at Berezovsky's order, government tough guys in jeeps arrived in Chechnya, and "we immediately realized that we had already been sold, and that they had now arrived to betray us. This was the Hasavyurt Agreement: senseless victims and a disgraceful campaign. And we, the generals, understood all of this, and this was why, it was important for us not only 'to get the enemy' but to also save the entrapped and deceived, and to bring the truth to them. I once saw a captured Chechen, about 20 years old—he was almost a child, and his hunched back had caught my glance. A lump rose in my throat even though I had seen many battles and death. His image clearly showed the cost of dirty political and financial deceit."

Savin spent two years in the Chechen Republic. In August 1996, when he was about to fly to Moscow for treatment of a serious injury, the commander detained Savin's airplane and informed him that Kolesnikov was being dismissed as Chief of the General Staff and replaced by someone Savin knew, Samsonov. Shortly thereafter, there were two new appointments—Samsonov as Chief of the General Staff and Igor Rodionov as Defense Minister. "I spent some time in the hospital, and when I was discharged, Samsonov received me as one of his own. But we did not work together for very long on the second go-around."

In May 1997, Yeltsin dismissed Samsonov and Rodionov, and Marshal Igor Sergeyev was appointed Defense Minister. That evening Pyotr Aven, the president of the Alfa Bank, called Savin to tell him that Army General Anatoli Kvashnin was going to be appointed Chief of the General Staff. "I should mention that though a banker, Aven's forecasts turned out to be a great deal more accurate than the predictions of any astrologer. After he once secretly whispered to me that it was his opinion that 'Volodya Putin' would be appointed Prime Minister and then later President, I then took Putin's climb up the ladder of power for granted. Very few people knew who Putin was at that time, but apparently, everything had already been decided. Sometimes I joked that Pyotr Aven was a super-talented seer, however it was not the case—the choice of Putin was clearly a matter of backroom politics. The question arises: who elected the President of Russia—the people or those who had already chosen him? What kind of elections, what kind of democracy could one possibly speak about in our nation?"

Aven's prediction about Kvashnin's appointment turned out to be absolutely correct. In June 1997 General Anatolii Kvashnin, with whom Savin was already on friendly terms, was confirmed as the next Chief of the General Staff. He supported Savin's research in every possible way and adopted the decision to turn Military Unit 10003, which was still operating as a department of the General Staff, into a full directorate. The scope of their strategic tasks was expanded, and Savin's staff grew to fifty people.

This new development forced Savin to come face-to-face with the cream of the bureaucracy in Yeltsin's administration. It would seem that since his department was now a directorate, he would have automatically become its boss. However, given it was a higher position, he still had to go through the formality of presenting himself to the President's Administration. "When I arrived at the office, I saw a rather unkempt, semiliterate young man sitting there, putting on airs. Speaking with him was unpleasant, but this was just minor. More importantly, and for security reasons, I didn't have the legal right to describe my work to him. Here he was—without a security clearance—evaluating my work and me! It was a real bureaucratic gem of a situation!" When Savin returned home, his superiors called to tell, "They don't want to confirm you in the new position; they say you're working on the wrong things." Fortunately, Kvashnin made a call to someone, and General Savin was confirmed at once. The question one might ask is, "What was the point of this show?"[4]

After some time, Savin was recommended promotion to the rank of lieutenant general. "The paperwork was sent to this boor again, but I simply didn't go to present myself." A reaction was not long in coming and he received a call on a Friday evening from the Executive Office of the President. He was told that he "had to come in for a talk, i.e. a tongue lashing, on Monday with Sevastyanov, the personnel policy expert. I decided to use my own methods, and spent the weekend applying my own extrasensory techniques. I tried to make the best of the situation through 'harmonizing' with it, even though I didn't feel well physically."

On Monday morning, he woke up in a great mood feeling that it was a marvelous day, and that his weekend psi work would result in a positive outcome. He turned the TV on and heard the news that Sevastyanov had been dismissed. Two weeks later, a presidential decree conferred the rank of lieutenant general on Savin. "These were the kinds of unconventional methods that I sometimes had to resort to in order to counteract the bureaucracy. Of course, I'm not claiming that there was a direct cause-and-effect connection here; rather that it was a case of Jungian synchronicity. Nonetheless, evidence that the harmonization ESP techniques are effective exists, and they are linked to the new scientific paradigm."

In the meantime, the work continued. In 1998, Kvashnin approved Savin's proposal to create an Analytical Center within his Directorate. One of the tasks of the Analytical Center was researching issues related to military education, and Kvashnin himself initially drew on their research. At the time, a reform of military education was being developed, with the goal of introducing a system of quality into military education. Kvashnin charged Savin with formulating the criteria that define quality in military education and developing special methods to improve the system.

One of the first goals was the elimination of hazing, "which arises from the low intellectual and cultural levels of servicemen," said Savin. He continued:

Hazing disappears when these levels are increased—we proved this in practice. This was—and is—not only an issue within the Army, but also a question of the educational system in general, the overall cultural level and social climate in the nation as a whole. We had to work not only with soldiers, but also with officers for whom it is at times more expedient to turn a blind eye to violations in the Army, and easier to control their men through the institution of hazing. High levels of intellectual and cultural development had to become the main criteria in selecting cadets for military school and in their training—only then would our Army change qualitatively. But this would be possible only if continuity between the general educational system and the military education system could be established. I began to introduce methods to develop human mental, intellectual and physical potential, and I developed off-site methods to keep the entire education process uninterrupted. Unfortunately, all this work remained in project form and all the plans came to naught after I left.

One real achievement of their Analytical Center at that time was the creation of a set of computerized psychological testing programs, which made it possible to evaluate the professional and personal qualities of individuals from their photographs, handwriting, signatures, and voice recordings. The statistics gathered in the completed evaluations and their further practical research were highly accurate. "But we must immediately qualify this by adding the proviso that the help of a well-trained psychologist or sociologist, as a rule a Ph.D., is indispensable in working with this suite of programs. A computer can be a serious aid to a psychoanalyst but it cannot itself replace one. A human operator is essential in order to make up for the deficiencies of a computer system." According to Savin, they were able to determine:

hidden character traits

level of intellectual development

thinking proficiency (operational performance; judgment, etc.)

moral qualities and communication skills

ties to corrupt and criminal organizations

motivation

temperament

emotional qualities, character, etc.

This suite of computerized testing materials is now being used in both security and commercial organizations (an abridged version is used with software screened by the FSB). "We cannot say that everyone responded positively to our undertaking. To be sure, the introduction of our system of computer psychological testing turned out to be a serious blow against dishonorable, apathetic and incompetent directors and staffers."

The Analytical Center also collaborated with other ministries and departments, and external organizations such as the Emergency Control Ministry. The head of this ministry, Sergei Shoigu, still uses psychics in its work to this day, including those Savin trained in his program. These psychics have rescued many lives. However, this is a different subject, and we will have to explore it in another book.

By the year 2000, there were over fifty people in Savin's Directorate in the General Staff, half of them civilians. They included specialists from various general fields in addition to military affairs, and many talented psychics including some who held a Ph.D. or M.D. Some of them possessed truly extraordinary ESP skills, such as Lyudmila Osipova M.D., who was able to map out a patient's blood count in detail on the basis of the patient's name, and Margarita Mishkina, who was able to read other people's thoughts, evaluate their characters, and describe their biographies and the circumstances of their lives without seeing them in person. "These specialists, my deputy and very talented manager, Major General Alexander Prozritelev, and I made a very powerful team."

With more power came more responsibility. In 2000, Savin did an analysis of their work performance in order to find additional ways to increase productivity. Initially this goal seemed unachievable as people were so loaded down with work that no additional push could have achieved the desired outcome. However, on one occasion, while using an ESP technique that had been designed earlier for picking up information about complex situations, Savin suddenly came to the stunning realization that he was the one who was excluding the most outstanding, self-motivated, and talented staff members from the creative process. "In fulfilling my assignments, they were involved in a daily grind, which consumed the greater part of their mental, intellectual, and, to some degree, physical energies!"

Savin asked the question, "How do we treat those members of our staff who have excelled the most at work?" and then answered himself with "We promote the individual, burdening him with still more administrative concerns. If he proves to excel in his new position, we promote him again, piling even more administrative work on him, and so on down the line. In this way, we keep distancing him farther and farther from the creative process and scientific inquiry in which he excelled most remarkably and powerfully. As a result, by advancing the most talented people along the executive path with our good intentions, we so greatly impoverish the intellectual and creative potential of the entire team that we are forced to ask our superiors for additional staff and to hire new people who, in turn, distract us from our work since they need to be trained, nurtured, managed, and so on."

After some reflection on this process, Savin suggested creating an unstructured directorate in which all the intermediate positions and departments would be eliminated, leaving three main areas: the staff, the scientific, and the economic sectors, which he and his deputy would oversee. The head of the General Staff, General Kvashnin, supported the idea, and it was soon implemented.

Savin kept the day-to-day administration unstructured so there was independence, but strict discipline and a system of quality control as well. He did not wish to cultivate officials of any type, even uncommon ones. He wanted his staff to be involved only in creative work. "The talented people whom I fostered had the opportunity to engage in real work without superfluous bureaucratic hassles."

These changes introduced new, intense competition and the motivation to advance in the career track. Positive results were not long in coming, and there was a real increase in work effectiveness, productivity and quality. A society of equal opportunity was created, and anyone, even a civilian, could now aspire to occupy Savin's position, that is, become the head of a Directorate in the General Staff. This was great for work, but very dangerous for the mass of uniformed functionaries ensconced in the General Staff as their irrelevance became completely obvious. "Backroom politics began to fester. Grey bureaucratic mice in general's uniforms set their sights on gnawing away at our directorate in order to secure their own cozy futures."

Savin went on to say, "A group of deeply envious persons (there's no getting away from them!) began to form and Kvashnin listened to them from time to time. Rumors about me had already been circulating that I was a magician and the General Staff's soothsayer and astrologer, that I knew everything but didn't want to share my secret knowledge with anybody, that I was capable of reading minds, and inducing illness. Sometimes the generals behaved like old women in a huddle, gossiping." These rumors propagated, and were furthered by happenstance. Savin lost three of his personal drivers to death: one slipped and had a bad fall while walking his dog, the second was a closet alcoholic who died of a heart attack, and the third one died of a ruptured ulcer.

"Rumors immediately spread that this was my doing, that I had either put a hex on them or murdered them telepathically. Some people were afraid of my gaze. On one occasion, the three of us, Colonel General Anatolii Sednov, Kvashnin, and I, were on a flight to Moscow together. They were talking with each other, while I was thinking to myself, looking out the cabin window right through Sednov. When he arrived in Moscow, Sednov convened an annual work review meeting at which he said, 'I flew to Moscow with Savin. The way he looked at me just made my flesh crawl.'"

Savin remarked that at many times it was ridiculous, but these situations sometimes could develop into full-blown plots that he always had to be aware of. One example he recalled had to do with a particular annual review by the Minister of Defense. At the end of a session, Kvashnin said, "And so, the chiefs of staff, the commanders-in-chief, and Alexei Yurievich will now go to lunch with me," referring with the patronymic to Savin.

The generals exchanged wondering glances, indicating they questioned whether this could actually be happening. "It was as if they were saying things like 'Savin must have hypnotized Kvashnin' and 'he's aiming for a higher post' or 'Kvashnin didn't even invite his deputies, but by all means Savin is welcome' or 'hey, he's even addressing Savin on a first name and patronymic basis!' I could feel their unkind, envious eyes on me, and thought that I'd better opt out of having lunch with my superiors, or I would have to pay dearly for it."

As it happened, Savin had already made arrangements with colleagues whom he hadn't seen for a long time, to get together during a break in an out-of-the-way back room to knock back a drink and have a heart-to-heart. "So that's what I did. When we all came back after the break, Kvashnin asked me, 'Why weren't you at lunch? If the Chief of the General Staff invites you, you are obliged to come.'"

All the folks at the meeting appeared happy that Savin was raked over the coals right in front of them. At the end of the meeting, Kvashnin invited him to his private office. The other generals followed him with looks of sympathy, assuming that his dressing down would continue. But instead, Kvashnin started asking Savin about how his work on the new book about military education was progressing. "It was hot in his office and he was in his shirtsleeves while I was wearing my service jacket. He was drinking fragrant green tea, and offered me some. When I walked out of his office, I was all red-faced and perspiring from the hot tea. The envious generals were exultant that it appeared I had been torn to shreds and I nearly got a round of applause. They followed me with sympathetic looks as I left and winked, 'Hang in there, fella, we're with you!' As you can see, the fame of being a psychic and hypnotist isn't always that rewarding."

There were denunciations all through those years, and at times accusations were even leveled at Savin's department. In one instance, there was a cadet who "went crazy at the Flight Academy, and the envious ones seized the occasion to cast the blame our way, alleging that this had happened because our psychics had worked with him." An investigation was begun, and the Ministry of Health and the FSB became involved. "It's a good thing that we found the cadet's data on file at a psychiatric clinic just in the nick of time—it showed that he had been experiencing nervous breakdowns since childhood. In response, we demanded an official explanation to our questions—how could a person with an unbalanced mind have been granted access to combat aircraft? What would have happened if he had broken down during a flight carrying a load of missiles? That was how we survived that particular head-on collision with our enemies."

A major assault on their work and the directorate by a group of political enemies, "including two deputy ministers of defense," followed, with the clear intent to shut them down. "A commission was organized to review our activities. Its findings were honest and objective, and the commission cleared our name. But I was beginning to see that working on the larger mission was impossible with the present leadership, and that the time of great leaders had come to an end. A different era had dawned."

Anticipating the threat of being misunderstood by the leadership, Savin began to wind his program down. He handed over certain projects to other sections of the Ministry of Defense, where they were reasonably well developed. He put other programs on hold until better times, and began to work on some projects either independently or jointly with "particularly dedicated associates, among whom I would single out Colonel Viktor Melentiev."

The growing negative tendencies intensified when General Yuri Baluevskii was appointed Chief of the General Staff. He soon formalized the demise, and a presidential decree about the elimination of Savin's Directorate appeared at year's end in 2003. Savin wasn't even informed about it, "I found out about it after Baluevskii signed it. The day after the decree appeared, I just did not go to work. In early 2004, my personal aide sent in my papers and I retired. I had no desire to work in any government agencies or private firms—for me the happy period of creative scholarly and literary activity had finally arrived."

Savin often asks himself the question "Why was our research axed?" He believes it was most likely because the top brass was frightened by the knowledge and skills they possessed. "I feel that it takes a great man to dare to work with a team of grand masters, and not everyone can do it. I certainly wanted to leave a group of specialists in the General Staff who would train grand masters, but this did not happen. Nonetheless, from my point of view, our mission in the General Staff had been accomplished: we had perfected the methodology itself." Savin believed that they had not only discovered the methodology to allow them to "start accessing the database of the Universe, we had gained a philosophy. The path is open to those who are capable of advancing further. Authorities come and go, but universal concerns remain."

For his part, Savin is endeavoring to pass on his knowledge and techniques to students who are ready to accept them. Thus, he turned over some of his projects to Viktor Melentiev and has advised him on many occasions. "I should mention that Viktor established Mevil, a private ESP diagnostics and healing center, which 'harmonizes situations' and offers assistance in solving many other problems. We jointly outlined the course of our future work, namely, the establishment of RAMEX, a Russian-American center to engage in similar activities at the international level." Currently, Savin is also contemplating the possibility of organizing an international school to develop extraordinary human potential and to train psychics using his methodologies, which have been proven by many years of practice.

What can he say in concluding his account? What might onlookers say about him?

That Savin is a general, a former communist who believes in God and communicates with higher beings. That he's "a real oddball" or that people like him should be put into prison so they don't mess up people's minds. "But what kind of person would say such things? Only someone of limited intellect or spiritual outlook. In fact, raising the cultural and intellectual levels of such people and broadening their horizons of understanding the world became my true mission."

Savin believes that his group finally achieved their goal of devising a methodology that "enables us to train different types of professionals—professional military men, social workers, government officials, and philosophers—in developing extraordinary human capacities. This methodology is not our unique achievement; it is the common heritage of recent decades."

In the initial phase, they were developing a system for training people based on a selection of techniques that already existed in the nation and elsewhere in the world. They supplemented the work with the scientific achievements of many foreign scholars, primarily, of Americans. The group considered them scientific partners, not opponents or competitors, because all were working on common universal challenges. Said the General:

In order to improve and fine-tune our techniques, we supervised a specific group of people in these methods, who, as a result of this training, were able to control the process of connecting with and entering the universal information field when necessary. Plato, Tolstoy, Solovyov, and Tsiolkovsky were pillars of philosophy; they gave us the foundation upon which to base our work, but we took a path different from those who came before us.

We understood that a new cosmology is essential to the future of mankind, as it represents the morality of the future, relationships of the future, maybe even future industrial technologies. Using simple techniques and practices, we can open the path to extraordinary new capacities and a new way of viewing the world for average children, which will inevitably instill a higher level of culture in them. And, once an individual attains a high cultural level, he possesses a powerful immunity to banality, moral filth, insolence, and crudeness, and he will not become a gangster, a thief or a rascal. We may get puffed up about the prestigious school or elite university that we graduated from, but that's not what is important. We should be seeking a place where we can learn to be good, decent people. The Universe needs us to be morally advanced individuals who can rise to a new level of understanding of universal processes, of our own places in them, and of our own most vital human concerns. We are confident that our techniques, which are based on the humanitarian philosophy of cosmic consciousness, will be capable of meeting the challenge of developing such individuals.

Perhaps these are lofty goals, but based on past success, perhaps these goals can be achieved—provided such programs are not subjected to political or bureaucratic restraints or academic prejudice. In the following sections, we'll consider the closure of the various programs in the US and Russia, some reasons why the governments decided to close them down and even prevent them from resurrecting, reactions from the academic/scientific communities to the declassification of the programs, and whether there is a future for the children of the ESP Wars.

NOTES:

1) According to May, this is quite similar to the quip from Lou Alan of the US Air Force who said "I believe in ESP; it is the work of the Devil, kill the program" in response to the US psychic spying efforts.

2) Ed May relates a parallel story in the US, of a viewer giving him "a ton of unsolicited material about an attack on the State of the Union address during the Reagan Administration. Tons of details and I passed it along to the DIA Rep Jim Salyer." Salyer asked May if he were giving it to him officially. "What does that mean? Well the Government would take action and God help me if I were wrong!" May said, "That led to the most difficult 24 hours of my career. In the end, the only parts of the 18 pages or so that were correct were (a) Reagan would have a foreign head of state at that address with him and (b) there was a pink hat associated somehow. Margaret Thatcher was next to him and was, in fact wearing a pink hat, and pictures appeared in the next days' papers."

3) While this may surprise some of our readers, the subject of reincarnation has had serious study even in the West, especially of

children who report remembering previous lives. The late Ian
Stevenson from the University of Virginia spent a major portion
of his career studying reincarnation cases in the US and other
places around the world, and such work continues there today.

4) According to May, this kind of political silliness also occurred
on the US side. "I had to play that game effectively including
pitting government types against each other. High risk/high
pay off!"

THE SHUTDOWNS AND FOUNDATIONS FOR THE FUTURE

CHAPTER 10

A LOOK BACK BEFORE GOING FORWARD: THE WEST

Authors' Note (April, 2014): Given the recent clear examples of ideological disagreements between Russia and the US—as evidenced by the statements and actions of Vladimir Putin and Barack Obama—and military actions by both countries, one has to wonder if the end of the Cold War was really only a suspension. It may be that this section is already obsolete even as we prepare for publication. Let's hope not!

The world was turned upside down at the beginning of the 1990s. The communist bloc fell apart, followed by the Soviet Union, itself. The political and ideological confrontation between two opposing social systems vanished. "Enemies" disappeared. The Cold War was over, at least the one between the USA and USSR. This turned out to be more brazenly effective than the magic of Merlin or that of the ancient Egyptian soothsayers. Only yesterday, there were plenty of "wild Russians" and "aggressive American imperialists" ready to devour one another, but suddenly they were all gone. People everywhere turned out to be the same, and to have the same aspirations, desires, joys, troubles, and concerns. It became apparent that no one wanted to attack anyone else, and never did.

What sort of ESP miracle can compare to this?

It's likely curious to many that none of the psychics, including the famous ones, were able to accurately predict these global events, at least publicly. People identifying themselves as psychics certainly made predictions as they always do, but their forecasts lacked exact (or even close) dates and details, making the predictions essentially useless. One has to wonder whether predictions are necessary at all, especially given that many psychics won't even go there, claiming the future is not set in stone and therefore always includes an element of unpredictability (and a good chance for them to be "wrong"). Yet human beings do want to know the Future—we consult a sort of "oracle" every day that even helps us plan our day and especially our wardrobe (you know—the weather-guy/gal on TV or radio or the Internet).

In the West, research supports the vagaries of predictions. In carefully designed experiments, we find that remote viewers appear to have statistical access to possible, even probable, futures that are likely to occur, even if in actuality they do not.

So there were no ESP-related miracles preparing either side of the Iron Curtain for what was to happen, though plenty of other experts in numerous fields made their own predictions relating to what was happening, and what was next. It's hard to point to anyone who predicted what actually happened.

With the fall of the Soviet Union came a disappearance of the imminent threat of global war at the time. This led to the shutting down of many strategic military research projects and changes in defense spending on both sides. In the Soviet Union, most of the research and development of the newest types of armaments, including psychotronic weapons, was discontinued. People who had been trying to develop psychotronic generators or information transfer equipment began thinking about civilian applications for these inventions, primarily in the medical and ecological spheres. However, stories about collaboration between Russian Special Security Services and the military on the psychic front continue.

Included in the US program closures was Star Gate. More of the story of its closure, the politics around that, and what was next for some of the principals involved is the subject of this chapter. Star Gate's last director Edwin May provides us with the "death throes" of the program, which lasted several years after the fall, and ended in 1995. Joseph McMoneagle tells the story from his perspective.

How the program came to be known to the public and scientific community, the fallout from that, and the closure is itself quite a commentary on how the ESP Wars were bound up in politics and scientific prejudices.

EDWIN C. MAY

Many people are unaware that the program suffered an earlier closure, which led to the shift from SRI to SAIC. "In 1989-90, for the nine months following the closing of our program at SRI," began May, "I was basically unemployed. During this time, I was in full marketing mode. I would call my Senate Staffer contact and lie to him by saying that I was going to be in Washington on other business, and would he and his Senator boss have 1/2 hour or so to meet with me?" On those occasions when he got a yes, May would scramble to make all the flight, car, and hotel arrangements so that he could make the meeting in Washington. "I am not sure how many visits I made during this time, but I spent probably close to $20,000 of my own money for travel expenses."

This practice was "sort of" successful. Looking for six million dollars, "what made it through the appropriation committees and the House/Senate conference committees was only two million." However, this was only the beginning of the problems that arose. "Congress can increase the budget for some Executive Branch agency, which in turn can provide a contract to individuals or corporations, but they can't do it directly." May and the project had two major problems: no receiving company for the future contract, and, at the time, no agency to do the contracting with the freshly appropriated funds.

"I hit the road again, trying to solve the contractor problem," said Ed. His wanderings took him to some of the top defense contractors. Many of their CEOs strongly supported the concept, but at the end of the day, they opted out. "I was getting a little desperate so I called a former Air Force client friend of mine, Colonel Joseph Angelo (now retired from the Air Force) to seek his advice. After all, I did have a virtual suitcase full of a virtual $2M in cash! That should stand for something, I thought." Lucky for May he'd guessed right. Col. Angelo had loved the work and asked, "When and where do you want your office with Science Applications International Corporation," the company where he was working at the time.

The project was almost set for a new home, though Col. Angelo told Ed that he would have to convince Angelo's boss of the worthiness of the potential new program. A meeting was set up for a few weeks later at SAIC headquarters in San Diego between May and Angelo's boss, Tom (name omitted for privacy).

They met and, after some pleasantries, moved to a conference room where May asked Tom what Joe Angelo had told him about the briefing. "Joe said that he respected your work and you were a physicist," Tom said.

"Is that all?" May asked.

"Yep," he replied.

May was ready to cancel the meeting, fly to Florida, and "choke Joe with may bare hands! How could he NOT tell his boss that I was going to talk about ESP? For all that Tom knew at that moment was that maybe I was going to speak about some nifty new over-the-horizon radar or some other physics intelligence gadget."

May recalled that he swallowed hard and waded into uncharted waters." Five hours or so later Tom was asking me for a job. He was riveted on the idea. Thus the government-sponsored ESP program had an industrial home, and a very good one at that."

There was still the other bigger problem, the question of which agency would take responsibility for the contract. Given the SRI Program history with the Defense Intelligence Agency, it seemed a natural fit, but the 3-star General in charge flatly refused the program. "That started a war with the Senate which, by definition, the Senate wins," said Ed. "I was shown a formal letter addressed to that recalcitrant 3-star commander from the senior member of the Senate Select Committee for Intelligence, who had visited me earlier at SRI, informing him that he had 24 hours to show why he was not in formal contempt of Congress by refusing this program. Let me assure you, this is not a happy letter to get from Congress to further one's career." The letter worked its own "magic" and the new program ended up at SAIC with the contract coming from DIA.

What does all this have to do with the eventual closing of Star Gate? "Plenty. Naively, most people think that the military chain of command rules the day," said May. "Generals tell Colonels who tell Majors who tell Lieutenants what to do. Well not exactly. Most often senior officers respect the judgments of many of their junior officers and professional staff and rarely overrule them. At times when this is violated, the so-called letter of the law is followed, but often not the intent. There was a well-known example of this during the Carter administration. The President had a scientific interest in UFOs and dropped in on NASA to ask the director to look into this phenomenon. The director said, 'Yes Sir!' the President left, and NOTHING further happened."

In 1990, the 3-star commander of the DIA followed the Congressional wishes but only to the exact specifications of the request. "For the next four years DIA did everything they could to create road blocks to make it as difficult as possible for the program to flourish or for that matter even survive. With one exception, the DIA brass assigned total career-ended incompetent people to run the Ft. Meade remote viewing program. Morale plummeted within the unit. So much so, in fact, that on many of my frequent visits to Ft. Meade, different staff members of the unit would take me to lunch and beg me to intervene on their behalf. I did so but with absolutely no effect whatsoever. The word had come down from the top: Make the program vanish."

On the plus side, the SAIC portion of the program prospered for a bit more than four years and produced a number of peer-reviewed publications. Like during the previous incarnation of the program at SRI, they had a Scientific Oversight Committee to assure their sponsors that they were doing the best possible science, an Institutional Review Board to assure the ethical use of human subjects in the experiments, and a Policy Oversight Committee to assure that the work remained in compliance with the Department of Defense's overall mission.

As the geopolitical climate began to shift with the ending of the Cold War, their funding began to run out, with the intelligence requirements slowly shifting from mostly strategic to mostly tactical. Ed May provides an example. "Let's say there was a site in the Soviet Union that we were watching for some time and wished to know what was happening at that moment. Tactical intelligence is more concerned with the immediate circumstances, such as 'tell us where the downed aircraft is in the next hour or so.' Strategic intelligence is concerned in the long term." In addition the political support and cover for the program also waned. Finally SAIC slowly began to pull the plug.

Word came to May from his management that they had to reduce staff and give up their functional and comfortable offices in Menlo Park, California, and move a skeleton crew to an existing San Francisco office of SAIC. For May, that meant a 20 minute walk to work turned into a difficult hour or so by train and bus commute. More importantly, however, was the shift in emphasis from research to cleaning up the contractual loose ends and to start a storage and archival activity. Fortunately, most of the staff found other jobs, and the close bond they shared on the job survives through to today even though they have all scattered across the globe.

Finally SAIC asked May to move once again for a brief period to an SAIC office in Palo Alto. The good news was that he could ride his bike to work; the bad news was this was the end. His main role was to box up reports and declassify others. "However, in parallel to all this moving, I was given a small mandate to support a Central Intelligence Agency's program review."

The terrible situation of the Senate Select Committee for Intelligence having to cram the program down the throat of the DIA—a win that wasn't—was recognized by one of the Staffers for Senate Appropriations Committee. He decided to take the program away from the DIA. His mechanism of choice is called a Congressionally Directed Activity (CDA), which was part of the Department of Defense's Appropriations fiscal year 1996 bill. The CDA asked the Central Intelligence Agency to conduct a retrospective review of the 20-year ESP program to determine its overall efficacy as a tool for intelligence collection. Moreover, if the CIA found that the program had merit, the CDA ordered them to assume responsibility for the program including transferring all the associated DIA personnel to CIA.

In compliance with the CDA, the CIA let a small contract to May via SAIC to assist, as needed, in their evaluation by supplying requested documents. "That I did and acquired a tan from the copy machine with all the reproduction I was asked to do!" said Ed. Initially, he was excited to work with Dr. Andrew Kirby, a physical chemist working for the Science and Technology directorate of CIA. At the start, Andy was not knowledgeable about the topic but "his enthusiasm was refreshing given the gloom of the DIA people for the last few years."

However, it slowly dawned on May that something was amiss. The earlier incarnations of the Star Gate program had more oversight within the Department of Defense including from the office of the Secretary of Defense, than perhaps any other current program. These reviews had been ongoing since 1985, but there were also some dating from the earliest days of the program. The program passed muster with regard to the Department of Defense's mission, the science and methodologies of the contractors (SRI and SAIC), and it had met all guidelines for the ethical treatment of humans in experiments.

"So I thought that CIA's internal review would have a substantial leg up given the myriad of published government reviews—the CIA could begin where these had left off." Unfortunately, Kirby told May that the Agency would only look at the results of the last few years, which included the period of the terrible morale mentioned previously. Furthermore, the Agency contracted out to the American Institutes for Research (AIR) to conduct that limited review. "At first look, AIR's approach looked reasonable. They assembled a team of experts who had open minds on the topic. But sadly the fix was in!"

Three Ph.Ds—Michael Mumford, Andrew Rose, and David Goslin—prepared the report for AIR on the Star Gate program. This report was based on the expert evaluation of Professors Jessica Utts (dubbed as representing the pro-psi group) and Ray Hyman (considered a skeptic). The tasking for the reviewers was to cover four general areas:

Was there a statistically significant effect?

Could the observed effect, if any, be attributed to a paranormal phenomenon?

What mechanisms, if any, might plausibly be used to account for any significant effects and what boundary conditions influence these effects?

What would the findings obtained in these studies indicate about the characteristics and potential applications of information obtained through the remote viewing process?

As Mumford, Rose and Goslin (p.3-80) report:

One of Dr. Hyman's first comments about Dr. Utts' review was that he considered it perhaps the best defense of parapsychological research he had come across. We concur; likewise, we feel that Dr. Hyman's paper represents one of the clearest expressions of the skeptic position we have seen.

At the outset, it should be noted that the two reviewers agreed far more than they disagreed. One central point of agreement concerns the existence of a statistically significant effect: Both reviewers note that the evidence accrued to date in the experimental laboratory studies of remote viewing indicate that a statistically significant effect has been obtained. Likewise, they agree that the current (e.g., post-NRC review) experimental procedures contain significant improvements in methodology and experimental control."

Their technical paper can be downloaded from www.lfr.org/ LFR/csl/library/AirReport.pdf.

AIR's September 1995 final report was released to the public two months later, and according to May, "the bottom line was nearly schizophrenic." As a result of AIR's assessment, the CIA concluded that a statistically significant effect had been demonstrated in the laboratory, but that there was no case in which ESP had provided data that had ever been used to guide intelligence operations. The conclusion was that ESP was not useful for the intelligence community—in direct opposition to a substantial number of Department of Defense documented investigations to the contrary. Classified and unclassified versions of the report were written and presented to Congress in compliance with the CDA. "Oddly I was denied access to this report—even the unclassified version. Some of the authors of the report were allowed to review the material and add comments or in some cases submit complete papers in the form of a rebuttal to other sections of the report—a minority opinion so to speak." May went to Washington to visit the Senate Staffer who wrote the CDA and complained that he had not been allowed to see the report on the program of which he was the contractor director. The staffer gave May his own copy.

Reviewing the report, there are some interesting highlights. Jessica Utts, a professor of statistics at the University of California at Irvine, and formerly at Davis, stated as part of her analysis:

Using the standards applied to any other area of science, it is concluded *that* psychic functioning has been well established. The results of the studies examined are far beyond what is expected by chance. Arguments that these results could be due to methodological flaws in the experiments are soundly refuted. Effects of similar magnitude to those found in government-sponsored research at SRI and SAIC have been replicated at a number of laboratories across the world. Such consistency cannot be readily explained by claims of flaws or fraud.

The second expert reviewer, Ray Hyman, a professor of Psychology at the University of Oregon, while agreeing on the statistical evidence, felt that competing explanations for the phenomena have not been eliminated, a viewpoint that is disputed by Utts. However, considering these are still relatively early days in the investigation of psi phenomena, and there is a growing body of research from other groups and laboratories, in the spirit of science and inquiry, we need to continue with this investigation and attempt to address the most vital question, the how of psi.

There are also a host of technical reviews of the experimental literature on parapsychology, known as meta-analyses, which merge together most of the available published research directed toward a particular topic. Utts published one such review paper in the prestigious statistics journal Statistical Sciences, and psychology professor Daryl Bem from Cornell University, along with the late Charles Honorton, published a notable review of the literature in Psychological Bulletin investigating a type of ESP research methodology known as the Ganzfeld—a procedure where psi is observed when the participant is in a mildly altered state of consciousness. Furthermore, since the publication of the AIR report on the Star Gate program, scientists have continued evidentiary and explanatory studies using improved methods and technology, the results of which cannot be dismissed outright.

Although doubts have also been raised against the utility value for military purpose, it is important to note that many eminent scientists, including academicians and Nobel laureates, supported these programs. Prominent scientists have been involved in the exploration of these phenomena from the early days of its experimental investigation in the late 19th century. While officials of the American government involved in the Star Gate program may be reluctant to "come in from the cold," once again it's fair to mention that McMoneagle's Legion of Merit award is evidence of their support and satisfaction with the applied aspect of the program. Needless to say this acknowledgement does not support the doubts raised by the reviewers of the program on the value of psychic espionage as one of the methods of intelligence gathering.

A copy of the AIR report was leaked to the US press and media before its official release. "At this time I was still a paid employee of SAIC, and I went to my management to inform them that that there would be a public release attesting to the fact that the US Military and Intelligence communities had supported ESP research and that SAIC had been one of the contractors." May's boss asked him to keep him informed especially because SAIC's corporate culture at the time included complete media avoidance. By this time they had physically closed the program doors at SAIC's Palo Alto office and May was placed on administrative leave without pay, but his medical insurance was kept in place and his security clearances were kept active.

"I told my boss, who by the way was always supportive of our program, that I had received a call from the American Broadcasting Company's news division and was cooperating with them. I told him it was extremely likely that I would be asked to appear on a popular late-night news magazine show called Nightline with Ted Koppel. I received a go-ahead nod from my boss, but clearly this put him and the company in some immediate stress."

It happened, and May was invited to go on Nightline opposite former CIA director Robert Gates (who later served as Secretary of Defense) and a CIA analyst who was described only by his first name, Norm.

"Again, I informed my boss that this was happening and told him the scheduled date and time of the program." Unlike most of the other Nightline shows, which were always broadcast live, this one was being taped a few hours in advance of the air time. A few hours before he was scheduled to drive to an ABC studio in San Francisco for the taping, Ed May received a most difficult call from his boss.

"Ed, you are on speaker phone with my management and SAIC corporate lawyers. We order you NOT to go on the Nightline show."

Ed actually thought he was kidding given their very friendly relationship and mutual respect. As a result, he promptly made the first of a number of mistakes during this life changing—at least for May—phone call. "Why are you saying this?" Ed asked.

"Well, we are all concerned that you will reveal classified information."

"My response was mistake number one. 'Look,' I said, 'I've been working in classified environments since I was 20 years old in 1960, and if I were going to reveal classified information, I would not do it on some TV show; rather, I would sell it to the Russians for a huge bunch of cash.' I thought this was a funny joke. WRONG. Dead silence followed my wise crack." In a flash, May realized he had just stepped in it and had better stop joking around.

Finally, after what seemed an eternity, his boss said in a very somber voice, that now they were afraid that he would reveal SAIC company propriety information. He responded with purposeful intent that he had "been invited on the show simply to keep Director Gates honest in that he knew, and that he also knew that I knew that he knew, that our program was useful to the intelligence community. Moreover, I was only going to speak of research issues that could be found in the journals in the library and, as part of my agreement with ABC, I would not mention, nor would they, SAIC's involvement." They had reached an impasse. Clearly SAIC was not going to back down and May was faced with a terrible choice, which he did not handle well. "On the one hand, this show was one of the media's top venues and this would be the first public extensive exposure ever of the formerly classified program—how could I not do this? Yet, even though I was on unpaid administrative leave from SAIC, I did not wish to burn any bridges to a company I admired and to a boss I liked and respected."

"In retrospect, even now, close to two decades later, it is difficult to tell if I made the right decision. Instead of entering into a negotiation to ascertain about what they would give in return for me not going on the show, I told them that my resignation letter would be on their desks within the hour."

So they knew that May was going on the show and they could not stop him. "What happened next was both frightening and terribly disappointing. In effect, I was directly threatened that both the CIA and SAIC lawyers were going to watch the show carefully. Now in a shaky voice but reverting back to my 'humorous' approach, I wished them well and hoped they will enjoy the show, perhaps they should get some popcorn."

Sadly for Ed May, that severed his relationship with his boss, "a most competent scientist, a supportive manager, and all around delightful man," said May.

After hanging up the phone, Ed told his wife Dianne about the conversation, "and she was as shaken as I. What to do? I was determined to go forward with the show, but she did not want me to."

They contacted Dianne's ex-husband, a competent lawyer, seeking advice. "Don't do it," he said, "it's too risky on a number of legal and personal dimensions."

Nonetheless, in the face of all this personal and legal advice, May did the interview, the transcript and video of which is still available online from a few sources. As it turned out, all the angst was unjustified. However, while there were no legal consequences, May's private research life via government contract came to an immediate and seemingly permanent end.

A multi-year and mostly unpleasant media feeding frenzy followed the Nightline exposure. Just as this began, on one of May's many visits to the senior Senator on the Senate Select Committee on Intelligence who started the SAIC era of the program with his visit to SRI back in 1989, he was asked if he could rebut the AIR report. "I told him that it would be embarrassingly simple." He told Ed to do it and pull no punches. May's report, which is a scathing review of the CIA's methodologies, demonstrated beyond a doubt that the CIA had determined the result of their investigation before they actually conducted the study. "I think my subsequent paper is another example of winning a battle but losing the war. Sure it was easy and great fun to ridicule the CIA and their methods, but I think that had long-term consequences that may exist through to today." That published report can be found at www.lfr.org/LFR/csl/library/AirReview.pdf

May provides us with a summary that points out the technical and administrative reasons why the Star Gate program closed. First the technical:

The intelligence mission shifted from mostly strategic to mostly tactical. This shift sharply lessened the efficacy of ESP intelligence collection.

The research did not solve a very pressing problem. How do we know, in advance, if an ESP-generated intelligence report should be taken seriously enough, in totality or in part, to justify taking any action? Director Gates said on Nightline that no action was taken on the bases of ESP intelligence alone. He was right and my remarks were edited out of the show. "Mr. Director, you are correct, but it is also true that one should never take action on the bases of a sole source." Yet in a related problem, we never did develop a protocol about how to integrate ESP intelligence data into the general intelligence community.

Unfortunately, the general level of ESP performance is not as good as it is often described in public venues. The scientifically certified performance could not and did not live up to these expectations.

Aside from these technical difficulties, which perhaps could be solved in some later program, the administrative reasons for the closure of the program were nearly insurmountable. These included:

The Congressionally Directed Activity order to the CIA to accept the program including all of its current personnel given that they found it to be useful. "In my view, this placed a significant burden upon CIA. In general, a shift in program means a fresh start and I think no one would want to be saddled with potential problems associated with a previous administration of such a program."

Contrary to public impression, the Star Gate program survived only in part because of its intelligence and scientific successes. For its 20-year lifetime, the program was always in the cross hairs of one group or another in trying to close it down regardless of its merits. "The principle reason it survived, then, was because of the significant courage exhibited by a very few senior government people who, in some cases, put their own careers on the line to keep Star Gate in place. By the time of the AIR retrospective review, most of these remarkable individuals had either retired, or in some other way moved on. In short, we lost our political cover."

During this sensitive time, a few well-meaning, but ill-informed, government project personnel thought they were trying to save the program, but their enthusiasm was taken, correctly so, as serious exaggerations of the capacity of ESP-derived intelligence. "In short, through the life of 20-year program, we were often hurt more by the support of our 'friends' than any of our critics!"

There were other person-centric issues that both helped along the demise of the program and prevented it from being picked up again by any other department or office. One involved an inter-office "entanglement."

In business, managers at all levels have to deal with a problem: romantic (or just plain sexual) relationships that interfere with the structure or workings of the business, especially between managers and subordinates. Often these liaisons lead to destructive consequences for the organization, and at the end of the day, no one wins: not the man (married or not), the woman (married or not), nor the organization. The military is not exempt from this general societal problem.

Neither was the Star Gate program. A very powerful government official (unmarried) began dating one of the women (unmarried) way down the "food chain" within the heart of the program. Sadly—though predictably—this caused a major managerial problem.

During the final days of the project, May had developed a close working relationship with the aforementioned Dr. Andrew Kirby at the Science and Technology Division at CIA, but now a senior physical scientist at CIA's Intelligence Technology and Innovation Center. As mentioned, he had been assigned to head the CIA's internal investigation of Star Gate, in accordance with the Congressionally Directed Activity. Kirby was initially quite neutral with regard to matters psi, but as is often the way with honest scientists, he became fascinated with it, and his relationship with May warmed. So much was his fascination that he had planned to attend, as a CIA scientist, the 1995 Parapsychological Association[1] (PA) annual conference being held in Durham, NC that year.

As part of a lengthy phone conversation May had with Kirby, Ed informed him of this difficult romantic liaison. Ed also said that should the CIA take the program as directed and include all the Star Gate personnel, they would be in for major problems. Furthermore, Ed suggested that Kirby not believe a word of what he said but verify, or not, his contention. Kirby thanked Ed and hung up.

About a week later, May received a most distressing call from Andy Kirby. "He said 'Ed you have grossly underestimated the extent of the problem. A decision has been made at a much higher pay grade than mine, so I cannot ever speak to you again.' He abruptly hung up the phone, and to this day nearly 20 years later I have not heard from him," said May.

This romantic entanglement certainly did not cause the closing of Star Gate, but equally certain it was a contributing factor.

Another individual-driven issue came up when May and Joe McMoneagle found themselves caught in a sort of character crossfire.

Long after Star Gate had closed, Joe and Ed spent considerable time and money in trying to get various arms of the military intelligence community interested in starting something up again at a very low level of activity and very classified.

In part, the motivation for this was the apparent lack of interest of the DIA upper management. In 2000, with Russian General Alexei Savin's blessing, May and McMoneagle wrote what is called in the business a "contact report." In this lengthy report, they described in detail their meeting with the Russian version of the Star Gate program, Military Group 10003. In addition, they provided photographs of the principals involved and an outline of an organization chart displaying how exactly the Russian program fit into the larger picture in Russia. Moreover, the report was explicit in Savin's request for a joint effort to address the common problem of terrorism for both countries. May handed a copy of this report directly to the three-star commander of DIA at the time. It appeared to be good timing, as that commander was scheduled to travel to Russia to explore joint operations with his counterparts. This seemed like a natural for the psi people. For some reason, however, nothing ever came of this.

McMoneagle and May ran into this same problem for seven or eight more years. That is, at the working level, the people were vitally interested and willing to offer monetary and other support. Yet any new effort that involved psi was killed in the "board room" that is upper management in the military.

There was one exception to this. One of Joe's military colleagues and friend (who must remain nameless here) invited Joe and Ed to come to a base in Hawaii for a week to write a proposal for further work. They were offered $10,000 for the job plus expenses. So, off they went for a week on Oahu.

Upon arrival, they briefed the appropriate "brass" on the project, who turned out to be a senior female officer in charge of intelligence.

They were given the go-ahead to write a proposal, but the requested funding was to be limited to only $200k—very small in terms of military budgets. A week later, they had prepared a proposal that fixed many management and expectation errors of the operational side of Star Gate, set unmovable goal posts to define success, and provided many exit points on which to cancel the project should the on-going tests not work. During their exit briefing to the officer, she asked if they could provide political cover in the Pentagon for this obviously controversial program. May said he would check.

May scheduled an appointment with a former colleague from the Senate Select Committee for Intelligence who by then had a civilian job with many high-level ties to the management within the Pentagon at that time. "Through this man's effort," said Ed, "we obtained the blessing to move ahead by one of the few Assistant Secretaries of Defense—mission accomplished."

Two weeks or so later, May received a phone call from the comptroller for the Pentagon saying he was ready to fax the statement of work and move ahead with the contract. Ed told him he no longer had a classified fax machine. To which the comptroller replied, "Not to worry, the effort is unclassified."

At this point May admits he made one of his most devastating mistakes of his career. Instead of calling his Pentagon contact and inquiring what was up (with the project not being classified), he contacted the female senior intelligence officer in Hawaii. "She was overjoyed that I had saved her 'six'—which is military jargon for one's behind. For obvious reasons, it would have been both genuinely dangerous for the project's participants, as well as open the military for media ridicule should word of it have gotten out at that time." She cancelled the request to the Pentagon.

"That action caused the proverbial shit to hit the fan," said Ed. "I received an angry phone call from my friend and Pentagon contact saying that I had substantially hurt his business and the reputation he was building. That rift took many years to repair."

May and McMoneagle found out later that the Assistant Secretary of Defense had it in for that "uppity female" intelligence officer and was going to use their program to embarrass her. He knew full well that the program should be classified but also knew that unclassified, it would be only days before it would be a major news story.

Ed commented that, "We never did see the promised $10,000, and it took years to finally be reimbursed for an expensive week on Oahu."

May concluded his account with, "As far as I know, and I think I would know, the US Government has had no formal program to use ESP to help with the intelligence gathering in our troubled world since they closed down the Star Gate program in September, 1995."

Regarding Edwin May's recollections, it is important to emphasize that, although it may seem as though Star Gate was shut down due to bureaucracy and internal politics, interest from government institutions such as the Department of Defense, the CIA, and the DIA was also waning at the time.

Could Star Gate have survived? Yes, but only in a different form, working on current problems such as terrorism, organized crime, locating missing persons, and so on–just as the Russians were doing internally. Naturally, this would have required international cooperation, and the American bureaucracy was clearly not ready for this shift in thinking. It also would have required interpersonal issues, like the ones mentioned above, to remain at a minimum (or better still, non-existence).

The former Star Gate program participants were indeed prepared to move forward with the research, and made attempts to get the project going again in different forms. Ed May visited Russia many times in the 1990s. In 2000, he offered his program colleague Joseph McMoneagle the opportunity to come along on one of the trips. For Joe, who as an intelligence officer had been involved in espionage targeting the Soviet Union, this offer caused conflicting feelings. On the one hand, Joe had never visited Russia, and it was interesting for him to look at a country with which such a large part of his career had been involved, and to witness the changes occurring there. On the other hand, the image of enemy was still not fully erased from his picture of Russia. Therefore, his attitude to the trip was ambiguous.

But Joe, along with Ed, was capable of altering that image and of rejecting the stereotypes that had dominated the relationship between the USA and Russia for so long, though this did not prevent him from being critical of the residual Soviet mentality. In the following section, we present Joseph McMoneagle's story about this trip and his meetings with his Russian colleagues—military men and intelligence agents who had once been his opponents, but who by now had become his friends.

JOE MCMONEAGLE

In October 2000, Ed May asked Joe McMoneagle if he felt up to a trip to Russia. May had obtained sufficient funding for them to travel to Moscow and was confident that they would be able to arrange a possible meeting with some of the major players from the Russian military ESP program. It was just over ten years since Perestroika and, while there were some very major changes taking place under the Russian leader Mikhail Gorbachev, there weren't many changes with the people's way of thinking and doing things. "So, I was both very interested and also somewhat nervous about the trip," said Joe. "This was my point of view as a retired Army officer, whose job in the past was to spy on the Soviets."

Immediately, it was clear that the old Soviet way of thinking and doing things still persisted. In order to obtain a visa for the trip, Ed had gotten an official invitation from General Alexei Savin. But since the official copy of this invitation was being held by the Russian Counsel on the West Coast where May was located, it required communications between him and the Russian Embassy in Washington DC where Joe needed to pick up his visa. "My trip into Washington to obtain the visa quickly expanded from a simple matter of a one hour visit to the Russian Embassy to two days of bureaucratic nightmare," said Joe. "While they acknowledged that the official request existed (albeit on the West Coast), they couldn't seem to find anyone within the embassy authorized to issue the visa without an actual copy of the invitation being held there." This required forwarding the invitation electronically from the West Coast to the East Coast, a process that took almost 48-hours. Eventually, they called McMoneagle's hotel and informed him that he could pick it up on the second day, less than 72 hours from his actual departure from JFK in New York. Joe and Ed had agreed to meet at the airport in London where they were scheduled to fly out to Moscow together. May had the itinerary in his possession, as well as hotel reservations, and other necessities they needed for their trip.

Unfortunately, Ed never made it to the rendezvous in London. "I checked on his arrival time and knew that his plane had landed, and he was probably on the ground somewhere," said Joe, "but he couldn't get through customs in time to catch the flight to Moscow. I stood at the boarding door until the senior flight attendant told me that she was shutting the door and, if I wasn't on the other side of it, the plane would be leaving without me. I reluctantly boarded, knowing that I was headed to Moscow, with only the name of the hotel in my pocket and a foolish inability to even ask where a toilet was in Russian. Our colleague and translator, Larissa Vilenskaya was already in Moscow and we were supposed to meet there."

On Joe's arrival in Moscow and clearing customs at Sheremetyevo International Airport, he retrieved his baggage and caught a cab to the hotel, finding a cab driver who could read the English name for the hotel. "Ed had made reservations for the Marriott Hotel because, as an American hotel chain, it supposedly met Western standards. Unfortunately, they had not yet been able to accustom their employees to operating it as a Western hotel is normally run." Joe's attempt to check in resulted in some major complications as Ed had made the reservations for the suite, and had put the reservations on his credit card. "They wouldn't let me check in because I wasn't Edwin May. After about an hour of arguing with the manager they agreed to give me the room, but only if I transferred the charges from his credit card to my own. Fortunately, we were able to eventually straighten out the situation, since back in those days the costs were so high, it nearly wiped my card limit clean."

This caused a bit more in this comedy of errors. When Ed arrived after catching a later flight, the hotel wouldn't honor his reservation because he no longer had one—it having been transferred to Joe—and they wouldn't let him up to the room because it was under Joe's name. Eventually they called McMoneagle down to the lobby and they were able to straighten it out at least temporarily. "During the entire two week stay, we were required to report to the front desk every morning to trade our old electronic room keys in for new ones because the codes wouldn't operate on the doors for longer than a 24-hour period. Eventually, Ed and I were able to sit and have a long conversation with the very pleasant Concierge, who was trying very hard to please everyone, and some changes to their rule book were made."

It took some time to arrange the official meeting, so Ed and Joe spent a few days relaxing and visiting some of the general areas of Moscow. This was very exciting for Joe because "up until the trip the only thing I knew about Moscow was what I had seen in training films, or bits and pieces I'd gotten in briefings about the old USSR. There were a number of things that struck me as being both interesting and strange. While visiting Lenin's Tomb, on exiting I noticed that directly across Red Square from the tomb entrance sat a huge department store—GUM. The interior of GUM had been completely changed from the way it used to be under the rule of Communism. It now contained hundreds of shops carrying the very latest in fashion from around the world. It was well lit and as beautiful a shopping mall as you would find anywhere in the United States. I wondered what Lenin would think about that were he able to suddenly sit up and see it."

Just down the street a ways, there was an even better shopping mall just off Red Square, constructed almost totally underground. Three floors of shops, containing everything and anything one might need. New restaurants were everywhere, including a three story McDonald's with seating for 500 people. "It was evident that the Russian people were already thoroughly enjoying the significant changes taking place within their capital city. If you looked closely though, you could see that it was still in that difficult process of change."

While they waited, Ed and Joe were invited by Professor I. M. Kogan to give their standard presentation on remote viewing at the famous Moscow State University, which had a significant number of people in attendance. Joe noticed there were a number of military officials at the rear of the presentation area during their delivery. They fielded a lot of questions during the presentation, "including the one we've never been able to answer—how does remote viewing actually work?"

The day finally came when a black Mercedes arrived mid-morning at the hotel with driver and escort to take them to their official meeting. "Ed and Larissa didn't look nervous, but I was. I was finally going to get to meet the people who were my counterparts for so many years during the cold war."

They drove for some time to the outskirts of Moscow. Once

leaving the major urban center, they entered an area, which would have to be called rural, eventually leaving the paved track of road and entering a gravel roadbed not unlike the road that leads to Joe's home in central Virginia. It took the better part of an hour to get to the destination, which was a very modern looking dacha (essentially something on the order of a summer home) with a wall constructed of wood around it. The gates opened and they pulled inside and parked. Waiting at the door was Lt. General Savin and Security Service General Boris Ratnikov, along with a woman security officer and numerous others. "They greeted us warmly and took us inside and gave us a tour of the facility. It was clear to me that this was possibly one of a number of meeting places they might maintain, this one being one of the more recent ones constructed. There were facilities for meditation and study, as well as a briefing room, which probably was also used as a school room. There were offices and a general lounge area with kitchen facilities. Attached to the main building they had underground lab facilities, as well as computer facilities, and even a rest and recreation area that included a wet sauna. It was far and away better than anyplace I had ever done remote viewing."

After the tour, they were formally introduced to the Russian psychics who were present. Most were much younger than Joe. They had what appeared to be the same approximate mix of male and female that existed within the Star Gate unit. "I was introduced to their Number One viewer, a woman named Elena Klimova, who I sensed was probably about as nervous meeting me as I was her. We later learned that she had earned a high Russian decoration for her psychic functioning during the Chechnya War, working from a front line, main battle tank. I suddenly felt like a wimp."

After introductions, they retired to the classroom where they received a lengthy briefing on what the Russians were doing in their work. "At this point, I must confess that I took a lot of notes. The Russian culture is somewhat different from the typical American's. So, there were a lot of things in the psychotronic area which I was not familiar with but which they seem to have an exceptional and long-lived background in. I spent more time listening than speaking or asking questions."

After a number of hours, they broke for refreshments and moved to the lounge and kitchen area. "In the course of my years in the Army, I traveled extensively, and socialized with numerous cultures all over the world. In the course of that socializing, I've probably drunk enough to float a battleship. But, I have to say that of all the celebratory social gatherings I've ever attended, the Russian military really know how to throw a party." The table was piled with food and bread from end-to-end and everyone sat around the table, as one would within a family dining room. As soon as McMoneagle began eating, someone handed him "what I would call a small juice glass in America. They filled it with vodka and once everyone's glass was full, someone stood up and made a formal toast that was exceedingly nice and which went on for some minutes, at the end everyone downed the vodka and slammed their empty glasses onto the table. I realized by the time I had downed three glasses of vodka, they were working their way around the table, eventually reaching me." Joe stood at attention and held his glass high–"and hopefully straight—and gave a toast from my heart. I honestly can't remember exactly what I said at the time because Vodka does that to you, but whatever it was, it must have been the right thing. I got a bear hug from both sides." After the party, they returned to the hotel where Joe promptly spent the next 15 hours recovering.

Joe and Elena just after their joint RV session.

They returned to the facility the next day. There were more briefings, and Joe was able to participate in an experiment with the Russian's top female psychic, Elena Klimova. Completely isolated in a totally darkened underground chamber, Joe was asked to draw whatever came into his mind that she might be drawing. He was told that the starting signal would be a bell that he would hear through headsets. Klimova was in another part of the facility doing exactly the same thing under the same conditions.

"It is very disorienting to sit quietly in a totally black room, where you can't hear anything, for a period of approximately 30 minutes, and then have to draw on a digitizer pad with an electronic pen something that you can't see. But, that is what the task was and I decided to give it my best shot." He heard a bell in his earphones and decided that he would simply "let her guide my hand remotely on the digitizer board." When the second set of bells rang, the task was ended and Joe was taken back to the office area. They made a comparison of what the two had drawn. "The drawings were almost perfect mirror images of one another. I think everyone in the room was greatly surprised."

During the last few hours of that second visit, Joe asked if it would be possible to take photographs. This initially caused some degree of anxiety with the security officer, but after discussing it with General Savin they were given permission with the provision that we wouldn't publish the photos until given official permission to do so. "We agreed. These are now being shown for the first time within this book."

Joe McMoneagle and General Alexei Savin

Before they left Moscow, General Savin made arrangements for Ed, Larissa and Joe to tour the Military Veterans Hospital on the outskirts of Moscow. The Commander of the Hospital took time out from his busy schedule and gave the three an extended tour of his facility, which he was very proud of. "I cannot blame him for being proud. Back in those days, the New Russian government didn't have a great deal of money, and maintaining the facility was a tremendous difficulty. One could readily see that there were improvements that could be made to the buildings and interiors. However, the entire hospital was very clean and well maintained to the extent it could be."

What impressed Joe the most was the approach they had in the care of their wounded. Active duty veterans who were in the hospital were not being rehabilitated for discharge into the civilian work force. They were being rehabilitated for discharge back to their military units. This included limb-amputees. "I spoke with a few of them and they assured me that they would be returning back to their units as soon as they were declared fit enough. They wouldn't be going back to the same jobs of course, but they would be given jobs fitting their rank and service time that they would be able to handle. They seemed to think that it was better for the unit morale to send the men back after they recovered, rather than force them from the service. That way the country could benefit from their expertise and they wouldn't become a burden on the state because they couldn't obtain a civilian job. I'm sure there were some who would not be able to rehabilitate, however it wouldn't be as great a percentage as those who were obviously wanting to go back." In fact, Joe was offered an invitation to return to this hospital as veteran patient any time he wanted and the care would be free of charge.

Joe and Ed played tourist for a number of days and met with other people in the research field, but eventually the visit came to an end and they had to depart. They were told by the concierge at the hotel that the terrible lines and difficulties at the airport could be avoided if they paid a simple charge of only $350 dollars apiece beforehand. They talked it over and decided that it might be worth the effort. For the money, they received a comfortable Mercedes ride from the hotel to the airport at 5 AM. "Our car was stopped three times in route by police, who were obviously checking for something other than us. When we arrived at the airport our luggage went to a side door where we received preferable treatment from our own private customs agent who gave our bags a cursory check and then tagged them through to New York." They were then escorted to a private bar on the second floor where they had free drinks until another customs official came and took them to the aircraft. They walked down the other side of the glass wall where all the other passengers were waiting to board to the side entry of the aircraft and boarded before the First Class passengers.

"It was a great first trip and one in which I learned a lot about my counterparts, as I'm sure they did about me. It wouldn't be the last trip and Lt. General Alexei Savin and I would become good friends over time. But by the time we cleared Moscow air space I was again thinking of home."

Joe McMoneagle flew to Moscow several times and met with his counter-parts, the men and women he worked against for so many years. "We now live in a new remarkable world; some things about it have changed greatly, while others have changed very little. The Cold War ended in what now seems like a long time ago. In visiting Russia," he continued, "what I found were reflections of myself. Wonderful human beings, thoughtful and insightful, curious and dedicated to exploring the very issues I have spent the past three decades of my life investigating–looking deeply into the shadow world of the human spirit. They are as committed to the protection of their nation as I am to my own, but the difference now is that we share many of the same goals, particularly in the exploration of human consciousness and how it might be used for the good of human kind."

It's clear from Joseph McMoneagle's story, and from the accounts of the Russians themselves, that the end of the confrontation of political systems led to a deeper understanding between the two countries, and set the stage for them to cooperate. However, there were differences still in the opportunities for Russian psychics. By the time of his trip, Joe had already traveled all over the world, presenting the potential of ESP. In fact, for several years Japanese television had broadcast an annual show featuring him locating missing persons. It was so popular that about 30 million viewers watched these shows. Openness to this extent may have seemed quite natural to a retired American psychic agent, but major changes in Russian society had to take place before a psychic who had worked for the Soviet security services would be able to perform in this way.

NOTES

1) The Parapsychological Association is an international professional organization of researchers of parapsychological phenomena. After an impassioned plea by Margaret Mead, it was voted into the American Association for the Advancement of Science as an associate member organization exactly similar the American Physical Society and the American Psychological Association and so forth.

CHAPTER 11

A LOOK BACK BEFORE GOING FORWARD: THE EAST

Authors' Note: As with the material in Section Three, the following is based on interviews with those described and quoted, with an eye towards keeping even the narrative in context with the quoted material.

The same opportunities for international cooperation emerged for citizens of the countries of the former Soviet Union as for those from the US. This is apparent the relationship of Russian psychic Tofik Dadashev with the Turkish security services in the 1990s. This would have been totally impossible during the Soviet heyday, when citizens of the USSR were rarely allowed to maintain acquaintances with foreigners, much less work for foreign security services. This story also reflects changes in the mutual relations of psychics and the security services in the post-Soviet period as a whole.

PSYCHIC TOFIK DADASHEV

At the end of the 1980s, Dadashev decided to stop working with the Special Security Services completely because he was doing more and more private consulting and did not want the two activities to intersect. But as reality often contradicts one's wishes, there were exceptions. On one occasion during the 1990s, he was staying by invitation at an out of town government housing complex not far from Baku. "Suddenly one of the security guards weapons went missing," said Dadashev. "The Special Security Services became alarmed because members of the President of Azerbaijan's inner circle lived nearby. They contacted me to help and, given the hospitality that was being extended to me, I could not refuse." Before looking at the suspects, he asked to see the security guard whose weapon was missing.

Dadashev barely had a glimpse of him and said "Don't look any farther, he hid the gun himself."

"That can't be!" the security officer said. "Why would he do that? Is he planning a crime?"

"'No,' I assured them," said Dadashev. " 'It's an ordinary reason, like an argument with his wife. He just did a foolish thing. Give me your word that you won't charge him.' They gave me their word, and the very next day the psychic's accusation was confirmed. The security guard confessed to everything, and was later simply fired."

In the mid-90s the Special Security Service of Turkey invited Dadashev to work with them on one case. He happened to be in Istanbul in transit, and they called to request that he help a young man who had been in a serious accident. The man was the son of Nedzhmeddin Arbakan, the head of the Islamic party, which led to the Security Services handling the situation. Dadashev changed his plans, arrived at the requested location. He conducted a psychic diagnosis. They asked him, "Will he live?"

"He will live, but he needs a complex operation. It's better to have it done in America or in Germany. And he will remain confined to a wheelchair. This will be difficult both for him and for his family, but it's not the end of the world. He has enough energy to lead an active life in the future. I see that he will become a Member of Parliament, and incidentally, his father will become the prime minister within the year."

The security officers were amazed. "How can Mr. Arbakan become prime minister within a year, if elections aren't going to be held during this time?"

"I don't know how, but he will," said Dadashev.

It seems the psychic was correct. An unexpected shakeup did occur within the Turkish government soon after, and Nedzhmeddin Arbakan became prime minister in June of 1998. Dadashev immediately received an invitation to move to Turkey and take up residence there. "I was offered a private house and special working conditions there, but I refused, mainly for patriotic reasons," his loyalties remaining mainly in Russia.

In another situation involving terrorism in the mid-90s, he

was working in Baku again providing private consultations. "One time my assistant told me that a journalist passing through town from Belarus had stopped to see me for a consultation," recalled Dadashev. "I asked her to show him in. However, as soon as the journalist appeared at the door, I felt an inner impulse and said to him right away, 'Stop! Leave your bag in the hallway behind the door. Do you have a bomb in it, by any chance?'

"Outwardly, it seemed like a joke, but he was taken aback. He did not smile and put the bag in the place that I'd indicated, entered my room, and sat down facing me. An awkward pause ensued."

"What do you want?" the psychic asked, breaking the silence.

"I want to write a piece about you for my newspaper," he answered.

"We chatted for a bit, and he left. A few days later, I found out that the Azerbaijan Special Security Services had arrested this 'journalist' on a charge of terrorism. It turned out that he had already blown up a train in Belarus earlier and was planning to do it again in Azerbaijan or Russia. At the trial, this man said, 'Tofik Dadashev blew the lid on me.'

"I must admit that I had not informed the Special Security Services about him myself because I wasn't one hundred per cent sure this time that I had a terrorist in front of me. But it became clear that the apartment I was working in was bugged by the Special Security Service, and for good reason. They had taken note of my words about the bomb and had checked this person out, just in case. Many human lives were saved as a result."

As for incidents in recent years, Dadashev cites the case of the kidnapping of the wife of Dzhakhangir Gadzhiev, the president of the International Bank of Azerbaijan that occurred in February 2005. The kidnappers nabbed her as she was walking out of a beauty salon, drove to parts unknown, and demanded a ransom of 20 million Euros. The next morning a close friend of Dadashev's from Baku called the psychic in Moscow about this incident. The banker had contacted Dadashev's friend, asking him to persuade the psychic to help search for the kidnap victim. "An oppressive pause ensued because I felt that there was more than just foul play involved, and my principle is not to get involved in such matters," said the psychic. "On the other hand, I couldn't refuse my close friend, and I expressed my reasons to him."

The friend was so stunned by what he heard that he asked whether the banker could call Dadashev directly so that this could be repeated personally. Two minutes later, the banker Gadzhiev called. "I immediately asked, 'Have you notified the Special Security Services?'"

"Everyone is already engaged," he replied.

"Have they made any guesses?" asked Dadashev.

"No, absolutely none."

"She wasn't kidnapped by mobsters," said the psychic, "but by people in the intelligence services of the Ministry of Internal Affairs, very high-level ones. That is why they have so many opportunities to track the situation. I'm sure that this isn't the first time they've done this. But I'm also experienced here. Several years ago, I helped some high-level people whose son was kidnapped, and in their case, the kidnappers were also people from intelligence. You have to stay strong and not panic, and to maintain control of yourself. If you show any sign of weakness, you'll only play into their hands."

"Can you come here?" Gadzhiev asked.

"The danger is that if I come on the scene, the kidnappers will find out, and they'll get rid of her—they'll kill her and hide the body. I'm sure that their man is close to you, they know all your plans and are monitoring you."

In responding to the question of what might happen to the man's wife, Dadashev told him that her relatives need not worry, that she would be safe and sound, there would be no violence or abuse, that these were not ordinary bandits who would cut off her nose or ear or bully her. The psychic also asked for her photograph, "so that I might positively influence the outcome, that this was my method. And I repeated that if I came on the scene, it would ruin everything. I could only come after the hostage was freed. I said all this to the banker over the phone."

Two hours later the woman's photograph was delivered to Dadashev in Moscow. He conducted a session to "psychically harmonize the situation and influence its success." Shortly thereafter, a special operations team from the Azerbaijan Ministry of National Security conducted an operation to neutralize the criminals and freed the hostage. The kidnappers were all taken by surprise. The head of the criminal gang was Gadzhi Mamedov, a police colonel on the staff of the Main Directorate of Criminal Investigation in the Azerbaijan Ministry of Internal Affairs. The banker El'chin Aliev, a family friend of the Gadzhievs and Mamedov's nephew, turned out to be directly involved in organizing the kidnapping, confirming Dadashev's perception that "their man" was close to Gadzhiev.

Naturally, it's next to impossible to draw a conclusion that Dadashev's session with the kidnapped woman's photo had any real effect. But events turned out well for all but the kidnappers. "Those who took part in the operation received high ranks and decorations. Although my role in this story was kept confidential, it was natural to expect an expression of gratitude of some kind. Therefore, I was surprised that none of the participants even called me after it was over."[1]

Tofik Dadashev's stories, as well those of Joseph McMoneagle, provide us with a context for the position of a psychic working for special services and the military. The narrations of Ed May, Alexei Savin, and Boris Ratnikov represent both the researcher and the organizer of these investigations, while others involved in the Russian work provide additional layers of the history of the ESP Wars in that part of the world.

The following, from Colonel Vyacheslav Zvonikov, M.D., provides some of the rest of the story. Zvonikov, a psychic and a research physician, began working at the Ministry of Internal Affairs in the early 1990s and established a large center there to study and develop the practical utilization of ESP, post-USSR. In his narrative, we can also see the radical changes in the state institutions' attitudes toward ESP, such attitudes particularly characteristic of the final Soviet period. At that time, the abrupt breakdown of the old ideology forced officials to open their eyes to new, unconventional ideas and approaches to decision-making with regard to social problems, even though many (perhaps most) in the West might consider such ideas and approaches too "New Age" or "mystical." This period of openness to new ideas in Russia's governmental bodies ended for the most part in the middle of the 1990s.

PROFESSOR VYACHESLAV ZVONIKOV

Vyacheslav Zvonikov's interest in human potential and extraordinary capabilities stretches back to his childhood, as it does with so many parapsychologists in the West. In his case, the interest led to entering the world of medicine. But he noted that he also possessed psychic abilities himself and, "when I conduct ESP experiments, often it is to participate in them personally. But it is worth saying that I always look at the problem of miracles through the 'lenses of science,' with an objective approach."

His affiliation with ESP research began in 1989. He was working at the Institute of Aviation and Space Medicine and had written a report for the government about the existence of extrasensory perception, explaining that the subject needed to be taken seriously. The report focused on the potential for ESP as applied to military purposes. The paper was well received and interest was shown in his ideas. As a result, he became acquainted with Colonel Michael Bazhanov, who was in charge of similar subjects at the Ministry of Defense. Bazhanov also offered Zvonikov a job at his department in the General Staff. "I was tempted," said Zvonikov, "as this would have allowed me to remain within the Ministry of Defense but, in contrast to my job at the time, to have major opportunities for research in the field of parapsychology. For some time I oscillated between the General Staff and the other interesting offer from the Ministry of Internal Affairs."

In the end, Zvonikov chose the Ministry of Internal Affairs. Within a year, 150 persons were working for him in the center. The first department there, consisting of 12-15 people, was engaged exclusively in ESP research. They created a huge program, with more than a hundred institutes and laboratories under Zvonikov's direction. At that time the Prime Minister of the USSR, Valentin Pavlov, and the Chief of the Department of Defense of the CPSU Central Committee, Oleg Baklanov, were greatly interested in extrasensory questions, and they helped support the work.

Zvonikov worked in close cooperation with the KGB and the Ministry of Defense. "Thus, I met with Colonel—later General—Alexei Savin who replaced Bazhanov in the General Staff, to discuss and debate ESP research, especially with regard to the ways extrasensory influences affect people. At first, Savin proposed experiments using technical devices, such as using a psychotronic generator to measure extrasensory effects. I held the contrasting view that the usefulness of such machines had not been proven. In my opinion, it was important first to study carefully the phenomenon of extrasensory influences on humans, and only then to use technical modeling methods."

For nearly three years, they worked together and achieved a great deal. Using policemen as their subjects, many were found to have extraordinary abilities. They selected 20 to 30 from about 400 officers and prepared them for work as operatives. These were engaged in the search for criminals using ESP, and the results were quite impressive.

One important case that Zvonikov reports working on involved the first murder of a foreign businessman in Moscow. "During Soviet times all foreign business was connected to the state, and such things simply did not happen," said Zvonikov. "But after perestroika the dividing-up of the Soviet state's wealth had begun, and the clash between private interests brought the potential for violence." In 1991, a Polish businessman was killed in a hotel. Through access to his hotel room and items found there, his psychics put together accurate descriptions of the perpetrators, their base of operations, and their motivation—namely that the murder was connected to the oil business. Through this information, the location where the criminals were hiding was found, and they were later arrested at the very location specified by the psychics.

Concurrently, there was a large-scale analysis of ESP abilities of Russians as a whole, using a sample of several thousand people. According to the data, about 1.5 percent of Russians possessed extrasensory abilities. "There are regions of Russia with populations more advanced in ESP, for example, in the Kuban.[2] We also found that, among those claiming extrasensory abilities, not more than 5-7% truly possess them."

As with all human experiences and endeavors, humor pops up even in the psychic world. "While I worked in the Ministry of Internal Affairs," said Zvonikov, "I was constantly persecuted by the inventors of psychotronic generators. In spite of tight security in our Ministry building, inventors somehow managed to get through and knock on my office door. As a result, by the end of the third year of my work, half of our conference room was jammed with all sorts of psychotronic generators that were stacked up to the ceiling, some of them with designs that were quite exotic. Most of these inventions were pure rubbish. This is not to say that all such machines are worthless. I simply had no time to test them." One wonders if word of the number of diverse psychotronic devices Zvonikov received somehow made its way to the West, given often outlandish rumors of Russian psychotronic weaponry reported.

When the Extreme Situations Agency (which later became the Ministry of Emergency Measures) was created within the Ministry of Internal Affairs, Zvonikov's center offered its cooperation. Using ESP in emergency situations seemed, and still seems, like a natural fit. Unfortunately, for a long time the Ministry of Emergency Measures had too many organizational problems and its longtime head, Sergey Shoigu, simply could not pay sufficient attention to the matter. Zvonikov added, "The ministry's psychological division was headed by his daughter Yulia. I discussed the idea of developing ESP services in the Ministry of Emergency Measures with Yulia Shoigu, but before the concept had time to be realized, I had left the Ministry of Internal Affairs."

In the late 1990s, the Ministry of Emergency Measures used the psychics trained in General Savin's programs, but the scale of work was much less than Zvonikov had originally envisioned. "The potential for ESP in that field is huge, such as the possibility of predicting and preventing accidents, of finding people under avalanches, of revealing the most effective strategies for firefighting, and so on.

"There should almost always be a professional intermediary between the psychic and the clients, for example, for someone on a rescue mission," said Zvonikov. "It is necessary to train professionals who can act in a role of 'translator.' The government agencies for emergency measures in all countries undoubtedly have a need for ESP support; it could save many lives and resources. I believe that, eventually, such a center could be created at the international level." Zvonikov emphasized that the work should be given serious scientific consideration, with a strong medical, psychological, and physiological research framework.

They continued their work until 1993. During the period that followed, Zvonikov organized a private center where they worked with subjects supervised by the Federal Security Service and also personally by General Boris Ratnikov, with additional help from General Nikolai Sham. The Service gave the orders, and Zvonikov's operatives, trained in ESP techniques, carried out these orders. They investigated criminal cases and shipwrecks, and predicted earthquakes. They drew up composite sketches (identikits) of suspects and locations from representational extrasensory perception.

By this time, terrorism loomed as a huge, global challenge. The Security Services briefed Zvonikov and his people on several explosions on Moscow trolley buses. The police could not locate the terrorists, as they had left no hard evidence. "Our psychics worked together with a conventional operative group in our investigation. The psychics, with their unique access to past events, made identikits of the terrorists, and they were shown on TV." Using extrasensory means, they also located places where the criminals were hiding out. "Our psychics surveyed the license numbers of cars," said Zvonikov, "with the conventional operative group following up on that information. From that, the corpse of a terrorist was indeed discovered in a car. But when we traced the mastermind of these terrorist acts, our operations were curtailed abruptly." Zvonikov speculated that "there were obviously high governmental connections. We surmised that either power lines were being redrawn, or some political intrigue was being played out."

As to the current state of Russian psi research and application, Zvonikov said, "Our experiments continue to this day. We prefer not to work with stray people from the street, and those who claim to be great psychics are also not welcome here. Instead, we test people, then we work with them, using the techniques developed in our center to develop their ESP abilities. Thus, I know that I can reliably produce amazing results in any, even the most strictly controlled conditions, with a high likelihood of success. And if it doesn't happen, I almost always know precisely why it has not worked. We have a success rate of about 75-80%. This satisfies the strictest scientific criteria of reliability and repeatability."

Ed May added a comment to the preceding statement from Zvonikov. "This is very much like our side with one exception," said May. "Throughout the Russian material they use the word train or training as if it is a given. Maybe they can do it, but our side failed at this and not for lack of trying. Our psychic hit rate (i.e., % of selected populations) was of the same order as theirs."

In addition to his research, Zvonikov teaches at the Moscow Humanitarian University. At this state university, they offer special courses of study in the department of psychology, in particular on the psyche's unknown reserve potential. "Research into ESP has never been more important than it is today, as mass media interest soars while little real scientific research is done. From my point of view the potential for the development of ESP abilities in ordinary people is simply enormous," said Zvonikov.

From Colonel Zvonikov's account, we can see that ESP research in Russia was being conducted at the governmental level during the early 1990s at institutions that had never shown interest previously, such as the Ministry of Internal Affairs. In addition, the KGB now supported the development of these new and unusual methods for practical use. This was a major ideological breakthrough for Russia.

However, the forces of reaction soon struck back. By the mid-1990s, ESP research within the Ministry of Internal Affairs and Security Services had slowed to a trickle. Among government institutions, real work was only being done under a wing of the Ministry of Defense. A backlash was to be expected, but it is curious to note that debate on the issue of ESP already mirrored, not the ideological divide between communism and capitalism, but opposing views on the question of a progressive attitude towards science and society.

We move now to General Sham, whom we've heard from previously, about how a united program of ESP research and related areas was created, and regarding the further prospects for ESP in Russia. As mentioned, he was the last Deputy Director of the KGB, and at that time headed all KGB development of ESP and new technologies.

MAJOR GENERAL NIKOLAI SHAM

When he was appointed to the position of Deputy Director of the KGB in September 1991, Sham set himself to the task of identifying everything that was being done in the sphere of non-ordinary technologies, ESP, and parapsychology in his nation. He wanted to evaluate their levels and prospects, to rigorously establish priorities, and to designate a special division in the KGB that would work on special unconventional subjects on a daily basis. This division was designated as a department in the Second Main Directorate (subsequently Directorate P), headed by Colonel Nikolai Dmitrievich Sharin.

"We began developing contacts with the Americans and came up with the idea of collaborating on new technologies and joint efforts to organize a system to monitor all the research that was being conducted in this area. It was too dangerous to allow it to go unregulated by the government," said the General. Sham's idea was to single out this special issue, and to create administrative departments to track the situation in the Soviet Union as well as in other nations and analyze the research in order to come to specific conclusions and decisions at the government level. There was historical precedent for this kind of an approach.

As Sham previously mentioned in this book, no focused, consolidated work was conducted in this field during the 1980s in the USSR. There was nothing comparable to the US Star Gate program, "but graduate-level courses were taught at the KGB on subjects such as investigative psychology," said Sham, "the substance of which was learning how to read an individual's mind and his motivation and learning methods of covert questioning to get needed information and of coercion." Interdisciplinary research in psychology, parapsychology, and technology on classified topics was also conducted there, and a multitude of military and civilian experts, scientists, engineers, psychologists, and psychoanalysts stewed in this pot.

Sham continued, "To the uninitiated, some of these project designs could seem totally unbelievable—like something from a science fiction novel. But these designs were real, and were being worked on by the most highly qualified scientists and engineers.

Many of them produced concrete, effective results for practical use."

However, there was no integrated government program. Some plans in certain areas did exist, but the main problem was that all the institutes were government-financed and had to fit into the budget. They had to officially disclose their subject and get their own funding. Conducting the work in a systematic way would have required a single analytical brain to formulate the objectives and tasks, organize how specific problems were resolved and issues were addressed, obtain feedback, and analyze the data gathered. But in reality, there were masses of indirect, subjective processes and sources: contacts, friends, and the command's priorities, all of which produced a tower of Babel, more than a little chaos.

"Each institute stewed in its own juices and there was no unified center. Nevertheless the activity continued, strengths accumulated, the R&D projects from various institutes came together, and people concluded that they needed to combine their efforts into a single serious, comprehensive joint program."

From the late 80s to the early 90s, Sham said that they "were confronted with the fact that these special abilities were beginning to be used for criminal purposes. For example, the same con men who used methods to manipulate the minds of individuals also used bona fide ESP coercion, turning people into bio-robots that fulfilled all their demands. When the victims regained consciousness, they often could not recall what had happened to them. It's entirely possible that in some of these cases the generators, created in the laboratories of the military-industrial complex, could have been stolen and used by criminal gangs for mercenary motives." This fits in with some rumors and fears running through media and other discussion of Soviet psychotronics in the West at that time, though even coming from someone like General Sham this begs to be questioned with more than a little skepticism.

General Sham provided a story dealing with such criminal activity in the early 1990s, which happened to the daughter of an associate of his. "Criminals put her into a kind of trance right on the street, using a kind of ESP-hypnotic influence. She gave them all her cash, then used her bank passbook to withdraw all her savings and gave that to them as well. She was in a confused mental state all day. It wasn't until midnight that she emerged from this state, and at that point she nearly hung herself. This particular story turned out to a good outcome, because her husband was a colonel of internal service, and he spotted this criminal group. However, this was a single success in defeating such people while we really needed a comprehensive system."

At the end of 1991, after analyzing everything, a program was created under a single conceptual system, which included the dozens of topics that were being developed in the field of parapsychology and non-ordinary technologies, and began to establish a unified code for them. "I personally supervised this program, which systematized all the R&D into ESP functioning and unique unconventional technologies. In the end, this work was expected to move up to the highest level of government and to acquire the status of a national program."

But Sham did not manage to see this work to its conclusion. He became the Deputy Chairman of the KGB under Vadim Bakatin just before the dissolution of the USSR. After the August 1991 coup, the leapfrogging—a rapid succession of changes in governmental appointments—began with the reorganization of the Special Services. The KGB was split up, and became the MGB at first, but then the names and structure began changing. About a year later, Victor Barannikov became head of the security agencies. All of Sham's attempts to interest the new leadership in these subjects went nowhere—everyone proceeded to divide up the money. "I turned in my resignation and left the system," he said. Once again, the parallel with what went on in the US is noteworthy.

He did not stop working with ESP and non-traditional technologies after he left the Special Security agencies. "In the mid-1990s we created our own center as a commercial enterprise, and it grew rapidly. We received contracts to investigate acts of terrorism and to search for missing ships and planes. This began after we had a brilliant success in investigating the blowing-up of a trolley bus in Moscow, previously described by Colonel Zvonikov, with our psychics identifying perpetrators and clients in this affair, who were quickly found and arrested by Special Services."

They also began developing an idea that they'd come up with in 1991, to create a set of equipment that would make any site on the planet accessible, and allow information pertaining to people, plants, animals or habitats to be transferred to that site. They started to implement this idea and to construct a generator that was on a larger scale than an earlier prototype. "However," he said, "with a generator like this we were confronted with a moral dilemma: it would be possible to transfer any type of information, good or evil, including how to wage climate wars. According to our data, military research organizations in several countries had already been working on contracts to fulfill climate orders for a long time. This can be useful in many cases, but the unregulated use of such generators and climate wars could destroy the Earth's ecological balance and cause environmental accidents. We shelved our designs, so as not to facilitate these destructive tendencies." Whether it could have actually worked in practice is unknown, of course.

"From the Russian perspective," says Sham, "Humanity has the capability of creating a system that might make it possible to perform detailed medical diagnoses, and to formulate procedures and regimens of rejuvenation based on these diagnoses.

"Modern technologies, based on the information and field transfer, make it possible to revolutionize everything related to agriculture—plant cultivation, animal husbandry and poultry farming. From the same foundation, we can create technologies that do not impact or pollute the environment, ensure any amount of gain in growth, that provide organic food, and that solve energy-related problems (that is, secure energy without pumping oil and gas). Clearly, it's impossible to stop our oil consumption instantaneously, but it is possible to extract oil in unconventional ways using resonant technologies, to make extraction less ecologically destructive, and to do this while reducing, not increasing expenditures."

He finished with the sentiment that "Money is what drives humanity now, but mankind must aspire to a completely different path, on which the thirst for personal gain is not paramount. We need to reconsider our objectives and concerns to change the patterns of our activity, both between people and toward the world around us.

"And ESP can help us a lot in this endeavor."

NOTES

1) The kidnapping incident caused a big stir in the Russian press at the time. This is the first time this account of Tofik Dadashev's role in this incident has been revealed.

2) The Kuban is a geographic region of Southern Russia surrounding the Kuban River, on the Black Sea between the Don Steppe, Volga Delta and Krasnodar Krai in the Caucasus.

PAST, PRESENT AND FUTURE

CHAPTER 12

LOOKING BACKWARD AND LOOKING FORWARD

For many decades, the US and Soviet/Russian governments set aside money to study ESP, and to a lesser extent PK, in an effort to apply psychic abilities to various tasks. While the programs in the East spent significantly more money than the West, we've seen that the psychic arms race—a race that during the 1960s and 1970s it was thought the US might be losing—was really neck and neck. There were no psychotronic generators or weapons that worked, no strong influence of the minds of others, and not even the probing of the minds of enemies.

The opponents of the existence of psi have gleefully said "See, what a waste of money," especially here in the West when the Star Gate program shut down. Undoubtedly some in the East would echo those sentiments, given the programs did not yield the weapons or energy sources they had been charged with developing.

Many would agree that neither country was ultimately successful as they would have liked given their goals. However, as you may have gathered from getting to know many of the individuals involved on both sides, we should be glad many of those goals were not attainable. After all, do we really want to have to worry about the enemy reading or controlling our minds? Or purely mental weaponry?

But as you also should have gleaned from the previous chapters, the programs were far from unsuccessful. While some of the accounts from our Russian colleagues, seem to have been somewhat dramatic in the telling, their successes and failures match up with or parallel research and research findings here in the US, both in the Star Gate program and contemporary psi research by parapsychologists. Let's review the past a bit before moving on to present and the future.

There were two levels of the story of the remote viewing program in the US: what the viewers were tasked with/how they did on their "missions," and how the unusual nature of the program was dealt with in the halls of the Pentagon and the Capitol.

We covered Edwin May's personal history and how he got involved in what many in the mainstream considered (then and now) a "wacky" idea. After May became Star Gate's contractor director in 1985, technical and administrative oversight increased sharply. Yet despite this scrutiny, the program proved even more successful than before, and on occasion sometimes influenced US policy and practices.

One early operational example was to see if the US's MX missile system—the idea of randomly moving long range missiles to launch stations situated around a 60 km circler track—could be compromised by psychic spies. After all, if US remote viewers could do it, then so could the Soviet psychics. While the psychics were not totally responsible for the cancellation of this very expensive program, a letter from Senator Warner (R-VA) to then Secretary of Defense Caspar Weinberger indicated that the psychic program was a contributing factor.

As with any bureaucracy, a number of very dumb rules emerged. There was an in-built tension between corporate and project welfare, and SRI and SAIC were no exception to this rule. May's story illustrated a few of these tensions and demonstrates how project tactical victories easily turned into strategic losses.

Joe McMoneagle, who became the project's Remote Viewer #001, provided us with his story. Joe had a number of psychic experiences with his twin sister during childhood. During his US Military service in the Vietnam War, he turned his unconscious psychic ability to a most important use: aiding in his survival during that dangerous conflict. A near-death experience in Austria in 1970 also foreshadowed his unexpected new role in the military.

Joe described these experiences, how he was recruited for the Star Gate program, his first trip to SRI International as part of a "technology transfer program"—remote viewing trials—and the process that vetted him as the number one viewer for the Army in 1978.

We also looked at some of Joe's psychic spying tasks, including a mission to rescue the US hostages in Iran in 1979, a lost Russian aircraft in Africa, and identification of the largest submarine in the world, which the West calls a Typhoon Class sub. All three of these cases produced useful intelligence data, some of which were briefed to the President of the United States.

A big part of the US program had to do with how success is measured for a complex program involving ESP, how one figures out the "usefulness" of information measured, and how the information gathered in Star Gate stacked up against other intelligence sources and their particular "usefulness."

Mixed reviews were to be expected of the military and intelligence community's use of ESP, given the controversial and complex nature of the program. In general, even for the best forms of intelligence collection, the quality of data is often separated from its intelligence usefulness. ESP-derived intelligence data is no exception. Even strikingly accurate data gathered by psychic means is useless unless it addresses and applies to the actual task.

Worse still, a controversial program tends to get the most unyielding and difficult problems that have not been resolved by more orthodox means. In other words, when all else has failed, what's to lose by calling in the psychics? Thus, the operational psychic missions were for the most part impossible problems that could not be solved using traditional methods.

Given such questions and circumstances, it's even more remarkable that the program garnered enough successes to survive for 20 years.

One indication of the program's successes was Joe McMoneagle's prestigious Legion of Merit award for excellence in psychic intelligence collection.

In another example, this time for law enforcement, data was supplied by remote viewer Angela D. Ford. Based on her psychic impressions, a US Customs agent who had gone "bad" was captured in an unusual and unexpected location.

Despite the successes, administrative and technical problems arose within the Ft. Meade psychic spying unit, and many problems arose when the SRI program was closed and before it was ceded over to a new contractor. The Senate Select Committee for Intelligence wanted to continue the funding at a substantial level, but there was no contractor to do the work. SRI was no longer interested and no government agency would agree to take on contracts in this controversial area.

The Defense Intelligence Agency was forced to accept funding from the Congress and to sole-source the funds to a new contractor, SAIC. Unfortunately this created a difficult atmosphere within its management. At almost every turn, the management set up the Ft. Meade group and SAIC for failure.

The application of ESP for intelligence gathering was clearly a success, and we discussed that. However, as you saw, internal politics and bureaucracy surrounding the program contractors seemed to make the end of the program inevitable.

At the end of the 1980s, the USSR disintegrated and strategic opposition from the West disappeared. The end of the Cold War eventually resulted in the end of the Star Gate program. Ed May discussed how the Star Gate program continued at the SAIC, and detailed his struggle with the bureaucracies of CIA, DIA, and Congress. We also looked at how an appearance on the TV show Nightline with CIA Director Robert Gates, and its fall-out, resulted in the end of the ESP program. The same politics and an ever-developing overt personal biases in and out of academia, coupled against psi research and applications kept the program from any sort of governmental reincarnation.

We also saw the development of a new understanding between the US and Russian counterparts where ESP is concerned.

Joe McMoneagle recalled his meetings with former Russian adversaries, now good colleagues. He describes the exceptionally successful remote viewing session in Moscow, which he conducted together with his counterpart, Russian psychic Dr. Elena Klimova.

Over in the East, the story that led to their program and that meeting was a little different.

The idea that so many had that the KGB was using psychics to spy on the West makes for a good suspense story. But the work that the KGB did with psychics was always more or less sporadic through the end of the 1980s. At the higher administrative levels of the KGB, no one would have dared to endanger their career by officially proposing such a program, due to the obvious "idealistic" bias against such non-materialistic things. However, elsewhere there were many attempts to develop so-called psychotronic weapons and naturally the KGB was indirectly involved.

The KGB held two opposing views of psychics at the same time: Officially, the KGB prosecuted them. Unofficially, they secretly used them.

The case of Edward Naumov was used to illustrate the official policy and the case of the famous Russian psychic Tofik Dadashev's work with the KGB and other security services from the early 1970s to the present demonstrates how they employed psychics covertly. Two high-level KGB officers described how a hijacker was thwarted by an extremely risky decision based upon Tofik Dadashev's psychic abilities. A second story involves Tofik Dadashev's work catching spies for the KGB–psychic counter-intelligence operations.

We also related the history of the Popov Radio-Technical Society's ESP Section, including stories of Brezhnev's psychic miracle worker Djuna Davitashvilli and the Gulyaev-Godik Laboratory where she was studied by the best Russian scientists using the most sophisticated scientific equipment.

KGB Major General Georgii Rogozin describes a story how he studied with psychic Sergey Vronsky and became a psychic himself. General Rogozin was widely known in Russia as the Deputy Director of the President Yeltsin's Secret Service, as the Kremlin parapsychologist and as the "Grey Cardinal" of the Security Service.

KGB Deputy Director, Major General Nikolai Sham, who contributed the foreword to this book, described how the KGB worked with psychics and discussed the USSR's secret psychotronic weapon designs that were supervised by the KGB. We also discussed the demise of the KGB and the formation of a new security apparatus, and a new home for ESP in the Russian Military and Intelligence.

From there we moved on to a bit of an inside view of the Soviet and Russian Military and Intelligence community, which came to us from the personal experience of KGB Major General Boris Ratnikov, and his involvement with the ESP Wars.

Ratnikov spoke of his work for the KGB from his early years in the 1970s, which ranged from keeping people from defecting in European ports, to more serious work in Afghanistan, in aircraft security and finally as Alexander Korzhakov's assistant in the

Security Department for the Supreme Soviet of the RSFSR, of which Boris Yeltsin had recently become chairman. General Ratnikov was a participant of the events surrounding the coup attempts in August 1991 and had an insider's view of the siege of the main Russian Government Building. He took over President Yeltsin's duties and ruled the entire nation for a very brief period, sitting in the President's armchair.

It was during Ratnikov's analytical work on the real and potential threats to the President and his entourage as well as to the government and the populace that he first learned about parapsychology and potential applications of ESP to military/ intelligence operations. The KGB recommended using Lt. Colonel Georgi Rogozin, an expert in psychic functioning, to develop mechanisms to neutralize the threat of these technologies. Ratnikov secured Rogozin's transfer from the KGB to serve as an advisor in his service, and Ratnikov's career underwent a drastic change of direction. Ratnikov's initial skepticism about ESP began melting away under Rogozin's tutelage, and we learned of situations where Ratnikov engineered President Boris Yeltsin's schedule, in part, on the basis of psychic data.

Lt. General Alexei Savin had several near death experiences and discovered his own extrasensory abilities, creating experiences and an interest that would follow him to a position as the head of the top secret military unit 10003. In its prime, Unit 10003 had over 100 psychic participants, arguably making it the largest psychic program in the world.

Under General Savin's supervision, many psychics have been trained for duty in the Armed Services, including Air Force pilots and missile specialists. We learned about Savin's background and how he came to run Unit 10003. We were provided with Savin's discussions of ESP-related issues with many high level politicians and academics.

Through Savin, we gained a unique historical sketch which describes the use of psychics during combat operations in Chechnya, as well as how ESP was used to clean up organized crime in Kalmykiya (one of the Russian regions), and to predict earthquakes and accidents at nuclear sites.

General Savin worked with seven Chiefs of the General Staff

and gave us his inside, personal impressions about their take on ESP research and psychic spying. From an insider's perspective, he told us about intrigues within the General Staff and the President's Administration and about underground games in the Russian political world.

Just as we got the inside scoop about the shutdown of the US Star Gate program, General Savin provided us the insider's view of the end of the military Unit 10003.

The psychic Tofik Dadashev discussed his work with the Security Services in the 1990s, including the case of the kidnapping of the wife of the President of the International Bank of Azerbaijan, and Dadashev's prediction of who would be the Prime Minister of Turkey.

Vyacheslav Zvonikov, M.D., a research physician (and psychic) with the Ministry of Internal Affairs provided us with his own narrative of work with ESP and how the work of psychics, including from General Savin's programs, fit into the shifting ideologies of the late 1980s into the 1990s. This was a time of change for as the Soviet Union fell officials were forced to consider new ways of thinking to deal with social problems, even if some of the ideas and approaches might have been on the fringe of what was previously and subsequently acceptable. Sadly, real openness to ESP in the Russian government ended for the most part in the mid-1990s.

Major General Nikolai Sham continued his account of the KGB's comprehensive program in ESP research and development of new technologies, many of which simply did not work, and finally the restructuring of the KGB. He was unable to interest the new leadership in the projects that may have held real potential, and "left the system." But he did continue his own work in the area of applied psi.

He concluded with his optimistic comments regarding possibilities for future development that could benefit Humankind, including the ones which are using ESP.

In general, while the politics of both countries were different, the approaches and amount of financial support and personnel involved also different, it seemed the results were quite similar. ESP provided a stream of actionable intelligence for a number of applications, from military situations to law enforcement opportunities to political issues. Unfortunately, ESP is also not able to provide actionable intelligence in all—or even most—situations. That the number of "missions" with the quality of information necessary was not really any better than other information sources already in place does somewhat undermine the use of ESP but also underscores weaknesses in those other information sources and intelligence gathering processes. Bureaucrats comparing the two (ESP vs. sources already in place) felt it was an "either/or" situation rather than considering that remote viewing was adding to the possible resources at our disposal. Any conclusion that it was duplicating effort based on the idea of the remote viewers providing similar percentages of actionable intelligence is a false conclusion. If remote viewing provided accurate intelligence in 15% of the missions, but other, in-place resources were about the same percentage, it does not automatically follow that it's the same 15%.

In the case of the Star Gate program, that the "missions" were those that already had hit the proverbial brick wall meant they were starting with what others deemed impossible missions. In other words, it was already accepted that the in-place resources could not gain accurate information. Consequently, ESP provided an additional potential information stream that added to our knowledge base. It was not a duplication of effort.

In the face of a mission impossible, there were successes completely inexplicable by those in mainstream science. The successes point at many interesting possibilities going forward, especially combined with many public successes of remote viewing tasks conducted outside of the realm of government secrecy in the parapsychological field.

Though the government support is gone, both American and Russian programs and the research outside of those programs put a spotlight on something very important: at least some humans are capable of retrieval of "hidden" information that can be applied in very practical ways. That the programs are gone, is not a result of lack of success, though one could reasonably ask whether things might have gone differently if the remote viewers were anywhere close to as accurate as the claims of some psychics in the media.

With the events of 9/11 in 2001, the question came up in several quarters as to whether the remote viewing program was "reactivated," or whether the US government was using remote viewers again to find terrorists.

"I think not," said Ed May. "Joe and I and others spent a decade after our program shut down, up to 2005, trying to get something started again. We ran into a problem that was so persistent that we gave up. At the working level, intelligence officers who were tasked with figuring something out were in favor of doing something because it's cheap compared to other things the government puts its money in to.

"But it was always turned down at the management level for its giggle factor," he continued. "In our era, with the Star Gate program, it was the same thing. It wouldn't have happened or continued if it weren't for a few people who we unfortunately do not have permission to name in this book, those few heroes who acted as a shield against all the people who were terrified that someone would find out the program was happening.

"A large part of the reason the program was so highly classified had nothing to do with protecting the US against the Russians, it was protecting it against Congress." This sounds familiar, especially given the political climate today.

"It wasn't the case that everybody loved the Star Gate program. Everybody hated it. That, together with not having the heroes to protect it, has made it all go away. And it turns out that it was the same problem in Russia, as Savin was saying." That leaves the future of research on the application of psychic abilities up to non-government funded researchers.

What lessons can be gleaned from a comparison of the US programs and the Russian/Soviet ones?

"One of them is how human the KGB guys seem," said Ed. Based on his experience with our Russian contributors, and his own experience with various agency personnel in the US, it's pretty clear that the Robert Ludlum/Ian Fleming kind of spies and agents are the rarity. Not every spy is James Bond, or a KGB assassin. Not everything such agencies do makes them the "bad guys."

However, one bit of fallout from the revelations of the Star Gate program was that "some of our colleagues are still angry with me for working for 'the bad guys'—meaning the US Intelligence community," said Ed. "But in fact, this was credible and even ethical work." The missions, while classified, were not directed at any offensive goal. "You cannot fight a war if there are no secrets. What we did was chip away at the secrets."

One can certainly say there are "bad guys" in every agency and every area of the government. This is applicable to the Federal, State and even local levels typically. It's applicable to many corporations and even many businesses. That's what whistleblowers are for. It is unfortunate we often demonize the whistleblowers, though because of their reasons for exposing what they reveal some of them may indeed be "bad guys" themselves.

Another lesson to learn here is how much misinformation came from the Soviets during the height of interest in psychic research behind the Iron Curtain. Several books were published in the West about the "secrets" and observations a number of people from the West made when visiting the USSR's psychics and parapsychologists. But in hearing from the Russians, it's important—and very interesting—to note that the bad information, the false front, was not created or directed at Westerners visiting, but rather seemingly to keep the funding flowing to the various labs and programs that were researching ESP and trying to advance the ESP Wars. This is hardly an uncommon practice even in the United States—tell them what they want to hear so you keep your job and/or funding!

"General Sham told me in person that he funded 40 different institutes specifically for the purpose of building non-lethal psychotronic weaponry. They could not make it work. That's pretty condemning," said May.

From the start, the Russians were pointing at research by the US government, and we were pointing at the Russians work. Due to the milieu of the Cold War, they were using us to get money and we were using them to provide justification for funding for the US side of the ESP Wars.

Research and application of remote viewing continues today, though not at the request of the governments. In the US, several researchers including Ed May continue the work to understand how ESP might work. If you do research on the internet, you'll find a number of people holding remote viewing training programs and seminars, some of them having been viewers within Star Gate and others trained by ex-Star Gate viewers. The programs are often based on what they learned from Ingo Swan during their tenure with the program, though they may have different methods from each other, with a favorite being Swan's method, called coordinate remote viewing or CRV for short that evolved into Controlled Remote Viewing instead.

"Many of the people offering courses are well-meant," said Ed May. "Nonetheless, with one exception, none of them are trained scientists. One of the things the government paid us to do was to figure out how to train others. The training process as Ingo defined it (CRV) did not produce actionable intelligence. It didn't involve double-blind conditions and there were other problems which can extend to the training." They were unable to come up with a training protocol that satisfied the conditions requested by the government.

"It turns out that not everyone has the aptitude to do remote viewing," he continued. "It's possible to train someone to reach their aptitude or skill level, but that's really about training people what not to do rather than what to do. This is something you'd see in Joe McMoneagle's book Remote Viewing Secrets."

That leads us to some important points about ESP, about psychic abilities in general.

People tend to call ESP a "gift" or look at it as some kind of super-power. "We tried to get the government off the idea that ESP, remote viewing, was a miracle," said May. "There are a lot of applications for miracles, but ESP is not a miracle." The proper approach in searching for applications of ESP is to assume that the current, laboratory-verified aspects of ESP are true and find applications that can benefit from that level of functioning. For example, suppose you wanted to use ESP to find a missing child. If you expect that a psychic can stick a pin in a map showing where the kid is, then you are in for a major disappointment. For sure, something like this happens from time to time, but it is extremely rare. However, if you reframe the quest for the child and say can we reduce the time and resources needed to find that child then, as it turns out, it is possible to reduce these by about 10-15% using ESP! That is, at times, just enough to save the child's life.

The late psychic Annette Martin, who worked extensively with our third author Loyd Auerbach, published a book that acts as a sort of workbook for people who wish to try all sorts of exercises with applications of ESP—with the rider that one will not be able to do everything, or even close to everything. (Discovering Your Psychic World by Annette Martin. Artistic Visions, 1995). Martin was not "good" at many of the things in the book, which is understandable: even the most psychic of psychics is only human. Most people miss the fact that we're not all good at (or even have the aptitude for) all psychic abilities. In fact, humans simply can't do everything they try to do. We all have a range of aptitudes for all sorts of physical and mental activities. That's what being human is all about.

That said, it's important to note that several people have been able to apply remote viewing to tasks like investing and archaeological research to some degree of success. More work needs to be done in this area to find the best ways to identify people who might be good at it, how to best bring out their talents and the information, and how to best understand the limitations of the information and set expectations with the people requesting the information.

There are two components to understanding ESP going forward. How the information gets from point A to point B is a physics problem. Once the data is on board (the brain), how it is processed is a neuroscience problem—though some in the field of parapsychology and other fields consider that consciousness is more than the physical structure of the brain, a point of disagreement with much of mainstream science.

Because what parapsychologists study has the "giggle factor" at so many levels of society and science, because there is a clear bias against even the possibility that ESP might be real in many academic quarters, and because the availability of funds to consider the question of ESP is so limited, the research suffers. "We are amateurs in our own future if we expect to really understand how ESP works from the perspectives of both physics and neuroscience," said May. "We can't really address the questions with the laboratory equipment and funding we have."

The question is how do we get people from outside of our discipline to look at the problem? "Funding needs to be available to people outside the field to bring new ideas, equipment from physics and neuroscience, and people into the field."

Then there's the problem of parapsychology's negative definitions; that is, ESP and PK are what happens when nothing else could or did happen. That, of course, tells us nothing about what these phenomena are! We study phenomena, experiences and abilities that are currently unexplained otherwise by science. If we find the explanations for ESP, does that mean that ESP no longer falls into the purview of parapsychologists? Or does that mean parapsychology as a field must adapt to where the explanations lead us?

Currently, and for some time, parapsychologists have been focused on evidential studies—gathering data that shows that ESP and PK do indeed happen. Research has also been conducted to understand what it is about certain people who are more psychic than others are, but the research outside of Star Gate has generally been conducted with "average" people rather than people who seem to have more skill or talent or even aptitude for the tasks.

That focus on evidence may have a lot to do with the lack of acceptance by mainstream science, and the continual statements of "skeptics" who insist on "extraordinary evidence" then seem to either ignore that any evidence exists, refuse to look at it, or say it's not good enough even when gathered under the best of controlled conditions. There's this idea that the acceptance of the phenomena is proportional to how much data you get.

But do we really need the evidential studies going forward? We have enough evidence.

From both the US and Russian programs, it's been clear that identifying and working with individuals with at least an aptitude for if not a prior demonstration of ESP skills leads to greater success. "It's very clear that some element of parapsychological work needs to be directed at identifying people who might have an aptitude for specific ESP tasks and abilities," said Loyd Auerbach. "How we do that without the test subjects hanging up a shingle that says 'psychic' when they are identified as having that aptitude is a difficult question. In the past, this has been a real concern, given examples of individuals participating even in standard experiments making claims after learning they scored 'above chance.'"

"Once identified," he continued, "we then have to figure out how to take those aptitudes and skills, bring them out, then apply them. Understanding how psi works is certainly part of this, though one can still apply a talent or skill without knowing how it works."

On the explanation front, Ed May stated: "There really are

some fundamental questions that need addressing. When does psi actually happen in the process? Does the information start coming into the individual's brain before the participant steps into the experiment, or once the trials begin?"

It's been shown that the capacity for the brain to process bits of information is limited (how many bits per second). "It would take much time, several months for example, for the brain to process enough precognitive information to guess specific lottery numbers on a particular date. Not the most practical process," said May. Yet it's clear that accurate precognitive information can come to conscious awareness. We just don't know when the process happens, or even begins for that matter.

Consequently, another question is: What is the duration of psi? "If it comes in five millisecond bursts, how can we even measure it?"

Then we're back to the question of to whom it actually happens. Evidence strongly suggests that the aptitude and even actual skill level has a genetic component, much like so many other human characteristics. Parapsychological research has provided us with some findings that other factors can affect the experience and expression of psi, including personality variables and personal beliefs, though these may support or suppress a genetically based aptitude. It may not be as simple as "nature vs. nurture," as both seem to be involved; the former in the aptitude, the latter in bringing out the aptitude's potential.

And finally, one of the most pesky problems of all. In experiments, who is the psychic? In parapsychology as well as in other human-oriented disciplines, it is generally assumed that the participant being studied is where all the action is and the experimenter is an objective observer. But what happens if the experimenter possesses an unconscious psi ability? That is, the experimenter makes decisions, which are slightly biased with that ability, in the design of the experiment including who will be the research participant? This could and has been seen in some psi research to mimic psychic functioning on the participant who, in fact, may have no ability at all. If this is true it raises a serious question for all statistically-based, human-oriented research!

LOOKING FORWARD

Going forward, the questions around ESP needs to be addressed by a spectrum of researchers including those from disciplines other than parapsychology. Funding to address those questions needs to be available to even attract those people—and the funding needs to be great enough to entice those people in the current atmosphere in mainstream science and academia of strong prejudice against those who even want to consider the questions around ESP, including the possibility that it might even exist.

Researchers who have come out of the proverbial closet and admitted their interest in the possibility of psi or in the evidence gathered by parapsychologists have been publicly denounced and even ostracized by colleagues in their field. The question of the existence of ESP and other psychic phenomena and abilities is a polarizing one. That so many scientists have denounced interest in reported psychic experiences is highly unscientific. Analysis of research and conclusions and criticism based on such analysis is scientific; dismissal of or bias against doing the research is not.

However there are many scientists from other disciplines who have privately expressed their interest and even their own psychic experiences to those in the parapsychological field over the years. Given the competition for funds in so many fields, if appropriate funding was available we might see some of those interested parties hardening their skins against the verbal onslaught from their colleagues for admitting their interest (and perhaps jealousy from those colleagues because the new research was getting funding instead of their own projects).

People have psychic experiences. What's behind those experiences, whether ESP or something else, is the question that needs researching. To ignore them or dismiss them without research is unscientific.

Some people seem to have an aptitude for consciously initiating ESP. The results from the US and Russian programs during the ESP Wars, and results from psi researchers otherwise support this.

Some task-based conditions, such as used by the US and Russia, seem to bring out the talent embodied in the person's ESP-aptitude.

ESP can produce useful, actionable information in a percentage of the attempts. Perhaps most important, ESP can produce information in some situations when no other source of information is available.

Going forward, we can take the lessons learned during the US and Russian programs to find people with an aptitude for ESP, to best work with them to bring out their potential, to bring them into situations and conditions where information is otherwise unavailable, and to apply information gleaned from working with them in a practical way. On the other hand, we must also always keep in mind that ESP is a human ability with limitations as to how often it's able to produce significant information so as not to rely on it to any great degree, at least for the foreseeable future.

Until we know more about how (and even whether) we can bring an individual's skill level up to the full potential of his or her aptitude, and how (and even whether) we can find people with an aptitude for greater continual success, ESP may still be a tool of last resort for many applications.

We must also garner support where we can, whether hidden in the closets of academia or government or amongst the general public—so many of whom believe in ESP—and mobilize them to open up, all the while pushing back at the outspoken opponents in science and religion who would have us ignore the research and experiences because understanding them might upset the status quo (something most of us in the field do not believe).

That may sound pessimistic, but let's consider what all the research and the US and Russian programs have actually shown: Some human beings can retrieve information without the use of their senses, without logical inference, and to a much higher degree of detail than any guesswork could provide. They can do it even if thousands of miles separate them from their "target." They can apparently do it even though the target has yet to be decided upon (in other words through time).

Even if only a few individuals in millions can do this, even if they can only do it a small percentage of the time and attempts, is it not worth looking into how and why they can do so? Given the value of information, is it not worth finding those individuals and working with them?

Most important perhaps is this question: What do these abilities/experiences say about those individuals—and the rest of us—as

Human Beings? We have long been on a quest to understand the Universe around us, and to understand ourselves and what it means to be Human.

The history of Science is filled with examples of people with "outside" or unconventional concepts that seemingly challenge part of the status quo being the subjects of derision and exclusion. Some have been shown to be wrong (often to the inappropriate glee of their opponents). But some have been proven correct, their concepts allowing us to expend our understanding of our Universe and ourselves. Imagine if people like Galileo, Newton, Einstein, Edison, the Wright Brothers, and others actually gave up because so many said they were "wrong" or even committing some kind of heresy?

What came out of the ESP Wars is much more than actionable intelligence: strong evidence that human beings are much more than we previously thought we were, that the limitations of being Human are not as restrictive as we thought.

To repeat General Nikolai Sham's comments in our Foreword, and his final comments in the last chapter:

"I am convinced that it is precisely these results of our work that will most significantly contribute to strengthening the mutual understanding between people and will in some way help solve the difficult problems facing the human community as a whole today.

"We need to reconsider our objectives and concerns to change the patterns of our activity, both between people and toward the world around us.

"And ESP can help us a lot in this endeavor."

Going forward, the ESP Wars will not be fought between nations or even nationality-based ideologies. The ESP Wars will be fought between those who wish to understand ourselves better and look into possibilities that may not fit the current paradigm of most in mainstream science and those who won't consider certain "outside" ideas—including those who refuse to even allow others to consider the concepts.

On which side do you want to be?

APPENDIX

In 2000, the CIA declassified and released 86,347 pages of the Star Gate record. The released data consist of proposals, final and draft reports, RV session details, experimental data, notes, memos, transmittal slips, routing slips, handwritten notes, academic literature from published sources, newspaper clippings etc. The three documents presented in the Appendix came from that collection to illustrate the high level of support the program enjoyed and to show the level of analysis and support for the program.

The three formerly classified documents as part of the US Star Gate program presented in the Appendix A include:

Defense Intelligence Agency's Science Panel Report: SRI Studies in Remote Viewing: A Program Review.

A memorandum of agreement between the Army Intelligence and Security Command (INSCOM) and the Defense Intelligence Agency (DIA)

Office of the Secretary of Defense review: Then enhanced human performance project: An assessment of the effort to date.

Appendix B comprises of brief excerpts from Joseph McMoneagle's Remote Viewing of Submarine Base in Severodvinsk, Russia.

A. SCIENCE PANEL REPORT OF SRI REMOTE VIEWING

APPROVED FOR RELEASE 2000/08/08: CIA-RDP96-00789R002800180001-2

SECRET

APPENDIX 8

SCIENCE PANEL REPORT
SRI STUDIES IN REMOTE VIEWING
A PROGRAM REVIEW

1 MARCH 1984

SRI STUDIES IN REMOTE VIEWING: A PROGRAM REVIEW

For the past eleven years, a small group headed by Dr. H. Puthoff has sought evidence that would support the case for extrasensory perception. In recent years, the focus of these studies has centered on "remote viewing" by subjects claiming to visualize the scene at a point beyond the field of vision, and in many cases, in a remote part of the world, typically not known to them by actual experience. The implication of success in remote viewing, if it exists, are revolutionary; since as described to the review team, it is manifestly incompatible with currently accepted scientific principles. Remote viewing of future events—"precognition"—evidently violates causality; real time remote viewing clearly requires a transmission mechanism other than any known process: electromagnetic, gravitational, etc.

The lack of a physical model should not be taken to preclude the existence of the capability to view a remote location. However, this circumstance has thus far limited application of the classic methods of scientific investigation to less cogent issues, such as controls for inadvertent cueing, statistical evaluation of the incidence of positive findings, estimation of false-positive and false-negative responses, and in particular, the design of experiments that would limit as far as possible intrusion of extraneous factors relating to personal interaction and observer biases.

The evidence shown to us is too impressive to dismiss as mere coincidence. Certain similarities between the SRI and Princeton results, obtained in very different circumstances by unrelated investigators, are particularly compelling. The Princeton work is somewhat more quantitative than that at SRI and leads to an estimate by Dr. R. Jahn that the phenomena he has observed could be explained by a transfer of information above noise at a level of about one bit per thousand. This of course raises the question of how much information is required to construct the impressions gained by remote viewing, a question which the investigators cannot presently answer. Therefore, the review team feels that remote viewing is either real or due to some sort of experimental interference from one or some of the participants; something one might describe as "inadvertent cueing." Although, on the basis of our brief exposure to the SRI program, we found no obvious evidence of cueing or collusion between the viewer and the experiment monitors.

The briefings strongly emphasized the investigator1s ability to train others in their techniques. This training program has developed over the past five years through the dedicated participation of Mr. Ingo Swann. His diverse talents have been devoted to self-training which he now feels competent to impart to others. Approximately a dozen trainees have completed instruction to various levels of claimed competence. An important aspect of Swann's contributions relates to his dissection of separate elements in the perceptual process. Under his guidance, the technique centers around the use of a coordinate method to describe the remote location, expressed in degrees of latitude and longitude. It is here that any attempt at a rational understanding of the perceptual process is lost. Since the significance of the coordinates so expressed is unknown to the viewer in most instances, it is impossible to understand why such a method should be translated in the viewing process into a precise delineation of geographic characteristics of the target site. The arbitrariness of this approach has not escaped the investigators, but repeated attempts to elicit a rational basis for this procedure, or to secure definitive information about possible success or failures with other methods that they may have tried, were uniformly unsuccessful. The investigators' attitude was that since they had found the coordinate method to work, they were not disposed to query the mechanistic basis of its applications, nor to seek an appraisal of other potentially successful methods.

Mr. Swann has distinguished three phases in his subjective interpretation of his viewing capabilities. The initial percept appears very rapidly with a latency stated to be as short as 1/50 of a second. Thereafter, for a period that may persist for several minutes, increasing detail may be added. Thereafter, and only after as much material has been added to the initial percept as possible, is the subject encouraged to examine his subjective image in a critical way, or to make syntheses or judgments about the significance of the perceived material. Swann pointed out that intrusion of a judgmental or interpretive attitude too early in the building of the percept was generally destructive, and to be discouraged in the course of training others.

A considerable variety of material was presented with photographic backup in support of the validity of the perceptual method. Much of this was highly impressive. The data showed the effects of training on the success rate, which typically reached a sustained plateau at a level higher than prior to training, both for groups of subjects as well as for individual trainees.

What then may be anticipated if the program is continued? In the absence of a physical model for the perceptual process, no predictions are possible about higher success rates in larger groups of viewers concentrating on the same target, nor about the effect on success rates to be expected if the technique were extended to those with special intellectual abilities or professional backgrounds.

Exploration of the phenomenon should not be restricted to specific applications. Rather, remote viewing should be studied as a scientific research program aimed at establishing the existence or non-existence of the phenomenon. In this way, a comprehensive and credible evaluation of the phenomenon should be available from continuing effort over the next five to ten years. The potential impact of this phenomenon is clearly profound. Therefore, a mandatory requirement would be the existence of independent but related programs conducted by others, with the free exchange of techniques and results. Only through independent reproducibility can a phenomenon so unconventional ever become accepted.

It is our conclusion that Dr. Puthoff's team warrants cautious continued fiscal support, and that the research should be conducted as much as possible in an open unclassified mode so that its reproducibility and accuracy can be independently verified by others.

W. ROSS ADEY _____

F. ZACHARIASEN _____

1 March 1984

THE ENHANCED HUMAN PERFORMANCE PROJECT:
AN ASSESSMENT OF THE EFFORT TO DATE
PROJECT REVIEW GROUP
14 APRIL, 1987

At the request of MG Philip K. Russell, MC, Commander, United States Army Medical Research and Development Command, the following individuals met at the Pentagon on 6 March 1987 to assess the work of the Enhanced Human Performance Project:

Ms. Amoretta Hoeber, TRW
Dr. Michael A. Wartell, Humboldt State University
Dr. Nick Yaru, Consultant (Chairman)
Dr. Chris Zarafonetis, Biomedical R&D, Inc.

Others in attendance at this meeting included:

BO Richard T. Travis, MC. Deputy Commander, USAMRDC
Col. Philip Sobocinski, MSC, Special Assistant for Biotechnology
Col. Peter J. McNelis, MSC, Project Manager/COR
Mrs. Jean Smith, Principal Assistant Responsible for Contracting
Dr. Edwin C. May, SRI, Principal Investigator

In preparation for this meeting, copies of all Project reports for Fiscal Year 1986 along with the Scientific Oversight Committee's comments regarding these reports and the contractor's responses to the comments were forwarded to each of the above-mentioned individuals for their review.

The Project Review Group was asked, via correspondence (MG Russell, 12 January 1987; Col. McNelis, 12 February 1987) and by BO Travis in his welcoming remarks at the meeting, to address the following questions concerning the Project:

Is the science underlying this research effort essentially sound?
Does the evidence to date support the existence of an anomaly?
What is the potential value of this effort to the DOD?

DEPARTMENT OF THE ARMY
UNITED STATES ARMY INTELLIGENCE AND SECURITY COMMAND
ARLINGTON HALL STATION
ARLINGTON, VIRGINIA 22212

REPLY TO
ATTENTION OF

MEMORANDUM OF AGREEMENT
BETWEEN
USA INTELLIGENCE AND SECURITY COMMAND AND THE
DEFENSE INTELLIGENCE AGENCY
SUBJECT: INSCOM CENTER LANE Project OPCON to DIA (S/NOFORN/WNINTEL)

1. (S/NOFORN/WNINTEL) PURPOSE. This Memorandum of Agreement (MOA) places the US Army Intelligence and Security Command (INSCOM) psychoenergetic intelligence collection capability (CENTER LANE) under the operational control (OPCON) of the Defense Intelligence Agency (DIA). The OPCON action will attach all INSCOM CENTER LANE Project (ICLP) personnel, documents, equipment, and office space to DIA to form the nucleus of a prototype operational group that will conduct psychoenergetic intelligence activities for the U.S. Intelligence Community. This course of action is an interim measure until Congressional approval is obtained for GDIP billets for DIA for the ICLP.

2. (U) REFERENCES.

(U) Memorandum, INSCOM, IACG, 17 July 1984; subject: INSCOM CENTER LANE Project (U) (TAB A).

(U) Memorandum, OACSI, DAMI-ISH, 1 August 1984; subject: CENTER LANE (U)—ACTION MEMORANDUM (U) (TAB B).

(U) Letter, OACSI, DAMI-ISH, 10 September 1984, subject: INSCOM CENTER LANE Project (U) (TAB C).

(U) Letter, OACSI, DAMI-ISH, 4 October 1984 subject: Memorandum of Agreement (U) (TAB D).

(U) Document, 6 June 1984, subject: INSCOM CENTER LANE Project
Training and Applications Procedures (U) (TAB E).

3. (S/NOFORN/WNINTEL) BACKGROUND. USAINSCOM has invested considerable effort and resources since 1977 to develop an operational psychoenergetic capability. Intelligence consumers

in the US Army, US Air Force, DIA, NSA, CIA, and NSC have all tasked this capability to augment other intelligence systems. These agencies have recognized the value and potential of the intelligence application of psychoenergetics; it is likely they will continue to task the system. Since INSCOM has disestablished CENTER LANE, existing resources must be put under the operational control of DIA or the Intelligence Community psychoenergetic capability will cease to exist. The transfer of ICLP to DIA OPCON must be done in such a way as to maintain continuity and momentum of effort, as well as state-of-the-art expertise.

4. (S/NOFORN/WNINTEL) SCOPE. The transfer of operational control of ICLP to DIA affects DA (ACSI), INSCOM, and DIA.

5. (S/NOFORN/WNINTEL) AGREEMENTS, SUPPORT, AND RESOURCE REQUIREMENTS. ICLP has been an active intelligence collection unit since 1978, and it is therefore intended that it will continue as an operational element under the operational control of the appropriate organizational element of DIA. Defense Intelligence Agency accepts the entire responsibility for mission-related training, mode of employment, applicable requirements of the "human use" issue, and the operation and security of the former ICLP and its assets for the OPCON period. The period of operational control will be no longer than one calendar year from the implementation date of this MOA. If, by the end of this period, DIA is successful in obtaining requisite positions and funding allocated for continued psychoenergetic activity, INSCOM agrees to assign affected personnel and other project resources to DIA as will be deemed appropriate and mutually agreed upon. This assignment will be by a separate MOA. If the aforementioned funding and resources are not approved in the FY 86 General Defense Intelligence Program (GDIP) submission, ICLP will revert to USAINSCOM to be reassigned or utilized at the discretion of the CG, INSCOM.

(S/NOFORN/WNINTEL) Personnel. All ICLP Personnel will be encouraged to continue with the project as it devolves under DIA control. Direct participation in psychoenergetic activities by CENTER LANE personnel is strictly voluntary and falls under the guidelines of DoD Directive 5240.1-R, AR 381-10, and Code of Federal Regulation, Title 45, Part 46. The ICLP manager will ensure that ICLP operational personnel understand that they will be performing operational remote viewing in support of the DIA psychoenergetic program under the guidelines of established procedures outlined in reference 2e.

(S/NOFORN/WNINTEL) Documents. All documents maintained by ICLP will remain under INSCOM control until such a time as need dictates a separate agreement be concluded transferring pertinent documents to DIA. Upon the event of such a contingency, INSCOM will in any case be permitted to retain access to command and control and historical ICLP documents. Documents generated after transfer of OPCON to DIA are the property and responsibility of DIA, but may be administered by the project manager of the INSCOM element at DIA direction.

(S/NOFORN/WNINTEL)Equipment. All ICLP equipment, rental agreements, and on band supplies will remain 1NSC0M property during the OPCON period.

(S/NOFORN/WNINTEL) Facilities. The ICLP will remain at Ft. George G. Meade, MD during the OPCON period.

(S/NOFORN/WNINTEL) Funding. Funding for all project-related training and operations is the responsibility of DIA. Funding for personnel, administrative functions and Army career development training remains the responsibility of INSCOM.

(S/NOFORN/WNINTEL) Security. CENTER LANE will be discontinued as a Secretary of the Army-directed Special Access Program (SAP) and the nickname CENTER LANE will be deactivated upon initiation of OPCON status. Responsibility for project security passes to DIA on the effective date of OPCON.

(S/NOFORN/WNINTEL) Administration. During OPCON period, all ICLP military personnel will remain assigned to INSCOM for rations, quarters, administration (personnel, finance, and medical records) and UCMJ. Civilian personnel will continue to be supported by their current civilian personnel office.

(C) The Project Manager of the INSCOM element will, as appropriate, update CG, INSCOM concerning current developments relating to the program and the involved INSCOM assets.

(U) RESPONSIBILITIES.

(U) CG, USAINSCOM will:

(S/NOFORN/WNINTEL) Attach the ICLP to DIA.

(S/NOFORN/WNINTEL) Appoint the ICLP Manager as POC for

the eventual transfer of ICLP to DIA.

(U) Director, Defense Intelligence Agency will:

(S/NOFORN/WNINTEL) Accept operational control of ICLP and assume full responsibility for the operations and training of INSCOM CENTER LANE assets during the attachment period.

(S/NOFORN/WNINTEL) Direct the development of a plan that will permit the eventual total assignment of ICLP to DIA and an operations plan that will manage, operate, task and evaluate operational psychoenergetic activities.

(S/NOFORN/WNINTEL) Notify Congress of transfer of operational control of CENTER LANE to DIA.

(U) EFFECTIVE DATE. This MOA is effective on the date signed.

HARRY E. SOYSTER
Major General, USA
Commanding General, USAINSCOM

11 Feb 1985

JAMES A. WILLIAMS
Lieutenant General, USA
Director, Defense
Intelligence Agency

B. JOSEPH MCMONEAGLE'S REMOTE VIEWING OF SUBMARINE BASE IN SEVERODVINSK, RUSSIA

The following are excerpts taken from a 157 page transcript of a 1979, formerly classified remote viewing session by Joseph McMoneagle. The target was a building in Severodvinsk in the Northern part of the Soviet Union. At the time, our side did not know what was going on inside, and Joe was tasked to tell us. It was learned later that the building was an unknown (to the U.S.) Soviet submarine base and the first Typhoon class submarine (termed by NATO) was under construction. In the dialog, #01 represents Joe and all other comments are of the monitors for the session. The accuracy of this viewing was later confirmed.

Summary Analysis:
Remote Viewing (RV) Sessions C73 and C74
This report provides documentation of two remote viewing sessions conducted in compliance with a request from OACSI, DA.
The viewer had not attempted any remote viewing for over one month and he had some difficulty getting started in Session C73. After a period of time, however, he was able to resolve relevant target imagery. He had no trouble at all in Session C71 (and was highly motivated by the importance of the target and the information he was providing.

The protocol used for these sessions is detailed in the document, GRILL FLAME Protocol, AMSAA Applied Remote Viewing Protocol (S), undated.

Following are transcripts of the viewer's impressions during the remote viewing sessions. At TAB A are drawings made by the viewer reference his impressions of the target site. At TAB B are analytical comments. On file in TAB C of Session Report C54 and C55.

∽⁓

TRANSCRIPT: REMOTE VIEWING (RV) SESSION C 73
[#66 = Session monitor; #01 = Viewer]
#66: This will be a remote viewing session (edited for security).
Pause
#66: It's time now to focus your attention on the target for today. Go to a large concrete building located in the vicinity of xxx:
Pause
#01: First impression I have is three large white numerals 251...I don't know what that mean but that's the impression I have. I'm kinda

going down a…some kind of a slanted type walkway with a rubberized or plastic flooring that's…interconnecting…uh…two spaces in the building…two areas in the building…and…uh…as I come out of this walkway and then a…and then a., end of a large open type bay. Some kind of a raised open area on the left. Looks like a Ford that's jacked up for some reason. There's a lota bright light and noise.

Pause

#66: What's going on in this room?

#01: I…I'm sensing a…brilliant flashes of light…uh…sparks… like someone is cutting some metal.

[The following figure represents an overview of the facility]

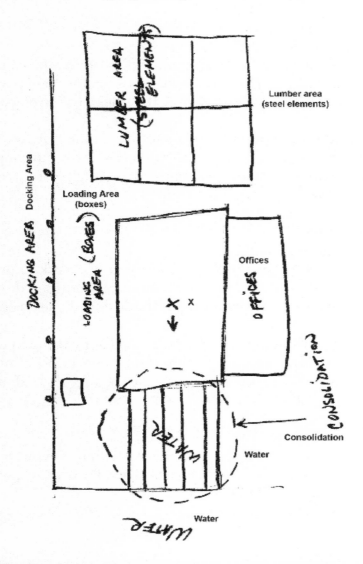

#01: I'd go to the pit.

#66 And what happens in the pit?

#01: I'm looking at the pit crossways and I'm seeing...the top edge looks like there's water flowing over it. And it fills up...and then the water goes out the bottom and empties, but its continually filled and emptied but it' not full now. And these things go in this... go...go...they go in the pit...they are put in the pit but they don't leave them there. They just go in the pit for some reason.

#66: Alright. Fine. Is the pit in this same room?

#01: Yes. It's in the far left corner of the room.

#66: Is there anything in the pit?

#01: Nothing in the pit now.

#66: What belongs in the pit?

#01: Water. I get a...I get a strong impression of...work...don't work with...associated with the pit...like they use it and they don't use it. I don't understand it. Like a...the pit, the sides that the objects leave the building.

#66: If the objects were put into the pit, or had something to do with going to the pit, how does the pit help them leave the building?

#01: They...a...they're...the environment changes. I don't understand. They do an environment change.

#01: Nothing in the pit now.

#66: What belongs in the pit?

#01: Water. I get a...I get a strong impression of...work...don't work with associated with the pit...like they use it and they don't use it. I don't understand it. Like a...the pit, the sides that the objects leave the building.

#66: If the objects were put into the pit, or had something to do with going to the pit, how does the pit help them leave the building?

#01: They...a...they're...the environment changes. I don't understand. They do an environment change.

#66: Is there an object in the pit filling the...

#01: They check them in the pit, and look at them in the pit.

#01: Get the feeling of pressure in the pit when it's used. Heavy pressure at the bottom then little pressure at the top

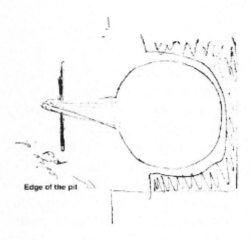

Edge of the pit

#66: Light up of what.

#01: It looks like the back deck and the sail portion of a submarine. But it's not...you know... it's not a complete ship of any sort.

#66: Move again from this area, exploring through the walls move again.

#66: Where are these?

#01: They're in the open part of the back deck of this...uh... structures.

#66: Where are the structures?

#01: They're on the ships on the submarines.

#66: Where are the submarines located physically?

#01: They're sitting in the parking bays. Very square, and the water's...water's kinda boiling up around 'em, bubbling up around 'em for some reason.

#66: Now, back into the description of what they're doing with the back decks of the submarines. Tell me about those.

#01: There's large, large black tubes sticking up and there's, there's people inside the tubes and they're working.

#66: Alright.

#01: Don't know what they're doing. They're in these tubes. There's twelve tubes on one...from what I can see.

#66: How many submarines are there?

#01: I see four, but the right bay is empty. The right, front right bay is empty. They're working on the second from the left.

They're doing something with tubes.
Pause

#66: How far along are they in their work?
#01: It appears...that they're taking out old tubes and putting in new tubes...Some are...some are out and they haven't put in the new ones yet. Putting in a different kind of tube. They're putting in another kind of tube. One tube's almost out now; the rest are and except for two, three, they're changing the top.

#01: Uh these...uh...(pause)...these are... uh...these are good... these are high-class submarines. These are biggies. These aren't new...they are old ones. I...I've...I'm getting the heavy nuclear feeling about them. I cannot.

#01: There's something funny about the submarines. I don't see any kind of marking on it...no flag or anything. I just see small numbers. There's no flags, no colors on the submarines. Seems kind of unusual.
#66: And what do you see...what kinds of markings are there?
#01: Just numbers.
#66: On the submarines, where are these numbers written?
#01: They're on the front top, right corner of the sail looking from the sides. They're small...very small letters.
#66: What color are they?
#01: The color of the numbers...is white. White on black.
#66: How many numbers...how many digits...how many different numbers are there?

#01: They're...a, it's like they're new all uncovered...all the plating is gone and they're canted and they're being removed... being removed.
#66: How many of them are there?
#01: I see twelve, twelve tubes. Twelve, ten or twelve. I can't see the last two very...very clear. There's a...two that really look different.
#66: How are they different?
#01: They're very small, very small. They don't appear to...uh...

have the same functions as the others. They're just different, different size. I don't know why they're different, but they're different.

#66: What's to the rear of the submarines?
#01: A wall. A wall and some doors.

#66: How do I get the submarines out of here?
#01: You open the wall.

#01: I don't...any other time, yeah, any other time and...uh... sails on the submarine. I don't...first...uh...the back deck comes out of the water like this. This is like...uh...let's call this water here; there's like a rise, thick rise in the sail. There is a sail, and it's shorter than our submarines. The front deck goes out like this and drops way in the water. And the submarine is actually much larger, and here, it's like rectangle on down the side of the numbers. On the sail...there's nothing at all that I could see protruding up above the sail on the sub...but this area back here is where all the plating was opened up and they were...they were working here. There's like tubes canted this way. Those are tubes. Yeah...and, there's a very large hatch up front. There's a very small hatch here. There's no other markings on the submarine. Very strange. And, I don't see any apparent ornament of any sort. I can't think of anything else.

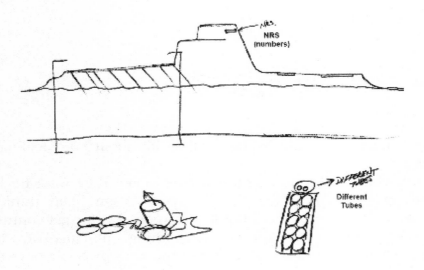

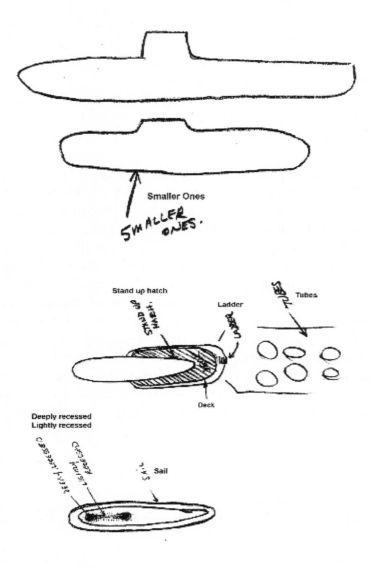

#66: Okay. Can you explain a little bit about your feeling of nuclear?

#01: I was trying to decide whether or not they were nuclear powered or nuclear armed. And, for some reason, I kept thinking powered, nuclear powered. But I, you know, I get, I get confused when I start trying to detail nuclear anything, but, I just know that there's something nuclear about 'em. I think it's probably powered.

Some reason I couldn't say armed. Couldn't say armed for some reason. I don't understand why, but I just couldn't do that. As they're sitting in those bays, they're just nuclear powered. Let's put it that way.

#01: Yeah…and…I'm not looking at any other part of the submarine and they could very well be even…you know…some other severe modifications to it somewhere, you know. Like a… double the width or something. I don't know. But, I almost get a sensation like this section of the submarine in its entirety is being modified or changed…that I put in brackets here. It's like that whole thing…I mean superstructure and all has been changed. But, that might be wrong. That might be analytic. I just get that feeling.

#01: Now…I don't know if it's…maybe it's my perspective of the larger submarine. Maybe looking down on 'em I get the impression of a small submarine because a lot of it is hidden in the water, and the side view I'm seeing the entire thing, I don't know if it's that or if somewhere in the area of this building or in this building they're not doing a like version of this submarine only a smaller variety…I just get…I'm getting flashes of a more compact submarine. Essentially the same design but a more compact model so to speak. Sort of like a pocket battleship's you know.
#01: A battleship, but nevertheless, but a smaller version. This is a good profile submarine. It's definitely what it looks like.

#01: They're working on one of them.
#66: Tell me about the submarine they're working on.
Pause
#01: They're working on some tubes.
#66: Tell me about this work.
#01: They're hanging tubes over the submarine. They're putting the tubes in the submarine.
#66: How is this accomplished?
#01: They're…uh…they're on the tubes and the…uh… into a work area inside the submarine. Looks like a room. Some kind of a room. They're stacking them together. They're putting them on their ends. There are holes in the floor. They go through a section of

floor in the submarine. It doesn't make sense. They got holes in the floors and the tube slides through the holes…go through the floor… and the

#66: Tell me about, where you are, where you're perceiving this. What's your position now?

#01: I'm inside the submarine.

#66: Very good. Tell me more about the tubes.

#01: (Mumbling)…they got these tube shapes and they're coming through the ceiling and they go on through holes in the floor.

#66: Walk down by the holes in the floor and tell me about them.

#66: How far along are they? How long before they will be through with this that they are doing?

#01: Long time. They're working very carefully.

#66: It's now 1 January 1980…You say it will take them a long time.

#01: Maybe 4 months. Over 100 read days.

#66: On the work right now or on the total modification?

#01: They're…uh…(mumbling)

#66: How much of this work has been done from the 100 days it takes them to do this work? How much has been done on this one submarine that they're working on.

#01: Uh…they…they've done almost all of the work. 100 days it takes.

#01 I don't know. This is an older sub. Older submarine. It takes longer with a…with a… it's a different submarine.

#66: Where is your perspective now?

#01: I'm seeing work done on submarines. I'm seeing a bunch of submarines. Different submarines.

#66: Where are you now?

#01: I'm looking up the tube from the bottom. They're very, very tall…(mumbling)…I'm very far down in the tube.

#66: I want you to concentrate now, and try to be very accurate. You told me previously, in another session, that these were not vertical but that they were slanted slightly. I'd like to know, if you'd like to describe that again. Tell me what your feeling is now about these tubes?

#01: Feel they're slanted in the hull.in the water they're not slanted. They're vertical to the earth but slanted on the hull. I don't understand that. They're...'they're installed slanted but they're vertical.

#66: For what purpose is this slant?

#01: They're longer. The tube is longer. Something about the end of the tube.

#66: What was this that you saw?

#01: Some kind of a vent. I was trying to find it alright. Don't know where it was. It was a vent. A strange looking vent. Like the top of the sail has a vent.

#66: The top of the sail has a vent.

#01: A recessed vent, or a hole of some kind. I can't...some kind of recessed or hole.

#66: OK. Is there anything else about the sail that you would like to tell me at this time?

#01: You can only walk around the side of the sail. You can't walk around the front or the top but you can walk around the side...in the rear of the sail.

#66: OK. Anything else?

#01: There's a ladder on the back of the sail, and there's a...there's a stand up door on the sail. That's all. That's all I can see.

#66: Alright. Is there anything you would like to add?

#01: No. No. I felt very bad when I was on the very bottom of the tubes.

#66: Describe your bad feeling.

#01: Intense excitement. I wanted to get out of the bottom of the tubes. They had very strong sensation of high pressure.

#66: OK. What's your perspective, right now?

#01: It's side of the submarine.

#66: Disregarding data that you've told us before and concentrating only on this submarine, right where you are right now, 1 January 1980, I am interested in knowing how OK. I have one other question now before we move. Many tubes there are.

#01: Eighteen tubes. Eighteen tubes. See eighteen tubes.

#01: There's a…I see two small hatches. I see one 20 feet out from the sail and I see one at the very tip. There's a very large, very large hatch and it's in two pieces. It opens in half.

#01: Wide, and it's flat. There's a large rectangular shape (mumbling) and there's, there's smooth holes. There's smooth holes there.

#01: Page 2, I explained to you. I was talking about when I look at the deck, I would have drawn the deck horizontal. Like this. And I look at the tubes. They're canting. This angle appears to be something less than 90 degrees. Like 80 degrees, But, then sitting in the water the deck is angled just a little bit as compared to the water and the tubes appear to be straight up and down. It's like they're canted, so to speak in order for them to be verticle while it's in the water.

#66: When you were looking at the tubes and perceived them canted was the submarine in or out of the water.

#01: I don't know. I don't if it was or not.

#66: Alright.

#01: Inside the submarine is clearly canted. Where it goes through the ceiling is clearly canted. I get the impression, standing on the first floor the tubes go through the floor. That cant is much less noticeable. It's almost as if the floor was put in…can't as well. I'm not sure I understand why, but I get that impression.

#66: Alright.

#01: And…a…on page 3 looking, if you were to look down on the top of the sail the center portion on the top of the sail is an oval like this. Right up here on top there is a…I was getting a very clear impression of this kind of a vent opening or hole. While this was recessed, here, this portion was very recessed. Much darker area.

#01: Yes. That what I kept trying to see but in the other one all there was smooth hole. Like you could rub your hand across the top and you could just perceive an opening. Not an indentation or anything. You just perceived the outline a little. May be a well sealed hatch. Or a disposable hatch. That would be interesting.

MEET THE AUTHORS

EDWIN C. MAY, PH.D.

Ed May's interest in serious research of parapsychological phenomena in 1975 when he joined the on-going U.S. Government-sponsored work at SRI International (formerly called Stanford Research Institute). Having spent the first part of his research career in the discipline for which he earned his Ph.D. in 1968 from the University of Pittsburgh, Parapsychology was a bit of a leap. Before leaving that career in Low Energy Experimental Nuclear Physics, he had published 16 papers in the peer-reviewed physics literature including his report of the first measurement of the singlet state of the deuteron, which appeared in the prestigious journal *Physical Review Letters*.

He did advance studies in his new area, and in 1985, he became the SRI program's director. In 1991, he shifted the effort to Science Applications International Corporation (SAIC), another US Defense Contractor. His association with government-sponsored parapsychology research ended in 1995, when the program, then called Star Gate, was closed by the US Government.

When the research was declassified in 2000, Dr. May was able to publish groundbreaking results and theories in the peer-reviewed literature—the latest of which appeared in an abstracted medical journal.[1]

Dr. May has managed complex, interdisciplinary research projects for the US federal government since 1985. He presided over 70% of the funding ($20M+) and 85% of the data collection for the government's 22-year involvement in parapsychological research. His responsibilities included fund raising, personnel management, project administration and planning, and he was the guiding force

---

1   May, Paulinyi & Vassy (2005). Anomalous Anticipatory Skin Conductance Response to Acoustic Stimuli: Experimental Results and Speculation About a Mechanism. *The Journal of Alternative and Complementary Medicine. 11*, 4, 695-702.

for and active in the technical research program. Currently, Dr. May is the Executive Director of the Cognitive Sciences Laboratory, which now resides within the Laboratories for Fundamental Research.

Dr. May's approach has earned him an international reputation for his research rigor and excellence even though the topic is considered highly controversial. He is the author or co-author of a large number of papers, reports, proposals and presentations from both of his career activities.

He recently was honored to give a public talk about intelligence collection at the World War II famous site, Bletchley Park, in the UK. His presentations—mostly to skeptical audiences—have been accepted worldwide, including such venues as Harvard University, the Universities of California at Los Angeles and at Davis, Stanford University, the University of Edinburgh, Trinity College Cambridge, Eötvös Loránd University, the University of Stockholm, and Imperial College London to name but a few.

The Parapsychological Association, an affiliate member of the American Association for the Advancement of Science, granted him the Outstanding Achievement Award in 1996. For his contribution and research excellence and the Association presented him the Outstanding Career Achievement award in 2007. He was President of The Parapsychological Association in 1997 and has served often on its Board of Directors.

To learn more about the Star Gate era and the research since then, including the complete set of publications, please visit www. LFR.ORG.

VICTOR RUBEL, PH.D.

Victor Rubel, Director of the Media Laboratory for the Laboratories for the Fundamental Research, was born to librarian parents in Stavropol, a southern region of Russia, in 1959. In 1976, he enrolled in the Moscow Institute of Physics and Technology (the Russian equivalent of MIT) and in 1982 graduated from the Moscow Pedagogical Institute, School of Physics. Following that, he served 2 years in the Russian Army as an officer with the rank of lieutenant.

After his military service, he taught physics and mathematics at the Pedagogical College and then was offered a position as a head of the Professional Orientation Laboratory at the Moscow Department of Education. In 1986, he enrolled in the post-graduate course (on methodology of science) at the Moscow State University, where he also taught students philosophy at the Departments of Physics and Mathematics.

From 1989 to 1992, he travelled to the US several times and started his further education in transpersonal psychology with Stanislav Grof's Transpersonal Training. Being certified in 1992, he established the Moscow Transpersonal Center and became its Director, providing Holotropic Breathwork™ training and transpersonal psychology seminars for psychologists and medical doctors in Russia.

During that time, he also established one of the first private companies in Russia and worked in the Russian TV and film industries, producing and managing a number of projects. The biggest one was an attempt to establish the first digital TV-movie studio in Russia in collaboration with Japan, which was halted by the collapse of the USSR in the 1991.

In 1993, Rubel immigrated to the US, where he worked as a manager of the Russian Cultural Center of San Francisco. In 1997, he enrolled in the Ph.D. course in the California Institute of Integral Studies. He earned his degree in Humanities in 1999 and began working as a consultant at the Laboratories for the Fundamental Research in Palo Alto, California. In 2003, became Director of the Media Laboratory there, managing a number of projects, including the Holographic Cinema Technology, in collaboration with the Russian Cinema and Photo Research Institute.

Victor Rubel is the author of three books: *Astrology without Astrologers and Horoscopes* (Sophia Publishing House, 1998); *The Principles of Forecasting Systems* (Ripol Publishing House, 2009) and a fairy tale written with his wife, Nina Wiese, *The Secret of the Enchanted Christmas Tree* (MediaVremia Publishing House, 2012) published in Russia.

LOYD AUERBACH, M.S.

Loyd Auerbach is best known as a field investigator and educator in the field of Parapsychology. The author of eight books, and dozens of published articles on the psychic/paranormal for the general public, he is Director of the Office of Paranormal Investigations, President of the Forever Family Foundation (2013-2016), a Professor at Atlantic University (Virginia Beach, VA) and at JFK University (Pleasant Hill, CA), and creator and Instructor of the Certificate Program in Parapsychological Studies at HCH Institute (Lafayette, CA). His first book, *ESP, HAUNTINGS AND POLTERGEISTS: A Parapsychologist's Handbook* (Warner Books, 1986), was named the "Sacred Text" on ghostly phenomena by *Newsweek* in 1996.

He is a member of the Board of Directors of the Rhine Research Center, on the Advisory Board of the Windbridge Institute, and the Scientific Advisory Board of the Forever Family Foundation. He was a Consulting Editor and columnist for FATE magazine from 1991-2004 and is quite active in the parapsychological community.

He has appeared in thousands of radio, podcast, and print interviews, and hundreds of national and local TV shows including *ESPN's Sports Center, Coast to Coast AM, The View, Ghost Adventures, Larry King Live, Oprah, Criss Angel: Mindfreak, Sightings, In Search Of, the Today Show, Unsolved Mysteries,* and *Late Night with David Letterman.* He can be seen frequently on A&E, Bio, the History Channel, the Travel Channel, SyFy, the Discovery Channel, and TLC (as many of his cable appearances are in eternal reruns). He's often sought after to consult behind the scenes as well, given his ability to translate the science of Parapsychology (and its often technical jargon) into plain language for the audience.

He is a professional mentalist and psychic entertainer, performing as Professor Paranormal—a title that follows him into his more serious work. He is a past President of the Psychic Entertainers Association, and served several years on their Board of Directors in another capacity, continuing as their annual meeting coordinator.

His knowledge and experience of magic and mentalism, coupled with his background in Parapsychology and broad knowledge of other sciences has led to a number of researchers to consult with him, especially with regard to laboratory controls and where potential for psychic fraud has existed.

Loyd Auerbach holds a BA in Cultural Anthropology (though he started out in Astrophysics!) from Northwestern University (1978), and an MS in Parapsychology from John F. Kennedy University (1981).

He earned a certificate as a Professional Chocolatier from Ecole Chocolat in 2009, and offers his services as a Chocolate Maven (guided chocolate tastings) and making exceptional chocolates.

JOSEPH W. McMONEAGLE, CW2, US ARMY, RET., CSTS

Mr. McMoneagle has 37 years of professional expertise in research and development, in numerous multi-level technical systems, the paranormal, and the social sciences, including work for military and civilian intelligence purposes. He is currently owner and Executive Director of Intuitive Intelligence Applications, Inc., which has provided support to multiple research facilities and corporations with a full range of collection applications using Anomalous Cognition (AC) in the production of original and cutting edge information. He is a full time Research Associate with The Laboratories for Fundamental Research, Cognitive Sciences Laboratory, Palo Alto, California, where he has provided consulting support to research and development in remote viewing for 17+ years.

As a consultant to SRI International and Science Applications International Corporation from 1984 through 1995, he participated in protocol design, statistical information collection, R&D evaluations, as well as thousands of remote viewing trials in support of both experimental research as well as active intelligence operations for what is now known as Project Star Gate. He is well versed with developmental theory, methods of application, and current training technologies for remote viewing, as currently applied under strict laboratory controls and oversight.

During his career, McMoneagle has provided professional intelligence and creative/innovative informational support to the Central Intelligence Agency, Defense Intelligence Agency, National Security Agency, Drug Enforcement Agency, Secret Service, Federal Bureau of Investigation, United States Customs, the National Security Council, most major commands within the Department of Defense, and hundreds of other individuals, companies, and corporations.

He is the only person who has successfully demonstrated his ability as a remote viewer more than four-dozen times, live, double-blind, and under strict scientific control while on-camera for national TV networks and labs in six countries.

His background includes serving as the Detachment Commander at two remote intelligence collection sites overseas, providing field intelligence collection, analysis and reporting at theater, region, country, and city levels. He has also served on an Air and Sea Rescue team, in Long Range Reconnaissance, as a Quick Reaction Strike Force team leader, and rifleman in war zones. He has earned 28 military decorations and numerous awards, to include a Legion of Merit for his psychic intelligence support to the Nation's Intelligence Community. He holds the rank of Knight Commander in the Order of St. Stanislas.

Joseph McMoneagle is currently a full member of The Parapsychological Association, a full member of The Writers Guild of America-East (WGA-East), a Life Member of the Disabled American Veterans, a performing member of the American Federation of Television and Radio Artists (AFTRA), and is a Retired Chief Warrant Officer in the Regular Army of the United States of America.

Made in the USA
Coppell, TX
14 March 2022

74950061R00239